THE $50-MILLION REFLECTION GIFT

Foreword
Need for a Title Revision

On January 28, 2011, I completed the text that would become this book. By the time I had placed the text into a publishing-ready format it was February 16, 2011. Back in those 'olden days' the printer-distributor had to load a new book on the donkey colt and walk it down the road to Amazon, and then wait for an audience with King Bookseller, before a title submitted could actually be purchased through that vendor. This book was then freely available for purchasing on Amazon (a Print-On-Demand book that was not in their actual possession) around March 1, 2011. I ordered fifty copies of the book to sell personally on March 2, 2011, which says a book submitted for publishing in mid-February took about a month to begin being a piggy going to market.

After this book had been available on the open market for no more than two months, on May 2, 2011 (actually May 1, 2011 in the Eastern Time Zone) the news flash was "Osama bin Laden killed!" Osama bin Laden was the point of the original title for this book – *The $25-Million Answer*. Shortly thereafter, the most wanted man in America, whose reward [I realized later] had been doubled to fifty million dollars, was removed from that list and the reward was said to have been paid to the informant who turned in bin Laden's whereabouts. With that news, my two-month old book was no longer necessary for any treasure hunters to purchase.

My wife bought a copy of this book from Amazon on May 1, 2011, which was billed to her credit card a few days later. So, now I have fifty-one copies of this book to sell, for anyone who wants one. Believe it or not, there is still good information in this book, although there is no longer any way to get rich off that good information.

The $50-Million Reelection Gift • *Robert Tippett*

One has to grasp the symbolism of May 1st. That was the day Americans were told that Osama bin Laden had been killed. May first is also called May Day. On the Wikipedia article entitled "May Day," the modern designations of that day are said to be this: "In 1889, May Day was chosen as the date for International Workers' Day by the Socialists and Communists of the Second International to commemorate the Haymarket affair in Chicago. International Workers' Day is also called "May Day", but it is a different celebration from the traditional May Day."

Simply because President Barack Hussein Obama was a Socialist-Communist- (Muslim pretender) [also known as a "community organizer" from Chicago] it would not be hard to imagine he gives more value to May Day than to Christmas or Thanksgiving. Some people believe in chance happenings; but just like the al-Qaeda attacks on the World Trade Towers and the Pentagon on September 11, 2001 could have been coincidence that September 11th (9/11) can also be the number a person dials on a telephone when there is an emergency [9-1-1], I tend to believe important events are planned, more than random. Just as the attacks on America by Muslim extremists were reasons to call for emergency help, so too was the announcement of Osama bin Laden's death being reason for Socialists to stand up and cheer for a president that was hellbent on destroying America. The one man all America hated, more than many hated Barack Hussein Obama, was Osama bin Laden; and, in one fell swoop President Obama was hailed as a hero for an achievement that made him look like he represented all Americans.

Now, when I heard the May Day news being announced on my television the least of my concerns was about losing the opportunity to sell books. I went into publishing my own books with the knowledge that I would pay more in towards making books available than I would ever take in return. I became a publisher to reduce how much those expected losses would be. So, no, I was not worried about book sales. I was worried that the leader of the United States of America had just pulled the wool over the eyes of the free world, giving the real Osama bin Laden a "Get out of being hunted! Free!" card.

Of course, there is no proof for anything I say here. I could be wrong. The opinions I immediately developed, based on the media's propaganda about what happened, including the movie *Zero Dark Thirty* that came out in 2012, is unbelievable. I base that on the ending of this story of American military stealth ingenuity being, "the Seal Team Six tested the DNA, found a perfect match, so they then ceremoniously [according to Islamic law] dumped the body into the

Arabian Sea."

Even the Jewish, Socialist-Zionist, Sacha Baron Cohen, in his movie *The Dictator* (also 2012), made references to Osama bin Laden still being alive, after a body-double had been killed instead. It does not take much wild imagination to come to that conclusion, based on how quickly DNA was analyzed and found to be a perfect match.

With that ability, the Navy Seal Team Six should be put in charge of retrying O. J. Simpson for the murder of his ex-wife and her bad luck visitor, just so they can sneer at Barry Scheck and make gestures to intimidate him, implying if he keeps up challenging their perfect test results, then he might also end up buried at sea, in order to get a conviction. With the Navy Seal Team Six also giving the evil eye to the racist jury that acquitted a murderer, justice done in that case might make it easier to overlook the injustice of proclaiming "Osama bin Laden is dead!" And, there being nothing anyone can do.

[Keep in mind they searched half the Indian Ocean for 227 bodies after MH370 went missing, so finding one body in the Persian Gulf is equally a lost cause.]

I had no plans to re-release this book, prior to about an hour ago. I have just published a new book that is about Nostradamus [a concordance to *The Prophecies*], which I did all the work for in 2015. I was doing so much writing and editing things I planned to publish back then that I developed severe carpal tunnel syndrome in both wrists. After two months of excruciating pain and three more months before all the scars of two operations had healed, I had turned away from Nostradamus and placed my sole focus on interpreting Biblical scripture. But this year has been my year for publishing, so the whisper in my ear an hour ago said, "Redo *The $25-Million Answer*," with a twist.

My wife passed away a little more than a year ago. Her soul-spirit has remained with me and together we have made 2020 a year for publishing. So far, I have published seven titles, with five and a half having been prior works that have been edited and placed into a publishing format. One and a half have been newly written. I have also republished four prior titles as e-books, something I had struggled with before. So, if I am hearing a whisper that says redo this book, then I trust that voice [and I trust that it comes from a place that knows the truth about May Day 2011].

Just this second, it has dawned on me that the 2020 Presidential election results is pretty much another episode of hearing the media propagandists saying, "Believe what we tell you to believe, even if it reeks of lies and corruption." Some people dance in the streets now, hearing the news they wanted to hear, just as they danced in the streets on May Day 2011 for the same reason. Anyone who does not believe what they hear is then "one of those racist, right-wing, gun toting, Bible thumping, white privileged, neo-Nazi, conspiracy theorists."

Oh well. Sticks and stones might break my bones, but words will never hurt me, especially if they are lies. Lies are like boomerangs, that always come back to haunt the liars, like karmic debt. So, I am going to reissue this as a second edition.

Certainly, all the sick humor above is just that. We live in a world that is sick with hatred, of all kinds. Politicians and extremist leaders are all doomed to fail, simply because their souls are black and guaranteed never to achieve heaven and a return to be one with God (also known as YHWH, but no other names fit). It was the God who Fathered Jesus, who was His Son reborn into the servant who went by the name Michel de Nostredame [a.k.a. Nostradamus], such that true Prophets of God are those sent with a message that needs to be heeded, lest they pay the price of failure to return and be one with God. Nostradamus wrote *The Prophecies*, which was a message to heed, dictated to him by the Christ Mind (because he was "in the name of Jesus Christ"), in 1555, to be believed and heeded once the Twentieth Century rolled around. The Holy Bible does not (and cannot) hold all of the divine documents of true Prophets, but to reject a divine message simply because it is not deemed canon is failure to hear the truth and act on it.

Nostradamus never once wrote the name Osama bin Laden anywhere in *The Prophecies*. He did write about someone whose description fits Osama bin Laden. If Osama bin Laden is indeed dead, as President Barack Hussein Obama said, taking credit for ordering his death, then the person described in *The Prophecies* just is not Osama bin Laden. This book tells where that person should be hunted, because that person is still alive and plotting a greater attack on the West than those which occurred on September 11, 2001.

The purpose of a divine prophecy is to elicit acts of faith as the response. That means accepting a true Prophet as such, so the message is known to come from God Almighty. The truth of a prophecy told by a true Prophet is not something that can be measured through hindsight. The people have to listen to the message and hear God giving them fair warning: change or face what the Prophet's message says. Change does not make the prophecy false, as the prophecy sent by God is always valid. Thus, change and then change back – the prophecy is still in effect.

The mistake so many have made in trying to interpret Nostradamus and find proof through hindsight is mostly wrong. Sure, some quatrains tell of events that have already come and gone. One big one was the recreation of Israel (1948), as a State government, which took place through the theft of Palestine. Nostradamus perfectly prophesied that even, nearly four hundred years before it occurred. Others of his prophetic quatrains have also come true, which fits a central theme that says the main players in his future epic tale would be Christians-Jews-Muslims. Along with the "reds" they will combine to bring about the greatest destruction the world has ever known.

In my mind, the simple solution would be to give Palestine back and punish the Jews; but the only reason for that solution would be: Nostradamus says change or the world will face a terrible end. Few are willing to listen to that solution. Fewer are willing to act towards that end; and, almost no one believes this is foretold by God, so no acts of faith are to be expected. That is regardless of what happened to Osama bin Laden on May Day in 2011.

Because this future is clearly written in quatrains that have never happened before and are not close to happening now, the events prophesied in the majority of the quatrains are still very distant. That means there is still time to change. If Osama bin Laden is dead, then someone just like him will take his place. Nothing has happened to tell God that anyone believes His Prophet and no one seriously is trying to change this evil that is clearly understood, but for some reason ignored. Therefore, because this future is still screaming a warning to "Stop!," I will republish this book.

I am not going to change the text to erase any references to Osama bin Laden. Personally, I believe he is safely hidden away where this book says to look. In that regard, I just watched a History Channel program about *Hunting Hitler*. I guess nobody told them Adolph Hitler committed suicide and died in 1945. Oh, wait. That was one of those media propaganda things, announced to get the people to dance in the streets. Well, that cable television production makes it seem Hitler was squirreled away to South America, where he plotted World War III. The program just said Hitler planned to go to war against the United States of

America, but then saw the Soviet Union was who they were going to let destroy the USA for them. All they needed to do was incite anger between the two hostile nations.

Wow! That is a good way to sum up what Nostradamus said was going to happen, in the quatrains. The exception being Hitler was not going to be the one to kill to prevent that end. Neither is (or was) Osama bin Laden. The only reason I wrote this book was to convey how reading the quatrains for divine meaning is possible, as long as one is divinely inspired and willing to listen to those inner whispers. Since the world has not changed for the better with me writing interpretations of Biblical scripture, I guess the time has come to again pass along this warning to change once more.

Always keep in mind that history is known for being repetitious. That means Napoleon getting defeated in Russia was repeated when Hitler made the same mistake. Same things happened, although each was specifically different. The same can be said about Osama bin Laden. Without a price on his head and nobody hunting him down, he could die of old age (another repeated theme). None of that means *The Prophecies* have been fulfilled, to any degree. The ones said to have already happened could all be set up to happen again. Same thing, same place, different people.

Let me add one last thing about the way I present the quatrains of Nostradamus. I do not make tabloid newspaper claims that are absurd and totally based on some flimsy translation. I follow a specific system of divine syntax that makes each word written bear importance that must be pondered. In that regard, I present many quatrains and elements of the letters Nostradamus wrote as evidence, which I present in a legal trial scenario. I give both prosecution and defense elements to consider. No one but me has learned this syntax, so I do not offer this evidence as if it is widely known. This means I offer deep explanation into words that takes the train of thought into past history, which needs to be understood in order to perceive it being repeated in the future.

So, if you are expecting some simpleton explanation about where Osama bin Laden (or someone just like him) is now, plotting a major invasion of Western Europe, then it is best you go back to drooling on your smart phone, thinking Osama bin Laden is dead. If you are ready to start putting a puzzle together, in order to find true faith and act to save your own soul, then - by all means - keep reading.

Preface

This work represents a logical, in-depth analysis of *The Prophecies* of Nostradamus. The discipline of logic, as a division of collegiate-level philosophical studies, has rules that govern such an analysis. A misunderstood publication from antiquity must be argued according to those rules, if any meaningful conclusions are to be found.

The arguments presented in this book begin with the premise that everything associated with *The Prophecies* has to take the presumption that typical syntax is not a given. To presume otherwise would mean that everything about Nostradamus' most famous work has been clearly understood. Since that is not the case, taking the side of standard language syntax being present in the poems of Nostradamus is an opinion that cannot be logically supported.

Such an error of reasoning is why there is so little that is truly known about the riddle Nostradamus left for the world. It is simply not enough to have "blind faith" that Nostradamus, the man, saw the future or did not see the future. There is no logical substantiation for belief that a human being can use a secret way to see the future. There is no proof that shows Nostradamus claimed to use some special techniques for conjuring visions, nor is there any proof that he attempted to use some form of magic. While some have proposed such hypotheses, such belief is without logical proof. Never in the history of man has any such feat been accomplished, before or after Nostradamus, such that it can be verified as anything other than trickery. This book does not request one to believe in Nostradamus as having achieved something all of humankind is incapable of reproducing.

Likewise, it simply is an error of reasoning to believe that Nostradamus produced a work of trickery, without taking the necessary steps to prove such a claim. The fact that no one in all the history of Man has been able to foretell the future, through "secret arts," has no impact on an argument that Nostradamus predicted the future. The use of a defense that it is impossible to prove a negative ("Nostradamus did not accurately predict the future" cannot be proved) is illogical in an argument that demands one look beyond Nostradamus and defeat such predictive tools as astrology, the Tarot, and other known metaphysical arts that Nostradamus may have used. All of these tools can be studied and scientifically tested, even found to have some degree of reliability; but to connect this level of accuracy to Nostradamus, one must successfully argue proof that Nostradamus claimed his source to be something proven to have a degree of inaccuracy. In other words, it is not enough to say, "There is no way Nostradamus could predict the future accurately by the use of known predictive tools, because we do not believe those predictive tools will be found to be anything other than magic tricks."

This work takes the logical approach that Nostradamus made the claim, in writing, that he encountered the Holy Spirit, in the form of Jesus Christ, and through that encounter Nostradamus was instructed to write about the future. As such, Nostradamus the man did not produce anything of a self-generated predictive nature. He wrote a true prophecy from a divine source, meaning the title of his work, *The Prophecies*, is duly named. Nostradamus also explained that his astrology-based predictions were divinely inspired, although without his being aware of that celestial influence. He further explained that a tool like astrology could only be so accurate, and only to the near future not the distant future, without the assistance of "angels." All of this explanation is written in the letters Nostradamus wrote, which accompanied *The Prophecies*; but few have ever been able to understand the writing style of those letters. This means no one has taken the logical approach that Nostradamus has claimed to be a prophet of God.

Just as it is impossible to prove a negative, it is impossible to prove there is a God or angels. What can become provable are the utterances of those who claim to be prophets. In all cases of this nature, the claim of a divine source must be accepted as true, simply because proof of the divine is impossible. The divine source becomes that "given" in a hypothesis, such that all said to be prophesied becomes that which becomes tested for truth. For the test of prophecy to be made, the prophecy must be understood. However, the writings of Nostradamus, those in particular under the heading of *The Prophecies*, have been so confusing that no accurate test of truth has been possible. To this point, everything has been nothing more than opinionated guesses, proving nothing.

In Greek mythology, as told by the tales of antiquity, the oracle at Delphi was where a prophetess always told the truth. She did so from divine inspiration allowed by the god Apollo. The problem in every tale of her prophesying the future was a misunderstanding of the prophecy. As such, one future was expected, but another future came. The result was always as the prophetess had prophesied, but it was only fully understood in hindsight. Nostradamus wrote of himself being compared to the prophetess at Delphi, because he knew his words would be misunderstood at first, and only afterwards would the truth become clear. The problem, again, is this comparison, written of by Nostradamus, has itself not been understood.

This work is founded in the premise that understanding *The Prophecies* comes from realizing it must be read differently than it first appears to read. It needs a new syntax by which consistent meaning can be gained. In that regard, I have come to realize that there are systems at work, which are embedded in the writing style used by Nostradamus, making overall understanding possible once one understands how to read in a new language.

This means that a new syntax must be learned. Reading by these systemic guides, which can be consistently applied when reading any of the verses and letters, makes seeing solid shapes stand out clearly, after the fog lifts. In comparison, Egyptian hieroglyphics were confusing until the Rosetta Stone was found and deciphered. The systems of Nostradamus are the breakthrough that makes solving the puzzle that *The Prophecies* have been.

This argument is completely logical, and defensible through the rules of logic. It addresses all aspects of a work of poetry from antiquity, respecting the aspects of symbolism and metaphor, while allowing great freedom for word definition. It also respects the explanations of Nostradamus, as the most reliable source of meaning. This is required when one is arguing for the meaning of something written long ago, where the author is no longer around to defend the work personally. Until someone stands up to soundly defeat my argument logically, all counter arguments are nothing more that useless opinions, full of faults and fallacies, and meaningless.

The point of this work is not to present this logical set of systemic rules that I have come to understand. That presentation is best left for its own in-depth publication. To some degree, I have included evidence that supports this premise

17

in another publication of mine (*Pearls Before Swine*). I have also written a much greater in-depth work of explanation, but I have yet to publish it (it is preliminarily named, *The Systems of Nostradamus*). That unpublished work is over 450 pages in length, going into minute details about how one must logically, and consistently approach *The Prophecies* of Nostradamus. Unfortunately, the lack of a demand for such a work, at this time, makes it too cost prohibitive for me to self-publish it. However, evidence will be presented in this writing based on my understanding of those systems; and, to some degree, an explanation of the basic systems (the new syntax) will be stated.

Because understanding Nostradamus requires one to learn a new syntax, the explanations of evidence contained in this work will be repetitive in explaining how repeating elements must be read. Each example presented is evidence to a premise that one specific provable prediction can now come from *The Prophecies*. This prediction is based solely on the words of Nostradamus, and logical interpretation of those words. The logical interpretation means the evidence must be explained based on a new syntax being present. The purpose of this work, however, is not to prove this systemic understanding; but the repetition acts as evidence towards that conclusion.

This work will present many pieces of Nostradamus writings, all from the letters and verses of *The Prophecies*. A logical analysis of each piece of evidence allows one to turn those writings into a present day prediction. The present day prediction is one of great importance, such that proving this prediction can be an assistance toward preventing other predicted events from taking place. This great importance requires serious evaluation and thus means this work is best read slowly. The reader should be willing to reread segments, to ensure an interpretation is accurately presented. This process should be seen as a necessary step towards proof of a claim, just as a juror should want to review some pieces of evidence presented during a lengthy trial. Logic demands one release all prejudice and be open to examine all evidence on its own merits.

One will notice in this work that the standard way I present the words of Nostradamus is by use of quotation marks. According to typical writing standards, a sentence that continues after a quotation will include a comma within the quotation marks. One example is my use the quote from the cartoon *Pogo*, where I state the famous line, "We have met the enemy and he is us." This quotation ends with a period mark, such that the period is actually part of the quote. However, if I made that quote part of a sentence that continued beyond the quote, it would be presented something as such:

> In the comic strip hall of fame for quotes, the famous "We have met the enemy and he is us," from *Pogo*, is an all-time favorite.

As one can see, the quotation marks above include a comma, whereas the actual *Pogo* quote ended with a period. In normal writing, the replacement of a period with a comma is meaningless, and required by the rules made common for proper grammatical writing. However, this is a rule that I regularly do not follow in this work, specifically when I quote Nostradamus.

The reason I do not follow that common rule is that one of the "systems of Nostradamus" involves how one approaches his presentation of punctuation. Whereas a period and a comma are today marks that represent pauses and stops, as one comprehends groupings of words, Nostradamus' use of punctuation displayed pauses and stops differently. Each presentation of punctuation is designed to be a specific direction to the reader. In this regard, each mark of punctuation written by Nostradamus must be read as its own separate quote of instruction. These marks cannot be arbitrarily changed. This means that I only place words Nostradamus wrote in quotation marks. Only if Nostradamus followed the words that I quote with a comma or a period, will I include them within my quotation marks.

For example, Nostradamus wrote the words, "*furibonde au mont Iouis*", without any punctuation following the word "*Iouis*" (in Old French, $I = J$, thus "*Jouis*"). Thus, one will note that I have placed my comma outside the quotation marks. This is because Nostradamus did not place a comma after the capitalized word, "*Iouis*". (← Nor did he place a period after it)

This series of words that I use as an example can also be seen to begin without a capitalized first word. The words shown above appear just as presented, having immediately followed the mark of an ampersand. The example words are the first four words in a series of words that represents a segment of words, which totals fifteen words. The segment ends with a comma. It is one segment of a string of five segments in a series, with the whole beginning with a capitalized first word and ending with a period. Such a collection of words would be seen by the standard use of syntax as one "sentence." However, the whole includes forty-nine words, which is far greater than any grammatically acceptable sentence.

This "sentence" includes the one ampersand, along with three commas. This is not a typical sentence, as one understands the grammatical rules of sentence structure today. The systems of Nostradamus require one to dissect these "sentences" according to the punctuation used and read each word as an individual statement. Each word then connects to other individual statements, which are connected as one flow of thoughts. As such, a segment of word from *The Prophecies* is more closely related, syntactically, to what one would call a paragraph.

It is then from that perspective that one addresses the quote of Nostradamus, "*furibonde au mont Iouis*". By including a comma or period within the quotation marks, one is incorrectly representing what was written, based on knowing that new systems of syntax make understanding Nostradamus possible. Therefore, I place a comma after the quote of words, as "*furibonde au mont Iouis*", because the comma is not part of the quote. I do not do so because I am ignorant of the accepted rules of modern sentence structure.

The purpose of this work is to give one specific prediction that can be gained from reading *The Prophecies*, based on understanding the systems incorporated into the writing style used by Nostradamus. The one prediction made is only one of the whole, where many predictions can also be made. The majority of what is presented in the quatrains (four-line verses) of *The Prophecies* is still to come and thus predictive. While much can be predicted, as events to come in the future with all predictions testable as to the accuracy of one's ability to make sense of what Nostradamus wrote, this work is only presenting one such testable prediction.

In order to present a logical prediction, evidence has to be presented as factual examples of what Nostradamus wrote. This written evidence supports the argument that leads to the predictive conclusion drawn. This evidence is the sole source that allows me to make this prediction; and, I have not encountered any extraneous material that suggests my conclusion is based on a preconception, consciously or otherwise. My prediction is solely based on a logical interpretation of words written long ago, based on realizing logical systems that allow for understanding. This is all that has allowed me to see more than a casual correlation between the meaning of the words written by Nostradamus (1555) and current events. Current events have led to a public desire for this prediction, separate from any inkling as to whether or not Nostradamus had any capability to foresee our current events.

Preface

The evidence presented in this work, as the basis for my prediction, is enhanced by being accurate English translations on an expanded level. These translations are verifiable by an Old French–Old English Dictionary, from the year 1611. That source is freely available on the Internet for others to utilize. The translations establish firm parameters within which any meaning can be gleaned, with any standard English dictionary providing the full scope of definition and clarity a known word contains. While some words written by Nostradamus are clearly not words found in any dictionary, all explanations of their meaning come from an established set of rules, as established in the consistency of the new syntax that governs reading for understanding.

The systems of Nostradamus recognize there is a need for a way to address "manufactured words" routinely. These rules are consistently applied to all such words found and they are consistent with known elements of linguistics, especially those that recognize the creativity in new word creation, puzzles, and poetry. Certainly, translations of such "non-words" are arguable, but such argument cannot be arbitrary. Reason must be the foundation for any argument for proof; and, this work does present reasoning, which addresses the systems that are necessary to understand. The reasoning is found within the interpretative analysis.

In the sense that logic states the author is the best source for explaining the meaning of his writings, one must support all hypothesis to the meaning of Nostradamus' words with evidence that Nostradamus himself supported that meaning. As such, Nostradamus wrote letters that become the necessary support for interpretation of the verses. This work includes references to these letters, and explains them as the confirmation for the interpretations.

This is a valuable step towards understanding Nostradamus. This step has been completely avoided previously, by the many others who have ventured into the arena of interpreting Nostradamus. The rationale for such lack of supporting evidence has been due to the letters seeming to be too difficult to interpret alone, much less be seen as explanations to the quatrains. The reason previous interpreters have not been able to associate freely the two together (the quatrain verses and the letters of explanation), such that each supports the other in revealing the same intention, is the others have not realized the systems of Nostradamus. The systems apply equally to the verses and the "sentences" of the letters, thus making all understandable. This powerful element is used in support of the prediction that is found in this work; and, it makes everything relative to being an explanation made by the author. The opinion I present is logical and unbiased, founded entirely in what Nostradamus stated *The Prophecies* would be found to mean.

Finally, this work presents a prediction that is entirely founded in the belief that the whole of *The Prophecies* is a divine prophecy, inspired by God. The prediction is based on what was written by a man recognized as a true prophet of the Lord, by those who knew him personally. Nostradamus had no ability otherwise to see our future, from his perspective of 16th century France. Further, this work has been made possible by no reason other than I profess to have been led by the Holy Spirit to "discover" the systems of Nostradamus. I have no abilities otherwise that have allowed me to understand all meaning pertaining to *The Prophecies*. Without the divine, there would be no prophecy, nor understanding of prophets.

The beauty of prophecy, just as is seen in the twists of mythological episodes of oracles speaking the truth, is that it appears to be one thing, when in the end it is realized to mean all things possible, within the realm of reality. Reality requires laws, principles, and truths, by which all things can be tested as real. This means that prophecy is of real happenings, which can be verified as possible by real means. Thus, the ability to understand prophecy can be verified by attaching logic to that understanding. The opposite is not true, as logic does not allow one to prophesy. Logic only allows one to project reasonable results, within the parameters of chance.

Mental acumen has proven incapable of solving the riddle of *The Prophecies* for centuries. There can be no debating that much more intelligent human being than I have tried their hand at solving the mysteries surrounding *The Prophecies*. None have been able to remove that sword from the stone. If it were up to logic to solve the riddle, then one would be led to think that I am insane for believing I have suddenly found the answer. I refuse to take credit for possessing any special intellectual abilities that have made me alone able to present the prediction found in this work. While the prediction comes from my head, it is based on prophetic words, inspired by a higher power. It is not for my ego, but for your wellbeing. As such, this work is presented purely as a work of faith.

This work is a challenge to all who profess a belief in God. The challenge is to all who claim to have faith in God, and especially to those who, through recital of The Nicene Creed, state belief because, "*He has spoken through the prophets.*" I proclaim Nostradamus is a true prophet, who delivered us a prophecy on the level of *The Revelation* of Saint John. I proclaim both prophets received their prophecies from the same source, Jesus Christ. All who believe in God should read these words as a test of that belief; and, they must either defend that belief by proving God has spoken through a new prophecy for humanity (my prediction is true), or prove me wrong, by exposing me as a false prophet (my prediction is false).

The challenge is also to all who claim there is no god. All who believe predicting the future can be nothing more than a calculated guess have to prove my prediction is wrong. I give rational interpretations of clearly defined words; and, using the rules of scholastic logic, I draw conclusions that lead to a testable prediction. It is unreasonable to proclaim faith in the systems of science and logic, as the tools of enlightenment that make those who believe in religion seemingly ignorant fools. The only fools are those who are unwilling to follow those rules to test a simple prediction.

God can never be proved through logical means. However, if a prediction that is founded on faith in God is proved, then it strengthens all reasoning for having faith.

The rules of logic say one cannot prove a negative, such as "prove there is no God." The test is then to prove my prediction is wrong, before there is any chance it could be manipulated into being found true. Since no one is predicting what I predict and I have no explanation for how I could make the prediction I make alone, based on the laws of probability, chance, and extensive detective work, now is the time to act on my prediction. The challenge is then to act immediately after reading this work, and prove what you say you believe.

From this perspective, I would like everyone to see this work as a gift. There is a monetary reward offered for proving my prediction. I do not care to collect this reward for myself. As such, one can see this work as a gift from me to you, from a divine source. Although there is a monetary reward for proving my prediction, proving it also gains one a much higher reward. In such cases, the reward will be felt as assistance in finding a deeper connection to God and greater faith in Jesus Christ. That comes by believing the prediction of this work is true and thus a sign to look for greater rewards beyond this realm. For those who have no use for such unseen goals, this work becomes the answer to your financial dreams. In a material world, large amounts of money rewards one with power, wealth, and influence. The monetary reward offered for proving the prediction in this book is minimally $27-million. To gain that reward, all one has to do is believe in the logic I present, make it your own, and then sell the information of this book to those willing to pay to know the prediction.

Afterthoughts: In my assertion that a new syntax needs to be applied to the writings of The Prophecies, this is not as absurd as it might sound. As one who has studied astrology, to the point of certification, astrology is a language that can seem rather simple to translate, when in fact it is much deeper than it first appears.

In astrology, words are understood differently, by different people, even astrologers of different levels of expertise. Astrology is a language that must be mastered; but even when that comes, after years of experience, nothing is one hundred percent accurate in prediction. This is because the same words are too wide scope (as variables) to be nailed down to certainty. That is why someone like Nostradamus, as astrologer, gave full credit to his accuracy (in his Almanachs) to God sending him divine insight.

I also mentioned my book The Systems of Nostradamus as written, but not published. I published that book after this book was initially published, in mid-2011. Its copyright is listed as April 28, 2010, because it was a completed work, still unpublished.

Chapter 1
Wanted Dead or Alive

On September 11, 2001 attacks were ordered on two American cities, New York and Washington, D.C. The collected evidence amassed by multiple international intelligence agencies points to those attacks having been planned and executed by Muslim radicals, often referred to as "Islamic terrorists". Osama bin Laden claimed responsibility in a recorded message that was released soon after the attacks occurred.

On October 7, 2001, President George W. Bush ordered the United States of America, with overwhelming world support, to begin a war in Afghanistan. The war was designed to crush the Taliban regime that had usurped control of the government of Afghanistan, with assistance from Pakistan. This Muslim extremist group had governed the Afghani people with an iron fist, while allowing Osama bin Laden to operate terrorist training camps there. It was to those training centers that the September 11 attackers were linked. Bush's invasion of Afghanistan was intended to destroy the Taliban and al-Qaeda and to capture (or kill) Osama bin Laden.

The operation that began on October 7, 2001 was named "Enduring Freedom." It was the first war in the history of the United States of America that had overt involvement by the Central Intelligence Agency (C.I.A.). That agency had directly provided guerilla warfare tactics training, as well as supplied armaments to the Mujahedeen, which made Osama bin Laden the nuisance of a man that he is today.

Sadly, after nine years of war in Afghanistan, it appears the "freedom" objective was only for the United States of America to be free to police the world as it wishes. Training Osama bin Laden to use terror tactics had nothing to do with allowing the Afghani people the freedom to govern themselves. If anything, the presence of the American-International Alliance resulted in an *"enduring"* war of occupation, with no end in sight that will justify the means.

If one recalls the onset of the Iraq War (Operation Iraqi Freedom), the soldiers were given a deck of "player cards" with fifty-two faces of people ranked high in Saddam Hussein's administration. Saddam and his two sons were three of the "aces" in those decks. The cards were produced so that everyone looking for bad Iraqis would be able to know what the bad Iraqis looked like. The result was highly productive, as most (if not all) of these men were identified and captured. Similar tactics do not seem to have been used in Afghanistan; or if they were, they did not have the same positive results. The "ace of spades" in the Afghan War is Osama bin Laden, who still is free to taunt America in front of the world.

By December 2001, or after about a month of fighting the Taliban, the U.S.-led coalition had pushed the enemy into the mountains along the Afghanistan-Pakistan border. With no bin Laden in their grasps, and instead of player cards being passed out, the F.B.I.-C.I.A. offered a $25-million reward for information that would lead to the capture (dead or alive) of Osama bin Laden. The thinking was, obviously, that it would take someone ratting on bin Laden to catch him. The decision to offer big money was based on the American greed model. As such, if Osama bin Laden were hiding in America, he would have been caught quickly.

Sometime around October 2002 (a year after the Afghan War began), a report surfaced that a man close to bin Laden (an al-Qaeda operative) had claimed the reward money. The report actually said that the man needed an extra $5-million ($30-million total), simply because he would need to be relocated to Great Britain. The cost of living was much higher in Britain than in Afghanistan, especially with all the private security he would need to hire (ala Salman Rushdie), to keep him alive long enough to enjoy the fruits of his ratting out bin Laden.

In November (12th) 2002, another bin Laden audio tape surfaced, which was followed by another in February (12th) 2003. On July 13, 2007 (5 ½ years after the war began, and 4 ½ years after the report of giving someone $30-million), the reward for Osama bin Laden's capture was approved by the U.S. Senate to be doubled to $50-million. The next day (July 14, 2007), a new bin Laden video clip was made public. Since February 12, 2003, up until October 2, 2010, there have been twenty-seven videos-audios of Osama bin Laden that have been made public. Yet another was announced in the news recently (October 27, 2010). Obviously, they have not yet captured Osama bin Laden, meaning the reward is still on the table for all takers.

All the news reports have indicated the belief bin Laden is in some mountain cave in Pakistan, where the local people are protecting him from Pakistani authorities, C.I.A. operatives, and American satellite surveillance-led drone attacks. The idea of reward money does not seem to be attractive in the Islamic world, regardless of all reports of interested people wanting to cash in. Certainly, one can expect that the news does not fully report all that is really happening. Still, the news recently reported that some crazy American had been arrested and questioned in Pakistan, partially because he was carrying a knife and a rifle, while camping out in the mountains there. It seems he admitted to being on a personal search to find and kill bin Laden. The point here is that while no one knows where bin Laden is, everyone is being led to look in the mountains of northwestern Pakistan.

This reminds me of the Warner Brothers Bugs Bunny cartoons, in particular those where we find Elmer Fudd trying to hunt the elusive "wabbit" by standing at a hole in the ground with a rifle pointed at the hole. Invariably, Bugs Bunny would come up from behind Elmer and ask him what he was doing. It is always funny to see Elmer react to having been outsmarted…once again. Obviously, the cartoon makes the point that a rabbit digging a hole, and going into that hole, does not mean the rabbit has to come out from that hole. In fact, as far as being smart goes, it makes good sense to always be some place not being searched, if one is "on the lam" or being hunted. Predictability can be bad for one's health, in those cases.

By November 2002, I had been working on a book about the story of the prophecies of Nostradamus for the better part of a year. During that year, I had taken six months off to work at a real paying job, at which time my work with the book was greatly curtailed. I had yet to do any of my own translations of the French text, but based on the translations of another author of Nostradamus' quatrains. Even from that translation perspective, I could clearly see how the war in Afghanistan was stated in one story told by some quatrains. I could also see the focus moving towards Iraq, before public talk went in that direction. Additionally, I could see where Osama bin Laden was hiding out (generally); and, it was not in Pakistan or Afghanistan. He was nowhere near that wabbit hole, meaning both Bugs Bunny and Osama bin Laden know how to be "waskilly wabbits".

I became unemployed in November 2002, due in part to the burning whisper in my head that said, "Your work with *The Prophecies* is not finished yet." I needed time to edit my book, find a publisher, and try to get news of Nostradamus' story public. Unfortunately, telling the world about Nostradamus offers no way to pay bills. I needed some source of income to make it possible to focus all my attention on writing about what Nostradamus offered. It was for that reason that I made an effort to "turn in Osama bin Laden" for the reward money.

I was living in the Dallas, Texas area at the time, so I contacted the Dallas office of the F.B.I. I talked with an agent about having information about where to look for Osama bin Laden. I stated that it was based on knowing how to read Nostradamus for understanding. I asked the agent if he would meet me at a coffee shop in the vicinity, so I could give him a better idea how I came to my conclusions. He said he would have to talk to his superiors about it and he would call me back. I gave the agent my name and number and then I waited patiently for a call back.

He did not call me. Instead, I called him a week or so later and reminded him of our previous call. His response was to have only a vague memory of our conversation, but with cobwebs detached he remembered us having had talked on the phone. Instead of the advertised reward money, I had suggested that I be paid as a contracted worker. I would be, in effect, a prophecy consultant. His answer, after I had called him back was, "Oh yeah, I remember now. No. The F.B.I. does not pay for information." I thanked him and hung up the phone.

I was glad I was turned down, regardless of how financially difficult my life was at the time. As soon as I made my initial offer to be a government consultant, I had visions of everything I provided being used for purposes that would have had no positive effect on the outcome of the story of Nostradamus. I could see people being killed in the name of goodness (preemptive strikes), with myself playing a role of responsibility for that outcome. I have since realized just how corrupt government has become, and government agencies are part of the problems, not part of the solution.

The purpose of telling this story now is that I have never clearly advertised what I would have told the F.B.I. in 2002, as to where they should look for Osama bin Laden. While I have alluded to where this place is to friends, and discussed it in a small part of my book *The Letters of Nostradamus*, and probably in some blog materials that I have posted online, I have not made it widely known where bin

Laden is, why he is there, and how I have come to that conclusion. As it turns out, what I would have presented to the FBI agent, at a local coffee house in 2002, pales in comparison to what I can present now. I want there to be a public record that Nostradamus explained where Osama bin Laden is in hiding; and I want it to be clear how I come to that conclusion.

Afterthoughts: From the 20/20 clarity of hindsight, nine years after 2011, in 2020, it dawned on me as I read this chapter just now. Nine years is a common theme. I wrote of Osama bin Laden spending nine years fighting in Afghanistan. After the events of September 11, 2001, he then spent nine years on the lam. It is now nine years later that I reissue this book. Nine is a number that is representative of completion ... numerologically speaking. A period of completion means a new beginning is next, after all loose ends are finally tied off or cut away.

Also, relative to the Federal Bureau of Investigation, one needs to realize the reality and not the hype. It is still the same private power organization that was begun (and aggressively micro-managed for decades) by the cross-dressing god of government – J. Edgar Hoover. The media has done a great job promoting how high and mighty that organization is, most assuredly because the media has been paid lucratively to provide such propaganda.

The current television series *F.B.I.* (which I have never watched) is in a long line of propaganda that projects them as having the ability to solve every crime. This goes back to the *Untouchables* and runs through all the C.S.I.-themed shows. The public is groomed to fear the F.B.I. in ways the Germans feared the S.S., the Russians feared the K.G.B., and the evil nemeses of the world feared James Bond, Agent 007. Everything comes from the minds of Hollywood propagandists, who listen to paid advisors with agency experience, before making everything up.

Keep in mind how much Hollywood loves to make movies and History Channel presentations about the few that invariably get away: The brothers that escaped from Alcatraz; D. B. Cooper; and the Oklahoma bomber, are just a few. Then, there are the colossal mistakes that clearly say the F.B.I. is nothing more than an organization run by flawed human beings, who kill innocent children in the name of justice: the Waco massacre and the Ruby Ridge, Idaho assault, both showing an impatience during sieges.

The television series, like *Person of Interest*, *Blindspot*, and *The Blacklist* (and many others) make it seem the F.B.I. has forensics capabilities that make

Nostradamus' ability to see the future minuscule, compared to their all-seeing eyes. However, when one sees how the F. B. I. has been run by political crooks that use the agency for personal gains, one comes to conclude the F. B. I. would never catch anyone with a brain (like the Unabomber or the MacDonald's Monopoly game fake winners) if it were not for people calling them and offering information.

Realizing that adds to my excitement (in hindsight) that my offer to be a prophecy consultant was not accepted.

Chapter 2
Why Now?

On October 27, 2010 there was another warning made public by Osama bin Laden. He warned the French that their citizens would be killed because of their support in the U.S.-led war in Afghanistan. He added that their discrimination against the practice of Muslim women wearing a hijab (or burqa) in public would also condemn them. This last part was obviously due to recent French laws against such public wearing of face-covering veils; it was included as a way to give the latest recording a way of being dated as current.

In this new release, the Associated Press quoted bin Laden as saying:

> "It is a simple and clear equation: As you kill, you will be killed. As you capture, you will be captured. And as you threaten our security, your security will be threatened. The way to safeguard your security is to cease your oppression and its impact on our nation, most importantly your withdrawal from the ill-fated Bush war in Afghanistan."

He also reportedly said,

> "You need to think of what happened to America as a result of that unjust war. It is on the verge of bankruptcy ... and tomorrow it will retreat beyond the Atlantic."

For me, knowing what I know about the prophecies of Nostradamus, reading this message by bin Laden directed to the French makes me see how it comes from a position of strength. I do not see it in any way as an idle threat or unrealistic boast. The Associated Press stated that the message was interpreted as a reference to six French uranium mine employees (previously reported to be five French nationals and two Africans), who were taken hostage in Niger in mid-September 2010. That makes bin Laden's threat become a direct statement about French colonial involvement in Africa (specifically Niger), which influenced several Islam-dominated countries. The message is also a statement about "turn about being fair play," where bin Laden is quoted as saying,

> "If you deemed it your right to ban (Muslim) women from wearing the hijab, then should not it be our right to expel your invading men by striking their necks?"

To hear bin Laden's words as coming from a position of strength, one must be aware of the fact that Europe has been glutted with Muslim immigrants. The "hijab law" is because the French have become nervously concerned about accepting it as normal that foreigners can walk around being concealed from public view. This nervousness is because Muslim terrorists now represent a threat to Western nations, and Western nations have become glutted by Muslims. Concealment makes it easier for terrorists to operate more "openly" in the lands they plan to subvert. The parallel, the reason Osama bin Laden openly makes such statements, comes from France's past involvements in foreign lands, covertly subverting those governments to do their bidding. Thus, the turn about – "Our scarves? Your necks." Osama bin Laden is calling out the French as specific targets for Islamic retribution.

France is one Western nation that has meddled in the ways Middle Eastern nations have governed their citizens. They have caused governments to act contrary to the customary application of Islamic Law, making it easier for a Western presence to oversee their "foreign investments" in the Middle East and Africa (primarily). Osama bin Laden knows that Muslims are now living in Europe for the same purpose of disrupting Western laws.

The concept of law in all "Christian" nations is democracy, in the sense that the will of the people (not simply majority will) cannot be trampled upon, without protest. The Muslims are now treading on Western freedoms, protected by Western laws that allow all citizens rights, for the purpose of disrupting the systems of law in the West. They have long been infiltrating Western countries, using the protection of the laws they wish to subvert. It has become a cat and mouse game, where the mouse has outgrown the cat. The mouse now seeks to make the cat feel what it is like being chased and terrorized.

France not only has a history of African colonial involvements, but it also was one of the designated Protectorates (over Lebanon and Syria) that were named by the League of Nations following the surrender of the Ottomans at the end of World War I. Italy and Spain also are targets of bin Laden's grand plan, due to their histories against Muslims, but France poses the greatest threat. It represents more of a resistant power, to a planned Islamic (plus mercenary allies) invasion of Western Europe. That story, which has yet to be fulfilled (a prediction of the future), is clearly written in *The Prophecies*.

It is so clear that Rene Noorbergen mapped out the waves of attacks (complete with bold directional arrows – from here to there) in his 1981 book, *Nostradamus Predicts the End of the World*. It is beyond any doubt that the verbiage some of Nostradamus' quatrains predict an invasion of Western Europe, in a way that has not yet occurred in history. It maps out a Mediterranean Sea (naval) invasion, with multiple points of entry. One in particular is into southern France. The same future awaits both Italy and Spain. Therefore, Osama bin Laden's latest recorded threat, which is directed specifically at France, reminded me that I know where he is hiding.

If you think about it a little bit, you might ask yourself, "How does Osama bin Laden, a man in hiding, keep abreast of the latest news?" The answer that comes to you might be a dawning of awareness. Surely, with every rifle the U.S. military has pointed at the mountain holes of Afghanistan (Elmer Fudd-like), they would see the paperboy riding up with the latest newspaper, making a delivery where nothing but mountain goats would be. That would be so suspicious that bin Laden certainly would be found. Even if he has a ham radio, trying to tune in on the latest news broadcast by Radio Free Europe (is that still in business?), modern surveillance equipment would detect that and he would be found.

I guess it would be possible for an Afghani poppy farmer to meander into a secret cave entrance and, after some hiking reach Osama bin Laden, he could tell him all the latest news he had memorized. However, I did not know about the French miners being taken by African al-Qaeda members; and, I watch Fox News every night. So, how would some uneducated Afghani be up on the latest French news?

The answer might be as simple as imagining a clean-shaven Osama bin Laden, wearing the local garb of a French grape grower, sitting at a table on a French sidewalk café, sipping a latte, while reading the latest French newspaper. He would read one that would tell all about the latest law changes, including the recent kidnapping of French miners. That would be how Osama bin Laden could be so riled up about the latest news about the French people persecuting poor Muslim immigrants. That would explain how he got the idea for a new video. In this vision, and in Bugs Bunny terms, one would realize that Osama bin Laden would not be where all the guns are pointed; and, he would not be looking like everyone expected him to look.

Afterthoughts: From the 20/20 perspective of hindsight in 2020, the "Why now?" must be understood as being **someone** is still leading the organization known as al-Qaeda. There has been an expansion, where other groups designated as terrorist organization are around the globe. If Osama bin Laden was not actually killed on May Day 2011, then he is hiding where Nostradamus said to look. If Osama bin Laden was killed when the world was told he had been, then someone like him is where Nostradamus told to look. The reason why is danger is still afoot. The reason why now is that danger has worsened.

It is undeniable that France has become a hotbed of terrorism, since May Day 2011. The Wikipedia article entitled "List of terrorist incidents in France" shows there have been thirty-eight specifically named 'incidences' since Osama bin Laden was announced dead, with over 170 listed per year. Nine of those specifically listed occurred in the year 2020. Over 270 have died in those specifically named "incidents," with over 960 injured. The top three specifically named "incidents" were: "Shootings, hostage taking and suicide bombings," in November 2015; "Vehicle ramming," in July 2016; and, "Shooting," in January 2015. That last specific "incidence" was the attacks on the *Charlie Hebdo* office in Paris, where cartoonists were among the dead.

This focus on France implies that there is a strong presence of organization there. This area of the world is where Nostradamus told to look for a terrorism 'mastermind' in 1555. When he wrote of what would befall his native land, there was little to worry about of this nature.

Finally, I wrote of the "hajib law." I hope the readers will see the way that has become a "turn about is fair play" circumstance, now that the Cornoavirus pandemic has caused France (all every nation in the Western Hemisphere) to mandate mask wearing. On the back cover of this book is a graffiti artist rendition of a terrorist (found in Marseilles, France in 2012), who wore a mask. Today, one would think nothing of someone looking like that.

Chapter 3
Eh ... What's Up Doc?

In early 2003, before I began my first attempt at translating Nostradamus' quatrains into English, I had seen where he indicated Osama bin Laden would go to hide out. This revelation was told as a part of the whole story that I initially saw, coming from 200 of the 943 quatrains at my disposal. The author of the only book I had ever seen about *The Prophecies* had translated all of those 200 (Erika Cheetham). From that portion of the whole (200 is roughly 21% of the total), I had seen much of what clearly points to bin Laden's hideout. The remainder that I later looked at (the other 740+) added to the clarity of that location, while confirming what I first understood. From those first months after I began to understand how to read Nostradamus, I could see the framework of a story line that would only get stronger and clearer as I advanced and progressed in my work towards full understanding.

My offer to an F.B.I. agent was made before I had actually prepared any presentation. That was part of the reason why I suggested a coffee house meeting in the first place, as a scheduled meeting would give me time to prepare such a presentation. Because I was turned down by the agent (and because I was unemployed and could not afford to waste printer ink and paper), I simply kept what I knew in my head. As I look back on that time now, eight years later, I do not know what I would have presented to him as evidence worthy of compensation. I knew, comparatively, very little then, relative to what I know now.

The story that I first saw is still the story. Overall, it has not changed. Since the time I first became aware that the 200 quatrains told a story line, I have gained much greater insights from translating all 948 quatrains, and two of Nostradamus' letters. I have translated the Old French to English several times, using multiple sources and tools, with each translation allowing me a level of concentration that has revealed deeper and deeper meaning. My growth in awareness has been like carefully peeling away the layers of an onion to reveal the core. It has never ceased being an onion, but I have seen more and more of what makes up that one onion.

It is, therefore, from that level of knowledge that I now prepare a presentation that explains where Osama bin Laden can be found. If I were to go to the F.B.I. today, I would map out the logic that is involved in understanding what Nostradamus wrote and how that understanding becomes a perfect match for finding bin Laden. The story is one where bin Laden is an important character; and, this correlates to the present, where bin Laden is an important character. We know he is an important character because every time he releases a new video and everyone, in particular the F.B.I., flocks to see it. The story presents characters who play roles that act to bring about a great devastation in the world (as would be a multi-pronged naval invasion of Western Europe), with persecution being a major theme. The latest video condemning France is a perfect example of this play being well under way.

I will make public where Osama bin Laden is, in an attempt to present a provable prediction told by Nostradamus. My intent is to promote belief that God still acts through prophets who are chosen to help mankind become aware of going the wrong way (turning their backs to God). Prophets speak divine utterances for the purpose of getting mankind to beg God to help them out of another mess they have brought upon themselves. I will now expose where Osama bin Laden is in hiding, because I want the world to find reason to repent and ask God to come save the day: from people like Osama bin Laden; from human beings that we allow to lord over us; and, from aspects or our own selves that thus makes it possible for evil to control our lives.

According to what Nostradamus wrote, it is possible to see that Osama bin Laden is inside the Pyrenees Mountains. If this is proved, he will be found there training an army of would-be France-Spain invaders. He will have the protection of the indigenous, non-Muslim, ethnic people along those mountains, from which there are several to choose. All have long fought for their own sovereign authority, against that imposed by Spain and France. He will be found there for the symbolic purpose of reclaiming land once possessed by the Moors, before a Christian Inquisition finally forced them out of Europe.

The stories told in *The Prophecies* expose the bin Laden plan. Accordingly, he and his companions will have already called upon all non-Muslims, those with some axe to grind with Western Europe, to follow him and the Islamic Jihad he leads. He offers a promise to such would-be mercenaries, one that says they will be rewarded generously for their efforts, from the spoils of another war fought on European soil. The Muslims see themselves as being above the trappings of a material world, which the West seems to lust for; but they recognize the feelings those who have lived in poverty have within them. Those who have done without for so long, in particular Eastern Europeans (the Slavs) and black Africans (the slaves), deserve their time to also wallow in the riches the world can provide. This story line tells how the boasts of Osama bin Laden come from the comforting position of knowing his allies are fully committed to stand with him, prepared to act upon given notice and invade the lands of his enemies, letting all their anger flow freely.

Nostradamus, as a Frenchman, was allowed to see the future of his homeland. Overall, the stories of *The Prophecies* are Eurocentric, as France is an important part of the whole of that continent. Moreover, Nostradamus was Christian, and France was the land of the original "bloodline of Christ." That means France stands for one seat of influence ("*kings*"), which would become the first royal rulers to unite all the lands of Europe under Christianity. Since the stories of *The Prophecies* are all about the conditions that would arise in Europe after the kings would lose their rule, in particular in France, they tell of a land no longer led by Christian values. As such, Nostradamus was shown how all future World Wars would be fought in his homeland; and in that regard, the greatest war humanity would ever face would be waged specifically on the grounds that border the Pyrenees Mountains.

To assist bin Laden's training plan, which is designed to help conquer Europe, waves of Muslim immigrants, both legal and illegal, have been pouring into Europe (North America has not been exempt) over the past twenty years. Africans seeking refugee status from civil strife in their homelands have assisted this number. It has also been increased by freed Eastern Europeans (including Russians) seeking to embrace the comforts of capitalism previously denied them. This total immigrant presence in Europe has long been causing many problems for all the Western nations.

France certainly has a swelling problem with a rising Muslim population. I personally witnessed this while visiting the port city of Marseilles, in 2006. Simply by looking like a tourist walking around the Vieux Port (Old Harbor), we were frequently approached by Muslim beggars asking for Euros. In a tour of Italy that I was part of in 2008, the tour guide warned us of the "gypsies" (a.k.a. Roma) that we would encounter at each tour stop. In every case, between the bus and the attraction we were stopping to see, we would pass by foreigners selling their wares. These immigrants (many from Africa) stood in designated areas (I imagine determined by official ordinance). Prior to visiting Europe, I had read of many immigration problems arising in all of the Western European nations, beginning after Saddam Hussein invaded Kuwait, leading to the first Gulf War (1991).

The quatrains clearly say to look to the Pyrenees Mountains. With the Pyrenees Mountains being the natural border between France and Spain, this would be a logical place to sneak in an army of Muslim men, who could be living and training in natural caves there. This would be logical, in line with the story line of *The Prophecies* telling of a planned future naval invasion, where a pre-established land force is predicted to help add to the confusion of a preemptive attack. Communities of Muslims have sprouted up in those lands, where none had existed before. Where do they all go after a long day of begging tourists for Euros and selling trinkets?

Begging and selling trinkets affords them a source of income, enough to keep them healthy enough to bear the babies that mothers are glad to show to tourists, to make them feel guilty that, as they spend, spend, spend on vacations, a poor baby could be starving. The socialist states of Western Europe provide some sources of sustenance to those who appear to have nothing, with little chance of ever making a life for themselves in a world that shuns the poor like the plague. In addition to these funds, news reports have proven terrorist cells regularly receive funds sent through Muslim "charities," with the subversive elements receiving funds through more secretive channels.

All of this means that the presence of Muslim soldiers in Europe is not expected to be obvious and overt. This element simply can be seen as small groups of Muslim men, which would not seem strange or out of place. Even Osama bin Laden, sans beard, sandals, headdress, and robe, could openly walk about the countryside or cities of southern France without being recognized. Just like Bugs Bunny, he could walk up to an armed French soldier and ask, "Eh, what's up doc?"

It is a fact that the CIA-American-led coalition forces in Afghanistan are looking for Osama bin Laden in some mountain hideout. Shortly after the invasion of Afghanistan, the Taliban retreated into the mountains there. The news of that war effort reported that sophisticated cave lairs had been discovered. Inside these caves were found copies of a terrorist training manual, which included instructions on how to make a dirty bomb (radiological material dispersed by conventional bomb explosives). These cave lairs were said to be quite extensive and capable of hiding, even housing, hundreds of soldiers. All of this information makes it possible to understand the importance of bin Laden being a "mountain man."

In this modern world of high-tech surveillance systems, the U.S. military can pay a soldier to sit in a command center in California and have him or her watch a computer monitor screen that shows satellite images of ground movements in northwestern Pakistan. This command center employee can coordinate the launching of a drone aircraft from Afghanistan. He or she can then direct it to where suspicious activities are taking place. Drones with surveillance cameras can get a closer view of who is involved; and, Predator drones can attack those who are identified as enemy combatants.

This ability amounts to a strategic "height" advantage in a declared war. It has historically been ideal military strategy to take the high ground on a battlefield. American forces would suffer heavy losses trying to march uphill, in mountainous terrain, to attack a suspected enemy stronghold. The history of Afghanistan in warfare is that it eventually wins all wars, simply due to the mountainous terrain. Ultimately, in Afghanistan, all significant battles must be fought in the mountains. However, the enemy in Afghanistan-Pakistan (al-Qaeda or the Taliban) cannot gain control of the height of a satellite orbiting around the earth.

The problem with this technology is it cannot see through rock, or inside a mountain. It can only see what is exposed to the sky. This makes a mountain the perfect protective cover for clandestine plotting for the demise of the West, through secret attacks and invasions. If one recalls several of the James Bond themes (books and movies), as well as other movies that portray an evil villain with unlimited money and tremendous intellectual powers (Dr. Evil for instance, in the *Austin Powers* movies), their lair was inside a mountain (or fake island volcano). The reason is no one ever thinks of a mountain as being hollow inside. From the outside, a mountain looks as solid as rock.

Wherever there are mountains there are caves. There are mountains in Europe, which is where the Pyrenees Mountains are. Osama bin Laden and his band of al-Qaeda are known to be mountain guerrilla fighters, as was his previous band that joined the Mujahideen (he was technically an "Afghan Arab"). What becomes important to realize, if for nothing more than symbolic purposes, is that Mohammed received God's revelations in a mountain cave near Mecca. One also must accept the possibility that, since the Pyrenees Mountains have a history of having been occupied by Moors, there could well be some old Moorish maps of caves in the Pyrenees. Perhaps, those maps were used by the Moors to hide people from the Spanish Inquisition. All of this history makes the naming of the Pyrenees Mountains by Nostradamus in *The Prophecies* suggest a viable place to look for a presence up to no good.

The possibility of belief exists, regardless of how improbable something is. This is where the language of Nostradamus enhances that possibility. This enhancement is magnified when one believes that Nostradamus was actually a prophet of Jesus Christ, chosen to write a message that would be used much later, at a time of great need, to solve a problem that before seemed unsolvable. This is particularly relevant now, since modern history has designated public enemy number one (at least on the FBI "Ten Most Wanted" list) as Usama bin Laden (more popularly known as Osama). He is known as a mountain-hiding man. This makes Nostradamus' use of the word "*mountain*" an important marker.

Afterthoughts: In my statement that finding Osama bin Laden in the Pyrenees Mountains would lead to a full understanding of *The Prophecies*, this needs to be explained further. A full understanding of *The Prophecies* cannot be understood as having some ability to boldly predict the next tragic event to happen, listing which quatrains point to that end, and then sitting back as the world destroys itself, just as one interpreted Nostradamus wrote it would do. That is not the purpose of divine prophecy. Seeing enough come true precisely as prophesied, such that it would be humanly impossible for some man in the mid-sixteenth century to even guess something so specific and never before happened, has to elicit faith that Nostradamus was a true Prophet and God. That then becomes faith that God is the source (with Nostradamus having been reborn, in the name of Jesus Christ). Faith in God then does everything humanly possible to stop causing the madness to grow larger and fester more greatly. Again, I say one must demand that the land stolen in 1948 be given back to Palestine and the Jews removed. That solution would force the Muslims to stop their terrorism. If they refuse to stop, at least God would be on the side of those who tried, in **good faith**.

Chapter 4
A Latte and a Long Table, Please

In the world of crime versus crime fighters, people informing authorities where criminals are, were last seen, or possibly could be, leads to more criminals being caught than good detective work does. With apologies to the memory of J. Edgar Hoover, Efrem Zimbalist, Jr., and people who believed in the ideals and concepts behind the Quinn-Martin Productions *F.B.I.* television series, agents for the F.B.I. are simply people who are trained to listen carefully to conversations.

They are good at mentally analyzing the slightest piece of memory told by a witness, a suspect, or someone remotely connected to someone involved in a crime. Their education in crime solving techniques means they can take those leads and then make arrests and convictions. In other words, agents of the law are not super-heroes who solve crimes without the help of many other people. They desperately need informants – consultants if you will – for most criminals to be caught; but that does not include the "mastermind professional criminals" who stay on the "most wanted list" for decades at a time.

I was not taken up on my offer to make a rational presentation as to where I believed Osama bin Laden could be found, based on a logical interpretation of prophetic words related to the crime of September 11, 2001. So, I can only imagine how I would have make such a presentation then, today. Since I am not about to go try to twist anyone's arm in an attempt to have someone believe in God, I leave it for someone else to make an actual presentation that would offer evidence to prove this point. Nostradamus only could have known where Osama bin Laden would be, then and now, by having been shown by God. That means belief in my opinion requires belief in God. Since government agencies have been separated from such belief, this book makes it possible for someone else to take up that baton and run with it – all the way to a $25-million reward.

The evidence I present represents what lawyers would call a "preponderance." This means that the amount of evidence Nostradamus provides can be defined as "superior in weight, power, importance, or strength."[1] There is such a wealth of evidence coming from the words of *The Prophecies* that only a fool would disregard it as unimportant. Since F.B.I. agents are not fools (they catch fools), they would have to look at this preponderance with very discerning eyes and test everything for any potential validity. The preponderance comes from many quatrains and both letters of explanation; and, while I have my opinion as to the meaning, with logic as the guide, then everyone should come to the same concluding opinion.

I will spread out my reasoning before the reader as would a trial attorney in a court of law. The reader becomes the jurist that sits and listens to the evidence presented, and then weighs that evidence for accuracy and believability. In this manner, the counter argument is left up to the reader to determine. In effect, this work is a disclosure of the evidence that would be presented in a trial, leaving it up to the defense to develop a plan of action in response. In either case, as jury member or as defense attorney, the ultimate decision boils down to a judgment of belief.

The American judicial system is loosely based on logic. It fails this test in how emotional appeals can sway an argument, such that one shred of reasonable doubt becomes just cause for going against logical evidence. A college debate team is more inclined to follow logic to a truly reasoned judgment, with those casting their votes in the end having been trained to detect flaws of reason. This is how I wish this work to be judged, before any emotional opinion sets in. I want a judgment that has attempted to find the true flaws in my reasoning, such that one can step forward and declare, "Robert Tippett made a serious error in defining one word here," or "he erred by mistaking the true historical elements of that event there." Specifics are required in that regard.

That type of argument against what I present must also go to the next level, going beyond simple doubt. It must finally state, "I have contacted both the French and Spanish governments, and after a thorough combing of the Pyrenees Mountains, no evidence of Osama bin Laden being there exists." This is the ultimate judgment that can be made against my argument. It exists because I do not have personal knowledge of anything relative to the prediction I present. I

---

[1]   Fair Use, "preponderance," a word similarly defined by many dictionaries.

may be wrong.

Still, if I am wrong, it proves nothing about Nostradamus or *The Prophecies*. I did not write those enigmatic letters and poems. I am only able to understand them through a system of rules I have attached to them, as a new language that allows me to gain understanding. I am the one making the prediction that is clear as a bell for others to test. However, there may be some other very important person in the Pyrenees Mountains, because after all is said and done, Nostradamus never wrote the name Osama bin Laden.

I am completely satisfied that my prediction will be verified, or I would not be writing this book. I have nothing to gain in this material world by being found right or wrong. I feel strongly that God is the source of Nostradamus' vision of an otherwise unknowable future. I am certain that the Spirit of Jesus Christ assists my brain's ability to fathom systems being present, and insights that lead me to check to see if this or that has any relevance (when they always do). It has been through such insight that I realized just how logical everything is, when one is led to understanding; and, that a prophetic prediction that can be proved at all, demonstrates a revelation of God and His all-seeing powers. However, I am not so emotional that I have let my feelings about *The Prophecies* effect how I undertake a logical approach, as that can be the only way to have others see the truth that I see.

I want everyone to test this prediction because I am completely confident it will be proven true. It can raise the level of faith that Christians profess to have immensely, which could help the world avert what *The Prophecies* state is still to come. Testing this prediction can be the answer to more than a $25-million question. It can be the way to save the world from a self-inflicted wound, one from which it will not be able to recover.

To test my prediction and find it inaccurate would help the atheists of the world prove there is no reason to believe in prophecy. No reason to believe in prophecy becomes reason to believe there is no god. There are a growing number of people who would love to find this prediction woefully inept and totally wrong. However, to come to that conclusion logically, my prediction must be examined with the same lack of emotional zeal for their own opinion. Emotion can lead one to illogical bias and flawed reasoning. One must remain open to the possibility that my prediction can be true, if my logic is sound.

That is why a test must be done immediately, because if word gets out about a debate over whether or not to look in the Pyrenees Mountains for Osama bin Laden, that waskily wabbit might go down a hole and come out some place else. If that happens, nothing might be proved.

Afterthoughts: I would like to let it be known that I do not speak of the F.B.I without some personal knowledge. My ex-father-in-law (who I loved and admired) was a retired F.B.I. special agent. He was photographed at the airport in New York City, receiving the extradited suspect in the Martin Luther King assassination, James Earl Ray, who was sent to face charges in the United States by the British. My father-in-law did not hunt down and capture James Earl Ray. My father-in-law was also photographed at the scene where a young female kidnap victim had been buried alive, in a case that made the national news. He was there as they uncovered her in a coffin, still alive. My father-in-law did not solve that case, as he was sent there by his superiors. Finally, my father-in-law was assigned to surveil the KKK Grand Wizard, James R. Venable, who had an office above a bike shop in Tucker, Georgia. He made sure James Venable knew he was watching him. My wife, then his young daughter, would go on surveillance with her father. James Venable often met them and talked friendly with them. He offered to let her ride the horses at his Stone Mountain ranch, and my father-in-law let her do that. My father-in-law drew the line by not letting James Venable give her a horse, which he tried to do. James Venable was a lawyer, never once spending time behind bars for being convicted of any crime, which goes to show how a lot of F.B.I. activities never do much of anything. Preventing crimes means no crimes get committed. However, no police agency in America can stop a crime, simply because Americans are free to commit every crime on the books; it is after a crime has been committed that one needs good investigators.

Finally, it is important to see how I made the point in this chapter that Osama bin Laden might not be the one Nostradamus was writing of, although his history certainly was a good fit. Certainly, the F.B.I. would have never turned over a large reward without first proving it wrong. That is what a "good investigator" does; and, Lord knows every crime has its share of leads that must be followed up on They might have been led to expose a secret underground network in the Pyrenees Mountains that was poised to do evil deeds, with Osama bin Laden not actually there. If that were the case, I doubt the F.B.I. would even say, "Thanks for the tip."

Chapter 5
Prosecution Exhibit A

The Presence of "Mountain" and "Pyren-nees" in the Letter to Henry II

In the whole of *The Prophecies*, Nostradamus penned some form of the word "mountain" fifty-one times.[1] He wrote *"monts"* ("mounts, hills, mountains") thirty times, *"montaignes"* ("mountains") twice, *"mont"* ("mount, hill, mountain") fifteen times, and *"montaigne"* ("mountain") four times. There are no specific references to any mountain in Afghanistan; and, only one possible reference (that I see) to a mountain outside of Europe, anywhere in *The Prophecies*. All references to what appear to be specifically named mountains are in Europe, being those along France's border with Switzerland (Jura) and Spain (Pyrenees), and Italy's central mountain range (the Apennines). Of all those references to specific mountains that Nostradamus named, only two are referenced three or more times.

One of those two is Italy's mountain range, the Apennines. Nostradamus specifically mentioned the Apennines in three quatrains (spelled as *"Apennis"* twice, and *"Apennines"* once). The focus on the Apennines is enhanced by three other references to a specific *"mont"*, where two require the translation be as "hill". In those cases, the word *"mont"* connects to a proper name that is a specific hill in Rome. The "Seven Hills of Rome" can be seen as part of the mountainous peninsula that makes up the majority of Italy, thus they are offshoots of the Apennines. The third specific reference becomes an indirect reference to the Apennines, such that *"monts Italique"* ("mountains of Italy")

---

1   Fifty are found in the quatrains, with only one found in the letters.

45

makes this identification. These references to Italian mountains place Italy as an important focal point in the future told by *The Prophecies*. However, the Pyrenees Mountains get much more attention.

The Pyrenees Mountains form the natural barrier that is the border between France and Spain. Nostradamus specifically referenced this mountain range twelve times,[2] spelled as either *"Pyrenees"* (9), *"Pyrennees"* (2), or *"Pyrens"* (1). Between those listings and the ones placing focus on other individual mountains in Europe (such as the Jura Alps being found stated twice, to name one reference), the naming of European mountains highlights a prophecy placing emphasis on Europe, Western Europe especially. The multiple listings previously stated show the importance of prophesied activity in Italy, Spain, and France. Still, the preponderance of reference to the Pyrenees becomes most important to understand, simply because it is the one specifically mentioned the most times.

Eleven of the twelve references are in the quatrains. The twelfth reference is the only instance of the word *"Pyrennees"* found in either letter of explanation (spelled in any form). This is further enhanced by that one specific reference coming alongside the only reference, in either letter, to the word *"mont."* One must realize that the letter to King Henry II was written to explain the meaning that would be found in the quatrains. One must also understand that the rules of logic say, especially when trying to figure out the meaning of something written long ago and that is difficult to interpret, the author is the best source of meaning. That rule, coupled with only one reference to the Pyrenees Mountains in an explanation letter means the one usage in the letter to Henry can be expected to be a guide to interpreting the eleven uses found in the quatrains.

That understanding makes closer inspection of Nostradamus' use of *"mont"* and *"pyrennees"* in the letter addressed to King Henry II important. As one piece of evidence that leads to a prediction that Osama bin Laden is hiding in the Pyrenees Mountains, the information coming from the letter must be able to match the information coming from the quatrains, and vice versa. If the two match, then logic supports a conclusion as to the meaning.

In that letter, Nostradamus wrote of a "raging in the mountain". The whole of that series of words containing "raging in the mountain" says, *"furibonde au mont Jouis descendant pour monter aux pyren-nees ne sera translate à l'antique*

---

2   This number comes from eleven references in the quatrains and one in the letter to Henry II.

monarchie".[3] This translates to state (in one specific literal case), "raging in the mountain Possessed-ones descending for to rise at them not Pyrenees-born-ones nor will be translated with the ancient kingdom". Do not be alarmed if this reads like a Shakespeare play where Old English is difficult to follow, because it is difficult to follow. It has little to do with the translation being Old French, as I will explain.

For this piece of evidence to make sense, it is important to remain focused only on the use of "*mountain*". One must not get too far astray, following the words that develop the context relative to a "mountain". That is how normal syntax works as an automatic process in your brain. It kicks in immediately, after one has spent years reading words with normal syntax applied. However, because normal syntax is not being used in *The Prophecies*, it is immediately difficult to follow too many words at once.

Reading too much at one time, from any part of *The Prophecies*, will result in difficulty in understanding the specifics of what is being conveyed. Everything written by Nostradamus is vitally important for full understanding to come, as each word adds the details that make up the whole. This is the same concept behind full understanding when normal syntax is used, but *The Prophecies* uses syntactical rules differently. Therefore, it is especially important to pay attention to the detail that comes from each word written, particularly in the letter to Henry II.

This letter from Nostradamus explains what one can expect the quatrains to reveal, as a general overview. As the first piece of evidence that Osama bin Laden is hiding in the Pyrenees Mountains, one needs to get a good grasp of the depth of meaning that comes from the series of words that surrounds the word "mountain". The only way to do that is to come to understand each word slowly.

The words that lead up to the word "mountain" can say, "furious in the mountain". The French combined preposition-article, "*au*," represents the words "*à+le,*" from which "in the" has been translated. The French preposition "*à*" can convey the meaning, "in, to, with, at, or from", such that it presents a direction for one to look. All of these possible directions are correct, such that one can read, "furious at the mountain", "raging in the mountain", "mad with the mountain", "fury

---

3   The 1566 Lyon edition shows "*Pyrenées*", as a capitalized, non-hyphenated word. The hyphenation of the 1568 Lyon edition [my preferred reference] is due to the printer, and the word ending one line, and being continued onto the next line.

from the mountain", and/or "furious to the mountain". This shows how multiple translations of *"furibonde"* are also all correct. Thus, the reader is being told that part of the story told in the quatrains will focus on an element of anger and turbulence that will be found directing people around one specific "mountain".

Capitalized words will always be found to denote importance. A name is a title of importance, such that the specificity of one is more important than a generalization of many. In this string of words, Nostradamus identified "the mountain" by creating the symbolic name *"Jouis"*, which I have translated as, "Possessed-ones". One knows this name is symbolic because there is no such mountain named *"Jouis"*.[4] This means Nostradamus has chosen the name[5] because it indicates the importance that one specific "mountain" presents in the story line.

The name is making the statement that "the mountain", which has anger (*"furibonde"* is translated as, "furious, fury, mad, raging") directed around it, is identified by those who own it. The reader is told of an important mountain that is identified as "a mountain" being "Enjoyed, Possessed, or Had" by the "ones" there. As such, this capitalized word is identifying the "ones" of the "mountain", as their presence is what identifies the possession, ownership, and/or occupation.

By understanding that from the symbolic name, one can understand that "fury" directed "at the mountain" has brought about a major "Enjoyment". Perhaps, that is due to "the mountain" having come into their possession. If so, then this is an indication that the "mountain" is being claimed, in some sense, by invaders or foreigners. Their arrival and a state of important occupation they feel in this "mountain" is reason for a new name to be created to denote that change.

I understand that what I have just presented is making little sense to many readers. Let me assure those who are confused that reading slowly cannot be

---

4   In Old French, the past tense of the verb *"jouir,"* is *"joui,"* which means, "enjoyed, possessed, held, had, occupied, used, taken the profit, received the fruit, and had the fruition of." As standard syntax does not have the past tense of a verb take the plural "-s" ending, as Nostradamus wrote in this "name" of a mountain, the syntax of Nostradamus requires the translation to add "those," or "the ones," who the past tense action then refers to. As such, *"mont Jouis"* translates as, the "mountain those Held". This can also become "mountain Possessed ones".

5   At all times when I make a reference to what Nostradamus meant, it is to be inferred that Nostradamus acted only as a vehicle for God, such that it would be correct to say, "the name chosen by God." However, that would become confusing.

over emphasized. By the end of this book, one will be much more capable of following what I write and hopefully be able to foresee what I will write, simply from seeing what Nostradamus wrote. However, let me quickly review how I came to my conclusions, based on these four words written by Nostradamus: "*furibonde au mont Jouis*".

Nostradamus has set forth four concepts, in four words. In one's normal syntactical approach to language, the same can be said for the four words, "mad at the mountain". Unfortunately, our syntax teaches us to grasp strings of words and quickly process them for meaning. It is not like that when reading *The Prophecies*. In those four words, God has stated through Nostradamus everything possible that comes from the meanings associated with the words "*furibonde*", "*au*", "*mont*", and "*Jouis*". As such, the reader is asked to understand "furious" as an emotional state, which leads to an outward expression of that state, as "raging". It is a state of anger and turbulence, due to one being "mad", to the point of no longer being able to control oneself. It borders on being insane with anger and pent-up rage.

Typically, such an emotional energy is directed "at" that which has caused the "raging". This means that state is "in" one's self, and shown "to" all as not being in a normal state. The state has come "from" something that is most probably unwanted and therefore forced upon one. It creates a state that all must live "with". Thus, the state of being is directed to all that surrounds the one in that state.

Standard use of the French and English languages places the object of the verb close by. As such, reading "furious at the mountain" leads one to think the "mountain" is where the anger is directed, thus making the "mountain" the source of the fury. This is not necessarily the case in *The Prophecies*. While that meaning may be relevant in some sense, it may not be the primary sense. In this case, the primary meaning is found by seeing the word "mountain" as indicative of where the "furious" one(s) can be found. Still, the word "mountain" can also act to state the size of the "madness", meaning that it has reached a peak.

No definition can be eliminated, which is why confusion abounds. Our learned use of syntax is designed to quickly process words and eliminate as many meanings as possible, so that word specificity creates a limited focus. When complex words are used, it restricts one's ability to understand the context an unknown word fits. This is not a problem when reading *The Prophecies*, because each word becomes its own context based on all possible meanings each word commands. That is why each word must be seen as its own statement, with a context that fits with all the possible contexts of the words surrounding it. But, the context of two words together can be considered only after each word is completely understood alone.

This is why a word like "*Jouis*" adds to the confusion. In French, the combination of a lower-case "*mont*" preceding an upper-case "*Jouis*" is read syntactically as "Mount Joy", which is totally wrong. The word "*mont*" is not capitalized, and it is not dependent on "*Jouis*" for its meaning. Additionally, the word written is "*Jouis*", which is an "*s*" added to the end of a past participle verb, "*Joui*". That word, in the lower-case, means, "possessed, enjoyed, used, and/or had". Since it is improper to make that past tense word plural, the word is seen as being a misspelling of some form of the verb *jouer*, which means, "to play, sport, game", and in general to have fun. When the premise is that *The Prophecies* is a work of divine origin, there are no misspelled words possible. That means the plural ending is an indication of the "ones" who acted "possessed, enjoyed, used, and/or had".

The capitalization of that past participle plural word simply shows that a symbolic name of importance has been applied to the meaning behind the name. The importance is elevated so that it becomes seen as the cause of the "furious" state. A "mountain" of "furious" people has become symbolic as "Possessed ones". In that sense, when the "madness" is seen as relative to a physical "mountain" it becomes the terrain of "those Used". The symbolic name acts to identify the importance of that preexisting state of being, through all meanings that can come from that moniker.

I have paused the analysis of this important section from Nostradamus' letter of explanation to his king because it is paramount that one be able to follow the meaning that is to come. All of the following quatrains will be strung from this meaning. I pause to give the reader a quick lesson in how the systems of Nostradamus are what is guiding me to write what I write. From this point on, I will not be doing this type of stop and repeat, although I am fully aware of the struggle one faces trying to grasp what I write quickly. Again, the words I have written are not designed to be read as fast as one can read them. It is important to realize a great need to slow down and take one's time contemplating what I am writing, because the reader's ability to understand is important to the outcome of all our futures.

With that now better understood, we look at how this major accomplishment of "Possession" is related to the "raging". One is then able to see how that has led "to the mountain", where next is found the word "descending". The French word written is "*descendant*," which is the present participle of the verb "*descendre*," meaning, "to descend, go down, come from, alight, light off, light down; also to cast down, take down, bring down, or lay down; as well as to fetch from a higher place unto a lower." Additionally, the word "*descendant*" can be like the English word, and mean, "the progeny or offspring of." All of these meanings can be applied correctly in this series of words written by Nostradamus, with each being relevant to those "Possessing a mountain".

With the use of "*descendant*," one must be open to the possibility of the translation, "going downwards," but not such that it necessarily means, "going downhill." The word used can be a sign of going inward, or below the surface. It carries a connotation of something swooping down towards something, as well as a process of degradation. When associated with a "mountain" (especially when "*mont*" means "hill"), one can see how a "mountain" has an advantage of height (to swoop from), caves (to go beneath the surface), and slopes (to go down). All of this meaning will be seen repeated in later pieces of evidence; but pay particular attention to the element of going below the surface. One's attention is brought to that possibility at this time because it will have an impact later. Still, that translation is not the only one, as the words of *The Prophecies* are selected for use with the purpose of bearing a multiplicity of meaning.

The reference to "*descendant*" also has an intended double meaning, being that "the mountain Possessed-ones" are connected, as kin, to that piece of earth where "a mountain" is located. This means the series of words can indicate that "the mountain" can be seen as returning to the hands a "progeny", or a "descendant", of a people who once before considered "the mountain" theirs. This lineage, or link to relatives as past owners, assists one in identifying why "rage, madness, and fury" would be directed "to the mountain".

Remembering the suggestion that "*au mont*" can mean, "in the mountain", see how this relates to the next word in the text, "*monter*". That French verb means, "to mount, ascend, rise, climb, to go up into or get up into; also to increase or to grow dear; and also to show in quantity, to amount unto; and to raise up, advance up, and/or to lift up." In that case, "*monter*" represents an exit, from within to without, as the opposite of "descending". It explains why one would be inside "a mountain", as "in the mountain" becomes the place where one "descendant" will "rise up", or "ascend" to "lift up" and "to advance".

One cannot help but also realize that the word "*mont*" ("mountain") is derived from the verb "*monter*", such that both words identify heights that require effort to achieve. When one connects "*descendant*" to "*monter*", with the next word, "*pour*" (meaning, "for, because, considering, instead of, in defense of, and/or against"), one begins to see a purpose developing. That purpose is "for raising", or "because to lift up" one's numbers of related people ("offspring"), would ensure one's new "Possession". As such, the "mountain Enjoyed", as the place of one's distant relatives, has to "increase against" those causing them to be "furious".

This assumption of numbers of people is confirmed in the next word, another combined preposition-article ("*aux*"), which is in the plural form. This is then taking the "*au*" previously stated ("in the, with the, to a, at an, from the") and changing the focus from an individual ("a, an, the") to more than one ("them, those, the ones"). As each word written by Nostradamus has to be seen as its own statement, nothing can be regarded as insignificant. Thus, the reader is asked to ponder the direction that will be taken by the action "to mount". One then begins to see the purpose ("because") being "to increase with them".

It is at this point that Nostradamus wrote the word "*pyrennees*", which is printed in the lower case in the 1568 Lyon edition.[6] This is clearly a reference to the Pyrenees Mountains because this word is used in the same segment of words where the word "mountain" is used. Still, by this name not being presented in the upper case (as a proper name, thus specifically identifying the place known as Pyrenees) it is placing focus on the history that is behind the purpose for naming the mountains Pyrenees. Remembering that Nostradamus has already named "the mountain Possessed-ones", it would be confusing to refer the same "mountain" by a second name. As such, "*pyrennees*", and in particular a hyphenated version (as "*pyren-nees*") is more likely a direct statement about the indigenous people of those mountains.

The etymology of the name "Pyrenees" is connected to Greek mythology, specifically the tale of Hercules tenth of twelve "Labors." In that story, Hercules finds the remains of a princess named Pyrene. As Hercules held some responsibility in the princess' death, he felt deep remorse upon finding her dead and dismembered body. So the world would always remember the princess,

6   It is also hyphenated, as "*pyren-nees*", and unaccented.

Hercules called upon the land to cover her bones, thus forming the mountain range known as the Pyrenees Mountains.

Still, in the lower case, "*pyren*" is representative of the Latin word "*pyra*", meaning, "funeral pyre." This translation can also be read as a "funeral pile", which becomes synonymous with the tale of Hercules, focusing on the land that piled upon the princess. The French word "*nee*" is then seen as the past participle of the verb "*naistre*," meaning, "to be born." The plural ending ("-*s*") makes "*pyren-nees*" read as "the ones born of the funeral pile." This becomes the root for "Pyrenees," identifying it through the etymology, and not by name. This places focus on the indigenous people of the Pyrenees, who were "descendant" to the royal family of Pyrene.

This concept is confirmed by the following words being "the ancient kingdom" ("*l'antique monarchie*"). During the times of Nostradamus (16th century), France and Spain were not the nations they are today, as various "realms" retained autonomy along their perimeters. Along the border that is the Pyrenees Mountains were the *Royaume d'Aragon*, and the *Royaume de Navarre*, which were primarily in Spain. The Kingdom of Navarre extended north into what is now France. Southern France was made up of lands ruled by Counts and Viscounts. That France of antiquity was divided into regions, such as Occitania, Gascony, and Aquitaine. Still, those entities were not long removed from the days of Nostradamus, enough to be truly classified as "the ancient". The point to realize is the Pyrenees Mountains were where several "ancient kingdoms" existed.

The *Royaume de Navarre* was "an ancient kingdom", and is today represented by the Basque people of the western Pyrenees. Equally "old" (alternative translation of "*antique*"), having been formally in existence many years prior to Nostradamus, was the "realm" (alternative translation of "*monarchie*") of the Independent Moorish States. This was a large area of land in central and eastern Spain, which went as far north as the central Pyrenees. The Kingdom of Aragon assumed control of most of the region, well before Nostradamus' times, before Aragon, Catalonia, Castile, and Leon united to form Spain. The Independent Moorish States represented a presence that had overtaken Visigothic Christian Hispania, in 711 A.D.[7] Spread of the Moors from Gibraltar to the Pyrenees ended with their defeat at the Battle of Poitiers in 732 A.D. The Basque people, who represent the earliest civilized human beings in Spain, resisted Moorish takeover

7 Atheists prefer C.E., but I am not an atheist.

of their land; but, the Basque eventually outlasted the Moors. Still, "the ancient kingdom" can be representative of either of those two, or both individually, as "a kingdom of antiquity" in the Pyrenees Mountains.

In order to make a clear determination of "the kingdom", Nostradamus next wrote the words, "*ne sera translate à*". This translates literally to state, "*n*ot will be removed from one place to another at". Reading these words slowly, one at a time, allows the true meaning to appear.

First, when one sees "*pyren-nees ne*", one possible understanding of this is as a negative (use of "*ne*", meaning "not") about being one of "those born in the funeral pile" known as the Pyrenees. This is then making a statement about "the ancient Moorish realm", as they are "not" originally "descendant" from there. Second, this becomes relevant to the Moors, by the same words explaining those who had once been born there, but had since been "translated", or "removed from one place to another". These are then "descendant", now known as Muslims. Thus, Muslims will be "at" the place that was their "ancient kingdom", where those who have always been "descendant" to the "mountain funeral pile" were "translated" to a smaller part of the "mountain" they have long "Enjoyed".

In the entire letter to Henry II, this is the only segment of words that contains the word "*mont*." There is no mention of a mountain in the letter of Preface to *The Prophecies*. This single reference is also found in a connected segment that also holds the word "*pyrennees*". One has to understand that nothing can be seen as insignificant in a work that has a divine source. In a letter that was intended to explain what can be found in the 940-plus quatrains, this one segment is explaining the importance of the Pyrenees Mountains in the story line. To this point, we can see how "fury" is a motivation, to return a "descendant" of "the ancient kingdom" "to the mountain" that kingdom once "Enjoyed", "for" the purpose of "rising". This is very important information, but there is still more associated with this series of words.

When published, the quatrains of *The Prophecies* were not presented in their proper order. When placed in a correct order the whole of *The Prophecies* becomes an epic tale, told in poetic verse. Further, each verse is an individual prophecy, thus the title. However, the presentation in a scrambled order increases the difficulty in finding meaning in the quatrains.

When Nostradamus was told to explain the meaning of the poems to his king, he wrote a letter that mimics that need for reorganization. This means that the letter to Henry II is also divided into pieces and reordered into a random presentation. The letter thus appears to make very little sense, just as do most of the quatrains, so one matches the other in its chaos. The reality is that the letter to Henry and the verses that the letter explains have to be reordered. When they are put in this corrected order, they match and tell the same story line, one general (the letter) and the other detailed (the quatrains).

In the reorganization of the letter to Henry II, the key indicators are certain marks of punctuation and combinations of punctuation. The identifying marks let one know where the letter can be dissected so that individual pieces can be determined. From disassociated pieces, like an unfinished puzzle, each can then be rearranged into an understandable order, matching one to another, until all are connected properly. Just as each puzzle piece has individual shape, when connected within the whole the outline of that shape becomes the marker that shows a mosaic at work. The pieces that make up the whole of the letter to Henry II have their shape marked by the punctuation that is present.

The dividing marks of word pieces in a letter are less visible to discern because of the normal use of punctuation one expects to see in a letter. Our brains are basically blind to that use, especially that most common use of a comma. A comma represents a separation from one segment to another, where the separation denotes importance, a time sequence, or both. Still, a comma by itself does not represent a breakage in the flow of information being presented to the reader. Our minds are not trained to see the comma as the border of a piece of a puzzle. The mind wants to keep running gleefully along to the next full stop (colon or period).

This is how a new syntax is built into *The Prophecies*. It looks like the syntax we are used to seeing. It has the same rules governing the use punctuation, but acts differently than we have been trained to read the written word. The new syntax plays upon the mind's inability to think differently. In other words, God devised a way to write prophecy so that it could be misunderstood, until the time came in which to understand it perfectly. Everything means what it means, but the application of that meaning can be different from that accepted as normal.

The segment that contains "*mont*" and "*pyrennees*" ends with a simple comma. The series of words that precede that comma are not parts of a sentence fragment or phrase. Each word is an individual statement, which contains the full breadth of definition and meaning that each word has, in all contexts. There is no need for internal punctuation, which means that punctuation is not a mark as typically viewed. Instead, it is a sign of transition. Thus, what Nostradamus wrote in the letter to Henry II that has been discussed so far here says, "furious – with it - mountains - Possessed-ones – descending – because – to rise – with them of the Pyrenees – not – will be – removed from one place to another – those ancient – realm". That is how every piece of the letter to Henry II is read; and, it is how every piece of a quatrain is read.

As stated, that segment of words is separated from the next segment by a comma. That is a sign that the two segments are connected, thus related, but separated as sequential. One set leads to the next set. In that regard, the following words indicate what will follow in time, after a "furious" people are "to rise up" "with them in the mountain", as "descending from the" Pyrenees Mountains. Next, Nostradamus wrote, "*sera faicte la troysieme inundation de sang humain*". On a very literal level, this can translate to state, "will be done there a third inundation of kindred civil".

In this segment, one is immediately told what "will be done there". On one level of understanding, this represents an explanation of the prophesied future that involves those in and around the Pyrenees Mountains. In a most direct way, it is referencing "the ancient kingdom," as that focus ended the previous segment. The continuing explanation can then be seen to take the focus to what "will be made" be relative to another "kingdom, realm, monarchy, and/or government of one absolute prince". This sense of individuality matched the oneness of "descendant", as being one "progeny" who will rename the Pyrenees Mountains "the mountain ones Used". The reader is then led to see what "will be done", relative to a "realm".

This is where the number "three" explains a "cause, commitment, exploit, and/or deed" (translations of the verb "*faire*", the infinitive of "*faicte*"), as being an ordinal number that is designed to state a "third kingdom made" in the Pyrenees Mountains. Still, on a separate level, "the third" becomes representative of one added to two. Since the Pyrenees Mountains border the two nations of France and Spain, finding a "third there" would be an indication of being neither French nor Spanish, but instead "a third line" of descendancy. Further, on a percentage basis, one is allowed to see "a third" of the population of the Pyrenees Mountains being "raised up" by an influx of Muslim immigrants.

PROSECUTION EXHIBIT A

This view is sustained by the use of verbiage that says "overflowing" will take place. The word "*inondation*" can be read just as the English "inundation" but also as "overflowing, deluge, and/or surrounding." This makes it synonymous with "flood", but one cannot make the assumption that this is to be from rising waters. It is primarily a reference to an uncontrolled, rapid increase (an overwhelming) of people, which will be "overflowing" as a "third" race present, one "surrounding there [a] third" of the Pyrenees Mountains.

This is supported by the connection to "*de sang*", which typically is translated as "of blood". This can make this series of words take on an ominous meaning, such that an "inundation of blood" is typically found at times of war, when the flow of "blood" can be vastly "surrounding." While this theme is certainly within the context of the story line in *The Prophecies*, meaning war can be read into these words, such a reading must be seen as secondary. The primary translation must be based on the word "*sang*" being translated as "stock, race, kindred, lineage, parentage, and/or royal blood." In the context of this series of word, following the previous segment, that meaning allows one to see how this sequential series of statements connects to the first series, where "descendant" was used.

The word "*descendant*" carries the same connotation of a line of people. The word "*sang*" must then be read within that context first, such that the concept of a "descendant" of "an ancient monarchy", one once found "in the Pyrenees Mountains", "will be" the one who will have "caused" a "deluge" of fellow people. This would occur during a time of warfare, which would be secondary to having first assembled such an "inundation" of "kindred". As such, dual meaning expands the same words to have a present value, followed by a future value.

This meaning then connects to the final word in the segment, which is "*humain*". The Old French–English dictionary shows this word as translatable as, "gentle, courteous, friendly, civil, mild, affable, tractable," while also acting as "humane," in the sense that it is relevant to an emotional expression of human beings, and not animals. This is further advanced by reading "*humain*" as "manlike" and more specifically as "of, or belonging to, a man." When one recognizes that the first segment of words ended in the word "monarchy," which can also be read as, "rule of an absolute prince," one sees how the continuation of that individual statement is clarified as being a "civil government" (alternate translation of "*monarchie*" is as "government of an absolute prince"). This is a clarification of the type of "kingdom" that "will be made".

When one recognizes that the two "governments of absolute princes" (i.e.: kings) that existed at the time of Nostradamus writing *The Prophecies* were those of France (under King Henry II) and Spain (King Phillip II), one is now able to see "there" (the Pyrenees Mountains border between these two) "will be made" a "third". The two rulers of France and Spain were accepted as princes through a divine "bloodline". That "descendancy" is related to Jesus Christ, such that God has deemed the "blood" of kings holy, enabling them to be Christian rulers of nations. This second segment is then also identifying a form of "government" that will not be so divinely enabled, as it will be from the "blood of man".

This primary meaning of the numerical indication "third" can be seen as further expanded to fit a form of rule that is prophesied to seek a "third spilling of human blood". In the case of a "third inundation of human blood", it is not a stretch of the imagination to see how a third world war would do this. However, it must be recognized as being a statement that a "third line of civil government will be made". That would represent "the rule of a third kingdom" in the region, one that would duplicate "an ancient realm". All of this is pointing focus to a return of Islamic rule in France and Spain, after an "inundation of human kindred" to southwestern Europe.

Along the line of thought that a third world war can be read into this segment, one needs to look to the final segment in this section of the letter to Henry II. That segment is also relative to the Pyrenees Mountains. It begins by recognizing that the second segment of word-statements ends with a comma. This separates the two as either being sequential (a relative happening, later in time), or consequential (a logical conclusion, or an element of separate importance), as is the defined nature of a comma in language.

The last segment of words begins with the French word *"ne"*, which (unaccented) means, "not, nor, neither". When accented, as *"né"*, the word then means "born, bred from, risen from, descended from, proceeding from, grown out of, *issuing out of*, or *to come out of*." The written word does not include an accent mark but the absence of marks merely means there are no limitations put on the meaning of *"ne"* (in Nostradamus style of writing, relative to the "systems"). It can be read as both *"ne"* and *"né"*. Only when an accent mark appears in print does it place a limitation on the possibilities of meaning that one can derive from what has been written.

In the accented translation, we see how this sequential series is representative of a beginning, such as from a "birth, coming out, or rising from." This is connected to the major "Enjoyment" of the Pyrenees Mountains, such that troops are "in the mountain ones Used", from a motivation of "fury". This makes the "mountain" take on the essence of a womb, from which will be born" a "third line of monarchal rule". Because such a "birth" would not be allowed without extreme resistance, the "birth" would require a "deluge of blood human".

In the scenario where "*ne*" is read as written, meaning "not", the focus is placed on which "blood of man" will "not" be "overwhelmed" (a synonym of "inundation"). This negative word is then connected to the French reflexive pronoun "*se*", which translates as, "oneself, himself, herself, itself, and/or themselves." The Old French dictionary included the statement that "*se*' is "A Relative of both Numbers, and (always) placed before a Verb". This means that "*ne*", as "not", is relative to "the third" that "will not be found", as "*se*" is placed before the future tense form of the verb "*trouver*," which means, "to find." This is a clear indication of secrecy, such that these "human relatives" will "not" be out in the open.

This is another theme is important to take note on, and remember. This element, "not oneself will find", is a statement of secrecy, which will be repeated later. Here, however, in the context of this series of segments, it is supporting a translation of "*au mont*" as meaning, "in the mountain". This shows how one can be hidden "in mountain caves", by "descending" below the surface.

It will be from this secure position of "not oneself found" that they "will be found coming out" (as "*né*" meaning "birth", or "coming out"). This concept of secrecy is then advanced by seeing how "*trouver*" can also mean, "to invent, to contrive, to devise; to light on, to meet with, to take in the manner; and also to get, to obtain, and/ or to procure." This allows one to see the "birth" of a plan (use as "*ne*" as "*né*"), which "themselves will meet with" through the "descendant" of "the ancient realm". This means "oneself will devise" a plan. While many will be involved, "oneself will contrive", or "invent" how the secrecy and exposure will proceed. The plan is then relative to the "inundation of kindred", such that this growth "will be to obtain" the numbers of people necessary to make the plan work. It "will procure" everything necessary "to climb" (alternate translation of "*monter*") to reach a "third" of the whole number planned. This plan will come from one "human, who "not himself will be found", as Nostradamus then wrote, for a "long time".

59

The "birth" of this plan calling for an "inundation of human kindred" will be through a "flood of gentle people" (alternate translation of "*humain*") to Europe. In that location, there will be a "surrounding of humane Christians", by the children of Abraham "descendant" of Ishmael. This migration "will be procured" over a "long time", meaning it will be known "to" require an "extended" (alternate translation of "*long*") length of "time" to meet one other "third" of the total planned. We see this period spelled out in the written words, "*de long temps*". Such a peaceful migration of foreigners "not will be found" in the history of Europe, at least since the migration of banished Jews, those children of Isaac, who were scattered to the nations of the earth at the time of the fall of Israel and Judah.

This connection "to the times" of history will be a precursor "of the times" to come, which have been prophesied for a "long time". When one sees how the French word "*long*" can also be used to indicate, "slim; extended, outstretched; continual, tedious, and/or wearisome," one gets a clearer picture of difficult "times". Such "wearisome times" will be new for the people native of Western Europe, because they will "not" be able to accommodate such an influx of aliens without experiencing pains and discomforts. Europeans will see "themselves" as Christians and as capable of sharing, but they "will take in the manner" of "continual" immigration with much difficulty.

The last period of history when such tests "of humanity" were "found born", which are relative to now, comes "from" ten "long" years (1936 to 1945) that were the "times" relative to World "War" II, in Europe (from the use of "*Mars*", the god of "War"). The prophesied future can then also be "found to be" rooted in the "wearisome times" afterward. While Western Europe "will be found" able to recuperate and grow strong and wealthy from the assistance to rebuild that which war destroyed, the "times" of "War" in Eastern Europe did not end. Those nations fell behind the "Iron" Curtain ("*Mars*" synonymous with the alchemical metal "Iron"), suffering at the hand of their Communist overlords. This would become known as the "wearisome times" of a Cold "War".

This concept is confirmed by the capitalization of the word, "*Mars*", which identifies the importance of a major "War". While there is a history of "War" before, the plan "devised" will be for a new major "War". The Old French word "*Mars*" primarily means the month of "March", but it was also representative (in 1611) of the planet "Mars", the alchemist's element "Iron", and "Coarse corn". In modern French, one will often find the month of March written in the lower case, as "*mars*." The capitalized version is an indication of the planet with the proper name "Mars". The use as "Coarse grain" appears to have become archaic. Thus, this is where one has to look to the root language of French for the meaning.

Nostradamus wrote *The Prophecies* primarily in two languages, French and Latin. While other languages are found hinted at in the quatrains, the presence of clearly distinguishable French text, set apart by clearly distinguishable Latin text, in both letters,[8] shows that Latin is a language to be utilized in translation. Since French is a Romance Language, it is Latin based. When one recognizes one is dealing with a true prophecy sent to man by the Spirit of Jesus Christ, the Latin language use becomes important as representative of the language of the Holy Church of Rome. Therefore, logic supports one looking to find how a Latin translation of "*Mars*", as "War", becomes the intended primary translation.

The Latin word "*Mars*" is representative of "the (Roman) god of agriculture and war." In the transitive form, as the verb "*mars*," the translation is as "war, battle, fight." When one sees that the lower case is the more accurate way to describe the action of "war," the capitalization becomes a statement of major "War". Further, when one sees how the capitalization is the name of a specific Roman god, who ruled over "war" and the tools of "bloodshed", one can also see the parallel to the astrological meaning associated with the "red planet," named "Mars". The planet "Mars" symbolically rules over "war" and the energy of "battle and fighting," often symbolized by the "spilling of blood." However, when one utilizes the Latin translation, the capitalization becomes representative of, on the highest level of meaning, "Holy War".

When one makes that connection to "from long times", this is the "Holy War" known "to" come, prophesied in Scripture for an "extended" number of years. In the eyes of the divine, as written in the Holy Bible, it represents the "times" to come, which were foreseen "from" the beginning of "time". It will be the "wearisome times" of faith, which will precede the "times" of the "War" called Armageddon. That "War" has become synonymous with the End "Times".

This connection is an important one not to overlook, because the lack of faith in the present "times" makes it impolite to talk openly about this topic foretold

---

8   In the editions that include both letters (1566 and beyond), the typeset of the quatrains is in a standard font, while the letters are in a cursive style. In the style of each letter, a contrasting style is used to denote the Latin text, such that the Latin readily stands out from the French.

by the Holy Spirit's encounter with the prophet John (of Patmos). As such, one's head in the sand will keep one's eyes closed to what is foretold to come. From such a position of ignorance, one *"not will find"* what one should be on the lookout for, being the signs of the end. Those signs will persist for as *"long"* a *"time"* as necessary, to keep the flame of faith alive and to call upon the faithful to act to avert that end.

The final words of this segment are *"en caresme."* The word *"caresme"* represents an Old French spelling, as the modern adjusted spelling is *"carême."* The "s" has since been dropped, replaced by an accent circumflex above the first "e" (*"ê"*). The only translation of this French word is as the Christian season of "Lent". The capitalization of "Lent", in English, is not required in French, which makes this word similar to the word *"mars,"* in the sense that the French do not capitalize that word if it means the month of "March." While "War" has no strong relationship with "Lent", the month of "March" does.

The month of March is connected to the season of "Lent", because it can either begin or end in that month. As such, the use of *"en caresme"* can act as a timing factor, as an indication when one might expect the "times" of "War" to be taking place. In this case, it would depend on "Lent" being in "March". One example of such a time could be the Lenten season of 2011,[9] which will begin on March 9. On the contrary, the 2013 season will end on March 30. Still, because the word *"caresme"* is not capitalized, it is less likely to have the primary significance of a specific "Lent". Likewise, the primary meaning of *"Mars"* is not found to be the month of "March."

What is primarily important to remember is the capitalization and Latin translation of *"Mars"* as being representative of "Holy War." When this is led to connect to the phrase *"en caresme,"* the fact that *"caresme"* is a word denoting a Christian observance makes the "Holy War" be one that has come "upon" (alternate translation of *"en"*) those who recognize the season of "Lent". The symbolic reasoning for the season of "Lent" is the sacrifice that must be made after the Advent of Christ's birth and an Epiphany relative to that coming within. This period of sacrifice is linked to Christianity and therefore acts to define this major "War" as that foreseen to come in the New Testament. It defines the "War" as the one Christians see coming prior to the second coming of Jesus Christ.

---

9   This is NOT a prediction. The lunar cycle that determines the Lenten season is cyclic, meaning many possibilities of Lent in March are also possible.

Due to the word *"caresme"* being in lower case, despite it being typically written in that manner in French, its significance must be seen as being representative of the meaning behind the word. The word *"caresme"* is said to be rooted in the Latin word *"quadragesima,"* which comes from the Greek *"tessarakoste,"* meaning, "fortieth day (before Easter)."[10] The word "Lent" is said to come from Old English, and being representative of the "lengthening" of the days in spring, which lead up to Easter. Still, all of this is relative to a Christian observance, for the "times" Jesus spent in the wilderness, before beginning his ministry. For this reason, *"caresme"* becomes synonymous with "times" of abstinence, repentance, and prayer. On a symbolic level, a "third War upon" the world[11] would certainly place many humans "into long times of self-sacrifice."

This series of segments ends at *"caresme"* with a period mark, signaling that a full stop must be recognized at this point. All periods found in *The Prophecies* denote the end of a train of thought; and, this is true in every case, whether one is found in a quatrain or in one of the letters. As such, almost all quatrains end with a period,[12] such that a period mark allows for a complete shift to another topic of focus, either within the context of a previously begun topic or to a completely new topic. The placement of a period mark in the letters indicates the same shift in focus; but period marks are at a premium there. The average use of a period mark in those documents is somewhere in the neighborhood of four to eight per page, compared to my own paragraph that now contains five periods, in roughly a quarter of a page.

As mentioned before, the three segments I have just presented as evidence are the last three in a string of five segments that totals forty-nine words. Thirty-two words make up those three segments. Because of the need to dissect the letter to Henry II into pieces that can be moved to associate with other pieces (like a puzzle), these three segments that end with a period need to be joined with some other grouping that begins with a capitalized first word.[13] In that regard,

---

10 From "etymology" section of the Wikipedia article on "Lent."
11 World War I and World War II are numerically referenced wars of the 20th century, which involved many nations of the world. However, as a war that meets the criteria to be classified as a "world war" took place in the 19th century, each 100 years begins a new count. As such, the next World War, will be the first of the 21st century. It too, I would venture to guess, will be known as another "War to end all wars."
12 Some quatrains have internal period marks, meaning there is more than one focus placed on the main theme.
13 The first two segments in the string do not agree with the topic of the last three, with a "break point" mark being present, which allows the string to be broken

there is no guarantee that only one other segment adds to these three. There are pieces that become properly separated and have neither capitalized first word, nor period at the end. These fit into the middle of a series, and such a piece could be matched with this example three-part segment. As such, the forty-nine word "sentence" these examples appear in is incorrect. They have been incorrectly linked with words that properly link to another segment ending with a period. Still, the forty-nine word total is probably around average, if not on the short end of the scale, when measuring the "sentences" of Nostradamus' letters. In any case, the three segments presented here end the focus on the topic that includes "*mont*" and "*pyrennees*".

At this point, it is important for one to understand that these three series of word-statements were written in the letter the king of France. Nostradamus wrote that letter for the purpose of explaining the underlying meaning of the quatrains (the four-line poems). It was written because no one could figure them out, including the king and his wise men. The king had actually summoned Nostradamus to appear before him, personally, to do the explaining; but Nostradamus was led to write a letter that would forever hold the explanation, albeit an explanation that was as seemingly unintelligible as the verses had been.

The revelation of systemic properties makes understanding everything about *The Prophecies* now be possible. That means the three segments presented are an explanation of one small element contained within the story line told by the quatrains. Once the poems are properly linked together, the specific stories they tell are found to match the generalized explanation, as I have just revealed. The whole of this letter being placed in its proper order allows for the "sentence" that does connect to this three-segment series to appear. That then adds to the meaning I have just presented. However, as evidence to a provable prediction, the reorganization of the letter to Henry is off topic at this time.

This series of words is located by a search of key terms, "mountain" and "*pyren*". The search is done due to the numerous times those words are placed in the quatrains. By simply locating this section and knowing how that three-segment series of words separates into one complete piece, due to knowing the systems at work, one is able to see how the Pyrenees Mountains will play a role in the overall story. This explanation is then relative to every reference to "*monts Pyrenees*" in the verses. What I have presented here, as to the translation possibilities and meanings that come from those translations, now has to correlate to the translations into two pieces that join with other pieces found elsewhere in the letter.

PROSECUTION EXHIBIT A

and meanings found in those quatrains that also contain the identification of the Pyrenees Mountains. If that is found to be true, then the author is explaining the meaning of his work. My opinion is then based on that explanation.

To ensure that what I have presented is not a trick and that I have not slanted my interpretation to match a preconceived notion, I have given verifiable evidence that states how anyone should be able to come to the same conclusions I have stated. Simply based on the language written by Nostradamus, the accepted dictionary meaning of that language, and knowledge of a new syntax that allows for understanding, I have developed a theme that explains how the Pyrenees Mountains is an important topic worthy of closer inspection. I have explained the relative systems that come into play, to the degree that this work does not attempt to become anything other than a presentation of evidence that supports a prediction that can be proved. My opinion is then based on how the words written by Nostradamus match current events, something he cannot be expected to explain in more than general terms, and only through divine means. In that regard, it becomes important that one summarize the information that comes from the explanation letter before proceeding to the next piece of evidence.

The following numbered summations list the points made by the three-segment explanation made by Nostradamus in his letter to King Henry II. That section is chosen because it refers to his use of the words "*mont*" and "*pyrennees*".

1. Rage and fury are preexisting conditions that lead "to the mountain".
2. The "mountain" is identified as an important "Possession" held by "ones".
3. These "ones" are both "descending" into the "mountain" and returning to the "mountain" once "Possessed", as "descendant" from there.
4. These "ones" are there "for" a reason or "because" they seek "to ascend" or "to rise".
5. The place of the "mountain" is named as being the place of those who are "descendant" to the mythological princess Pyrene, thus it is the place of the "Pyrenees-born ones".
6. The "ones" there have returned, as they "will not be removed from one place to another".
7. They are "descendant" of "an ancient realm" that previously existed in the Pyrenees Mountains; and are thus Islamic kin of the Moors.
8. These people "will be there" for the purpose of "action" or having "made" themselves a "third" party, between the two other peoples who

65

claim the Pyrenees Mountains (France and Spain).
9. This growth will be from a "surrounding" or an "inundation", to the places around the Pyrenees Mountains, "from kindred" people.
10. The governments of France and Spain, because of laws that are "humane" and "civil", will allow this growth of foreigners.
11. The element of this growth that will be "in the mountain" and "not themselves will" be "found" says they will be out of open sight, or hidden.
12. A significant person "not himself will be found" for a "long time", which is a match to the "continual" search for Osama bin Laden.
13. This hidden presence will last for a "long time", meaning their numbers will grow steadily, but not so fast that it is readily seen as threatening.
14. This growth will be designed as a preparation for a major "War", one between the nations of Islam and the nations of Christianity, as a "Holy War".
15. The "War" will be the one that will precede the second coming of Jesus Christ, thus synonymous with Armageddon.

This summary shows that one individual can be found as an important "descendant", who will be the one leading others in the possession of "the mountain" of the Pyrenees chain. This would have to be a leader of significance, in order to devise a plan that will be far-reaching, requiring great patience. The only such person that fits that charismatic description today is Osama bin Laden, who is a known "mountain" man. Still, it is a tremendous leap of faith to see Osama bin Laden as clearly being portrayed in this one piece of evidence. However, the preponderance of evidence found in the individual quatrains will make this hypothesis become quite clear.

Afterthoughts: Simply because this segment of words from the Epistle to Henry II places focus on the root word for Pyrenees, and an "ancient monarchy," the history of the people of the Pyrenees Mountains that have fought with Spain for autonomy must be seen as allies in a foreign presence among them. In 2017, a referendum in Catalonia for independence from Spain was banned by the Spanish government, leading to some conflict. Catalonia is the eastern end of the Pyrenees. To the west are the Basque, who are not only in Spanish Pyrenees, but also in southern France. They too suffer under the rule of Spain. This becomes a base dislike in the Pyrenees that makes a willingness to protect a foreign element that offers to give them unconditional autonomy reason to see how someone like Osama bin Laden could safely be hidden in those European mountains.

Chapter 6
Prosecution Exhibit B
The Opportunity to Be in the Pyrenees via Escape

In a trial of proof, three elements need to be given merit. These three elements are means, motive, and opportunity. In a prediction that Osama bin Laden can be found hiding in the Pyrenees Mountains, it is a given that he is wanted for criminal activities. He certainly has the means, through an acknowledged terrorist group called the al-Qaeda, which he has accepted responsibility for heading. He has played a role in recruiting and training soldiers for acts of terror and he has confessed to planning the September 11, 2001 attacks, using this al-Qaeda network. That has been determined to be fact that involved Europe, such that Germany was determined to be a place that played a key role in the coordination of the events of 9-1-1. This means that Osama bin Laden has friends he can visit outside the core of his operation, which has been determined to be in Afghanistan.

He also has the motive to continue leading his terrorist group. In this regard, he has coordinated the production and release of personal statements made in tapes and videos. The latest motive for continuing to be a threat to the world was said to be due to French involvement in Nigerian affairs, while stating French laws against Muslims to be a reason for retribution. The most relevant motive is to seek the release of stolen Palestinian land, which he sees as an unjust theft by Zionists and their partners. He has made threats that promise destruction in the West, unless there is a cessation of meddling in Muslim affairs by Western nations. This means his motives are not only in Afghanistan, but everywhere his enemy operates; and, in particular those places are where Muslims live and are perceived to be persecuted. Thus, he has motive to be in any of these places, in order to stay abreast of the issues behind his anger.

The element that is most difficult to prove is opportunity. This is because the world has been looking for Osama bin Laden in the mountains between Afghanistan and Pakistan for a long time. This was his last known presence; but, after nine years, the element of opportunity for escape must be accepted as possible. Without anyone being able to nail down where he is now, or precisely where he has been since 2001, the opportunity exists that he could be in any place that offers asylum. The question then leads one to ask, is opportunity present in the Pyrenees Mountains, to the degree that Osama bin Laden could secretly reach that location and remain there undetected?

The last known location for Osama bin Laden is in Afghanistan. The reason U.S. forces are standing at that rabbit hole is because the last confirmed evidence showed that Osama bin Laden was observed to have been there. According to reports, the C.I.A. successfully infiltrated al-Qaeda with an operative during the last year of the Clinton administration. A meeting of al-Qaeda soldiers was planned, one that the intelligence said would be attended by bin Laden. The U.S. military was prepared to strike the meeting site with drone missiles, while C.I.A. ground troops were prepared to follow those attacks to the site and wrap the operation up. However, due to delays in getting proper channels to approve the drone attack, bin Laden left the meeting before he could be caught.

In late December 2001, during the Bush administration and after 9/11, a covert CIA team sent to kill bin Laden had intercepted transmissions said to have been from bin Laden's radio. Afghan operatives within bin Laden's camp confirmed this. His location was at a 14,000-foot ridge in the mountains along the Pakistan border, at Tora Bora. A battle was fought there, in which the Taliban was overrun; but bin Laden is said to have escaped by mule to Pakistan.

To confirm that he had not been killed in the attack, many of the buried dead were exhumed so their fingers could be removed for DNA analysis. Those tests were negative; and, a confirmed bin Laden video release in 2004 proved he was not killed. However, the failure of that battle to lead to bin Laden's capture has led to speculation that he is hiding in the mountains of Pakistan, protected by tribal leaders sympathetic to his cause.

It is also assumed that tighter security has surrounded him, making it difficult to plant informants inside his camp. That camp is suspected to be some hiding place that makes it impossible for high-tech surveillance equipment to pick up his trail, such as inside a mountain cave. Certainly, the C.I.A. is looking in Pakistan because they are being told to look there by informants whose information they trust. Unfortunately, the lack of success in locating him is reason to believe the informants are not giving the C.I.A. good leads. They may be giving bad leads on purpose, to ensure the focus of the manhunt remains at the last place on earth Osama bin Laden was seen alive; not leading them to look in some other place.

In all probability, especially since it has now been nine years since he was last located, Osama bin Laden could be any place on the face of the earth. It makes more sense that he would try to go to any place not near Afghanistan, Pakistan, or Iran. Because of heightened surveillance of those places, much less risk would be involved if he could manage to get to a place that was not on the list of the usual places to search for an escaped Islamic Jihadist. That makes a place like the Pyrenees Mountains a safe place to hide, simply because of a lack of intelligence that says he went there.

Osama bin Laden is undoubtedly a mountain man. He has proven a willingness to abstain from the comforts provided by major metropolitan areas. Being a mountain man is good strategy, as high ground is an advantage in military battles. There is safety provided by higher ground. The mountainous terrain in Afghanistan is why that land has a long history of eventually defeating all invaders, simply because the native inhabitants know how to get around and stay above their enemies. The Pyrenees Mountains would offer the same general type of environment as that found in Afghanistan and Pakistan.

All mountainous regions provide a terrain that is not easily navigated by those unfamiliar with the surroundings. Human beings generally inhabit mountainous terrain less densely, allowing for an isolation factor. Most mountains in the higher latitudes of the Northern Hemisphere are covered by forests and have natural water sources. Perhaps most importantly, mountains usually have an abundance of natural caves, which is a known characteristic of the Pyrenees.[1] The Pyrenees Mountains would offer all of those protections.

In addition to those natural similarities found in the Pyrenees Mountains, making them as protective as the Hindu Kush mountain range which he has known is the

---

1 Some of the caves on the French side of the Pyrenees are advertised by the Department of Ariège (found in the Midi-Pyrenees region, which borders Andorra and Spain) as "the most prehistoric caves of any department of France."

exclusivity they provide. The C.I.A. would probably not have the opportunity to roam freely around the border with France and Spain, neither with their troops nor with their drones. France and Spain are both allies in the War on Terror, so they would undoubtedly frown on the thought of the U.S. policing their territory. They would have to do their own surveillance, with American satellite intelligence being made available to them. However, given that Osama bin Laden's latest audio release has threatened France directly, one would have to wonder just how committed the French and Spanish are towards helping the United States make new enemies.

In that regard, another similarity makes the Pyrenees Mountains an ideal place for someone like Osama bin Laden. He would feel just as at home there as he has been in the mountains along the border of Afghanistan and Pakistan, where the local people are willing to accept him and his cause. The people in the mountains of western Pakistan are believed to have worked hard to protect bin Laden from view. That aspect is related to the inability of the Pakistani government to operate freely in the tribal regions of the Afghan-Pakistan border, because the government of Pakistan is at a disadvantage there. Although that region is technically a part of Pakistan, their army is limited in how effectively it can force the will of the national government on the people in the mountains. In essence, the Pakistani military would be no more effective than would be an invading army.

The same situation is in play in the Pyrenees, because the Basque people predominately populate the western Pyrenees (French and Spanish). That region is known as Basque Country and the Basque people have their own history of coordinating terroristic acts against the nations who they see as lording over them. The organization known as the ETA (meaning Basque Homeland and Freedom) is an armed separatist group responsible for a series of bombing attacks since 1959, primarily against Spain.

The 2004 Madrid train bombing, where 191 people were killed and 1,800 were injured, was immediately blamed on the ETA, as it fit their model. The one eventually found most likely to have been behind that bomb attack was a little-known North African group, with an al-Qaeda member immediately claiming responsibility shortly after the attack occurred. The point here is that Spain had been the regular target of the ETA, such that to have a Muslim group claim responsibility for a major bombing did not sit well with European authorities. The immediate aftermath was high level of worry in Italy and France which led to alerts of terrorist activity there. Such a response would not have occurred

PROSECUTION EXHIBIT B

had intelligence known it was a Basque separatist bombing in Madrid. In other words, if any non-Muslims were ever to see Osama bin Laden as a kindred spirit, then it would be the Basque people. They realize that "one person's terrorist is another person's freedom fighter."

All that adds up to the Pyrenees Mountains being a good fit for one Osama bin Laden on the lam. With a new suit and a close shave, he could fit in so well he could safely lie low for a decade or so, without worry that a bombshell would land outside his cave door. Throw in the Muslim history in the Pyrenees and Iberia, as the evidence from the letter to King Henry suggests, and it becomes a tighter fit. All that is needed to proceed further is something stated by Nostradamus that points one's focus from Afghanistan to France.

My prediction that Osama bin Laden is in the Pyrenees Mountains is based on the stories of *The Prophecies*. In the overall epic tale, told in 948 quatrains, roughly one-fifth of the whole story has already happened. It has happened exactly as prophesied in the 200 quatrains that have been fully fulfilled, with great detail from the words written matching precisely the details from historical records.[2] The remaining eighty percent can be foreseen as a logical expansion from what has already occurred.

The predicted future that was told in the stories of the quatrains is confirmed by the pieces of the letter to Henry. Thus, the words of Nostradamus tell of a future that is already unfolding around us, connecting what has already happened to what will happen next and beyond. This future is being stated as possible, if not probable, by people who have no link to prophecy of any kind related to religion. Those predictions are based on observation of current events and anticipating the most probable outcome We are now in the middle of a prophecy, which makes understanding the stories of the past the key to preventing the stories of our future from coming to fruition (in our lifetimes).

Some of the stories that make up the one-fifth that have already happened involve the events of September 11, 2001 and the subsequent wars in Afghanistan and Iraq. All of this is related to the other stories that led up to those events; and, those acts of violence are related to the acts of violence prophesied to happen in

---

2   In my book, "*Pearls Before Swine: Volume 1, Predicting the Past*", I write in great detail how 111 quatrains tells of the history relative to the instructions from Nostradamus' letter of Preface, leading in time up to the eve of the new millennium, which began on January 1, 2001.

the future (motive). Part of the focus that comes from the quatrains telling of the Afghan War is the escape of a leader. Two specific quatrains combine to tell of a significant person leaving that area of the world, detailing a route that would end in France. While neither of these quatrains mention the Pyrenees Mountains specifically, these two are important to understand here because they establish the aspect of opportunity. These are helpful as evidence that places Osama bin Laden at the scene of a future crime, which later will be specifically named as the Pyrenees Mountains.

The first quatrain telling of this escape reads:

Sus la minuict conducteur de l'armee	Above there midnight leader of the army
Se saulvera, subit esvanoy,	Himself will be safe, suddenly slipped out of sight,
Sept ans après la fame non blasmee,	September years after the renown not found fault with,
A son retour ne dira oncq'ouy.	With his returning neither will say never heard.

Realizing that such an English translation is for demonstration purposes only, as most words have multiple translation possibilities, this representation offers a clear main theme of a "leader of an army", with a clear focus on an escape, as "suddenly vanished," or "quickly slipped out of sight". It does not take much imagination to see how well this could fit an escape by Osama bin Laden.

The supporting details to the main theme statement (found in line three[3]) identify "the army" as those "renown" for an act in "September". To see that translation, one must realize that the French word "*sept*" (in the lower case) is an accepted representation of the month "September". As the French do not typically capitalize the months of the year, the capitalization acts to show an importance to that month. As such, the events of September 11, 2001 are very important. They were events that have been claimed by Osama bin Laden as from his plan, initiated through his command as the "leader of the (stateless) army" of militant

---

3   This is relative to the systems of Nostradamus, such that all line ones state a main theme, with all line twos stating a secondary theme, relative to the main theme. Thus, in line with the ABAB rhyme scheme, all line threes offer details that support the main themes, and all line fours offer details that support the secondary themes.

PROSECUTION EXHIBIT B

Islamists known as al-Qaeda.

The combined word, "*l'armee*", when seen accented, as "*l'armée*", can translate as, "them armed with weapons". One does not need to see a formal uniformed "army", as might be expected. In addition, the use of the word "*conducteur*" can mean, "ringleader, guide, conductor, and/or one holding the rank of Captain." This choice is more in line with denoting someone who is less-than-officially recognized for a position, rather than seen as a solid statement of official title, earned through national military service. It recognizes a rank that has come from "fame, credit, report, renown, and or reputation" (from "*fame*") as a "leader", relative to an important "September". Still, there is another important meaning for "September", which is related to the theme of this quatrain, and the theme of jihad against the West.

This other connection is linked to another "army" of "renown" that makes "September" an important marker and of which Osama bin Laden is supportive, if not directly descended. That group is said to have been responsible for the attacks made during the 1972 Munich Olympics, as those who called themselves Black "September".[4] This connection identifies an "army" of terrorists, and their creation is due to the theft of Palestine by Zionist and their supporters. It represents an unofficial "army" due to the inability of Middle Eastern leaders to command regular military actions towards similar ends, as those had been influenced to allow this theft of Palestine. Those leaders had been put in place artificially, to be beneficial to the West.

Still, one can also see the word "*Sept*" as being a significant number, as "Seven". This then connects with the word "*ans*", which only translates as "years". As an important number of "years after the conductor of the army suddenly vanished", one must be led to see an importance in the "years" 2008-2009, based on the battle of Tora Bora having taken place in mid-December 2001. This timing factor would then be relative to the "reputation" or "fame" of that "vanished leader", which could be a renewed thought that bin Laden had died.

A report by the new Pakistan president Asif Ali Zardari, in April 2009, suggested that Osama bin Laden may have died. He stated that Pakistani intelligence believed that theory to be the case. However, one can see "Seven" as representative of the

---

[4] The use of "September" in the name is said to be due to the September 16, 1970 declaration by King Hussein of Jordan, which expelled thousands of Palestinian refugees from that Arab land.

single-digit number for 2007, which is when the U.S. Senate voted 87-1 in favor of doubling the reward for bin Laden's "death or capture" to $50-million. In such a scenario, the number of millennia is unnecessary to state, such that the year "Seven" is important as the only "*seven*" in a count from "one" to "nine hundred ninety-nine" with the one-thousandth year represented as "zero."

Whichever direction one takes with the translation of "*Sept*", it represents an importance that is relative to "the army" and "suddenly vanishing". That then leads to the realization of "the fame" developed in Afghanistan (or stated as "there renown"), where that "renown" is "not" "condemned" or "rebuked". This is a statement that the legend of the leader is one of "blame," but where he will be "Seven years after", so "there" people will find "no fault with" what others have "accused" him for having done. This supporting statement is making it possible to see an escape to a different place, where the people will accept the "conductor of an army".

The supporting details for the secondary theme (line four) then tell that the "sudden vanishing" will be followed by a "return". As such, the capitalized "*A*" can be seen as either the directional preposition, "*à*", or the third person present form of the verb "*avoir*," meaning the one "slipped out of sight" will later be found "In, At, To, and/or With" "his return", and/or the "leader" will be found to "Have his coming back". This is making a statement that any talk of Osama bin Laden's death is premature.

The remainder of this statement tells of "speaking" and "hearing", on a level that "never" will be expected. It says the "returning will not be told", which means there will be no informant leaks that will let anyone know where the leader has fled. It also means that those whom he has fled to also "will not speak" of his presence there.

The use of the word "*oncques*" is defined as, "an Adverb of time", which makes it related to use of the word "years," in line three. It means that "not once" in that period of time will "his returning" be known, as no one will be talking or listening in the right place. However, this line four is saying that the "conductor will say" what "never" must happen.

This is related to the regular messages Osama bin Laden "speaks", which are always "heard" by those looking for clues to his whereabouts. The messages are like the one recently made to the French about their miners in Africa and their laws against Muslim women and veils. It is a message that a future retribution will come, as one has "never" known before. It is a threat to those who "never listen", that the enemies of Islam keep digging themselves a hole from which they will "never" escape.

With the same numbered list summary of this quatrain as I presented with the three-segment evidence from the letter to Henry II, the evidence is clear to see. One must take the position that the given to be considered is that all of *The Prophecies* is from a divine source. With that given, then everything will eventually be found true. Since there is no set time frame known from the written text, all of history's events are possible for consideration. However, to be found true, all historical events must perfectly match the themes established by the letters and quatrains. With that in mind, one must ask oneself, "Has this ever happened before in history?" If the answer is "No," then this quatrain is telling of an incomplete present, or the future still to come.

1. The main theme is about a "leader to an army".
2. The secondary theme is related to this "conductor" being "safe".
3. In regard of that safety, actions are "quickly" taken, which lead to a disappearance of this person.
4. "September" is an important identification that will last for "years".
5. "Seven" is an important number that is related to the leader's "reputation".
6. This "fame" is "reputed" by some, while his supporters see "no blame".
7. This person will "Have his coming back" from the "vanishing".
8. The event of "his coming back" will cause people to "talk" like "never" before.
9. That which "will be spoken" will "not" be "heard".

When all of this is linked to one central theme of a great leader, there is one element I have purposefully skipped over which further links this "*conductor*" to Islam. The words that begin the main theme, "*Sus la minuict*", can now act to greatly narrow one's choices in this regard. Without a deep discussion at this point, look at those individual words as saying, "Above – there – midnight". From those three acceptable translations, let the capitalization be seen as identifying the "Overseeing" power that is a leader" who controls an "army" and chooses a "guide" for it. Understand how the use of the adverb "there" acts independently to point to the region of the world that is under or below that power "Above". If one can see this development, one can find "midnight" as a statement of darkness and an implication of that which rises "Over the darkness", which is the moon. By being able to see this, one has just identified the great "conductor" as one who is a servant to Islam, which is a repeated theme in the quatrains, where the sun symbolizes Christianity and the moon Islam.. Everything else must be seen through that lens.

In my mind, this quatrain tells the reader that Osama bin Laden "slipped out of sight or vanished". He long ago left Afghanistan and that explains how he has not been seen since. Constant C.I.A. snooping, satellite surveillance, drone spying, and insider mole information has not benefited the search for this leader. There has been no confirmed sighting since the end of 2001. The reason is simple. He is not inside the rabbit hole in Afghanistan, where the hunters are patiently waiting for him to pop out. This quatrain tells the world he will not be found there.

Afterthoughts: From the 20/20 clarity of the year 2020, knowing that President Barack Hussein Obama declared Osama bin Laden was dead, within two months of this book originally being published, one needs to see how the last line of this quatrain (uttered by Nostradamus through the Holy Spirit's influence) cannot be changed by human manipulation. The words *"A son retour ne dira oncq' ouy"* plays a role in this announcement. The statement now says, "Has his return born will say never heard."

The declaration "born" (from accenting *"ne"*) is not that of Osama bin Laden, but by President Obama. The death of Osama bin Laden meant "never" again "will speak" Osama bin Laden, so his declarations will be "heard." This means the importance (indicated by the capitalized *"A"*) that "Has his return" is the importance of the person identified by Nostradamus, whom history calls Osama bin Laden. He "returned" to the news, through President Obama, just as he "returned" in 2009, when thought dead by the Pakistani president. If that thought was later deemed wrong, then can be seen just as wrong on May Day 2011.

The absence of verbiage that says "dead" in line four says (without directly being written), the announced death of Osama bin Laden will keep him from publicly making more videos and tape recordings about France. He will be "heard" by his actions, once he has that cover of escape.

Chapter 7
Prosecution Exhibit C

The Itinerary to France

To expand on this evidence, Nostradamus wrote another quatrain that explains the route of Osama bin Laden's escape. If the reports of his *"sudden vanishing"* are correct and he did escape the attacks on Tora Bora on a pack mule, then this quatrain tells what happened next. This quatrain states:

Du pont Euxine, & la grand Tartarie,	To the bridge Hospitable, & there great Asian-Russia,
Un roy sera qui viendra voir la Gaule:	One king will be who will come to see here France:
Transpercera Alane & l'Armenie,	Will bore through Alania & the Armenia,
Et dedans Bisance lairra sanglante Gaule.	And within Byzantium will leave bleeding beaten by a big rod.

When one looks at the flow of places that are identified by capitalization, this quatrain takes one's attention from Asia to Europe. In this regard, the word *"Euxine"* is found to be the name of the abyssal plain in the center of the Black Sea. That sea is located where Eastern Europe meets Western Asia. The Greeks named that body of water *Euxeinus Pontos*, which means, "Hospitable Sea." Nostradamus wrote *"pont Euxine"*, which gives the impression of identifying that place; but that is not the only meaning. While it is helpful to have the initial focus be towards Asia, where the Black Sea is central to the places named in the quatrain, the true meaning comes from realizing *"pont"* is the French word meaning, "bridge". The true initial focus of the main theme statement is therefore saying "To the bridge Hospitable".

This statement is half of the main theme, as a comma placed after *"Euxine"* separates it from the remainder of line one. The combination of a comma followed by an ampersand indicates a point of separation that is consistent throughout all of *The Prophecies*, its letters and quatrains. This means the main theme is in two pieces, with the ampersand indicating that the second piece is also important, just as beginning with a capitalized word indicated the first piece is important. Thus, the main theme of this quatrain is telling of two important, yet sequential, elements.

As stated, the first element is the important movement that is "To the, From the, Of the, and/or With the," from *"Du"* stating *"De + le."* One can then see *"le"* as capable of being modified to allow this preposition-article to be a stand-alone statement, saying, "To him", where *"le"* is representative of the masculine personal pronoun, "he." In all cases, the direction "To him", who could be running "From them", or be escorted "With them" (the implied plural), would be "To the bridge".

This makes the importance (denoted from the capitalization) of the direction make the "bridge" a place important to reach. One must then realize that a "bridge" is nothing more than a structure of some type, which connects one place to another. A "bridge" often acts as a span for passage over a barrier, like a river, chasm, or gap. This makes the story of Osama bin Laden's escape at Tora Bora important to revisit.

Tora Bora is located near the Afghan border with Pakistan, in the Safid Koh mountain range, which is a southeastern extension of Hindu Kush. The place that makes it possible to travel between Afghanistan and Pakistan is called the Khyber Pass. A pass is in essence a "bridge" that is a narrow passage between mountains. Tora Bora is importantly located in Afghanistan close "To the bridge" that is the Khyber Pass. This leads to Pakistan, where the people have been known to be importantly "Hospitable" to the fleeing Taliban and al-Qaeda soldiers. The first half of the main theme is telling about an important escape route for Osama bin Laden.

The second half then begins with *"la"*, which becomes important as representative of "there" (accented as *"là"*), which is where "the bridge" connects and provides passage "To" another place. Nostradamus then wrote the word *"grand"* which in all cases found in *The Prophecies* means one of the world's "greatest" nations or

PROSECUTION EXHIBIT C

superpowers. In this sense, the superlative is seen in the word itself, as a noun, and not as an adjective. The specific "great" is then identified as being "Tartary".

The ancient region that was once known as "Tartary" is that which was ruled by the Mongols (Genghis Kahn, etc.). That region was rather vast and as the Mongols declined in power the area of Asia known as "Tartary" was divided into geographic sections: Muscovite Tartary (Siberia), Cathay Tartary (China & Mongolia), East Tartary (Manchuria), and Independent Tartary (western Turkestan). One must see the significance of "*Tartarie*" as being representative of the region of western Turkestan. The Russian Czar, Ivan the Terrible, conquered this region of "Tartary" the year *The Prophecies* were initially published (1555). As such, Russia has to be considered one of the "great" powers in the world today; and, it can be thus identified in this quatrain as "great Tartary", which is a specific region under Russian control, once part of the U.S.S.R.

Today, the region that was Independent "Tartary" borders in the West at the Caspian Sea, and tracks along the south, to the east, along the Iran-Afghanistan borders. This includes the former lands of the Soviet Union now known as Tajikistan, Uzbekistan, and Turkmenistan. Afghanistan has an extension of land that produces a narrow "bridge" that runs between Tajikistan and Pakistan, along the line of the Hindu Kush mountain range.

Relatively recently, Tajikistan news announced the completion of construction on a half-mile long "bridge" across the Pyanj River, which forms the border between Tajikistan and Afghanistan. That $37-million "bridge" was made possible by financial assistance from the United States, the nation that is the number one "great" in *The Prophecies*. The construction was done to make truck transportation of supplies to American troops in Afghanistan more viable. Transport from Tajikistan was previously quite limited, due to the typical ferry crossing, which quite often was impossible due to the rushing waters of the Pyanj. This "bridge" was visualized in 2005 and planned for an April 2007 opening. A somewhat surprising lack of bureaucratic delays allowed it to be officially opened in August 2007. This information makes it possible to see "To the bridge" link to the important number "Seven" in the last quatrain, which was "years after" the "sudden vanishing" of a "conductor".

The secondary theme follows a comma at the end of line one, making it separate from the two-part main theme that referred to a "bridge" in "Tartary". This secondary focus then goes to the capitalized number "One", which shows the importance of being number "One". This is relative to the use of "great" in the main theme's second half statement, such that it can be a reflection of American assistance to Tajikistan; because, after the fall of the Soviet Union, America became the number "One great". However, that becomes a secondary meaning, as the primary importance of "One" is to identify a person who is "king".

Just as the word "great" can always be seen as a noun in *The Prophecies*, the use of *"roy"* (spelled *"roi"* in modern French) is always significant. The stories of the quatrains tell of a future that would become diametrically opposite to the way things stood in the 16th century. In the times of Nostradamus, the use of the word "king" would identify a person who had ascended to the throne of a nation, based on being the number "One" male in a royal bloodline. However, in modern times, there are very few of those royal figures left in power, keeping them from being referenced in the stories. As such, the lower case use of *"roy"* is an indication of a "chief, and/or the head man of a company," "One" of common blood. In modern terms, a *"roy"* must be seen as a president, prime minister, or "conductor" of many people.

The identification of a most important leader leads one next to find Nostradamus indicating the "One" is found identified as, "will be who will come". This is saying that the "One king" is not yet recognized as having such official rank, but he "will be" that "One king who" is expected "to arrive" (alternative translation of the root verb, *"venir"*). In this regard, towards meeting such an expectation, this person "will proceed" towards that goal. That goal is also something that is within sight, as all are "to see" this event happening.

The use of the verb *"voir"*, meaning "to see" and (as *"veoir"*) "to perceive, to view, to look, to behold, to oversee, to survey; to pry, to spy; to mark, to note, to heed, to examine, to search into, to consider of, to devise, and/or to find some means for," acts to set up how those goals "will be" achieved in the future. This breadth of meaning allows one to understand that "to see" is relative to physical sight, to introspective understanding, and to visionary planning. Following the main theme's sense of travel along a "bridge" to "there" in "Tartary", the secondary theme is setting the sights to further movement, which will allow "One to see in that place" (alternative translation of the "adverb of place – *là*"). The reader next sees "that place" is named "Gaul".

The place known as "Gaul", which existed during the times of the Roman Empire, was called *"Gallia"* in Latin. "Gaul" is generally all of Western Europe, including portions of the British Isles; but it is most commonly associated with France. The use of an ancient name for modern Tajikistan is now being balanced with an ancient name for modern France. The secondary theme is making the statements that "One who will be king will go to see France", and thus, one will "observe One who will arrive to be king there in France". It makes the important statements that an important "One" is going to be in "France" as a "leader of an army", "to see" the land he will conquer. Once his quest "will come" under his power, he then "will be" elevated, as a common man lording over many peoples, to "king".

This powerful secondary theme statement ends with a colon. A colon is a punctuation mark that indicates more is to follow, which will act to clarify that previously stated, or it will further specify that which has been stated by the presentation of examples. This means that the third line will clarify the meaning of "One who will be king", while also maintaining its responsibility of supporting the main theme (line one).

In regard to line three supporting the main theme, a theme presented in two important halves, one finds it too is divided into two parts. This division is realized through the presence of an ampersand. This line begins with the capitalized future tense verb, "*Transpercera*", which translates to state an important "piercing through, thrusting through, and/or striking through" that will take place.

Whereas the first half of the main theme was focused on "To the bridge", the support for understanding this half-theme comes from realizing that "bridge" represents how one "Will pierce through". This acts to support the concept of an escape through the Khyber Pass, into Pakistan, as that "pass" represents a natural "bridge" between mountains where one can travel safely. The act of "piercing through" can be seen as a mountain "rabbit hole," where "One" will have directed the excavation of rock, so that an exit to the Khyber Pass would have been prepared beforehand. This would be in case of emergency, making escape from Tora Bora possible.

As a clarification of "One who will become king to see in that place France", another important "Piercing through" will take place. This action of "piercing" will be found repeated in the other quatrains that specifically name the Pyrenees Mountains. Those will be found to indicate the placement of people "in the mountain", just as the discoveries in the Afghan mountains have exposed. It clarifies how an established complex of caves, enhanced by engineering techniques that are used to bore tunnels, allows for *"an army"* to safely reside in mountainous terrain.

The supporting element of line three also adds the important (recognized through capitalization) word *"Alane"*. This is the ancient name for the medieval kingdom "Alans", which is the place now known as the Republic of North Ossetia–Alania. This place has been in the news in the last year or two, as where the Russians took military action into Georgia and South Ossetia, which had become independent nations. The North Ossetians have hyphenated their name to include "Alania", because of a desire to retain their history as an independent nation. However, it remains a vassal (federal subject) of Russia.

This identification of North Ossetia acts in support of the theme of a *"bridge there"*, in the part of Russia connected to Afghanistan and Pakistan, known as "Tartary". It adds to the picture of a travel path being established. "From the" southeastern part of Asian Russia will be an important "Piercing through" to the southwestern part of Asian Russia. That makes Russia a "bridge" to "France", while also identifying North Ossetia as a place on the "bridge" of land between the Caspian Sea and "Black Sea" (*"pont Euxine"*).

North Ossetia, incidentally, is known for the Darial Pass. That is a "bridge" that is along the border of Russia and Georgia. The Terek River is said to "pierce through" the Darial Gorge. All of this allows one to see a "penetration" (synonymous with definition of "pierce") along a path made possible by Russia.

Following the ampersand, which is a mark of punctuation that indicates importance in Nostradamus' writings, one finds the stand-alone statement, *"l'Armenie"*. This translates to state "the Armenia", and becomes important (through capitalization) as being representative of history's greatest version of "Armenia". This historical "Armenia" is nothing like the one that exists in a diminished state today. It represents the times when "Armenia" was a kingdom.

Under Tigranes the Great (140-55 B.C.), the Kingdom of "Armenia" stretched from the shores of the Caspian Sea to the Mediterranean Sea, covering parts of what is now Iran, Iraq, Turkey, and Syria. An important factor in Armenian history is that it was the first nation to accept Christianity as its official religion. As such, "the Armenia" is referencing an important "bridge" between the Persian Muslims (those of "Tartary") and Arab Muslims (those of Iraq, Syria, and Turkey). Due to this eastern threat, "the Armenia" became closely allied with

PROSECUTION EXHIBIT C

the Byzantine Christians.

An ampersand that separates two parts, with no other punctuation marks present, also acts like the word "AND", joining the words before and after it into a combination of meaning. This is how most people typically read an ampersand. In this case, Nostradamus wrote "Alania AND Armenia" (where French typically attaches an "*l'*" to a word, with only the word meant, such as "*l'France*" means "France"). The symmetry surrounding an ampersand becomes a focal point, such that there is a similarity or difference present. In this case, the two nations mentioned are small (similar) and located on the Caucasus Isthmus between the Caspian and Black seas (similar). They were once both independent kingdoms converted to Christianity (similar), and allied with the Byzantine Empire (similar). However, one fell under Soviet domination, while the other fell under Ottoman domination (a similar difference).

This combination then points to "the Armenia" as the one that will stand most alone. As a support to the second half of the main theme, it represents a reflection of the "great" of "Tartary". In a sense, both have been "pierced through" by the history of empires seeking to "thrust" its religious preference on the small lands their empirical "greatness" consumes. The people of both "Tartary" and "Armenia" have had those more powerful than they persecute them into servitude and compliance.

In the case of "them [of] Armenia", (where "*l'Armenie*" can be seen as "*les Armenie*") they faced a genocidal campaign against them by the Ottoman Turks, one that was so massive the word "genocide" was coined to describe that specific carnage. Beginning in the late 19th century, at the time of the reign of the Ottoman Sultan Abdul Hamid II, and lasting until the times of World War I, millions of Armenians were killed because they were Christians. Czarist Russia had once acted as a defender of Christian minorities in the Middle East and Russia fought the Ottomans during World War I. The genocide of "the Armenians" was excused as if those peoples were resistance fighters for the enemy. Following the war, the advent of communism mean both Muslims and Christians were persecuted by the "great" Soviet Union.

As a supporting detail to the main theme of "Tartary", that region was predominately Muslim and of Persian descent. The Soviet control of that region persecuted those of all religions. This was more prevalent under Stalin, who deported many Crimean Tartars (Muslims). The Soviet Union has had constant problems forcing its will upon the Muslims of the Caucasus region, especially in Chechnya. Chechnya wants autonomy from Russia, but the Russians will not release them for fear that Tatarstan (a predominately-Muslim region with a strong economy) would want to follow suit. Chechnya is known for its acts of terror, as are the Russians known for bloody retaliation.

Line three supports the main theme of a "bridge" that is importantly "Hospitable", which is "there" in the Muslim region of southeastern Russia. This "bridge" will then be the means by which the "One king" "Will strike through" to the northern Caucasus ("Alania") and end up in the Ararat Mountains region of Turkey, at the border of "Armenia" and Iran. This appears to be a path to safety, taken by a Muslim with protective friends.

It also promotes a common theme of mountains. The security of a mountain lair in Afghanistan could be duplicated in all of the subsequent regions. It also hints at the historic conflicts that European Christians have had with the Islamic people in the Near East. This plays a role in clarifying why someone like Osama bin Laden would want "to see France", or (on a wider scale) "to behold Western Europe" (the bastion of Christianity), not as a tourist, but as conqueror. He wants "to see Western Europe [Gaul]" under the rule of someone who would make the genocide of "the Armenian" Christians seem tame.

The fourth line then adds the supporting details to the secondary theme of "One who will be king [that] will come to see France". In that regard, the colon at the end of the secondary theme statement makes line four also act as a clarification of "Gaul". As mentioned, the name "Gaul" is relative to the Roman name "*Gallia.*" Line four begins with the written word "*Et*" which means, "And, Likewise, Also, As well, and/or Both," and it must be realized that Nostradamus did spell out this conjunction when it was necessary to be included in the verbiage. It only appears written as a capitalized first word of a line, meaning it is always written when an important additional aspect must be known. Nostradamus never wrote an ampersand as an abbreviated way to state "and," such that it never was intended to have that meaning primarily.

The important addition to the secondary theme, which adds clarification to "Gaul", is the phrase, "within Byzantium". This can also be translated to state, "inwardly Byzantium" or simply, "in Byzantium".[1] This capitalized word becomes elevated

1   In Old French, and in particular with Nostradamus' spelling of Old French, several letters become interchangeable. Two are "*y*" being interchangeable with "*i*",

in meaning, so it acts to show the Christian association to that empire, as it was basically the Greek branch of the Roman Empire. This follows the second half stand-alone statement of "the Armenia," which also brought that history into its meaning. The addition of "Armenia", such that it is "Also within" the scope of "Byzantium", becomes a statement about the eastern branch of the Holy Roman Empire. Line four is thus beginning with the important focus (capitalization) on more than one nation ("And") being "within *Byzance*".

The name "Gaul" can then take on the meaning as "Western Europe", in the broad sense. The meaning of "France" is also valid, but as a specific element that was part of "Gaul". This means that line four is acting as a clarification of line two's last word, "*Gaule*", with the colon ending that line. Thus, the "One king" that "will be", as the "One who will come to see Gaul", is then known to additionally ("And") be "within" the realm of Christianity, which includes an eastern branch and a western branch. In this meaning, the word "*Bisance*" is seen as coming from its Latin roots, where "*Bis*" means an important state of "Twice", or "Two times".[2] From the theme of Christianity (stated through "Armenia" and "Byzantium"), there are "Two conditions" of influence (Roman Catholic and Greek Orthodox). This is in addition to the area of "Gaul" being known as "Two states", "Western Europe" and "France".

Further, on a historical level of meaning, "Byzantium" can mean the vast areas of influence of the "Byzantine Empire", which lasted a thousand years (306 A.D. – 1453 A.D.). The last remnant of this empire, after assaults from the east, was the fortified city that represented the center of this eastern realm. That went by the Latinized name "*Byzantion*". That city is today called Istanbul, but was also known as "*Constantinople*", named after the Roman emperor/pope Constantine who made it his center. As a clarification to the "*One who will oversee Gaul*", the statement "And in *Byzantion*" says this area of rule will be expanded greatly. The power that "One will see" will be as "king" over an empire.

Empires do not come by simply telling nations of people, "I want to be your lord." Leaders went with armies and militarily defeated each nation to bring them each under their control. This has been the same for all of history's greatest

---

and "s" with "z". As such, "*Bisance*" becomes "*Byzance*". The translation then becomes, "*Byzantium*", the Latinized name.

2   The Latin word "*bis*" means, "twice, two times", and the suffix "*-ance*" means, "state, condition, or action". Thus, "*Bis-ance*" means an important condition of "Two Gauls".

empires (such as Alexander the Great, Cyrus the Great, Napoleon, et al). This "One" will be no different. Nostradamus wrote that this significant person "will leave", the verb that indicates movement from one place to another, as an act "to depart". This means he "will see France" by exiting some place other than "France" in order to reach "France", and lay his eyes as well as his visions of empire building on his objective.

As a continuation of line three's stand-alone second half "the Armenia", a kingdom that was aligned with the "Byzantine Empire", and adding that to "Constantinople" (alternate meaning for "*Bisance*") it means the influence of Christianity in the Middle East "will leave". As a support for the main theme governing the whole of the quatrain, line four is saying that Russia (as the ruler of "Tartary") "will relinquish" its role as the defender against Muslim uprisings against Christians (in particular the genocide of "the Armenians"). That "abandonment" will allow this "One to leave for France", with hops along the way including North Ossetia–Alania, "Armenian" Turkey, "And in Istanbul" (alternate meaning of "*Bisance*"). All of these places represent an itinerary for an escape to the West for the purpose of being a "king".

Further, one sees how this movement will not be without warfare, as the wake that "will be left" will be "bloody". The use of "will leave bloody" can act as a statement about the "One king", such that it is an indication of having himself been wounded. This would be in line with the tremendous bombardment assault that took place at Tora Bora and could be justification for the thoughts that bin Laden might have died after his escape, due to wounds he received. However, that meaning would be secondary to the purpose of going "to see France", as that nation is in the sights of Osama bin Laden, for he plans "to see France left bloody".

Line four's rhyming word matches the rhyming word at the end of line two. Both words are spelled exactly the same. "*France*" is specifically named as the place that "will be left bloody". The problem with this specific identification is the system of Nostradamus that does not use the same translated meaning at multiple places in the text of one quatrain, unless there is only one possible translation. "Gaul" can specifically mean "France", or it can broadly mean Western Europe". These two possible meanings indicate that line two can refer to a sight-seeing tour of "Western Europe", followed by seeing "France bloody" and vice versa. However, there is another translation possibility to consider.

The capitalized word "*Gaule*" is found in a modern French-English dictionary as meaning "Gaul," but specifically when proceeded by the article "*la*", as "*la Gaule.*" In the use of "*l'Armenie*," I explained that the article combination makes that translatable as simply "Armenia". The same can be said about "Gaul", but there is no article present. This means one can look to the lower case spelling "*gaule*," which is found to be a perfectly good French word meaning "pole," in modern French as well as Old French. However, the Old French dictionary shows the past tense use of the verb "*gauler*," which becomes the accented version of the same spelling "*gaulé*".

The modern word "*gauler*" can translate to mean, "to beat (using a long pole to bring down fruit etc)" and specifically in reference to "(fruits) to beat down (with a pole)." The word "*gaule*" is defined in modern terms as a "long pole; fishing rod." Old French had a similar usage, but with an additional meaning. The word "*gaule*" is stated to be, "A pole, big rod; long staff, or perch [for use in falconry]". The accented version, "*gaulé*" is stated to have meant, "beaten with a cudgel [a short, heavy stick, or club]; beaten down with a pole [as would be fruit]; and also "robbed of, or despoiled of." The additional meaning is rather brutal, as an act of theft which would cause one to be "left bloody".

This expanded translation leads to an interpretation that is showing violence being what the "One who will be king will issue" (alternative translation of "*viendra*"), as he will come "to find some means for" (alternate translation of "*voir*", as "*veoir*") the specific nation of "France", and generally all of "Western Europe". Line four is thus supporting that secondary theme by saying that Osama bin Laden will come "to see France beaten down with a long pole".

This is where the main theme's use of "great Tartary" allows one to realize Osama bin Laden is not personally going to beat Frenchmen with a cudgel. It would be more appropriate to visualize him being at the command of a "big rod", the type that makes all that have it "great". That type of "big rod" is now called a nuclear weapon, in the form of Intercontinental Ballistic Missile (ICBM). There are many quatrains that support this line of thought but for the purpose of proving one possible prediction that evidence will not be presented here. However, one must be prepared to see a motive with a scenario where the Soviet Union would allow Osama bin Laden the capability to possess this "big rod", which all have long feared "would leave" the whole world "bloody".

Simply put, the motive for the Soviets is hatred of the West, in particular the United

States of America. The hatred is mutual. Osama bin Laden was elevated to be the "conductor" of guerrilla-style warfare against the Soviets, who had brought their strong-armed influence to the Muslim nation of Afghanistan. Americans are tickled at the thought that some drunken party-animal, a.k.a. Charlie Wilson (Democratic Congressman from Texas), could manipulate the office of the C.I.A. to ship surface-to-air missiles (little "big rods") to Osama bin Laden, for use against Soviet tanks and helicopters. They are tickled to think Ronald Reagan defeated the Soviet Union by simple economic punishments, as well as putting the fear of God in them by saying America actually had *Star Wars* technology. The West has celebrated being number "One" since 1990. However, this is all an American dream.

Nostradamus is indicating the whole break-up of the Soviet Union was a ploy, so that their enemy, who also hated the West, could help them out in their Cold War against America. Remember how the Basque were indicated to protect Osama bin Laden in the Pyrenees Mountains? The Basque used to war with the Moors centuries ago, because the Moors would have gladly killed the Basque and taken their land for their own use. They hated each other too, to the point of getting "bloody". The same concept makes a unity between the religious Muslims and the atheist Communists possible, because the concept of "The enemy of my enemy is my friend" is in play once again. Osama bin Laden is suggested in the story of the quatrains of Nostradamus as having said to the Russians, "Okay FRIEND, show me the nukes."

Summarizing this quatrain in bullet points; this quatrain states:

1. A "bridge" is an important direction of passage "To", "From", and "With".
2. The "bridge" leads to a place that is quite "Hospitable".
3. The "bridge" leads to the "Black Sea".
4. The "bridge" goes through "there", which is a place identified as the land of the "great", who are in possession of the land known as "Tartary".
5. "Tartary" represents southeastern Russia, as the lands of Tajikistan, Uzbekistan, and Turkmenistan.
6. A very important "One" is identified as a non-royal blood "king".
7. This "One will come" to "France" for the purpose of "seeing" the situation "there".
8. The path to "France" involves "Alania" (Russia), "Armenia", and "Istanbul".

9. The focus of going to "France" is genocide, as the Ottomans mercilessly killed Armenians (Muslims persecuting Christians).
10. The port of call the "One will leave" is Istanbul, the place formerly known as "*Byzantion*", where the "Byzantine" Empire of Christian influence to the East was centered.
11. This Christian influence "will be left bloody", with "France" a target, along with "Western Europe".
12. A "Beating by big rods" will do the "bloody" damages.
13. The importance of "Big rods" means weapons of mass destruction, including nuclear warheads on missiles.

Afterthoughts: From the clear view of hindsight being 20/20, from a perspective of the year 2020, this quatrain can be tweaked and twisted so it produces a picture of the events that supposedly killed Osama bin Laden in Abbottabad, Pakistan. The name of the Hollywood heroization of murder was *Zero Dark Thirty*, which fictionalized the events of operation Neptune Spear. The timing of that attack was after midnight.

According to the Wikipedia article entitled "Killing of Osama bin Laden," activity in the Situation Room at the White House began at 1:22 PM (or 11:22 PM in Abbottabad) on May 1, 2011. President Barack Hussein Obama entered at 3:00 PM (or 1:00 AM, May 2), "to monitor the raid." A Sentinel drone overhead supposedly gave them a an "Above" view. This fits the main theme statement, such that "the conductor of the army" was a Commander In Chief who had less military experience than had Osama bin Laden.

Because the main theme statement links to the secondary theme statement (in line two), the two theme statements typically differ. This is why the main theme is an A and the secondary theme is a B, in the ABAB rhyme scheme. Thus, if the main theme is placing focus on President Obama, the secondary theme would not be about him, but Osama bin Laden. That says bin Laden is the one "safe" and "sudden slipped out of sight." In regard to this possibility, the fictional movie showed a C.I.A. woman who was told the chances of bin Laden being in the compound were 60-80%.

The supporting details for the main theme statement about the "conductor of the army" is then the one given the "renown" for having killed the man responsible for the attacks of "September" 11, 2001. President Obama would then be reelected for a second term, based on the actions he oversaw on May 1-2, 2011. For all his faults as a president, including his lack of military experience and a heavy lean towards Muslim and Communist support, he was not "blamed" when time came for another time to vote.

As for line four being the supporting details for Osama bin Laden having "vanished" or "slipped out of sight," the man killed and thrown into the Arabian Sea was not him. According to the Wikipedia article that gives details of the raid, there were "5 killed, with 17 captured (1 injured)." Of the captured were women and children, some said to be children of Osama bin Laden. One can assume they were interrogated, with the possibility some said the dead included Osama bin Laden. However, line four points to the truth not being told, as "not will speak ever yes" with "*ouy*" read as the French word "*oui*."

This says the importance of "*A*," as "Has his return," is supporting the secondary theme of "sudden slipped out of sight." Still, when "*A*" is read as an important directional preposition, as "In his coming back" or "With his returning," the importance supports the concept of a body double, as one who stepped "In" as "his" identity, which was "suddenly swooned" by a "midnight" (1:58 AM) raid. The witnesses who were captured were then those who would "not tell at any time" who was really killed.

The implication of this scenario does nothing to reduce this quatrain as being evidence that Osama bin Laden escaped from Tora Bora. Instead, it shows how divine prophecy is never limited to only one event, as history is know to repeat. The element of a plot having been engineered that set this who charade up, beginning with the leader of the United States of America and the intelligence that fed their military, says America was led by people not in the know, or they knowingly ceased all hunting for Osama bin Laden.

Chapter 8
Prosecution Exhibit D

A Duplication of Spelling ... Pyrennees

The realizations from the last quatrain make the taped words of Osama bin Laden have a much more powerful effect. When he is seen prophesied as "One who will be ruler" over an empire, his latest "threat" to "France" acts more as a promise, than as a threat. A promise is based on a position of confidence and an ability to fulfill an obligation, whereas a threat is more centered in anger and not necessarily founded in any reality. When these recorded messages are written off as baseless anger, everyone becomes vulnerable to the possibility that his threats do indeed come from a position of strength.

Such a position certainly can be considered, based on the hypothesis that Iran has secured all types of weapons of mass destruction from the arsenals build up by the former Soviet Union. This is more than just fantasy thinking, as there are facts that support such a hypothesis. The Cold War that everyone thought had ended after the collapse of the U.S.S.R. has instead changed temperatures. It has become heated through the acts of terrorism, which escalated from other parts of the world soon after 1992.

Since then, the news has been filled with attacks that come out of nowhere, for example, in 1993 (the first World Trade Center bombing), 1998 (the U.S. embassy bombings in Africa), 2000 (the U.S.S. Cole attack), and 2001 (the events of September 11, 2001). The new Cold War has become the declared War on Terror. The same fears of a nuclear holocaust exist but instead of the Soviet Union and America exchanging a barrage of ICBMs, Americans and their allies now fear suitcase nuclear bombs detonated by suicide bombers.

Since terrorist organizations do not have the real capacity to make these weapons, the enemy has not really changed. It is still the Soviet Union, in the lamb's clothing of many separate nations. Instead of being an overt enemy, they have gone underground. Their weapons have been placed into the hands of those who do not care what happens to the world after they are used; and, when they are used, Mother Russia can claim it had nothing to do with it.

This is how Osama bin Laden can tell the West exactly what "will be" and what "will arrive" and "will leave bloody" those who do not listen to and obey his commands. In his messages, bin Laden says this is what will happen should the West not stop its perpetual motion of hatred. The "out" from this proposed end is stated by the same one promising the end; and, this becomes the answer to averting those "bloody" actions.

This makes the last quatrain's line four stand out, when one sees how Osama bin Laden "will be" the "One king", and "his return" will "not" be expected "to come". Denial, or unwillingness to listen to what the messages truly say means the West "will be told" they will hear the words he says, but they will "never" once believe it possible. Nevertheless, the time is prophesied "to come" and then it will be realized his words spoken were "never listened unto."

By accepting the possibility that Nostradamus wrote about the escape of Osama bin Laden to "Western Europe", in particular that part that totally encompassed what is today called "France", and with a mission to plot the destruction of Europe, one needs evidence that places focus on a specific part of "Gaul". As the "One" most known for hiding in mountainous terrain, it would be logical to assume this "conductor of an army" would likewise seek a mountain base, with "France" having the Alps, its Central Mountains, and the Pyrenees Mountains to choose from. The preponderance of quatrains that specifically name the Pyrenees Mountains makes them worthy of inspection, simply to see if the information stated in the letter of explanation (the Henry letter) matches the information in the quatrains that contain the words "*mont Pyrenees*" (in some form, as stated before).

There are eleven quatrains that contain some form of the word "Pyrenees". Those eleven are not all together in one "*Centurie*" (the title word used for each of the ten sections of 100 verses), which means they are not in an order that presents them as somehow connected. Likewise, the three segments of words that included related information (stating, "*mont Jouis ... monter aux pyren-nees*") are found randomly placed in the middle of the letter to Henry II. One section is amid other sections that have nothing to do with mountains. The quatrains are thus in no logical order, with the letter that explains them equally illogical. However, the repeating of key words, in this case *"mont"* and *"pyrennees"*, link the pieces together.

This means the verses of *The Prophecies* and the letter to Henry II must be viewed as puzzles. Everything is a piece of a whole that has been purposefully put into a scrambled condition. The quatrains need to be placed together properly, so one grand picture can emerge. The letter then needs to be put in the correct order that matches the order of the quatrains' stories. Each then verifies the other.

The process that makes putting a complex puzzle (of 1,000 pieces) together properly first requires comparison of similar elements (color, straight edges, corners, etc.). This sorting divides the pieces into similar groups. This is a standard step in puzzle solving; and, with the quatrains, key word repetition acts to help one perform this task. The next step is to do a close inspection of each piece, looking for details and shapes for the completed picture. In the quatrains, the nouns, verbs, and use of unique elements bring out the details that surround the key terms. The last step is the time-consuming trial and error approach, where one tries to see if the shapes make a perfect fit by physically putting two pieces together. While one can see two pieces having the same traits, they need to be pieced together in the perfect order for the whole picture to become crystal clear. These same steps will be used in this presentation of evidence that says Osama bin Laden is in the Pyrenees Mountains.

At some time in life, most people of minimal means and intelligence have attempted to put a complex puzzle together. Regardless of how successful or unsuccessful, the process of puzzle solving is always the same. In complex puzzles, one piece includes several aspects that are repeated throughout the completed puzzle.

For instance, the last puzzle I put together (over 1,000 pieces) depicted a country dirt road, with leaves on the ground and trees featured to one side of the road, and with a split-rail fence, a pasture with horses, and a red farmhouse on the other side of the road. The dirt road curved to a central point of perspective, with a blue sky, scattered with wispy clouds, and the extended branches of the tree's leaves were in the upper-center portion of the overall picture. Obviously, this puzzle is a picture with many points of focus, and the most valuable pieces usually included elements of more than one point of focus.

To clarify this point, a piece that included part of the tin roof on the red farmhouse also had part of the background trees, behind the farmhouse. Part of a piece that depicted the country boy's barefoot and blue overalls had evidence of the brown of the dirt road along which he was walking. This happens when a completed work of multiple points of interest is cut into pieces for the purpose of putting the pieces back together. Having to look for minute details adds to the complexity of matching pieces together; but that is what makes putting puzzles together both challenging and rewarding. There is a sense of accomplishment when each section of the puzzle is completed, even while the other sections are still scattered and unrecognizable.

With that remembrance of how puzzles work, transfer that knowledge to each of the quatrains. Most of the four-line verses will deal with more than one point of focus. While all aspects of each piece are vital in the recreation of the completed whole, it is unnecessary to explain the presence of all the details. For example, to say that a red farmhouse is in the picture is factual evidence to that point of focus. It is unnecessary to detail everything that is pictured aside from the red farmhouse. Each of the pieces that contribute to the completion of that singular focus, a red farmhouse, may also detail some dark trees behind it, or a gray gravel driveway that leads to it, or some green grass of the pasture alongside it. It is understood that all aspects of the pieces contribute to understanding the wholeness of the total picture, which is greater than the part that shows a red farmhouse. Similarly, this work is not focused on the whole picture; it is only concerned with the details that show one prediction contained within *The Prophecies*.

To this point, I have gone into great detail about the meaning of two quatrains and three segments from the letter to Henry that explains the quatrains. In each of those cases, the whole view has been important to realize. The two quatrains make it possible to see a match to the fact that a character like Osama bin Laden exists, has been missing for some time, and keeps producing videos threatening a Day of Reckoning. This Day of Reckoning is the whole view of *The Prophecies*, and it is the whole view that assists one in understanding the who, what, when, where, and why of a prediction that Osama bin Laden is hiding in the Pyrenees Mountains. Now, however, the presentation of evidence will show a narrow point of focus found from the "mountains Pyrenees".

The following eleven pieces of evidence will focus only on the parts of the quatrain that make the case relative to Osama bin Laden being in the Pyrenees Mountains. I will only detail the red farmhouse, so to speak, and not address the parts that lead one's focus away from that point. While the parts I do not explain are important in understanding the whole view, those parts become superfluous as evidence that supports that prediction.

From this analogy, each piece of evidence from quatrains of *The Prophecies* can be expected to deal directly with the whereabouts of Osama bin Laden by uniformly pointing to the Pyrenees Mountains. Each of the eleven quatrains that will be referred to in this regard will contain the words "*monts*" and "*Pyrenees*", mostly spelled that exact way, with all shown as side-by-side words, and with all in only one line of a four-line poem.

Based on the systems of understanding that place an importance on order, such that each line bears a specific role as being either theme or supporting details to a theme, the line of placement is an important factor regarding how much relative information needs to be gleaned as evidence. This means that the placement of "*monts Pyrenees*" in the main theme will mean the majority of the quatrain (if not all) needs to be explained. Conversely, if those key words are in line three, it may be unnecessary to explain line four. It would be like the pieces that make up the red farmhouse; it would be irrelevant to explain the grass beside it, or the trees behind it.

The eleven pieces that point to the Pyrenees Mountains need to be brought together so they tell a story, as they are found scattered randomly throughout *The Prophecies*. There is some trial and error to this process. Like separating eleven puzzle pieces that will eventually form a red farmhouse, all would be mostly shades of red, and those would then need to be fitted together by trying one with another, until two of them match perfectly. In piecing the quatrains of *The Prophecies* together, as a word puzzle, one has to look at the fit that comes from the flow of information, which then creates a cohesive picture that is relative to the Pyrenees Mountains.

The logic of organizing the quatrains into a good fit is based on the order of placement of "*monts Pyrenees*" in the lines. The quatrains that have it in the main theme will be fitted together first, followed by those that have those words placed in the secondary theme. Finally, I will finish this section off by discussing those having these words in the third line.[1] As with the pieces of the red farmhouse

---

1   None of the quatrains have "*monts Pyrenees*" in line four.

fitting together to look exactly like the whole picture on the puzzle box top, assembling the story of Osama bin Laden in the Pyrenees Mountains will be guided by the description set forth in the letter to Henry II. It is the guide one must follow, in order to reach the correct conclusion.

With these preliminary instructions understood, it is important to look first at those poems that make a statement about the Pyrenees in the main theme (line one). Of those, there are three; one of those contains the only spelling in the quatrains that matches the spelling in the letter to Henry, where an extra "*n*" is present ("*Pyrennees*").[2] This makes that one quatrain stand out as the first to present as evidence.

The quatrain states (simply translated):

L'Aemathion passer montz Pyrennees,	The Arabian king to hold on a course mountains Pyrenees-born ones,
En Mars Narbon ne fera resistance,	At War Narbonne not will make resistance,
Par mer & terre fera si grand menee,	By sea & country will resemble in sort great conducted,
Cap. n'ayant terre seure pour demeurance.	Capitulation not possessing land sour for remaining.

The main theme statement (line one) begins with two capitalized letters, such that the abbreviated article "*L'*" is denoting the importance of "One", as "THE". This makes the capitalized "*A*" of the main word "*Aemathion*" be the importance of a proper name. As such, the main theme is immediately drawing focus to the main topic as being relative to "THE One named Aemathion". This makes the translation of "*Aemathion*" quite important.

On occasion, Nostradamus will present words that have "*ae*" in them as "*Æ æ*," which is a representation of the Latin diphthong, with a traditional English name as its own letter, being called "aesh," or "ash tree." In French, the "*æ*" is used

---

2   The 1566 Lyon edition shows "*Pyrenneés*", which is capitalized and accented. It is not hyphenated because it appears in the center of the page. The 1568 Lyon edition, which I feel is a better representation of a holy document, shows it in the lower case, hyphenated, and unaccented, as "*pyren-nees*".

to spell Greek or Latin borrowings.[3] When looking up a word that is spelled with this double letter, one letter gets dropped. In this case, this name becomes searchable as "*Emathion*", which has meaning in both Greek and Latin.

The Latin meaning is derived from the name "*Emathia*" which is a district of Macedonia. The spelling "*Emathis*" or "*Emathidis*" represents a Macedonian. One spelling, as "*Emathides*" is said to be a reference to "the Muses," who were Greek mythological figures.[4] However, none of these spelling is an exact match for "*Aemathion*" as "Emathion", but Greek mythology does show an exact spelling as "The person named Emathion".

This character is said to be, "A son of Tithonus and Eos, and a brother of Memnon. He was king of Arabia, and was slain by Heracles."[5] With this information it becomes possible to see how this name from Greek literature can be used as a metaphorical representation of Osama bin Laden. He is a "descendant" of Saudi Arabia, and he is "One who will be king", as the "leader of an army". This is a good fit for understanding a puzzling name, but more reasoning confirms this opinion.

This use of "*Aemathion*" is repeated in three other quatrains (with two other similar spellings). Further, some representation of "Hercules" is found in six quatrains. The system used in interpreting Nostradamus' writings that allows for metaphorical representation of people, especially through poetic license and the system that demonstrates a regular use of Greek mythological figures to achieve this goal, makes it logical to see this main theme placing immediate focus on "THE" future's version of an Arabian king who is best represented by the pseudonym "*Aemathion*".

From this understanding, one then sees this important person acts to, in French, "*passer monts Pyrennees*". The French verb "*passer*" can be translated with a myriad of meanings. The Old French-English dictionary shows it as representing action, "to pass, wend, go, walk on afore; to proceed, or hold on a course; also to flit, remove, or depart from." It also means, "to surpass, overgo, overrun, overreach, overtop, overgrow, surmount, exceed, excel; also to pass, let go, suffer, give way unto; and to forget, omit, overslip; run slightly over". It can

---

3 Information found in the article on Wikipedia, entitled "*Æ*".
4 Per Notre Dame University online Latin Word Lookup.
5 Greek Myth Index, under "*Emathion*" - one of three references of this name being found in Greek literature.

mean in another context, "to transport over, convey, or carry over; also to strain through; also to decay, fade, wither; decease; vanish away." As is the nature of all words used in *The Prophecies*, each of these meanings can play a role in leading one to deeper and deeper understanding of the whole, by assuming that all meanings are correct, within specific contexts. For evidence purposes, I will go over a few at this time.

My basic translation stated that the important named one would be seen "to hold on a course". That becomes a "passage" relative to "mountains". This "course" can then be seen as one requiring a body "to surmount, to overtop, and/or to carry over," which relates well with how one is "to proceed" on a mountainous path. This relates to the main theme line in the prior quatrain that began, "To the bridge Hospitable". In that half-theme, the word "*Euxine*" is Greek, meaning, "Hospitable". Here, "The Emathion" is Greek, meaning, "The Arabian king". The "bridge" of that quatrain, as discussed, was (among other possibilities) a "mountain pass", where the Khyber Pass represented a "course" to the "Hospitality" of "mountainous" Pakistan. This makes this quatrain take on the "feel" of being associated with that quatrain previously discussed.

Just as the other quatrain developed a "*course*" as an itinerary leading to "Gaul", this course ends at the specific place called the "Pyrenees Mountains". Those "mountains" are indeed in "Gaul" as representative of "France" or "Western Europe". "Gaul" is a continent away from "Tartary", meaning movement is required to get from "Tartary" to "Gaul". The entire focus of this quatrain's main theme is placed on the "vanishing away" (alternate translation of "*passer*") that allowed "THE Arabian king" character to be placed among those "born of the Pyrenees" (the meaning of "*Pyrennees*").[6]

In this scenario, one is also reminded of being told in another quatrain of a "conductor of an army" who will be "saved" by having "suddenly slipped out of sight". The letter to Henry II further stated that a "descendant ... will be removed from one place unto another". This would describe one named for an ancient "Arabian king," who has not been seen for nine years. This makes all prior evidence become supportive of the main theme of this quatrain, which specifically names the "Pyrenees Mountains" as the end destination of a "course held". The rest of the quatrain becomes relative to this theme.

---

6   As discussed in the letter to Henry II, this is the root meaning of "*Pyren-nees*", spelled with an extra "*n*".

The secondary theme statement (line two) of this quatrain then tells the reader that an important direction is to be considered. This is understood by the first word being the capitalized preposition "*En*". This word has versatile usage in French, such that a modern French dictionary shows it being used in the contexts of locations, directions, times, compositions, descriptions, causes, and assorted combination usage with other parts of speech. In the Old French-English dictionary, several uses are listed individually, such as those uses "relating to a thing, relating to a place, and also those set before verbs of motion." However, as a preposition, its basic uses denote, "in, into; at, on, and/or upon."

As a capitalized word immediately following the word "Pyrenees born ones," as separated by a comma punctuation mark, one is asked to see the importance of being "In" those "mountains". As such, "In" means being inside them, more than a statement of being readily visible "On" them.

As the first word of a separate theme, this use can be seen as being "set before a verb of motion." In that regard, the following word is the capitalized: "*Mars*". Previous discussion has addressed this being rooted in the Latin, lower-case verb in the transitive, meaning, "war, battle, fight." The capitalization makes this verb represent a major (named) "War". Thus, one can see that a separate theme (line two) is placing initial focus on a time when the world is "At War". When this is related to Osama bin Laden, as depicted by the metaphor "The Arabian king", line two is placing focus on the international acceptance of a declaration having been made, for a "War" on Terror.

The next word is "*Narbon*", which is rooted in the Latin "*Narbo,*" meaning the town in southern "Gaul" that now goes by the name "Narbonne." The Catalan (local dialect of Catalonia Spain and Andorra) and Occitan (local dialect of southern France) spelling used by the people along the Pyrenees Mountains is "*Narbona.*" It is logical to read this place as the meaning to be found in line two. That logic is strengthened by the fact that the southern French city of "Narbonne" is near the Mediterranean coast, at the foothills of the "Pyrenees". "Narbonne" then acts as a metaphor for "France", which is an important player "In" the "War" that makes Osama bin Laden a most wanted criminal.

Following the word "*Narbon*", one finds the independent negative "*ne*", which means, "not, nor, and/or neither." Still, when the same letters are seen with an accent mark used, as "*né*", it becomes possible to also include the meanings, "born; bred from, risen from, descended from, proceeding from; grown out of, issuing out of, and/or come out of." One can see how "*Narbon*", as a symbol of southern "Gaul" or "France", has become part of the "War" on Terror. Perhaps some soldiers will have been "issued out of" this region, to go fight in Afghanistan. Yet, it can also mean that "Narbonne" is probably "not" a place that is hot under the collar for "War". The "War France" has gotten itself "Into" includes "Narbonne", but that does "not" make its people feel like they are "At War".

The next word is the future tense of the verb "*faire*" ("*fera*"), which makes a prediction about what "will be done, will act, will effect; will cause, will make, will form, will forge; will counterfeit, will resemble, and/or will imitate." As a stand-alone statement, this states what can be found in the form of action in "Narbonne", relative to the "effect, cause, or deed" of "War". This is then connected to the word "resistance", which states that the "actions" of the people of "Narbonne", or southern "France", will be in "opposition" to themselves being considered willful participants "In" (actually fighting and dying because America was attacked by Muslim terrorists) that major "War" effort.

As a secondary theme, separate (use of a comma) from the main theme, thus capable of stating a theme that is only relative to Osama bin Laden being in the "Pyrenees Mountains", line two says southern France would be a safe place for Muslims because the people along the "Pyrenees Mountains resist actions" designed to fan the flames of "War". This becomes a general theme for "France" historically, where the French prefer to fall like fainting goats when attacked. This method is preferred because protecting its national treasures is more important than angering those who might start trying to blow them up. It is harder to replace an Eiffel Tower, or a Château de Versailles, or The Louvre, than it is to outlast some foreign influence that is "At War" with the French government *en vogue*. This theme of the French people being "resistant" to "War" makes them less likely to look at Muslims as terrorists and therefore much less likely to look for Osama bin Laden in their midst.

The supporting details of the main theme statement (found in line three) indicate that "The Arabian king" will have reached the "Pyrenees" via some form of boat or ship. This is because line three begins with the capitalized preposition, "*Par*" which shows an important means to that end. It primarily translates as "By", but can also indicate "Through; Of, By reason of; For; and/or On." This allows one to see how "*Byzance*", which is the modern "Istanbul", is an Islamic port city that an "Arabian king" would "pass Through". That port of call allows one to understand an itinerary that leads to the Turkish shores of the "Black Sea" (alternate translation of "*Exuine*"), with an end destination of "Gaul" (which the previous quatrain presented). In this quatrain, one can see how a traveler reached a specific place in southern "France" ("Narbonne"), in the foothills of the "Pyrenees Mountains," importantly "By sea". The statement "By sea" represents one-half of the supporting detail of line three.

The presence of an ampersand breaks line three into two halves that each give support to the main theme about Osama bin Laden being in the "Pyrenees". The first half of line three contains the statement about how he got there. That method was "By sea". The second half makes the statement why he would go there.

In that regard, one finds the word "*terre*" written. The word "*terre*" means, "earth, ground, land, soil; also a manor, farm, close, field, piece of ground; also, a land, region, province, country; also the world, and/or the whole earth." The second half then becomes focused on the "region of the world" ("Gaul" as "Western Europe"), as well as specifically to the "country" of "France" ("Gaul" as "France"). However, it is also supporting the main theme, as a statement about the "piece of ground" named the "Pyrenees".

Again, the action verb "*fera*" is found repeated, so the translation used in the secondary theme line will not be used again in line three. All uses are viable in both uses, in both lines, just not repeatable at the same time when there is more than one translation possibility, allowing for multiple contexts. The secondary theme was seen focused on the action of "resistance" and "opposition" to a known "War", whereas the action of the supporting details are relative to an "if" situation (from "*si*" being the next word). It states what "will exploit" this situation, "if, if so be that, so, in sort, as, even as, and/or whether" the French will remain "withstanding" (alternate translation of "resistance") or "endeavoring against" the "War" on Terror.

Following the word "*si*" Nostradamus again penned the word "*grand*", which was last found used in the previous quatrain (used in the main theme line). Since every use of the word "*grand*" is related to a powerful nation, its use here becomes a clear indication of the "land" of the "Pyrenees Mountains" belonging to the powerful nations of "Western Europe", who act as "great" nations because of a history of imperialism. In our present world, this is also an indicator of those who are clinging to a "great" title, through an alliance with the "greatest" nation on "earth" (from "*terre*"), the United States of America. As a supporting theme to why Osama bin Laden will go to a "great land", the implication is that it will be to see "if" indeed they will be proved "great", through what they "will commit" (alternative translation of "*fera*") towards appeasing Islamic demands.

The last word of this third line is "*menee,*" which has to be seen as either the past tense version of the verb "*mener*" or the noun of the same spelling, "*menée*". Both words are accented, which confirms the theory that allows one to infer the absence of an accent mark, whereas the presence of one locks a word to that one spelling. The fact that two different meanings come from the verb and the noun supports the system that says the possibility of multiple contexts makes all translations play a role in deepening the level of understanding that one word can bring.

The verb "*menée*" meant, according to the Old French dictionary, "led, brought; guided, conducted, directed; managed; moved, induced, persuaded; also overwrought, subdued, fetched in." This meaning is reminiscent of the quatrain that called Osama bin Laden a "*conducteur*" which is a "leader, guide, conductor, director, and/or manager." The noun use of "*menée*" is then translated to mean, "A plot, conspiracy, practice; private faction; a shift, subtlety, device; a business carried closely; also the direct and outright course of a flying [leaping] deer." All of this is descriptive of the reason why "The Arabian king" would take a trip "By sea" to be with the people "born of the Pyrenees". It states that this leader guides a plot.

In the context that Osama bin Laden went to the "Pyrenees" for a purpose, "to exploit" the lack of will and determination of the West, while nations like "France" ride the coattails of "greatness" (variation of "*grand*"), he goes there to "conduct a plot" against that lack of commitment. In the context that Osama bin Laden went to the "Pyrenees" as the "conductor of an army" that is "At War" with the West, it is because "the world" is filled with supporters for his "cause" (from "*fera*"). Those "born of the Pyrenees" are examples "in sort" who are already counted as members of the "great", who do their own "plotting" and "conspiring" to disrupt the "great" nations that lord over them. For this reason, Osama bin Laden went to the "Pyrenees" to become "king" over all Christendom, to be the "guide" to all his supporters. He importantly will go to get them organized and readied, "Through" (alternate translation of "*Par*") "a plot" (from "*menée*") that involves building "an army" on "land" (from "*terre*"). That group will assist a planned naval invasion, which will come to "Western Europe" "By sea".

One must remember that this scenario was discussed in the interpretation of the terminology found in the letter to Henry II, which stated (in one syntactical sense), "the third inundation of blood human". Those words make it possible to see a "surrounding" (alternate translation of "*inondation*") that would "flood" the area of the "Pyrenees Mountains" "with kindred" people related to the "descendant" who would "rise" there. The reference to "third" allowed for the possibility of a "third War", as the word "*Mars*" expanded that meaning, as "the (third) times [of] War". This line is then combining the words surrounding the ampersand to see the strategic purpose (as an important "By reason of" from "*Par*") for being in the "Pyrenees" reflects a "sea AND land" action that will come by plan.

Line four of this quatrain then offers an element that I will not go deeply into interpreting. It pertains to the use of a period mark in an abbreviation. The word abbreviated is the capitalized first word, which means the word is making an important statement. However, the abbreviation leaves it wide-open as to the number of words possible to be read into the meaning of line four, as well as a multiplicity of support for the information found in the three other lines.

Nostradamus wrote, "*Cap.*" (with the period mark included by Nostradamus). All of the words (in French) that could be abbreviated "*Cap.*" are important to consider, as long as they support the main themes. Those themes are that Osama bin Laden went to the "Pyrenees" because he was a major player "In" a "War", to which the people of southern "France" ("Narbonne") "not will make opposition" to, as it is one they did "not" declare. He will find the "Pyrenees" accommodating because they "will effect opposition" to their involvement to that "War". In that regard, the only word that I focus on now, for interpreting "*Cap.*" along the line of those themes, is as "*Captif*".

The word "*Captif*" is translated in the Old French-English dictionary of 1611 to be, "Captive; taken in war, imprisoned by war; servile, subject that has lost his liberty." This makes the important statement (capitalization) that the people of "Narbonne" figuratively will be held "Captive" to the decisions made by their elected governors. They will reject (give "resistance") such forced acceptance to "War". It means their "Loss of liberty" (alternate translation of "Captive") is important enough "to cause" them "to make resistance" to a major "War".

While other words can be seen easily abbreviated as "*Cap.*" which are certainly applicable to the support of the main themes of this quatrain, I will only address that one possibility.⁷ Keep in mind that the use of a period mark represents a full stop, in all cases, such that all possibilities of "*Cap.*" must act as an important stand-alone statement. However, as the natural progression from the third line, as a separate element (use of a comma), "Captive" acts to expand the meaning of the "great" who are "led, directed, guided, and/or subdued." This is an important correlation to being manipulated, through "a plot" to do the will of the government, such that all citizens become "Servile" to the whims of a few leaders. This represents a mistrust of those who govern the people.

When this one possibility is understood, one sees the remainder of the line stating, "not having land – sour for staying." In this case, the use of "not" is built into the present participle "*avant*", making "not" the only translation possibility. As such "not having" relates to the sacrifices a "Captive" has forced upon him or herself. This relates to a "Loss of liberty" to do as one pleases, and this makes one become "sour" to this type of control over one's life.

This resentment, where "*seure*" means, "sour, sharp, tart" to the taste (relative to weaning a baby from suckling), is shown through acts of "resistance" and "opposition" to something one has become tired of tasting. On the other hand, the word "*seure*" also meant, "sure, safe, secure, out of danger; fast, assured, certain; trusty, loyal, and/or faithful." This is then pointing to a sense of self-sacrifice, where one has become "Captive" to something greater than self. This represents the nurturing of a "great" one, who wants to protect those under his or her care, to the point of "directing" everyone's roles in maintaining a "safe and secure" environment (the "land, nation, country").

The call for "national loyalty" (alternate translations of "*terre seure*") makes the demand set forth on everyone the need "for remaining Captive" to the status quo. One has to "trust" that the greater good is protected by those few chosen to lead the whole. It becomes representative of how "Captivity" is a "continuing" state of "not having", so the "land" can be "secure". This is supportive of the

---

7   Nostradamus used the abbreviated form of "*Cap.*" in 4 quatrains, making its repeated use become an indication that it is important to understand. In all, *The Prophecies* includes 17 words that begin with the letters "*cap-*", but six of those 17 are variations on the theme of "captivity." Those six spellings appear a total of 47 times, in as many different quatrains, with each '*Centurie*' including at least one representation. The word "*captif*" appears 22 times, "*captifs*" 17 other times, "*captifz*" once, "*captive*" seven times, and "*captivité*" twice, making it the one word most represented that begins with the letters "*cap-*." (Source: Index of the Centuries of M. Nostradamus, prepared by J. Flanagan)

secondary theme, which presented the people of "Narbonne" as being passive in the face of "War". Because they "will not make resistance" to the powers that be, who have deemed "War" necessary, it becomes the apathy that allows "The Arabian king to excel" in the "Pyrenees Mountains". It continues the third line's statement, where a "great" people will be "led" to the point of "not having [the] land safe" (from terrorists). That failure then acts as justification "for continuing" to toe the line of fear, being "Captive" to those in power.

As another reason for why Osama bin Laden would go to the "Pyrenees Mountains", such that he is a renowned figure seen as an "Arabian king" by many Muslims, line four relates to the whole "terrorism" movement as being linked to the people of the Middle East. There would be no threat of a major "War" if the "great" nations of the world would recognize the Palestinian issue. They are a people held "Captive" by all of the illegitimate reasons the theft of Palestine has caused.

The Palestinians "not having [their] land" is the most bitter taste that has "led" to Osama bin Laden "rising" to address their grievances through "War". He represents the complete and utter refusal to bend to the will of the thieves who stole Palestine. The call "for continuing" this arrangement of "dwelling" will be answered by a plot to make all Europe "Captive". The plan of Osama bin Laden calls "for dwelling" on stolen land, placing Westerners under the strong arm of an overseer. The reality Palestinians have long suffered is then to become a "Western Europe" reality.

Line four is making a strong statement about how turnabout can be fair play. The entire reason someone (anyone) like Osama bin Laden rises to power is the little people become fed up with the atrocities that punish them, keeping them "Captive". The people then "will make resistance" the impetus for a new power "to rise". This comes in the form of unstoppable revolution. Such swelling anger needs a "guide" in the form of a "conductor" who will devise a master plan. The plan of Osama bin Laden involves attacks "By sea AND land" made possible by training an army right under the noses of the enemy.

This quatrain supports the explanation found in the letter to Henry II, where the words "to long times [of] War" ("*de long temps Mars*") were relative to the future initiated by a "raging" which would take "to the mountain … for to show in quantity" that a people "will not be removed from one place to another". It tells that the "Pyrenees Mountains" will be the point of "land" troops, representing a "third" of the total "inundation" that is planned to come. It will bring about a "time" when those of Christian nations will be "subdued" (alternate translation of "*menée*"). Those who "will not act to oppose" their own government, nor "will act as great" people, will be trained to be "subdued". It predicts a coming period of Islamic persecution of Europe, which makes the statement, "See how you like having your land stolen and your people killed for resisting that theft."

The information that is gained from this quatrain is powerful, as it predicts the future "War" that is to come. It is equally powerful by naming Osama bin Laden "*L'Aemathion*". It states the motivation for being in the "Pyrenees Mountains" as being among those "born of the Pyrenees" who will make his presence "secure". It explains how a plot to overthrow Europe "By sea AND land" will be to punish Christians for not being Christ-like.

The element of the Creation of the State of Israel is the root cause of everything that has led to Osama bin Laden's rise to power. It alone will be the ultimate cause of Armageddon. Palestinians "not having [the] nation" that was Palestine "continuing" is detailed in an undeniably fully fulfilled quatrain (known as III-97) predicting that event well in advance of 1948. That corner piece to the puzzle explains line four of this quatrain and informs the reader that "*L'Aemathion*" will exact revenge "In War".

The summary bullet points of this quatrain state:

1. A major character is symbolically named to be representative of an "Arabian king" from Greek mythology.
2. This character will "vanish away" in "mountains".
3. This character will "go" to the "Pyrenees Mountains".
4. This character will be among the people "born of the Pyrenees".
5. The timing of the trip to the "Pyrenees" will be when the world is "At War", through an official declaration and use of military troops.
6. The "War" involves France, as symbolically named by the city in France that is "Narbonne".
7. The city "Narbonne" is in southwestern France, along the eastern foothills of the "Pyrenees Mountains".
8. The people of southwestern France "will make opposition" to their involvement in the "War".
9. The people of southwestern France "will not make resistance" to the fact that the world is "At War".

10. The travel to the "Pyrenees" will be "By sea".
11. The "land" of the "Pyrenees" (France and Spain) will be involved in the "War" as two historically "great nations" of the world.
12. The "nations" of France and Spain "will be led" by one "great" of the world, who officially put the world "At War".
13. The purpose of the "Arabian king" going to the "Pyrenees" is to make the lack of will in the French to fight "At War" a way to have them "subdued" through "Captivity".
14. The ultimate purpose for being "At War" is people "not having" their "land".
15. Those people have "soured" from the taste of foreigners "dwelling" on stolen "land".

Afterthoughts: While this book is only focused on producing evidence that says someone just like Osama bin Laden (if not him still alive) being in the Pyrenees Mountains, the "trees behind the red farmhouse" needs to be a different focus that addresses "*L'Aemathion.*" In the same way the key terms "*monts*" and "*Pyrenees*" addresses a place of danger, to which the West to be alerted, the double capitalized letter figure here, in this quatrain, is also found (with spelling variations) in three other quatrains. That repetition should be seen as a main character in this future.

In that regard, there was not enough explanation here about the root meaning of "*Emathion.*" There is evidence of Latin references to this name, in poetry, being allusions to Alexander the Great, because he was THE Macedonian of greatest importance ever. The original source of the name must be recalled to be that of a brother to Memnon, regarded as the King of Aethiopia. The name also relates to a Trojan prince and a king of Samothrace. This name from ancient history would have been more readily known by scholars in the 16th century, as Nostradamus was. This name can be seen to hint at the history of the Trojan War, which would suit this warrior prophesied to be hiding in the Pyrenees Mountains. The elements in the Iliad tell of a war of attrition, leading to a surprise ending, based on the enemy having been placed within an impenetrable stronghold by the Trojans willingly welcoming that danger within. The use of this name then says Nostradamus used it with the purpose of reminding the readers that history repeats, as a modern version to come.

By following that trail of quatrains separately, in the same manner that I explained in this chapter, one can get the impression that "*L'Aemathion*" is too young to be Osama bin Laden. He was born in 1957, meaning in 2020 he would be sixty-three years of age (if still alive). While that is not retirement age for a jihadist leader, it could mean the reigns of the troops will be given to a younger person, possibly one of bin Laden's sons. That can then be a reflection of the history of Alexander the Great, as he too was a young warrior who became emperor. This does not mean that Osama bin Laden was killed and a younger leader has taken his place, as it merely introduces a character that becomes the prototype of bin Laden.

This concept should be seen supported in the duality of the supporting details in line three, where "land AND sea" (from "*mer & terre*") become indicators of minimally two generals, one commanding ground forces and one commanding naval strategies. The use of "great" (from "*grand*") can then be read as a model from which all "great" nations are born, both offensively and defensively. This means the word "*menee*" indicates both the model that guides an assault and also the model that will "subdue" the "great."

Chapter 9
Prosecution Exhibit E

A Main Theme Statement Indicating ...
Monts Pyrenees

In the last quatrain interpreted, Nostradamus wrote *"montz Pyrennees"* in the main theme line, where a *"z"* and an extra *"n"* linked it to the letter to Henry II. That was explained as how those spellings best translated as "mountain ones born of the Pyrenees". The letter to Henry II, if one recalls, presented the word *"mont"* (singular), before the symbolic name "Possessed-ones" (translation of the plural past participle, *"Jouis"*). The addition of a *"z"* acted to add the word "ones" to "mountain". The spelling of *"Pyrennees"*, with an extra *"n"*, appeared with a hyphen (in the 1568 Lyon edition), which accented a point of separation, between *"Pyren"* and *"nees"*. That spelling actually meant, "those of the Pyrenees – born ones".

This is an indication of how nothing is misspelled, as every word of *The Prophecies* has been divinely chosen. Everything is spelled exactly the way it needs to be spelled.[1] Additional meaning comes from words that appear to be incorrect or flawed. However, in this quatrain, and the next nine quatrains, those

---

1   I have found the 1568 Lyon edition to be the corrected edition, and thus the one that holds all of the proper spellings. Each one of the other editions has differences in spelling and punctuation. The first seven *"Centuries"*, found in the 1557 editions (Utrecht and Budapest, copies of Lyon) mostly match the 1568 edition, while glaring errors and differences appear in the 1566 Lyon edition. I see the 1568 edition as being the work of those close to Nostradamus (he died in 1566) making sure the text was printed precisely as it appeared on the paper, thus the significant differences between the 1566 and 1568 editions. I believe they worked with the printer closely, at the request of Nostradamus, during the time before his death when he was too ill to travel to Lyon.

differences in spelling make the spelling in the last quatrain (and the letter to Henry II) even more pronounced, by demonstrating that Nostradamus knew the proper way to spell *"monts Pyrenees"*. The differences are how one confirms they are written with purpose and reason.

In Old French, a word could routinely end with *"s"* or *"z"*, with both being an indication of the plural number. A word that typically ended with an *"s"* in the singular number, would have its *"s"* converted to a *"z"* much as English adds an apostrophe. The confusion comes from words that do not have an *"s"* at the end in the singular, like *"mont."* The plural then becomes *"monts"*, but many words have a *"z"* substituted by Nostradamus, seemingly by whim. There are no such whims.

The presence of the *"z"* on the end of a noun is similar to the addition of an *"s"* or *"z"* at the end of a past tense verb. These have been mistakenly seen as merely making number agreement but that notion fails to pass the test of accuracy. This failure is detected through the many examples throughout *The Prophecies* where the surrounding verbiage does not indicate the plural. This failure is compounded when one realizes the system of Nostradamus calls for every word to be read as a stand-alone statement, with pluralized past participle verbs being nonsensical if the *"s"* ending is not read separately. All such words must be read as if the word "ones" has been an added at the end (ex. *"monts-z"*, *"Joui-s"*). As such, a seeming plural past tense verb is indicating the "ones" who did that action. Likewise, and in the case of *"montz"*, one has to read this as the "ones" of the "mountains", or "mountain ones".

When one reads line one of the last quatrain in this manner, one sees an expansion on the theme of "to pass mountains", such that it makes the line state, "to pass" along with the "mountain ones". That could mean "mountaineers" or it could be the army of men who were with Osama bin Laden in the "mountains". In other words, the spelling of *"montz"* is a statement that he did not "go" or "pass" alone. The word is not simply the standard French syntactical way of saying the "Pyrenees Mountains", where *"montz"* would usually be written in the lower case. This is because the word *"Pyren"* alone is representative of the "Pyrenees Mountains". The word *"montz"* must act as a stand-alone statement, as do all individual words in *The Prophecies*.

I bring this up because the next two pieces of evidence I will present have *"monts Pyrenees"* in their main theme statements, spelled correctly. This makes them important to discern, on the heels of the last quatrain. The first of these two states (simply translated):

Autour des monts Pyrenees grand amas	Round about to the mountains Pyrenees great amass
De gent estrange secourir roy nouveau:	From people foreign to help king new:
Pres de Garonne du grand temple du Mas,	Nearby with Garonne to the great temple of the Farmhouse,
Un Romain chef le craindra dedans l'eau.	One Roman leader them will fear in the water.

This quatrain begins with the capitalized first word "*Autour*", which is possible to translate as "About, Round about, In around". This makes it become an important statement of "Surrounding", which is one of the translation possibilities for "*inundation*". That reference was stated in the segment from the Henry letter, referring to an "inundation of kindred" that would be found relative to "fury at the mountain". Such synonymous connections in the quatrains can be seen from words mirrored in the letters of instruction. Still, there is another use for "*Autour*" that can add to the meaning of this quatrain.

In Old French, the word "*Autour*" is shown as also having a noun meaning, which is stated to be "(generally) a short-winged hawk; and particularly, the Goshawk." This title is significant as it names a subfamily of the diurnal birds of prey family (Accipitridae). That classification includes eagles, kites, and hawks. As a capitalized name that is symbolic of a place of importance, it helps to know that the United States, France, and the Roman Empire all have historic associations with the "Eagle".

When one sees the word "*Autour*" leading to the distinction of being "great", as stated by the words that follow "*Autour*" ("to the mountains Pyrenees great"), this immediately identifies the "French Imperial Eagle" as a possible interpretative meaning. That battle flag standard was used by Napoleon (well after Nostradamus lived); but it was an emblem copied from the Roman Legions, who used it in antiquity (well before Nostradamus lived). This makes "*Autour*" symbolize French imperialism, which has placed the land "Around the Pyrenees" under the flag of France (at least the northern half).

By seeing this perspective of "*Autour*", it makes it clearer to see that the "ancient kingdom" (from the segment of words in the letter to Henry II, which referred to the "Pyrenees born ones") is "In around" those mountains. This indicates a circumference, both north and south and from the east to west, that is "of the mountains". That area of land is possible to see as the "ancient" Kingdom of Navarre.

That region is now commonly referred to as Basque Country (not the specific autonomous community, but the general area), where an "ancient monarchy" was recognized. Independent Navarre, led by an independent king, was a "monarchy" on the French side of the "Pyrenees" during the times of Nostradamus. By 1620, this line was absorbed by a surrogate Navarre king, who was one in the official line of succession to the French throne. When the Navarre king became the King of France, the Kingdom of Navarre no longer had its own king as the French king also ruled their kingdom. That monarchal system lasted until 1792, when the French Revolution overthrew the French monarchy, leading to Navarre being seized for the Republic.

Line one certainly places important focus on the "Pyrenees Mountains" as being in the possession of the "great", such that France and Spain claim the majority "of the mountains" as their land (the tiny Principality of Andorra is the only exception). The last word of the main theme is then "*amas*", which bears the meanings, "A heap, or pile; a great number, sort, crew, rout; also a mooncalf, or tympany in a woman's womb." These latter uses ("mooncalf" and "tympany") are defined somewhat as a benign tumor, as "a mass" or growth in the abdomen (swelling) that is freakish or ugly to observe. This is rooted in the Latin word "*massa*", which means "lump".

This associates the people "of the Pyrenees Mountains" as being "in large numbers". While they are "great", as citizens of France and Spain, they are as much French or Spanish as is a tumor in a woman's belly actually being a baby developing. In other words, they are French or Spanish only because they are not strong enough to retain their own independence. They are, as the word in the letter to Henry II stated, "*Joui-s*" or "Possessed-ones". Thus, all "About" the "Pyrenees" are people who would like to be removed from their host's body.

This is an important statement to understand. As the main theme of this quatrain, it is introducing a strong indication of a subversive condition preexisting "Around" the "mountains" of "great" France and "great" Spain. Because this main theme line does not end with any punctuation marks, the secondary theme can be expected to describe a continuation of this "growth" in the "Pyrenees".

Line two immediately makes a statement about this "large number" of "great" by making the important statement (as indicated by capitalization), "To people". If you are American, you will readily see "To the people" as being an important reference to the principles of democracy. The power to govern one's self without a king or religious leader telling one what to do is written into the American Constitution. This acts as a confirmation of "*Autour*" being the Napoleonic Imperial "Eagle", which expanded the power "Of [the] people" of France through successful wars against kingdoms all across Europe. It also is stating how "a mass Of people" have become an ugly "heap", due to it having become a gathering place "To people" that disdain being part of the "great".

This sense of conquest and lack of respect is advanced by the next word "*estrange*", which means, "strange, uncouth, unusual; foreign, alien, outlandish; unaccustomed, unacquainted, also, harsh, crude, odd (in conditioning, or constitution)." From these possibilities, it is easy to see "great growth" in the direction "To people foreign". Still, when the word is accented, as "*estrangé*", it acts as the past tense of "*estranger*", meaning, "estranged, alienated, altered from, separated from; grown away from, or out of knowledge and acquaintance." This shows that the people of the "Pyrenees" are "foreign" to the concept "Of people" having the freedom to have a voice in their government, while being an "alienated" part of the "nation" (alternative translation of "*gent*").

This is explaining how one becomes "great" in the first place. One amasses "piles" of colonial underlings, who are "unaccustomed" to a "foreign" culture. The conquered see it as "outlandish" that one can believe freedom is a product of conquest.

When this history is read into both theme statements, the main theme comes into focus as being about activity that will be importantly "About", in reference "to them" (as "*des*" = "*de+les*") people of the "mountains". This would be indicating those making the "Pyrenees Mountains" their home; but the secondary theme can expand to mirror "Pyrenees", showing it as a place among all the "great" nations of Western Europe, in particular where "a large number" will be significantly "From" (alternate translation of "*De*") somewhere else. The "Pyrenees" will be filled with "people" coming "From" places "foreign", but this will be no different than other places of the "great" facing similar immigration "Of people foreign".

113

This view then supports a theme of an "inundation of kindred" who will join with a "descendant" that "will rise with the people born of the Pyrenees". The citizens of the "great" will become a "rout" (i.e.: a "rabble") against their lack of freedom, importantly acting "With people" to whom they are "unacquainted" (alternate translation of "*estrange*"). Those people would be Muslims, primarily, but also Africans and Eastern Europeans, all of whom would have immigrated to the regions surrounding the "Pyrenees Mountains".

The purpose of such association is "to assist, to comfort, to aid, to relieve, to second, to back, to help, and/or to further" (translations of "*secourir*") these "people foreign", because they too feel the pain of being "estranged, alienated, and separated from" that which they used to have. Thus, the "fury" that is "with them" both (from "*au*" = "*à+le*") makes the "mountain" that has been "Enjoyed" as their home, but "Possessed" by others (i.e.: France and Spain), a common bond (experiencing land theft) that joins them. Both (natives and foreigners) desire to rekindle their "ancient" glory days, when they both had "realms" that kept them from being "removed from one place and set in another" (from the letter to Henry II stating, "*furibonde au mont Jouis – pyren-nees ne sera translate à l'antique monarchie*").

At this point, it is important to understand that the word "*roy*" (or "*roi*" in modern French) is written in the lower case, becoming a distinction from an upper case spelling. A "*Roy*" is a real King or Pope (individually named), as a recognized leader by birth or holy decree. A lower case spelling denotes someone who is of lesser merit, but who wields the same power as a ruler.

The 1611 Old French-English dictionary states "*roy*" to mean "A king; also, the chief or head man of a company." In this day and age of political parties, I see this as referring to the leader of a political party or a faction of sect, religious or otherwise. Nostradamus differentiated between royal kings and elected presidents by the use of capitalization. Someone like Osama bin Laden represents one man of tremendous power and influence; but he was born without royal blood, nor does the Holy Spirit from God [YHWH] rest on him. However, he certainly represents a "new' or "rare" form of "king" (from "*roy nouveau*"), which is stated in the use of "*nouveau*" at the end of the secondary theme. The word "*nouveau*" means "new, fresh, recent; strange, rare; lately done, or made; uncouth, unused, unheard of before."

One can see how the use of the title "king", along with the distinction of being "new", is making a statement about a rekindling of "the ancient realm" (from "*l'antique monarchie*") seen in the letter to Henry II. That means those who are "to assist" (alternate translation of "*secourir*") Osama bin Laden in the overthrow of the "great" powers holding the "Pyrenees" will be the "descendants" of that land, through antiquity. The Basque people would be able to produce another "king", who would then begin a "fresh" (alternate translation of "*nouveau*") start in a "new" monarchy. Still, the primary focus is on one "king" with a "novel" approach. He will be one who will rise to power through acts that swell the "masses", allowing one man to elevate to the level of "head man" (alternate translation of "*roy*").

Just as it is the will "Of [the] people" to choose a "king" (one of common birth), thus being the result "Of people helping" one to power, the opposite is also true. A "chief" becomes accepted by the "people" by coming "to [the] aid" of his "kindred" (alternate translation of "*gent*") at times of need. This is then furthering the quatrain where the secondary theme was about "One king will be who will come to see France". Osama bin Laden "will come to see" the "people" of the "Pyrenees" and he will find a mutual vision shared by those he will call his relatives. "To [the] people" of Basque heritage this "foreigner" will be "helped" to become "king".

At this point, this quatrain becomes one that veers away from being evidence of Osama bin Laden in the "Pyrenees Mountains" and becomes informative about future events relative to his coronation as "king". Line two's secondary theme ends with a colon, letting the reader know that what is to follow is relative to the two theme statements that are one continued theme of two aspects (lack of punctuation at the end of the main theme line). Recalling our jigsaw puzzle metaphor, to go in this interpretive direction of clarifying and listing examples of how the "people" are going "to assist" one who would be "king" of a "new" realm would be like detailing the trees behind the red farmhouse. Therefore, I will not place deep focus on the remainder of this quatrain, as it does not enhance a prediction that is based on *The Prophecies* telling where Osama bin Laden can be found hiding.

Let me assure the reader that the last two lines of this quatrain do support the main and secondary themes, just as the systems of Nostradamus set them up to do. I welcome the reader to attempt to make sense of what he wrote there, based on the same style of analysis I have shown. One simply must make the words become clear through the application of a new syntax. However, the supporting elements of the last two lines are connecting this element of a "new king" to the plan of persecution against Christians; a theme which is greatly expanded in many other quatrains.

That plan becomes evidence of another prediction that is to come. That prediction will be vital to understand should Osama bin Laden not be caught in the "Pyrenees Mountains". It is a prediction that nobody, in particular Christians of Europe, wants to be proved as a divine prophecy come true. If the prophecy of Osama bin Laden hiding in the Pyrenees Mountains is believed, then the persecution of Christians may be averted with God's help. That help only comes to those who believe and act upon those beliefs.

Thus, to sum up the two theme statements in bullet points, we have read from this quatrain:

1. A bird of prey is an important point of initial focus, in particular the species into which the "Eagle" falls.
2. The focus also is placed "In around from mountains", which expands to the valleys and flatlands "Surrounding" a central core of "mountains".
3. The "mountains" are specifically identified as the "Pyrenees Mountains".
4. This territory involving the "Pyrenees" is under the flags of the "great" nations of France and Spain.
5. The majority of people "About" this region do not fit the mold of typical French and Spanish people, as they are like a "mooncalf", or false pregnancy, never to be born as those nationalities, while "swelling" to become an "ugly" faction.
6. This description "Of people" is also the history "Of [each] nation", who became 'great' through the imperial conquests of "foreign countries".
7. The secondary theme is focused "To kindred" that is "estranged" within their own land.
8. There will come "To [these] people alienated" a "large number Of people" from "foreign nations", in order "to help" them with their dilemma.
9. The "people estranged", in turn, will come "to assist" those "foreigners", who will be led by a "chief".
10. This "head man of a movement" will become "king" over a "new" realm.
11. This will allow "To people estranged" their own "new" realm, which

will elevate one of their own to become "president" of that "nation".

Afterthoughts: A way to view this quatrain overall is as an afterthought from someone in some high levels of government taking the prophecies I reveal in this book seriously. I doubt it will be because of anything I have written here, but from the sheer fact that an army being built in the Pyrenees Mountains to destroy France and Western Europe (a major theme of *The Prophecies*) will inevitably be "discovered" and approached. In that regard, the main theme statement can be read as the beginning of this confrontation, when "Around to those mountains Pyrenees great sort." Since the U.S. Navy incorporates McDonald Douglas T-45 Goshawk aircraft as trainer jets for pilots, the use of *"amas"* could be an indication of "sorties" flown in reconnaissance. Whatever the case, this is still a future event, at a most dangerous time, which tells that focus will finally be placed on the Pyrenees Mountains.

The lack of punctuation at the end of the main theme statement leads directly to a secondary theme, which is less about a military confrontation and more about who will order it. Because the governments of republics and democracies love the idea of electing their leaders, rather than be born to leaders born from royal families, *"roy nouveau"* becomes a statement that a new president of France will have risen to power. This makes the capitalization of the preposition *"De,"* leading a statement that says, "<u>With</u> kindred foreign to help" (from *"De gent estrange secourir"*). That becomes aid from Great Britain of the United States, who have come to the aid of the new French regime, where the importance of *"De"* says France is powerless alone at this point.

In this regard, there is a series of quatrains (quite a few) that place great focus on a losing battle or war strategy that plays out along the Garonne River, in southern France from Bordeaux, and the Garonne Canal that flows into southwestern France to Toulouse. those quatrains paint a sad picture of defeat and retreat, with the possibility of a nuclear weapon (or more than one) being used against this coalition. The verbiage paints a more dismal picture than the known historic defeat of the British (who were sent to defend France from Hitler's Germany) and their scramble to retreat at Dunkirk.

Again, this future event is not one that should ever be seen in hindsight, so one can remark, "Gosh. Nostradamus was right." Too many lives will have been lost by the time this defeat takes place. The point is coming to the realization now that something in the future will be focused on the Pyrenees Mountains. One must ask the question, "Why there?"

The answer demands one look at the divinity of *The Prophecies* and realize God sent Nostradamus as a Prophet with a most serious warning to believe and act upon, lest the future will be our fault. The man known as Osama bin Laden has made verbal "threats" to the West, in particular France, and even if he is dead then someone just like him is making plans now (and has for nine years as I write) that involve the Pyrenees Mountains. Those plans call for a most horrid attack on Europe, with surrender bringing horrendous persecution towards all non-Muslims. It is too late, at this point, to try and train the French military and French bureaucrats in how to be jihadists for a religion few believe (Christianity) and become anything more than those who will quickly throw down their weapons, raise they arms in the air and say, "*Je me rends*" or "*Je m'abandonne*" ("I surrender.")

The only way to delay this prophecy is to give the Muslims what they want, and then be prepared to go to war against the Jews. Even with that scenario, the Africans and Eastern Europeans will still want the wealth of Europe as their own. There might still be war to address, but maybe not everyone will be willing to die, in order to destroy the Western concept of superiority, based on how many things they can possess.

Chapter 10
Prosecution Exhibit F

Military Activities in the Pyrenees

This quatrain is another that states "*monts Pyrenees*" in the main theme line, showing it to be an important factor that will be found related to the whole quatrain. This is also another quatrain that need not be fully interpreted, in order to add to the evidence for Osama bin Laden being in the "Pyrenees Mountains". In that regard, the two main theme statements and the information found in line three will be brought forth here, with line four left for the reader to ponder.

This quatrain fully states (based on one simple translation possibility):

Bien contigue des grans monts Pyrenees,	Possessions close together with the great ones mountain ones Pyrenees,
Un contre l'aigle grand copie adresser:	One in opposition to the eagle great troops to direct:
Ouvertes veines, forces exterminees,	Opens veins, forces driven forth ones,
Que jusque à Pau le chef viendra chasser.	Which until in Pau the principal commander will come to pursue.

In the last quatrain, line one began with the typical preposition-adverb "*Autour*". Upon further inspection, it was realized that the word also had a noun application which was as a subfamily classification for birds of prey. This quatrain is similar, in regard to it beginning with a word that typically is seen as an adverb, while also being recognized as having a noun usage. Being capitalized, as the first word of the line, conveys a sense of important that must be applied to the translation.

The first word here is *"Bien"*. As an adverb, the Old French-English dictionary states its many uses to be, "Well, Good, Right, Content; Aptly, Fitly, Commodiously; Fully, Thoroughly; In good case, With good reason and/or As it should be." In modern French it is also often used as a value or intensive statement, meaning "Quite, or Much". A translation as an adverb makes it an important modifier of the following verb or adjective. However, the syntax of Nostradamus requires that each word be read as its own statement, before attaching to other words surrounding. Thus, this word works best alone as a noun.

The noun usage of *"Bien"* is also rather extensive. It can mean "Wealth, Substance, Chevisance [synonymous with Achievement, Profit, and/or Gain], Riches, Possessions, Goods, Patrimony [synonymous with Inheritance]; also, a Benefit, Pleasure, Favor, Good office, or Good turn; also, Goodness, Honesty, Virtue, Sincerity; also, a Good thing." Simply from these choices, one should be drawn to the translation that says "Possessions".

This becomes synonymous with the capitalized word found in the segment from the letter to Henry II, *"Jouis"*. We have discussed how that plural past participle meant, "Possessed-ones". While all of the above meanings have a role in deepening the understanding of the main theme, the importance of "Possessions" must be seen as the primary intended use here.

This then leads to the word *"contigue"*, which when unaccented acts as an adjective, meaning "near adjoining, fast by, close together, and/or touching one another." When this word is accented, as *"contigué"*, it acts as the action of having been "joined, laid near, or close unto." This gives the impression of a partnership, where the important "Wealth" of two has been "joined" as one. This allows one to see the important condition of two being "Quite close together". The "Benefit" of such a union is then seen due to one being "fast by" or "near adjoining" something of value.

We have discussed previously the element of imperialism that made both France and Spain "great" nations in history. The object of such expansionism was indeed for "Wealth" and "Riches", at the expense of lands that were undeveloped (seen as uncivilized) and unable to defend themselves against a larger, "Much" more technologically advanced invader. The quests that became the heights of

"Achievement" for France and Spain came during the discovery of a New World. Their successes led to a rush for foreign "Possessions" by several Western European nations. As such, France and Spain raised their flags over places that were "near adjoining" the others (for example, in the West Indies, North America [Louisiana-Southwest], and Africa).

France and Spain are countries that are "touching one another", but this closeness is more than simply the physical separation of the main European continent, (at France) and the Iberian Peninsula. As mentioned previously, the Kingdom of Navarre continued as a recognized independent kingdom, led by a king (1513 - 1589) until King Henry III of Navarre became the King of France (Henry IV). By 1620, the Kingdom of Navarre (north of the border with Spain) was absorbed into the Kingdom of France. Additionally, the Kingdom of Spain, due to cross-marriages of royal offspring, would come under the rule of Philip V (1700) who was related to the French King Louis XIV.[1] The point is that the relationship between France, the people of the "*Pyrenees*", and Spain was "Quite joined".

This view is enhanced by the presence of the word "*des*" following "*contigue*". That word is the plural form of the preposition "*de*", such that it is "*de*" plus the plural article "*les*". This makes it mean, "to them", as "*les*" indicates more than one being relative to the preposition meaning "to, from, of, or with". The word "*des*" is also often translated simply as "from". With all possibilities of translation allowable and expected to play some role in deeper understanding, one is directed to see movement that is relative to the condition of being "Well near adjoining".

The movement "of them, to them, with them, and/or from them" can be seen as movements by the "great ones", as "*des*" is followed by the plural word "*grans*". This use of the word "*grans*" is an accepted abbreviated plural form of "*grand*". It can be translated to mean the "greats", as a noun indicating "those" of "great" recognition of some type.

As discussed previously, when reading *The Prophecies* the addition of an "*s*" at the end of a noun, especially when that noun had to be abbreviated to accommodate the addition, means one can add the word "ones" to the noun. This removes the

---

1   This event caused Europe to be split by the imbalance of power this represented, with the ascension of Philip was contested. It led to the War of Spanish Succession, a Spanish internal civil war, and later to the War of the Quadruple Alliance (1700-1717).

generality of the word. Thus, "*grans*" becomes "great ones" and all references to "great" (in quatrains and letters) become a reference to the powers of Europe, who have histories of being dominant nations.

One finds the words "*monts Pyrenees*" at the end of the main theme line. Having seen France and Spain as two of the possible powers coming from the words "Riches close unto from them great ones", one sees only those nations when presented the "Pyrenees Mountains". Only two "great ones" are "joined" at that "mountain" range. However, the specific details jump out by seeing the word "mountains" separately, as that meaning brings out the deeper meaning of the theme, which will guide the whole quatrain.

The focus is on those who are "of them great ones", residing in the "mountains" (thus citizens of France or Spain), who are not necessarily "with them great ones". It is a "Favor" (alternate translation of "*Bien*") being granted by allowing one "close unto" their midst. The "great ones Benefit" by the land that has been taken "from" them "mountain ones". The important "Benefit" of being so "joined" would be to make a statement "to them great ones", about who truly owns the "mountains" that are named "Pyrenees".

This deeper meaning comes to the surface when one reads the words slowly, absorbing all of the meanings possible. This then acts as a serious theme that links to the evidence that Osama bin Laden is in the "Pyrenees Mountains". It shows how his appearance there would not lead to him being turned in "to them great ones", who have declared a War on Terror and are desperately looking for him. He would have to make an important impression of "Sincerity" (alternate translation of "*Bien*") to the Basque people, so they would be "joined close unto" a quest to take "from the great ones" all that makes them "great". This quest itself represents "mountains" that must be moved to make this happen; but it will all begin with a marriage of kindred spirits in the "Pyrenees Mountains".

From that perspective, it is easier to see the importance that can be applied from the capitalized first word of the secondary theme statement, "*Un*", meaning, "One or A". The secondary theme is separated from the main theme statement by a comma, such that it is freed to address a major theme that is relative to the main theme (a union of kindred spirits), rather than directly continuing it. This can then be seen as making the focus be on "One" that offers a "Benefit to them" of the "Pyrenees". While the main theme sheds light on the history of the relationship between nations "close together", the secondary theme is about

"One" who will most find a "Good thing" by being "fast by to the great ones", almost "touching one another with the great ones", in the "mountains" between two "great ones".

This important "One" is then "against, contrary to, much oppugnant unto [synonymous with combative, antagonistic], in opposition to; also, over against, on the other side; also, towards" (from "*contre*") that is then identified as "the eagle" (from "*l'aigle*" being the following text). This becomes confirmation to the word "*Autour*", seen in the last quatrain, meaning a bird of prey, in particular an "Eagle". However, there is a difference that comes from the lower-case spelling, as "*l'aigle*".

The last quatrain began with the capitalized "*Autour*", beginning a main theme that was about the "Pyrenees Mountains". This secondary theme is following a main theme that also focused on the "Pyrenees", becoming focused on "One" that is not from there. This is known because he is "One on the other side", and "One towards" there (alternate translations of "*contre*"). While this "One" is "against" the French, he is "One" who has come to be "the eagle", as a bird of prey. The lower-case is identifying the capitalized "One", becoming that singular person as symbolized by "the eagle". The capitalized "*Autour*" shows the difference of importance that makes it symbolic of a nation, rather than one man.

Still, in the sense that "the eagle" can be representative of the French battle emblem, the lower-case spelling can be a general reference to all nations who see "the eagle" as a symbol of one's ability to prey on others. This "eagle" can include the United States, without specifically identifying that one nation (due to being in the lower-case spelling). As such, the "One" of the secondary theme is "in opposition to" the way those who revere "the eagle" have allowed the "One" to become "close unto" them. This allows "the eagle" to represent those of both France and America.

Both are further identified by the next word in the line, which is a repeating of the word "*grand*". This is the fully spelled out word, which acts to balance the abbreviated plural use in line one ("*grans*"). As such, the reader's focus is drawn from more than one "great" to only one "great", in the singular number. Because the secondary theme is relative to the main theme and the main theme is focused on the "great ones [of the] mountains Pyrenees", "*grand*" represents "the eagle" France. Because the secondary theme is separated from the main theme (comma use), it is free to focus on the "One great eagle", which is the United

States of America. This means the secondary theme is about "One against the great eagle", America, who will get to them through France, by himself being "the eagle great".

This all gets deeper into its meaning when one realizes that Old French had a second use for the word "*contre*", which was defined "substantively" as, "to second, assist, help forward", with a musical meaning relative to "bear the burden." When that contextual usage is read into the line, it makes it clear that "One" of the "great ones" is "to help forward" "the eagle great". This is detailing France as a partner of the United States, and their declared War on Terror. Likewise, in the "mountains" of the "Pyrenees" is "One" significant individual, who also is "to assist". This relates back to the previous quatrain's secondary theme, which said "To people – foreign – to assist king new" (from the word "*secourir*"). It means "One" will be assisted by those whom he will help.

The focus of the secondary theme then turns to the word "*copie*", which in French means, "copy of a writing," but also "store of, plenty of, and/or abundance of." In this translation scenario, where France is seen as an assistant in the War on Terror, it ensures there will be "plenty of" military bodies available to backup those in the front lines. When connected to the word "great", it becomes a statement about the United States ("the eagle great"), as the land of "abundance". Still, the whole of those "great", as "One", becomes the West in general, who consider themselves "first world nations" because of their "stores" of wealth and resources. However, there is still another translation of "*copie*" that must be considered, simply because this word is often repeated in the quatrains.[2]

The use of "*copie*" is best translated as a French version of the Latin word "*copia*". That Latin word has a direct military meaning that translates as, "supplies, provisions, troops, and forces". In this sense, France represents a "great" power, with an "abundance of forces". The United States is the world's leading "store of" weaponry technology, with an "abundance of" capacity to produce more. The alliance of powers that make up the Western nations (NATO) allows those nations to have "plenty of provisions" with which to wage war.

This use of "troops", involving France, the U.S., and their Western allies, in particular in the wars in Afghanistan and Iraq, is why the "One" of this quatrain is "in opposition". It is why "One" will become "an eagle" perched high in the "Pyrenees Mountains", to create for himself a "mighty" (alternate translation of

---

2   There are 13 different quatrains that offer either "*copie*" or "*copies*".

"*grand*") army of "troops". If one recalls the quatrain previously interpreted, where the main theme stated (simply put), "Over there midnight conductor of the army", that "conductor" can be seen as the "One" of this quatrain.

Yet, if one remembers that the word "*contre*" has a musical meaning, another interpretation comes into play. The Old French word "*contre*" was shown to mean, "to bear the burden; or to sing the plain song whereon another descants." This makes the secondary theme also state that the "One" is truly a "conductor", just as one directs an orchestra. This "One" will be he who "bears the burden of leading the base theme, while incorporating the others to play the ornamental melody" (from a definition of "descants").[3] Those who will sing the high parts are "the eagle" and those "great"; and, also from the meaning of "descant", the high part can also be in a discussion on a theme. The "conductor" takes the "contrary" position in a religious debate over who has the right to make international decisions that ultimately lead to the loss of life through the use of "forces" ("*copia*"). It becomes a melody of war that "One" conducts.

The last word in this secondary theme is the infinitive, "*addresser*", meaning, "to address, to direct, to lead, to instruct, to set in, or to show the nearest [readiest] way into." This is making the statement's end focus be on a need for action, in the form of leadership. This confirms the meaning of "*conducteur*", as a "leader or guide". This allows one to see how "opposition" to a "great" nation of "abundance" requires "One" who is capable of "showing [others] the readiest way into" war, as coming from equal "might" (alternate translation of "*grand*"). It means the "One" is "to lead" those willing to follow, who will learn how to be an army of "troops".

On a historical level, "the eagle" is relevant to France, being that it was the symbol of Napoleon's Imperial Guard. That army of "troops" was a "melody" of groups, being the Old Guard, the Middle Guard, and the Young Guard. Those groups were divisions based on experience, with the Young Guard being mostly the best of the yearly conscripts. In this sense, Osama bin Laden is much like Napoleon, in how he has a Main Guard (Muslims), a Secondary Guard (Eastern Europeans), and a Third Guard (those with a history as oppressed by Western European colonialism [Africans and pockets of Western European regions seeking independence]. Still, he is quite different from Napoleon by being "contrary" in his direction "towards" France. He wants to raise an army to defeat France,

---

3   The Free Online Dictionary by Farlex shows "descant" with its primary definition being, "An ornamental melody or counterpoint sung or played above a theme."

and its Western allies, and cease the imperial ways of those calling themselves "great". The iconic representation of both can be seen as that of a bird of prey.

The secondary theme then ends with a colon. This is an indication that the following lines will act as clarification or examples of the "addressing" that will take place, relative to the "great ones" and the "Pyrenees Mountains". This first comes from the line that offers the supporting details to the main theme (line three), which one can see is divided into two phases of clarification, due to the presence of a mid-line comma.

The first capitalized word in line three is "*Ouvertes*", which is a plural ending on the past participle verb "*Ouverte*". That word in the singular means, "Overt, Open; Patent, Evident, Apparent; Discovered, Uncovered, Plain, Without color; also, Gaping, Wide, Broad, and/or Large." This is another example of the "*s*" ending being Nostradamus' way of denoting the "ones" of an activity. In this case, the supporting details line immediately places focus on the "ones Evident", or the "Uncovered ones". This is directly a clarification of what "One" is "to guide" and provides supporting detail related to the "Pyrenees".

This important element of something being "Evident" then joins with the next word, "*veines*", which means "a vein in the body", from which a "pulse" can be detected. It also can suggest a body of land, meaning, "a vein of the earth [relative to metals]". It is also a "style of writing" and relative to "vanity". The primary focus thus becomes "Opened veins", which are openings in the "mountains", which are in "Plain" sight, long ago "Discovered" by the earliest dwellers of the "Pyrenees Mountains". The immediate clarification of "mighty forces to make the readiest way unto" comes by "storing" an army of men in the known "veins" of the "Pyrenees". There will be no need to toil to make holes in the rock, as it is already "Opened", and known as "Discovered" caves.

The part leading to the comma is pointing one to see how existing natural caves and even discarded man-made mines in the "Pyrenees Mountains" are so plentiful that they will house a "great number of troops". This is important as it will allow the lifeblood of a major movement "against the great French eagle" to "pulse" regularly. Those "forces" will also be "Open ones", able to come and go in the "veins" as they see fit.

This element of natural openings in the mountains, or those openings previously created, are what makes the following (after a comma's use, marking that which follows in time) acts possible. Those are identified as, "forces driven forth, abilities cast out, strengths driven away, or powers undone". The use of the French word "*forces*" is directly linked in support of the word "*copie*", as "*forces*" bears the same meaning, when seen to mean "store, plenty, abundance, plenty of", and in particular, "*troops*". As such, the powers of the French can be undone by an army built up of those who feel cast out, or driven to enlist. This becomes an identity marker for the swelling numbers of "refugees" and "aliens" present (seen in the use of "*estrange*" in the last quatrain). These immigrants have arrived in Europe in large numbers, to France in particular, over the past twenty years.

The second part of the third line then begins with the word "*forces*", which clarifies the translation of "*copie*" as rooted in the Latin "*copia*". The French word "*force*" (unaccented singular) means "force, might, strength, power, ability, vigor, vehemence; virtue, effect, operation, energy, efficacy, powerful working; violence, constraint, compulsion, ravishment; and also store, plenty, abundance, many of." The sequential element coming from importantly having been "Discovered" natural "Opened veins" (sequence denoted by a comma) is the development of "*forces*". These "troops" will be those in need of "One" who is "to instruct" them in how to be a disciplined army, capable of being "violence ones" (the "*s*" at the end of "*force*").

These "forces" are then identified as "*exterminees*", where the main word is once again a past participle verb, "*exterminée*", with an "*s*" added at the end. The word "*exterminée*" means, "exterminated; driven forth, cast out, chased away; and, ruined, undone, destroyed (thereby)." This becomes both the make-up of the "troops", while also being their goal. They will be made up of those "cast out" of their own lands, "chased away" by those of their new land, and "driven forth" by the ideological principles of the "One" who will "lead" them. Due to war in their homelands, at the hands of the "great forces", some will have come to exact retribution for their land having been "destroyed". All will be trained as "violence ones", to be unleashed upon the "ruined ones" of Europe. As such, "*forces exterminees*" can be read as "exterminator forces".

The fourth line of this quatrain is not necessary to interpret as evidence relative to the "Pyrenees Mountains". Rest assured it supports the themes of this quatrain but it acts more to link this quatrain to others that detail events that will come from "exterminator forces" in France. The first three lines give ample support to the theme of Osama bin Laden being in the "Pyrenees", to train an army for being capable of persecution against Christians.

The bullet point summary of the first three lines shows that this quatrains presents:

1. An important focus is placed on "Possessions" that are "jointly" held.
2. The "Possessions" are "near adjoining with the great ones".
3. The "great ones" are those "touching one another" where the "Pyrenees Mountains" create the border.
4. This border represents "mountains" that have been taken "from" those who live there, and given "to the great ones".
5. Those local people are "Quite close together" and wish to take their land back "from the great ones".
6. There is a significant "One" who is "against" France, as symbolized by "the eagle great".
7. This "One" has come "towards" the "Pyrenees" from somewhere else.
8. This "One" has come to be a bird of prey, as is "an eagle".
9. This "One" seeks to raise "mighty troops" to use "in opposition to" France.
10. This "One" will be in the "Pyrenees" "to instruct" his "troops".
11. The "mountains" of the "Pyrenees" have "Opened veins" that allow access inside them.
12. These preexisting caves and tunnels will be importantly "Opened" for the "troops" of the "One".
13. These "veins" will "pulse" with activity and they will be "Apparent" in their presence there.
14. The "troops" in the "Opened veins" will be "forces" of "driven forth ones"
15. The "troops" will be "exterminators", prepared to use "violence" in retribution for having their lives "destroyed" by the "forces" of the "great".

Afterthoughts: This is a quatrain like the one before it, where the greatest value is as a still future event that is one not to be seen coming true. The main theme statement tells of the important time when the battle line will be drawn at the Pyrenees Mountains. When the importance of "Opened veins" is also seen as a major bloodletting, it is too late to change a terrible future from happening. That is why the focus on the Pyrenees should be realized well in advance, as a place where secrete plotting is already well under way. Osama bin Laden arrived on that scene soon after May Day 2011.

Chapter 11
Prosecution Exhibit G

The Reason for Judgment from the Monts Pyrenees

By this point in this presentation it should be obvious that, based on looking at the evidence, Nostradamus wrote about where to look for Osama bin Laden. Once one has practiced with the systems that I am slowly teaching, through their application in interpretation, understanding the majority of what is written becomes relatively simple. Some of the more difficult words will require seeing how the rest of the information in a quatrain develops. In those cases, it is like reading a book and coming upon a word that is unknown. One keeps on reading to a point where the unknown word can be assumed to mean something relative to the verbiage surrounding it. Of course, looking up difficult words, to learn their various meanings, helps one get full understanding.

Everything has to be read one word at a time, examining each word thoroughly to see how its full scope of meaning can enhance overall understanding. Sometimes one has to skip a word or line, to get to a point where understanding comes easier. Then one can go back with a better feel for how the threads are laid out. In the word-by-word breakdowns that I have presented so far, I have made frequent references to the system that recognizes how each line plays a set role, by having a relationship with the other lines in a quatrain.

If anyone is at all familiar with the verses that make up *The Prophecies*, by having looked at them in a book or by having seen them on television, one knows those presentations make little sense. The error comes from translating them and then changing the words into some form of prose, making them mold to preconceived syntactical structure. This becomes not what Nostradamus wrote; but instead become a paraphrase transformation into what some translator wrote, with punctuation changing, lines bleeding together and words that were not written magically appearing. That is how the quatrains of Nostradamus end up appearing to be nonsensical.

The systems of Nostradamus do not allow for such mixing and changing. No alterations to his text are allowed, as each line is exactly as it needs to be. Each line is self-sufficient, just as is each quatrain and each word. All words fit the lines, all lines fit the quatrain, and all quatrains fit the other quatrains, such that all comes together in a perfect order. That perfection is mirrored line to line and quatrain to quatrain (microcosm-macrocosm). The order of the lines is thus fixed and cannot be changed.

This element of understanding is essential to remember when it comes time for interpretation. Some verbiage is difficult to grasp; and, one may find that three of the four lines in one quatrain offer little that can be found coherent. There are many of this nature; and, one reason why some are so nebulous is those quatrains are dealing with very specific events in the future, well beyond what is known now. Those can be clarified by identifying the quatrains that link to them, some of which are easier to interpret as a future story, because those others have some basis in events which are currently known. One must work towards understanding the unknown from a position of the known. This same principle applies when one or more words or lines do not make sense.

In those cases, I have found there is always one line that does offer clarity from its word use. That clarity becomes the known element from which to proceed. Where clarity is found, this becomes the beginning point of interpretation, regardless of which line that information is presented in. By knowing a system exists that makes one line relate in a specific way to all the other lines, one can start at the beginning and work down, start at the bottom and work up, or start in the middle and work out. This is where it becomes important to recognize the independence of a line, while also seeing how all lines are interdependent, based on that independence.

On the broader scale, each quatrain has to touch other quatrains, as the quatrains also link together as independent entities that become interdependent on one another. Using the puzzle comparison, each puzzle piece has physical characteristics that make that piece clearly discernible as unique, although all pieces are of similar size and general shape. It is only when a piece becomes one with the whole that a greater meaning is found. A puzzle that is complete, except for one missing piece, shows how important one piece still is, as the attention is drawn to the space where the missing piece should go. This is because the other pieces are leading one's expectation as to what should fill that space.

So far, this work has shown how the words found in one element matches a word found in another element, either by being repeated verbatim ("*monts Pyrenees*"), or by being synonymous ("*Joui-s*" and "*Bien*" are variations of "Possessions"). The words are the links that connect the quatrains, such that one quatrain's keyword that is found in a main theme statement then matches a keyword in another quatrain's secondary theme statement, or supporting details line. When it is found that two quatrains do fit together, the meaning of one word comes with the meaning of a whole quatrain, so that its whole meaning expands into one word's use in another quatrain. This connection allows for an ever-deepening sense of meaning that accompanies the interpretation of each quatrain.

I have presented three quatrains that have the words "*monts Pyrenees*" in the main theme statement line (always the first line of a quatrain). The words of those quatrains have had matching verbiage linking them together; and, some verbiage found in the two "escape" quatrains (from Afghanistan) that I presented earlier repeat terms found in the three "*monts Pyrenees*" quatrains. In the same way, those five quatrains are linked to the three-part segment I interpreted that came from the letter to Henry II. The focus will now move on to five other quatrains, all of them having the same two words, "*monts Pyrenees*", with the only difference being that those five have these words occurring in the secondary theme statement line (line two). As such, these quatrains are producing additional evidence that suggests Osama bin Laden is in the "Pyrenees Mountains".

The systems of Nostradamus require that the secondary theme be interpreted relative to the main theme, either continuing the main theme towards a separate focus, or taking an entirely new focus from that theme. The next five quatrains illustrate this premise. The keywords found in the secondary themes of these five quatrains reflect their individual main theme lines, while their secondary theme statements also draw upon the entirety of other quatrains where those keywords were found to be in the main theme line. Thus, the linked quatrains act together, either as different information that continues the story's theme (adding more details about Osama bin Laden being in the "Pyrenees Mountains"), or as separate themes that require one to be aware of the story told in greater detail in another quatrain (referencing Osama bin Laden being in the "Pyrenees Mountains"). All offer perspectives on information and are evidence for one central prediction.

Just as it was not necessary to present all of the detailing elements in the quatrains whose main theme was about the *"monts Pyrenees"*, it is not necessary at this point to interpret the entire quatrain that has the same keywords in the secondary theme. One can actually start with the secondary themes in each of these five quatrains and then see how they link to and expand on a main theme. Then one can examine how lines three and four support them. Each will be found to be relative to the specifics of "One" going to the "Pyrenees" to promote "War".

The first quatrain of this group states (in simple translation):

De Sens, d'Autun viendront jusques au Rosne,	From Sens, to Autun will be coming until at the Rhone,
Pour passer outre vers les monts Pyrenées:	Because to pass beyond towards them mountains Pyrenees:
La gent sortir de la Marque d'Anconne,	There kindred to deliver the Mark of Ancona,
Par terre & mer le suivra à grans trainées.	By land & sea them will pursue with mighty ones traps for ravenous beasts.

The secondary theme of this quatrain states, *"Pour passer outre vers les monts Pyrenees"*. This can simply translate to say, "Because – to depart from – beyond – towards them – mountains – Pyrenees Mountains". This suggests purpose and action to a goal. It contains the verb *"passer"*, which we saw repeated in the main theme of the quatrain naming "The Arabian king". That main focus was set upon *"L'Aemathion passer montz Pyrennees"*. This significant keyword verb being repeated here links these two quatrains.

This quatrain states that the reason (seeing *"Pour"* as "Because", meaning "For that reason") the departure action (*"passer"* means, "to depart from") takes place as to get "towards", or "in the presence of" (alternate translation of *"vers"*) "them" (plural personal usage of *"les"*). The "them" of this quatrain is identified in this quatrain's main theme, such that the listing of three places in France is an indication of "them" being French. This confirms the other quatrain's use of a French town ("Narbonne"), to identify France as a reason for "going" to the

"Pyrenees Mountains".[1]

The three places listed in the main theme of this quatrain ("*Sens*", "*Autun*", and "*Rosne*") trace a path that tracks from northeast-central France ("*Sens*" is roughly 45 miles southeast of Paris), southeast (almost in a direct line) to Lyon (roughly 290 miles southeast of Paris), where the "Rhone River" flows south-southwest to Marseilles, on the Mediterranean Sea coast. As such, it is setting up an itinerary of travel, just as was established in the quatrain telling of a trip from "Tartary" to "Gaul".

The word "*Rosne*" is a dialect spelling of the name that some French people use to indicate the "Rhone River". This river flows from Lake Geneva, through Lyon, and empties into the Mediterranean Sea. It branches at Arles, where it creates a delta between the two outlets, which is called the Carmague. The two branches are called *Grand Rhône* and *Petit Rhône*, with Marseille being a major port city at the *Grand Rhône* end. The *Petit "Rosne"* empties into the sea at a commune [town] named "*Saintes-Maries-de-la-Mer* (Saints Marys of the Sea), which is the capital of the Carmague. Today, those who indicate the Rhône as "*Rosne*" are primarily indicating the "*Petit Rosne*", more than the main river; and, this spelling is seen as rooted in the Provençal [Arpitan]-Occitan languages.

I mention this translation because it is not one that is commonly used today. The spelling acts to identify the lower region of the Rhone River, more so than the upper region. The commune known as Saints Marys of the Sea is where three important Mary figures from the New Testament[2] are said to have landed, bringing a Christian bloodline to France (and eventually to all Europe). This history gives a feel for how the word can act as a simple anagram; such uncommon spellings are often best understood through that methodology. For example, "*Rosne*" becomes "*n'Rose*" (as "*né Rose*"), by the simple movement of the "*n*". This one letter moved makes the word mean, "born Rose", or "Rose-born".

The basic symbolism of a "Rose" is "love, honor, and faith", but as a capitalized word (thus an elevated meaning) it connects to the lore relating to the death of Jesus. A main theme that states, "will be coming until with the Rose-born", can then be seen as showing a purpose "For" being among Christians. The north-south travel shown in the main theme then shows the reverse route (by land)

---

1 Line two in the other quatrain stated, "*En Mars Narbon ne fera resistance,*" or simply, "In War Narbonne not will make resistance".
2 Mary Magdalene, Mary Jacobe, and Mary Salome.

taken to reach the same place as did the Saints Marys of the Sea. This represents a different reason ("Because") for being "at the *Rôsne*", symbolizing a contrary purpose. Instead of "coming" to spread Christianity, this aggression against the Christian West, as a movement, is "coming until with the Rose-born". This translation then gives the main theme a deeper meaning, more than a simple path of travel.

The secondary theme then can be seen to have the word "*outre*", which has been translated to mean "beyond". This is one of the adverbial translations possible, which were based on the Old French variation, "*oultre.*" In the 1611 Old French-English dictionary, the word "*outre*" referred also one to look up "*oultre*", such that one can see how the French language was making changes towards modern French by that date. Still, both forms can act (when accented) as the past tense verb "*oultré*" or "*outré*".

Both of those spellings mean the same, being: "pierced through, opened through, bored through, struck through; run through and through; also, sickly, unsound, and/or consumed in body." This last meaning can then relate to a third use of the word "*outre*", which is said to mean "over-ripe, more than ripe, near-hand spent, and/or past the best." That makes the adverb translations, "over, beyond, without; more, besides, further; moreover; or, and forwards" be relative to a state of being that has seen its better days in the past.

When all of this possibility is read into the secondary theme, it makes the statement begin with the reasoning that says, "Because to depart from sickly". When this is seen as a separate focus (comma use separating) on a main theme, where the meaning became "Rose-born" or "born of Faith" in Christ, the secondary theme is now exposing a time when Christianity will have become weakened. This would amount to a time when those adhering to the principles of Jesus would have become "past the best".

One can also read into the secondary theme the translation that says, "For to vanish away [alternate translation of "*passer*"] bored through in the presence of [alternate translation of "*vers*"] them [into the] mountains Pyrenees". This is then repeating a past theme of being in caves, thus "opened through" is relative to "Opened veins", seen previously. It also mirrors the meaning brought forth in the other quatrain with an itinerary, where line three began, "*Transpercera Alane*", which meant, "Will pierce through North Ossetia".

In modern French, the combination of words *"passer outre"* becomes an idiom that says, "to carry on regardless". This is a statement of dedication to a mission, by continuing "beyond" the point most people would regard as too far. In terms of Christianity, it sates how Christians will retain that overall title, while living in a way that is outside the boundaries of a Christ-like lifestyle. In terms of Osama bin Laden traveling through France to reach the "Pyrenees Mountains", it shows a relentless drive to "pierce through unto them". This terminology certainly has connotations of "War" plans, where Christians will be persecuted severely.

When one begins with the secondary theme (line two) and then sees how that theme relates to the main theme, the next step is to see how the supporting details relate to the information of the secondary theme. While the secondary theme is directly supported by the details of line four, the information in line three is always a natural progression from the secondary theme. As such, line three supports both themes, while giving information that can greatly assist in understanding the main theme. When line two ends in a colon, one is directed (by the punctuation) to look to line three for clarification and/or examples relative to the secondary theme. In the case of this quatrain, line two indeed does end with a colon. That makes line three the next place to look.

Without the need to interpret line three fully, it acts as a clarification by beginning with the capitalized first word, *"La"*. When this word is accented, as *"Là"*, it bears the adverb meaning, "There, Here, and/or Then". This makes the "Pyrenees Mountains" be clarified as "There", while identifying that as an important (use of capitalization) place to be. The reason "There" is important is the "people" (the next word, *"gent"*), who are "to come forth" (*"sortir"*).

This is parallel with the last quatrain, where the secondary theme was importantly (capitalization) "Of people alienated", while also "To people foreign". Both quatrains duplicate the use of the French word *"gent"*, meaning, "a nation, people; stock, race, kind, lineage, family, kindred." Both quatrains indicate the element of racism being part of the reason why two different "people" will "issue, go beyond, depart or go out of; assort, furnish, fit with, deliver out of, and/or bring out of" (translations of *"sortir"*) together.

The remainder of line three can then be seen as specifics that link to other quatrains. While important to know, they are not necessary to interpret as evidence of Osama bin Laden in the "Pyrenees Mountains". It is related to important Italian history, which is an example of what will be repeated by those "people" of the

"Pyrenees". However, to delve into that moment of history would add nothing to the cause of presenting evidence of a provable prediction.

Line four does need to be interpreted, as it is where one finds the supporting details for the secondary theme. The secondary theme made the statement about the "*monts Pyrenees*", which makes those supporting details relevant to evidence of a prediction of Osama bin Laden's presence there. This line also acts as a clarification to that theme, because line two ended with a colon. The colon use indicates that all that follows is relative to that theme. Thus, "*Par terre & mer le suivra à grans trainees*" is supporting the secondary theme, which stated the direction "towards them" ("*vers les*") of the "mountains Pyrenees".

First, the use of the ampersand should bring back memories of having seen one being used before, in particular with the words "sea" and "land" surrounding it ["*Par mer & terre fera si grand menee*", or translated, "By sea & nation will act as great led"]. This quatrain has reversed those repeated words, such that this quatrain is first showing (prior to the break of an ampersand) the importance (capitalization) of coming "By land", "By reason of country", "For nation", and/or "Through earth" (all variations of "*Par terre*").

This is supporting the secondary theme in many ways. It shows travel over "land" to get to the "Pyrenees" ("By land"). It tells what is important about that region ("By reason of" Basque "country"). It states why that place is important (to be sovereign again, "For nation"). It even acts to say how that place will hide people in caves ("Through" the "earth"). All of this is also relative to "There" and the "people" (line three), while pertinent to the main theme of France, and it being a Christian nation ("Rose-born").

Second, the ampersand indicates an important segment will begin, by stating the word "sea". This is an important element that is within physical proximity of the "Pyrenees Mountains". We had previously seen how the itinerary of Osama bin Laden traveled "By sea" to the "Pyrenees", in the quatrain that named him "The Arabian king". Thus, "By land" indicates the path that his supporters will travel to meet up with him, as a call to Muslims throughout France. The importance of the "sea" then becomes important as how others will later (sequence of events, from order surrounding a mark of punctuation) join "him" (personal singular translation of "*le*", the next word). These will come by "sea", when "*he* will pursue" or "*he* will go after" (from the following word, "*suivra*"), "at" the "great ones" (from "*à grans*"). This is an important statement of a planned naval invasion, which is another repeated theme related to the "conductor of an army".

Once again, when the use of an ampersand is seen to act as a symbol that unifies two principles (similar or different), it announces the "Pyrenees" will be a key place from which an all-out attack will be made simultaneously, "By land AND sea". The key word in line four then becomes the last word, "*trainées*", which acts as the plural of the noun that is a "trap [Old English "*traine*"] set for ravenous beasts, like wolves". Both venues will be "traps", designed to "pierce through" the "Rose-born" of France, Spain, and Western Europe.

When this word "*trainees*" is seen as the past participle of the verb, "*trainer*", with an "*s*" ending to indicate the "ones" of an action, that action becomes, "to plot, to contrive, to practice, to conspire, and/or to devise", as a plan "woven" [base meaning of "*traine*", with "*trainer*" the relative verb]. In this meaning, those to come "By land AND sea" will be the "people issued from There", the "Pyrenees", and "There" where those "will be coming until at the Rhone". It supports a theme of invasion, and supports the other theme of Osama bin Laden being the mastermind behind a "plot" that could only be "carried on regardless" by a very significant "One".

At this point, it becomes important to point out a second translation relative to the first French commune listed in the main theme. That place is "*Sens,*" which is just southeast of Paris. In the letter of preface that Nostradamus wrote as a foreword for how to read *The Prophecies*, he made the statement that there would be found verbiage "limiting them places". To see the place "*Sens*" as only "*Sens,*" is "limiting" to those who are trying to make sense of a main theme. As stated previously, the main theme of this quatrain seems, at first glance, to be simply an itinerary of "places". However, "*Sens*" acts to make it more than that (as does "*Rosne*").

A comma follows the word "*Sens*". As that mark of punctuation is showing a break point, separate from that which follows, that written prior to the comma acts as a separate statement. The capitalized "*Sens*" follows the capitalized first word preposition, "*De*", which begins the quatrain and represents an important direction, "To, From, Of, and/or With". The direction is relative to "*Sens*".

The additional meaning of the word "*sens*" (the lower-case essence behind a name) comes from seeing it as either a noun or an adverb. As a noun, it means, "sense, wit, conceit, apprehension, understanding, judgment, reason, knowledge,

137

opinion, thought; also, natural sense or feeling; and a sense, as one of the five senses; and/or also, the sense, meaning, or construction of a writing." As an adverb, "*sens*" is used to denote being, "topsy-turvy, top over tail, and/or upside down." When these translation possibilities are capitalized, one can then see how Nostradamus was stating extra importance, greater than the general usage. That new perspective makes much come to light as the primary focus of this theme.

It makes one aware that the main theme is relative "To Judgment". It indicates that what is to follow will take place "With Understanding"; and, the motivation could be "From Meaning of a writing". This then connects to "*Rosne*", such that the capitalization elevates this to be a religious theme, where "Judgment" is the theme of Armageddon. It is also leading to the confirmation in the secondary theme, of a "sickly" form of Christianity, as resulting from reaching a "Topsy-turvy" condition. This then connects this quatrain to the information of the preface, which told that the future would be of a time when "religions" will be "diametrically opposite ones".

Seeing this coming from the two separated word of the main theme, a new perspective can then fall on "*d'Autun viendront jusques au Rosne,*" especially in respect to the "place" Autun. As noted, this is a commune of France, but the history of Autun comes out when it is stated, "to Autun will come until with the Rose-born". That history is the "school of rhetoric" that Autun is known for, which was from the Roman influence in Gaul (250-700 A.D.). As such, Autun is known for being a center of philosophy. However, Autun also represents the most northern expanse into Europe of the second (or four) Arab caliphates (an Islamic empire known as Umayyad – 725-732 A.D.)

From this history that elevates the meaning of "from Autun" or "to Autun", one is able to see how philosophy that will overtake Christians. In this regard, Nostradamus wrote in the letters and quatrains about "new Philosophers" having an impact on the future. Such a "new Philosophy" that weakens Christianity is democracy, as the will of the people over the will of the Church. From that understanding of Autun, one can then see a repeating of history prophesied, where another Arab will gain control of Gaul, as far north as "to Autun", and reign for seven years (the length of time Umayyad stayed in power).

To summarize the evidence presented in this quatrain, one finds revealed:

1. The important element "Of Judgment" is the initial focus of the quatrain.

2. The naming of three places in France (*"Sens, Autun, & Rosne"*) makes that nation the main theme focus.
3. The history of Autun France is as a center of pagan philosophy, as well as the place representing the furthest north place held by an Arabian empire.
4. The three places listed trace a path from north to south.
5. The use of *"Rosne"*, as a southern France dialect name for the "Rhone" River, places focus on the commune *Sainctes-Maries-de-la-Mer*.
6. The spelling, *"Rosne"*, can act as an anagram for *"n'Rose"*, taking the main theme focus to a religious symbol for those "born of the Rose", meaning Christians.
7. The secondary theme places its initial focus on the reason France is the main focus, through the capitalized use of the word 'Because".
8. Travel through France is explained as "to go beyond", which is then stated to be "towards the mountains Pyrenees".
9. The word *"outre"* has multiple translation possibilities, based on context, which allow one a purpose from having "pierced through", with *"vers les"* showing an accompaniment, "with them" in the "mountains".
10. The use of "them" is identified in the third line, as "people", who are the important "kindred There", about the "Pyrenees Mountains".
11. "The people" are "to come forth" in a way similar to Italian history.
12. "The people" are representative of an important issue "By reason of country".
13. "There" will come "people" from across the "sea" to be with "him" who "will pursue" the "great ones" through "those setting traps".
14. These "snares" will involve both "land AND sea" operations.

Afterthoughts: Line three is enigmatic, in the sense that *"Marque d'Anconne"* appears to add Italy into the mix. The Adriatic town Ancona is generally thought to be the meaning of *"d'Anconne."* The better translation is as *"Ancône,"* which is a small French commune, but it is located on the banks of the Rhone River (the *Grand Rhône*), roughly halfway between Lyon and Marseilles. As a named place, that would explain the capitalization as the importance of how far a reach will extend (from *"sortir"* translated as "to go beyond"). However, the capitalization of *"Marque"* needs explaining.

The word *"marque"* means "mark, sign, token," but it makes more sense as an important indication (capitalized) of "a distress, arrest, or seizure of body." This becomes a marker place, relative to how far north, from Marseilles, the port city on the Mediterranean Sea, an invasion by sea would extend, causing distress to the French along that path.

Again, this information does nothing to explain where Osama bin Laden would be hiding in the Pyrenees Mountains. The story line developing, which hopefully is becoming clearer the more one is introduced to these quatrains, that an invasion by sea can only find success with assistance by land. The land base of this is the Pyrenees Mountains and the only reason that area would become a threat for the Western world to worry about is the leader promising destruction to the West has taken up residence there.

Chapter 12
Prosecution Exhibit H

To Pierce Near to the Monts Pyrenees

The second of the five quatrains that present the words *"monts Pyrenees"* in the secondary theme line can be seen represented by simple translation as:

Proche del duero par mer Tyrrene close,	Near from she sleeps by sea Tyrrhenian hedged in,
Viendra percer les grans monts Pyrenees	Will arrive to pierce them great ones mountains Pyrenees
La main plus courte & sa percee gloze,	There public authority more short & its full of holes exposition,
A Carcassonne conduira ses menees.	In Carcassonne will manage one's devices.

Again beginning with the secondary theme, the reader is immediately focused on an important (capitalization) event that "Will come", or "Will arrive". The future tense of the verb *"venir"* is stated, with the root verb meaning, "to come; to arrive, to approach, to draw near unto; to proceed from, to issue from, to be derived from; to spring, to prove, to grow; and also, to happen, to chance, and/or to fall out." All of these contexts can apply to this theme statement; but the theme of "coming" was found in the last quatrain's main theme line. There, one saw "will be coming until at the *Rosne*". This is also connected to the quatrain that told of the "One king will be who will come to see there France".

The purpose for this arrival is then found to be "to pierce" (from *"percer"*), which is a repeated term. It was found used by a synonymous word in the last quatrain discussed (*"outre"*). Still, the root word, *"percer"* was found in the quatrain that told of an escape from the East (*"Transpercera Alane"*). As a way of hinting at the act of penetrating something, while being an indirect use of descriptive words, one is able to sense a piercing in the quatrain telling of "Opened veins".

The object of this "thrusting through" is then explained as being "them" (plural personal use of *"les"*), who are identified as the *"great ones"*. The same spelling of *"grans"* that appears in this quatrain was seen directly connected to *"monts Pyrenees"* in the quatrain that offered the main theme statement saying, "Quite joined to the great ones" (*"Bien contigue des grans"*). Additionally, the singular use of *"grand"* was found related to *"monts Pyrenees"*, in the main theme that stated, "About to the mountains Pyrenees great amass" (*"Autour des monts Pyrenees grand amas"*). All of these uses make these quatrains connected, thus confirming the quatrains link together to tell one story.

This secondary theme is then advancing a main theme that appears to be placing focus on Spain and Italy. These two nations are in the same category as "great ones". The secondary theme becomes separated from that European focus (separation denoted by a comma at the end of the main theme line), while that main theme is relative to that which "Will come to pierce them", in the "Pyrenees".

The main theme begins with the capitalized adjective, *"Proche"*, which means, "Near, Nigh, Neighboring, Adjoining, and/or Close unto." As such, the main theme is saying what could be importantly (capitalization) "Near" Spain and Italy, which becomes a statement about what is not either Spain of Italy, but "Close unto" both. That makes a statement for France being the main theme focus, as it is the only nation that borders those two. Therefore, the secondary theme is presenting a sense of "Neighboring" those two, while not being in either.

Spain is not directly stated but is indicated through the use of the Spanish, through the words, *"del duero"*. The impulse is to see this as making the statement, "to the Duero," which is a major river in Spain. However, such a changing, from the lower-case spelling to an upper case spelling, as a proper name, is not allowed.

Everything in *The Prophecies* is divinely spelled, thus correctly written. This relates to the instruction in Nostradamus' letter of Preface, which says to beware "limiting them places". This alludes to proper names coming from words that have general meaning, before they become specific to one person, place, or thing.

By not limiting them as a name of a place, the two Spanish words ("*del duero*") can state, "from she sleeps",[1] or "to them she sleeps". It can even be seen as coming from the Latin root word, "*durus*", allowing for a translation stating, "with them enduring", or "of them hard (or strong)". Still, the fact that "*del duero*" is clearly Spanish makes that transition in language become a focus on Spain.

The meaning of being "Close unto" acts with the general meaning represented by "*del duero*". It means the main theme is about being "Near" enough "to them" (from "*del*" being representative of the French "*des*", or "*de+les*") that one is comfortable enough to "sleep" with the safety that company provides. This can be seen from the perspective of the one that is "Near" or from the one who "sleeps". With "*duero*" translated as "she sleeps", the feminine gender can become symbolically characteristic of a nation, where "motherland" is a common term used to depict one's country. The use of Spanish words makes "she" become Spain, which is "asleep" because France is "Near".

Through seeing Spain represented through the simple switch to the Spanish language, one can then interpret the translated Spanish, as it implies the proper name. This allows one to see "*del duero*" as having the secondary meaning that states, "to the [*Rio*] Duero". One can "come Near" this physical river, named Duero because Spain "sleeps". It also allows one to see how one "Will come" from a place "Neighboring" both France and Spain, where the Princess Pyrene ("she") figuratively "sleeps" under the "Pyrenees Mountains". This suggests the mythology associated with the spelling "*Pyren-nees*".

From this initial meaning coming from the first words of the main theme, the verbiage shifts to state "by sea" (from the next words, "*par mer*"). This has been found stated in two other quatrains, where an ampersand separated the words "*terre*" and "*mer*". The last quatrain's line four began by stating, "*Par terre & mer*". That supported the secondary theme of that quatrain, which stated (simply), "Because to pass – pierced – near (alternative translation of "*vers*") – them mountains Pyrenees".

The support showed how the "sea" would be where "he will pursue to great ones" (from "*le suivra à grans*" following "*mer*", in the last quatrain). Thus, one will reach Spain "by sea", from a place "Adjoining" or "Close by". A course to Spain "by sea" could be from Italy, France, or any European country with a port on the

1   Per InterTran translation site.

Mediterranean Sea, but a port "Close unto" Spain is more likely to be either in North Africa, or in the Balearic Islands. The Balearic Islands are "Close unto" Spain, as a Spanish province in the Mediterranean.

The words "*par mer*" then lead the focus to the capitalized proper noun, "*Tyrrene*". This is a name for the "Tyrrhenian" people, or an "Etruscan", an ancient one who lived in the region now known as Tuscany (then Etruria). Generally, that name is associated with the western coast of Italy, including Rome. The people of that region are the root for the name of the "sea" that is off the coast of Italy, named the "Tyrrhenian" Sea (or *Mare Tirreno* in Italian). The naming of an ancient people, who are synonymous with the Roman Empire because their civilization grew to become that empire, is the primary intent in this main theme.

In modern terms, this use of "*Tyrrene*" represents both Italy and those of Rome, as those powers who would cause France and Spain to "Come Near unto" their influence. Evidence of that influence is seen in the fact that both French and Spanish are Romance languages; but seeing "*Tyrrene*" as a variation of the Latin spelling ("*Tyrrheni*") shows the influence elevates to the shared religion that is Christianity. All uses of Latin in *The Prophecies* act in an elevated manner, as the language of Christianity.

The last word of the main theme is then "*close*", which is another word with multiple translation possibilities. The 1611 Old French-English dictionary shows it meaning "closed, enclosed; hedged in, shut up; also, barred, stopped; forestalled, prevented; also, finished, fulfilled, perfected, and/or accomplished." The spelling with the "*e*" at the end makes it the feminine gender, in need of attaching to a feminine noun. An example of this word's use (in the feminine) is given in the dictionary, as, "*Ville close*." That was then shown to mean, "A city or walled town," with "*Ville*" being a feminine noun. As such, "*close*" makes agreement with the use of "*duero*", as "she sleeps". That allows one to see that not only is Spain feeling secure enough to let down "her" guard enough "to sleep", but so too does Italy. Still, in Italy's perspective, France is "Neighboring", allowing the Italians to feel "fulfilled" and "accomplished".

This makes the secondary theme be about why one would feel a need to get "Near" to two "sleeping" giants ("great ones"). That reason is relative to the lack of security they have in place, especially along the shorelines between Spain and Italy (including France). They are "prevented" from protecting their shores because the world is at rest, or peace. Thus, all three are "asleep" to the possibility of a naval invasion. Those seeking to get into the important position of being "Close unto" Spain, in the "mountains" of the "Pyrenees" will do so to become "strong" (Latin use of "*duero*" root, "*durus*") and "hard". As such, all three nations (Spain, Italy, and France) will be hit "hard by sea". Once this barrage begins, both will be "enclosed" by an enemy already on shore. They will have not realized this presence because "she sleeps", when she should be alert.

The secondary theme of this quatrain does not end with any punctuation. In a case like this the focus of the secondary theme is continued on in the third line, although each line retains its own specific focus. The capitalized first word of line three is "*La*", which means "There" (from an accented "*Là*"). This becomes relative to the last word of line two, "*Pyrenees*". Therefore, the supporting details of line three are continuing the focus placed on the "Pyrenees Mountains". The supporting detail found in line three's focus on "There" then splits into two halves, due to the presence of an ampersand.

The first half states, "There hand more short", where the use of "hand" should be seen as continuing the theme of what "Will come to pierce". This carries a meaning of a "strong hand" or the meaning of the labor that would do difficult work, as a "hired hand." It also must be recognized that a body has two "hands," one each at the end of two arms. This is then continuing the secondary theme by saying "There" is an arm in the "Pyrenees" with a "hand" that will be a "plus" or lead to "more" (from the next word, "*plus*").

While representing "more", it will also be "short" (from the next word, "*courte*"). The term "*courte*" means, "short, brief, succinct, cut, compendious; low; also little, and/or small." As such, the "hand" will be "small", but also "succinct". This acts like the saying, "Big things ("more") come in "small" packages." Seeing that, the archaic meaning of "succinct" is, "encircled, or drawn up tightly." This is an indication of a "hand short" being representative of being close to a goal, but still not "There". Thus, this is supporting a strategic element that makes being "Close upon" beneficial to an enemy. A "hand" representing "more" or a "plus" to the whole gains that value by being a "hand" maintaining a "low" profile, waiting for the time to have its greatest impact. This becomes a "hand" that is strategically placed.

This meaning connects the third line's first half to the main theme, where it is designed to offer its optimum support. Thus, the first half of line three is relative to the Spanish half of the main theme. The theme of being "Near to them" as "she sleeps" is then supported with the details of "There" (Spain) the "hand" is "more", as it is only a "short" distance to Spain from the "Pyrenees". At this point, one also needs to be able to see another usage for the word *"main"*, the French word meaning, "hand".

While "hand" is the primary use for *"main"*, the word had several other uses, a couple of which were related to horses, sailing ships, and buckets on draw wells. All of these uses have gone away with the passage of time. The word *"main"* also had a meaning that was related to wine pressing, which may no longer be applicable, due to the mechanization of the wine industry that certainly has taken place. Still, it had two meanings that could be relevant today, one as "a quire of paper" [less than a ream] and the other as a legal term meaning, "a public authority, or power." This last use acts to bring out the first line's theme, especially concerning how it reflects "she sleeps".

"La" is seen as representative of Spain due to *"del deuro"* being Spanish words. The words *"del deuro"* then are seen as saying, "to them she sleeps", which makes the pronoun "she" reflect the "public authority" of Spain. The word *"main"* then acts as the "hand" of Spanish law. Spain will be unable to do anything in the *"Pyrenees"* because the reach of that "hand" is "low" or "little" (alternative translations of *"courte"*). This, in turn, allows those who "Will come to pierce" into the "mountains" of the "Pyrenees" "more" freedom to do so. The Spanish government may wish to do "more", but their efforts will come up "short". In other words, the supporting details to the main theme (from line three's first half) are saying that Spanish "courts" (play on the use of *"courte"*) will be "barred" or "prevented" (translations of "close") from acting, due to a forced or self-imposed "sleep".

This symbolizes how Western laws will be used to protect those entering Western nations as foreign minorities. They will enter for the purpose of doing harm to those nations; but as minorities they will be able to claim the law does not give them equal protection. Lawsuits will reach the point that the law makes it easier to look the other way than confront those challenges. Those countries are then "asleep", in order to avoid confronting this issue. This important element weakens a nation's ability to defend itself from attack.

The second half of line three begins after the ampersand, with the ampersand signaling importance is to follow. The word that absorbs that importance is the possessive pronoun *"sa"*, which means, "his, hers, one's, and/or its". It is the feminine form of *"son,"* meaning it seeks another word in feminine agreement with which to match. As the supporting details to the main theme, the feminine form of *"Tyrrene"* (feminine due to the word *"close"* following it and being feminine)[2] allows this agreement. This means *"hers"* is referencing the nation of Italy.

Italy is symbolized by the ancient name of the civilization that founded Rome and the subsequent empire. The Italian islands and the peninsula's western coast create the "enclosed sea" that bears the name "Tyrrhenian". Thus, the second half of line three is then focused on "one's" being "hedged in" or "shut up" by that "sea". An important one then becomes the focus, as to who is the "most" (from *"plus"*) powerful in that region of Italy. The answer points to the pope, who presides over the principality that is Vatican City, which is "enclosed by" the "sea" ("Tyrrhenian") and Rome. This means the pope is the sovereign of that city-state; and it will be "his" "walled" city that will be "pierced" (the meaning of *"percee"*).

Needless to say, the use of the word *"percee"*, which is only found accented, as *"percée"*, is a repeated term. It is the feminine past participle of the word *"percer"* and translates to state: "pierced, bored, gored, thrust into, or thrust through; transfixed; open, and/or full of holes or windows." This then acts as a continuation of the secondary theme, as an important explanation for an element that "Will come to pierce them great ones" through "her" own "open holes". It says that Italy will be "enclosed" by having its empire "thrust through", making its reach (the act of a "hand") "little". All of this is repeating the use of "to pierce" (*"percer"*), "Will pierce through" (*"Transpercera"*), "pierced" (*"oultré"*), and "Opened ones" (*"Ouvertes"*), which links all of these quatrains to the same focus of sudden penetration.

The last word of this second half of line three is *"gloze"*. With the letter *"z"* being interchangeable with the letter *"s"*, and with no word spelled *"gloze"* found, the words *"glose"* and *"glosé"* act to complete this thought. The word *"glose"* means, "A gloss; comment, or exposition"; and the word *"glosé"* is the past participle, meaning, "glossed; expounded, commented on." One of the archaic definitions of the English word "gloss" is "to use flattery; to explain away; to use deceit; and/or to minimize the importance of."

---

2   Nostradamus repeated this word in four times, in four spellings. The above spelling matches the use of *"Tirrene,"* as the feminine versions of the masculine *"Tyrren"* and *"Tyrrens."*

This word then acts to show how the Church of Rome and the power of the Vatican have been "minimized", especially since the days of Nostradamus. It also shows how the Vatican has become deceitful in its dealings, which have generated scandals that have been widely "commented on". Some of these topics (not all) include money laundering deals with the Mafia, the murder of a pope, and priests abusing children. In one sense, the piety of the Church has been "explained away", to the point of it being little more than a tourist attraction, when once it acted as the defender of Italy. Therefore, the supporting details of the "sleeping" Italian element of the main theme are saying Rome will be incapable of defense, because it will be an "exposition full of holes" (alternate translations for "*percee glose*").

Line four then follows the comma at the end of line three, making it a separate focus on general details that are relative to the main theme of an army of terrorists gathering "Close unto" two "sleeping" giants, Spain and Italy. It produces specific details that relate to the secondary theme, which placed focus on those who "Will come to pierce them great ones", from their training camp in the "mountains" of the "Pyrenees". The first word of line four is the capitalized preposition, "*A*", which can also be read as the third person present form of the verb "*Avoir*".

As the preposition, line four is placing immediate focus on the importance (capitalization) of placement around the "*Pyrenees*". The preposition allows one to see those who "Will come" as being, "In, At, With, From, and/or To", which gives a general sense of movement in and out of the "mountains", from within and without. As the third person present form of "*Avoir*", the first word is making an important (capitalization) statement about who occupies the "mountains". In that case, it begins by stating, "Has Carcassonne" (the next word), which is another example of "Possessions".

"*Carcassonne*" is a commune in the Aude department of southwest France. The Aude department reaches the base of the "*Pyrenees*", from which is sourced the Aude River (the root of the department name). The Aude River flows north to "*Carcassonne*", where it makes a turn to the east, and flows into the Mediterranean "Sea". The town is famous for being a fortified city, or a "*ville close*". It is in a region once known as Languedoc, in an area that is still called "Cathar Country" (people exterminated by Inquisition in the 14th century). Instead of French, the people speak Occitan, which is said to be a quite different language. This characteristic makes "*Carcassonne*" visible as "them" of the "great" nation

France, who are more aligned with the country surrounding "them", which includes the "mountains" of France, north of the "Pyrenees". Thus, line four is stating possession of that town ("Has Carcassonne"), to the point that the enemies staying in the Pyrenees are freely accepted "In Carcassonne".

With that possession, line four is advancing the possession of "its pierced gloss", from the second half of line three. Line two's secondary theme placed focus on who "Will come to pierce", with line three continuing to state, "hers pierced", which shows what will have "come" by then, to the point of being "commented on" (alternative translation of "*glose*"). Line four is showing the point of "piercing" to be "Carcassonne" and with that area in "their" possession, they "will conduct their conspiracies" (from the final three words, "*conduira ses menees*"). Those "plots" will be for the "practices" and "devices" (all translations of "*menees*") that "Will come to pierce the great ones".

The use of "*menees*" in line four of this quatrain can be seen, due to the "*s*" ending, to be the "ones" of "conspiracy". The singular meaning of "*menee*" is "led, brought; guided, conducted, directed; managed; moved, induced, persuaded; and also overwrought, subdued, and/or fetch in." This suggests those carrying out the plots are "ones" being "led." This use was repeated (in the singular) in line three of the quatrain that stated, "land will cause so – great directed" (from "*terre fera si grand menee*"). That quatrain also mentioned "Narbonne", which is the commune on the Mediterranean coast, where the Aude River empties. "Carcassonne" and "Narbonne" are both in the Aude department.

One cannot forget the first quatrain discussed, which stated in the main theme one who would be the "conductor of the army". The second quatrain's secondary theme told of "One king" who "will come to see France"; and, the quatrain referred to "Narbonne" in its main theme, adding "The Arabian king will proceed [to] the mountain ones", where they "will not make resistance". This information is linking solidly to a central theme of Osama bin Laden being the "guide" for the "ones" who will carry out "his conspiracies."

This is another quatrain full of information which acts as evidence to support the theme of Osama bin Laden being in the "Pyrenees Mountains". Therefore, it is important to summarize that information in bullet points.

1. The main theme is initially focused on the importance of proximity, due to the first word being capitalized, stating, "Near".

2. The use of Spanish words in line one ("*del duero*") places focus on Spain.
3. The Spanish translates to state, "to them she sleeps", which places focus on a state of drowsiness, or rest.
4. The use of the words, "*par mer*", indicates the Mediterranean side of Spain.
5. The name "*Tyrrene*" is a symbolic reference to Italy, with Rome as the center of a powerful civilization.
6. Focus is placed on the "Tyrrhenian Sea", which is "enclosed" by the islands of Italy, and the western peninsula.
7. The overall main theme allows one to see a lack of defense placed on the Mediterranean Sea coastlines, from Italy to Spain.
8. To be "Close upon" is reason for who "Will come to pierce the great ones", with the point of piercing being the "Pyrenees Mountains".
9. Those who "Will come" will represent a "hand" hold that makes "them great ones" only a "short" distance away.
10. The situation "There", in France and Spain, in particular in the "Pyrenees", will be that the "public authority" will become "more brief", as the law "to them (those who Will come to pierce) sleeps".
11. The Vatican becomes representative of an Italian "great one", which has had its reputation "pierced" to the point of being "glossed".
12. The southwestern "walled" city, "Carcassonne", is close to the "Pyrenees Mountains", and where a leader "will guide his conspiracies."

Afterthoughts: Once again, there is little that points directly at someone named Osama bin Laden, although there is a preponderance of evidence submitted that shows a Trojan Horse will have made its way into the Pyrenees Mountains. Once there, the same result of doing inner damage, while opening the gates for more to rush in, will lead to the element of surprise attack and panic leading to quick defeat.

This central focus on the Pyrenees Mountains needs to be accepted as a source that should be investigated, whether or not Osama bin Laden has secretly been relocated there. His threats regularly made available pointed to this theater of intended action, which came about well after Nostradamus penned these verses. It is safe to say that the announcement of Osama bin Laden's death made looking for his replacement anywhere other than the Middle East (the usual suspects) out of the question. All the while since May Day 2011, France has had a plethora of terrorist attacks; but no one knows who is leading them.

Chapter 13
Prosecution Exhibit I

The Ethnic Nation of the monts Pyrenees

The third of the five quatrains that mention "*monts Pyrenees*" in the secondary theme statement is found to fully state (simply translated):

Le camp du temple de la vierge vestale,	Him camp lodged to the temple of there virgin chaste,
Non esloigné d'Ethne & monts Pyrenées:	Not removed from Ethnic nation & mountains Pyrenees:
Le grand conduict est caché dens la male,	A great training is kept secret destructive there hurtful,
North getés fluves & vignes mastinées.	North wind violently sent forth ones flown ones & vines rudely handled ones.

This is one of two quatrains, in the eleven that state "*monts Pyrenees*", that have an ampersand placed so that those words stand alone to make a statement by themselves. In this case, it is in the second half of the secondary statement line. Because that stand-alone statement ends with a colon, line three will offer clarification, or an example of how those two words make that separate statement. However, before one addresses that second half, one must look at the first half of line two.

The first half begins with the capitalized negative, "*Non*", which means, "Not, or No". The capitalization makes this an important aspect of what has "Not" been done, which is relative to the main theme statement. This undone

151

condition leads one's focus to the past tense verb, "*esloingé*", which means, "removed far away, sent far away, set far away, put far away, banished far away, and/or driven far away." Therefore, the initial focus of the main theme is something that has been left as is, rather than "removed" from one's midst. It also shows that this has "Not" been done to an element that has been "sent far away", to get in another place.

This dual focus leads to the combination word, "*d'Ethne*", where the abbreviated and attached "*d'*" represents the preposition "*de*". That separate word indicates, "to, from, with, and/or of". When "Not removed far away" is the preceding phrase, it is natural to see the "*de*" be read as "from", rather than "to". Finding the meaning of the word "*Ethne*" is a challenge because it is not Old French. Modern French lists the word "*ethnie*", as meaning "ethnic group", but the capitalization means this word has a more important meaning, to the point of proper noun status.

The answer to this elevated meaning comes from the Bible, in particular Matthew 28:19, where the Greek language shows, "εθνη" (epsilon-theta-nu-eta, or "*ethne*").[1] Strong's Greek Dictionary (reference 1484) translates this word by stating, "probably from "*etho*" (reference 1486)," meaning, "a race (as of the same habit), i.e. a tribe; specifically, a foreign (non-Jewish) one (usually, by implication, pagan):-- Gentile, heathen, nation, people."[2] Thus, the French word "*ethnie*" is not far from this meaning, but the capitalization acts more on the level of the capitalized proper name, "Gentile".

The biblical verse from Matthew is translated such that "*ethne*" is shown to say, "nations."[3] It is a quote attributed to Jesus, as he instructed the disciples after his resurrection. Jesus said, "Therefore go and make disciples of all nations, in the name of the Father and of the Son and of the Holy Spirit."[4] This word, through its capitalization, is elevated to the level of being a word of Christ; and as such, "*Ethne*" makes "Gentiles" become representative of the "Pagan nations" where the Jews would be found scattered. The Jews have become "Ethnic groups" among the "Heathens". As such, "*Ethne*" is elevated to mean those where the spread of Christianity would go. Therefore, "Not removed far away" makes "d'Ethne" bear all the meanings: "to Heathens", "from

---

1	Matthew 28, Parallel Greek New Testament.
2	Strong's Greek Lexicon Search Results – "*Ethne*"
3	Matthew 28, Parallel Greek New Testament.
4	New International Version.

PROSECUTION EXHIBIT I

Christians", and "of Ethnic groups".

With the first half of the secondary theme having this meaning, the second half simply states *"monts Pyrenees"*. As a stand-alone statement, this becomes an important statement that these "Ethnic groups" are relative to "mountains". In turn, those "mountains" are specifically named the *"Pyrenees"*. This is supporting the themes that told of "people foreign" in the "Pyrenees" (from the quatrain that stated, *"De gent estrange"*, as a secondary theme), who were like a "great tympany" or "ugly growth" (from the same quatrain's main theme, which ended, *"grand amas"*). This meant those "people" were "strangers" in their own land, so to speak.

That concept was emphasized by the main theme in another quatrain, which stated, "Quite joined to the great ones", in the "Pyrenees Mountains", then following to focus on how "One" would be "against the eagle" (France) (from the main theme stating, *"Bien contigue des grans monts Pyrenees,"* and secondary theme following with *"Un contre l'aigle"*). That focus then continues here in this quatrain, where it is placed upon those "Ethnic groups" of the "Pyrenees". The Basque people are certainly one of those groups, as mentioned previously. However, they are not the only group of people in those "mountains", as there is another.

The Basque people reside in the western portion of the "Pyrenees Mountains". This is where "Basque Country" lies, and it extends both north and south of the border between France and Spain. To see who lives in the eastern half of those "mountains", one needs to see how this secondary theme is advancing the main theme statement (line one). That statement reads, *"Le camp du temple de la vierge vestale,"* which is a string of words that can be highly misleading.

The reason line one is difficult comes from the last two words, *"vierge vestale"*. Together, those two words are translated syntactically as meaning, "vestal virgin". This is a known entity that is related to the pagan worship of ancient Rome. Specifically, the "vestal virgins" (plural) were young maidens who were dedicated to service in the "temple" of Vesta. The main "temple" of Vesta is near Rome. This makes one see this main theme, which states "temple" and *"vierge vestale"* in one line, appear to be relative to Italy. If that were true, then a main theme focused on Italy would then find line two jumping to the border between Spain and France. That consistency problem is rooted in not seeing two separate words, *"vierge"* and *"vestale"* and translating them separately, in

153

that order, so that each makes a statement on their own.

When one reads each word separately, in the order written, one sees that "*vierge*" has two uses. The first is as a noun, being "a virgin, maid, maiden; and also, the sign of the zodiac termed Virgo." The second definition is as an adjective, meaning, "virgin, pure, clear, prime, unbroken, untainted, undefiled, and/or untouched."

As a separate statement, the word "*vierge*" is one of purity and innocence. Then, when one sees that the word *vestales* (made plural, and not offered as translated in the singular) means, "the vestal virgins, and/or the nuns of the heathenish Romans," one has to look at the singularity of that meaning. The word "nun" comes to the forefront, and the English definition of "vestal" shows it generally meaning, "a woman who is a virgin; nun; chaste, pure."

When one puts the two words together and looks for meaning from "virgin pure", one has to consider the relevance of the mother of Christ, the Virgin Mother. Mary, the mother of Jesus, was a "virgin" who became pregnant without intercourse. She represents "purity" as being the source of the physical body of Christ. The Roman Catholic Church views the Virgin Mary as "pure", thus saintly and holy. The Roman Catholic Church is where one also finds "nuns", who are the modern version of "vestal virgins", in the "temples" of Christian convents. This is how one must think of these two words, when both are seen first as separate and then later conjoined.

The simple translation of the main theme line can be shown as, "Him – camp – to the – church – of – there – virgin – pure". This begins with the capitalized article-personal pronoun, "*Le*", which has been discussed as standing alone by representing the third person masculine pronoun, "Him". This is beginning the main theme of a whole quatrain by focusing on one individual, where the capitalization makes this person most important to the story line. This person is thus "THE" (interpretation as the article, "*Le*", meaning, "The") one represented as "Him".

In this string of words, the word "*temple*" is equally translatable as "temple" (a Jewish distinction, but also pagan) and/or as "church" (a Christian distinction). When one sees the words, "*temple de la*", as representative of the "church of there", this relates "to Gentiles" of the "Pyrenees", both as "temple" and as "church". The words "virgin pure" then act to make the statement of a

Christian "church", and this becomes specific as a "church" dedicated "to the" name of the "virgin". This suggests one should look for a "church" in the "Ethnic" regions of the "Pyrenees Mountains" named for Saint Mary (the "virgin chaste").

One such "church" could be Santa Maria del Mar (Saint Mary of the Sea), which is located in Barcelona, Spain. Barcelona is the capital of the autonomous community of Spain known as Catalonia. That region includes the eastern third of the Spanish "Pyrenees". This "church" was built at the height of Catalonia's history, in the 14th century, with inscriptions on the façade in both Latin and Catalan (the local language). The inscriptions refer to the "Cemetery of the Mulberries" (*Fossar de les Moreres*), which the "church" overlooks.

The reason this "church" can be seen as relative to the main theme is the history that accompanies it, which connects it to the "Ethnic nation" that was Catalonia. In the War of Spanish Succession (1701-1714), when Philip V (a Bourbon king of Spain) ruled, the kingdoms of Castile and Navarre were sympathetic to that king's claim to Spain. The Kingdom of Aragon (which included Catalonia) was opposed to his ascension. For their support of the Austrian claims to sovereignty, Philip placed Barcelona under siege. Those defenders of Barcelona who died were buried in the *Fossar de les Moreres*, and a plaza was built over the cemetery in their honor. After Catalonia fell to Philip V, he issued decrees against them (the *Descretos de Neuva Planta*), which (among other issues) banned the use of Catalan in public documents. The regions under the Crown of Aragon (Aragon, Catalonia, Valencia, and the Balearic Islands) were forced to follow the rules and laws of Castile.

When this history is known, it allows one to see "The camp" as one important (capitalization of the singular article, "*Le*") place where "An army lodged". It represents one specific "field" where soldiers rested, which is relative "to the church" that overlooked that site. That "church" is specific "to there", where soldiers of the "camp" were laid to rest; and that "church" is a building "of there", prior to the need for "An army lodged to there". The "church" is named for the "virgin", who is recognized for her "purity" through sainthood. Thus, "The camp" at the basilica of Santa Maria de la Mar is that of the Catalonians. The main theme is establishing a site that has become important, because of persecution by those more powerful upon those whom they dominate.

This makes the capitalization of the negative "*Non*" show the secondary theme being initially focused on "Not" being "pure" to that "camp", as well as "Not" letting the memories of those "chaste" who died fighting for autonomy be forgotten. It shows that although they became part of Spain, "Never" was the culture "removed far away", as they continued "with Ethnic group" traditions and practices, including their native language. It also shows how importantly Catalonia, the Basque Country, Navarre, and Aragon are all "autonomous communities" of Spain, which means they consider themselves "Not" Spanish, but nationalities "set far away" from independence. Thus, all are uniquely "of Ethnicity AND" all are of the "mountains", with the unifying factor to all four being the "Pyrenees Mountains" element.

When one sees *"vierge vestale"* representative of the Virgin Mary, it takes on a Christian meaning that resonates with the word *"Ethne"*. Jesus "sent" the disciples "far away" to preach the Good News to Jews who had scattered throughout the world. In that regard, Spain has a strong historical connection to Jewish settlements, as well as to the persecution that took place in France and Spain, "of" that "Ethnic group" (the Inquisitions).

The earliest Jews in the Iberian Peninsula came during the times of Roman domination. In those times, Romans persecuted the Jews to the point that they hid in secret groups. Those Jews later welcomed the influx of Muslims (Moors) that drove the Romans off, and the Muslims offered them protection from the Romans. The Moors held the regions of Aragon and Catalonia until Frankish Christians assumed control of those lands along the "Pyrenees" and south into the eastern half of the Iberian Peninsula. After the Christians took control of Spain, the Jews found their first political prominence through the Crown of Aragon, and they thrived throughout the territories under their realm. That comfort made Jewish settlements safe and openly known, which allowed them to thrive as productive communities, until the Spanish Inquisition.

Between 1212 and 1492, most Moors and Jews were in a state of being "driven far away" from Spain. "The" Christian "camp" was "Not" being very Christ-like in this regard. They were "far removed" from acting as disciples of Jesus, as they were little more than crusading "armies of Gentiles". This history is relevant today in the regions of Spain that have seen a cross used as a battle weapon; and this sentiment is strongly felt by Jews and Muslims alike. In that sense, a lack of the "church" displaying "pure" motivations has made those "of Gentile" pasts "Not" believers of the Virgin Mary. They have been shown how the benefits of that religion are "set far away" from those seen as truly being "of

Paganism".

In this way, the minorities of the "Pyrenees" can find reason for unity, as "A camp" on the "field" of Christian nations. As such, "The army lodged" is in the midst "of them" who dedicate a "temple to the virgin pure". This makes the main theme also be relative to "The army lodged" in the "Pyrenees Mountains". It is "An army lodged" that does "Not" look like that, as the appearance of "The army camp" will be "put far away" from open sight, through the help "of Ethnic people" that support the reason for having an army. This makes the main and secondary themes fall right in line with the overall theme of Osama bin Laden being hidden in the "Pyrenees Mountains".

As stated before, the secondary theme ends with a colon, making line three clarify the statement of "mountains", in particular the "Pyrenees". In line three, Nostradamus wrote, "*Le grand conduict est cache dens la male*". This whole line can translate (simply) to state, "Him - great - conducted - east - hidden - dense - there - hurtful". Stated in this way, it is easier to see the connection to the information provided in other quatrains.

This directly connects the "*conducteur de l'armee*" when "*conduict*" is read as the past participle of "*conduire,*" which means, "to conduct, lead, guide, bring on; govern, sway, rule, wholly dispose of; also, to handle, and/or manage." The capitalized article, "*Le*", is then read as the masculine personal pronoun, making an important "Him" be the "conductor".[5] The word "*caché*", meaning, "hidden, concealed, kept secret; in covert, in corners; lurking in some odd nook or another; and/or conveyed away", is relative to "The army lodged" that is "Not" seen. This invisibility is because it is a "camp" in the "Opened veins" of the "Pyrenees Mountains".

The word "*est*" is the third person present form of the verb "*etre*" (in Old French, "*estre*"), which means, "to be." Thus, "*est*" commonly means, "is." However, it is also the spelling for the noun "east".

As a stand-alone statement, "is" becomes more limited in what it can mean; whereas "east" connects the information in this line to the travel itinerary that took Osama bin Laden from Afghanistan-Pakistan, in the "east", to the

---

5 Line one began with "*Le*" also, thus the "*Le*" beginning line two is a repeated word. This means if the first "*Le*" acts as the article, "A, An, The", then the second acts as a personal pronoun.

"Pyrenees". It also is an indication of the "east" part of the "Pyrenees", which is where Catalonia lies.

The word "*dens*" is seen as the abbreviated plural form of the French word, "*dent*," which means, "tooth; fang; tusk, and/or tush." The plural, in all cases, is "teeth", which becomes limited in its stand-alone meaning. Therefore, the word has to be seen as Latin, where "*dens*" means, "tooth" and anything resembling a tooth, such as, "a mattock, or sickle," and abstractly as anything, "biting, sharp, and/or destructive." The Latin word "*densus*" can also play a role in understanding how many "teeth" are "hidden", as that word means, "thick, close, dense," and when in the context of degrees of measure, "intense." This makes one word show an "army lodged" that has "destructive" capabilities, for "intense biting".

Finally, line three ends with the word "*male*," which means, "male, or a great budget." The Old French dictionary also refers one to look up the word "*masle*", which is limited to the "male" translation. This is certainly applicable to one who will make up the "army lodged", which will be "conducted" by the important "Him". However, the word "*male*" is also the feminine spelling for the word "*mal*".

When connected to the feminine article, "*la*", the word "*male*" is a fit as a feminine adjective. The word "*mal/male*" has many uses in French, but perhaps the best fits for this quatrain's theme show it as meaning, "ill, bad, naughty, lewd; scurvy; mischievous, hurtful, harmful, shrewd; unseemly, uncomely, indecent; sick, diseased, crazy, pained, sore, and/or ill at ease." This means line three ends by stating the "hidden teeth" are "there" (from "*là*") to be "the harmful" (as the feminine article "*la*" connecting to the feminine "*male*"). That is ultimately the purpose of an "army lodged", as it made "camp" to be at rest before going to war, when its purpose is to inflict hurt upon the enemy.

The secondary theme is always supported by the information contained in line four. As such, line four begins with the capitalized word "*North*", which brings out the meaning, "Not removed far away" from the "Pyrenees Mountains" is France, to the "North". This direction importantly includes the French portion of Basque Country, as well as the small region of southeastern France, known as North Catalonia. Old French used the word "*north*"; but by 1611, it was being phased out, as evidenced by the Old French-Old English dictionary referring the reader to see the word "*nord.*" That spelling has since been the standard French word for "north, and/or north wind".

That spelling cannot be overlooked as being similar to English. The history of France shows English rule in southwestern France, up to the "Pyrenees" border with Spain, between 1154 and 1453. This region was and is still known as Aquitaine, which makes an English spelling of a word represent this English influence (just as "*del deuro*" represented Spain in another quatrain). Therefore, the capitalization of "*North*" shows it is more than just the northern slopes of the "Pyrenees Mountains", but as far "North" as England.

With the secondary theme stating, "Not set far away", this is then seen as within the proximity of the "North", ranging from the "mountains" of the "Pyrenees". As a main theme statement, it says, "The army lodged there" is able to strike at a considerable distance "North". The use of "grand", in line three, can then be seen as referencing Great Britain, as it is certainly one of the world's "great" nations. Therefore, one is able to see how a "conduit is concealed" that can reach that far "North".

The word "*conduit*" is defined (partially) as, "a means by which something is transmitted," which makes one remember the repeated them of piercing. A hypodermic needle is a way of "piercing" into a body, for the purpose of being a "conduit" for medicine or the withdrawal of blood. On the other hand, a bite from a rabid dog also "pierces" the skin, "transmitting" disease into the one bitten. This analogy makes it possible to see how "hidden teeth there hurtful" can represent a method for "channeling" something "harmful" into the "great North".

The word "*getés*" is rooted in the Old French noun "*get*", and verb, "*getter*", which was also spelled with a "*j*" (as *jetcter*). This means "*geté*" acts the same as the past participle "*jecté*", with both meaning, "cast, flung, hurled, thrown; darted; violently sent forth; put or pushed forth." The "*s*" ending to yet another past participle is again an indication of the "ones" performing the action of "casting". This means "*getés*" says, "those violently sent forth", indicating more than one having been "thrown".

This analysis works more than one way, as is normal with the verbiage of Nostradamus. It is clearly an indication of "ones violently sent forth" to the "North"; but it also means that the "ones darted" have written on the side of them (the actual darts cast), "Made in the North". In this way, the manufacturer of the darts is not the one casting them. This would make the present fears of North Korea sending missiles to Iran relevant, but the capitalized "North", or "North wind", is a figurative metaphor for Russia, repeated often in the quatrains. They are known to have made ICBMs, with some "lost" since the fall of the Soviet Union.

Still, "ones darted" can state the reason "ones" would want to "put forth" an effort against the "North". This would be due to those of the "North" having had made those of the "Pyrenees" feel "flung" down. In this case, it verifies the past theme of stolen land. The loss of Palestine has been seen related to the hands of the French and English ("them great ones"), who had Protectorate responsibilities in that region of the world following World War I. The land that was Palestine was lost primarily due to a "concealed" unity among "kindred" spirits (Profiteers and Zionists). Thus, the "North ones darted" will exact "Judgment" on Christian "Gentiles".

The next word, "*fluves*", is not clearly spelled as a French word, but it certainly is rooted in the Latin word "*fluvius,*" meaning, "flowing water; a stream, and/or river." It can also be related to the Latin words "*fluus*" and/or "*fluere*", which are variations on a theme of "flowing" and that which is "to flow". From that meaning, the words "emanate, proceed from; and fall gradually" describe this action. Thus, something that can be "violently sent forth" then "flows" to its objective, to then "fall gradually" like a "stream". In war imagery, in modern terms, this is like the ICBMs previously discussed, and related to the quatrain where "*Gaule*" was explained as meaning "Big rod".

This shows that the proximity of Western Europe makes targeting Western Europe, "North" of the "Pyrenees", ideal for rockets with medium range capacity. It is known that Pakistan, Iran, and North Korea have medium range missiles[6] capable of reaching between 807 – 2,175 miles (1,300 km – 3,500 km). The driving distance between London, England and Marseilles, France is 1,192 miles.[7] The distance between Bilbao, Spain (the capital city of autonomous Basque Country) and Washington, D.C. is 3,744 miles. These distances are "Not set far away", when compared to a positioning in Pyongyang, North Korea (6,869 miles), Tehran, Iran (6,328 miles), or Islamabad, Pakistan (7,080 miles).[8]

6 Others known to have this capacity are the U.S.A., Russia, China, India, and Israel.
7 Per the website: Driving Distances Between European Cities.
8 All calculations between Washington D.C. and other places in the world are

The first three words of line four end at an ampersand. This ampersand matches the ampersand found in the secondary theme. As such, the statement about "North cast ones", in "flows", is supporting the theme of "Not far removed from" those "of Gentile nations". Although the "North" claims to be Christian, having heard the Gospel the disciples brought long ago, it is "of Paganism". Their support for Israel, which represents those Jews that have rejected Christ as their Messiah, shows a lack of knowing God through Christ. In this way, the Christian West has routinely supported actions that back the theft of land from smaller nations. The biblical story of David versus Goliath tells one how the smaller can fell the "great", with one stone "cast" causing the blood of a giant to "flow".

The ampersand, again, acts to show the importance of that which follows. The words that complete the line and the quatrain, are, "vines rudely handled ones." The word "vines" has to be seen as figurative, as "vines" have tendrils and are known for climbing, twining, and creeping along a surface. In a sense, "*vignes*" represents a "vineyard" where many "vines" grow, and those "vines" are managed in rows and pruned regularly. Still, with that management they do tend to intertwine and mesh together, especially when left alone. Wild "grapevines" can become impassable thickets. As a barrage of "cast ones", crisscrossing to various targets from multiple launch points, it would be difficult to "prune" such wildly arrayed "flows".

Still, as a stand-alone half-line of supporting details, aligned with the secondary theme's second half about the "mountains Pyrenees", "vines rudely handled ones" links to "hidden teeth" in line three. It gives the impression of entrances to caves being covered by a "vine leaf" design camouflage (if not real wild grapevines planted), with "mountain curs" (a mastiff-bred dog, where the alternate translation for "*mastinée*" is, "a big cur") acting as watch/guard dogs, should unwelcome visitors come near. There also could be traps, appearing like natural "vines" which act as snares. All would be designed to maintain the security of "The camp".

The religious elements throughout this quatrain represent one last element that should be interpreted. The main theme offered the "virgin pure", as the woman who sacrificed her own desires to bring the human gift of God into this world. Line two offered the Greek word, written by Matthew, as uttered

---

found calculated on the website: findlocalweather.com

by the resurrected Christ ("*Ethne*"). He instructed the disciples to go to all the "Nations", meaning "of Gentiles", to convert humanity to belief in the one God. As such, Christ is the "great conduit" of peace and love, by which the world will never grow tired. The use of "vines" then brings in Christian symbolism, as "vines" are represent the "necessary connectedness of the Christian to Christ."[9]

The use of symbolic words shows how "The army lodged" is because "of Gentile nations Not" truly accepting the "great conduit" to Heaven. Thus, those "Ethnic groups" are "Not" connected Christians, acting with Christ in their hearts. This lack of "vine" caretaking has people "hidden", with "teeth" ready to be "hurtful". It says the "North" will have "darts flown" at them, for their failure to represent Christianity truly. The "North" calls itself "great", as though it has been blessed by God, but line four says they are nothing but a "line of curs", who have "filthily used" Christianity to steal from others.

To summarize this quatrain's information, the bullet presentation shows:

1. An important "army lodging" is the initial focus of the main theme, as "THE camp".
2. This "camp" is "of the temple", and/or "from the church', as well as being "to them" of the "army lodged", they are a building dedicated to religious practices.
3. Logistically, "The camp" is near a "church" dedicated "to the virgin", which is sanctified as "pure" and holy.
4. The "virgin" is one known to have come "to there", a land "of Gentile nations", with Jewish settlements near the "Pyrenees".[10]
5. The location of "The army lodged" places them strategically "Not removed far away" from those "of 'told of the Gospel' nations".
6. These "non-Jewish, Christian nations" are "put far away" from the principles of Christ, as demonstrated by their "Not pure" actions.
7. The important focal point of "The army lodged" is the "mountains", and specifically those "Not set far away" from the "Pyrenees Mountains".

---

9   Wikipedia article on "Christian Symbolism".
10   The legend behind the naming of the southern France commune, *Sainctes-Maries-de-la-Mer*, must be seen as connected to the naming of a basilica in Barcelona, *Santa Maria de la Mar*. Both places surround the "*Pyrenees*", along the Mediterranean Sea coast.

8. This important "army lodged" in the "Pyrenees" is home to an important "Him", who has "led" soldiers to "there", from the "east".
9. The soldiers are "male", and have come to inflict "hurt and harm" upon their enemy.
10. This "army lodged" by "Him", who is "mighty" [alternate translation of '*great*'], "is hidden" from view, although their numbers are 'dense".
11. This "great army" will become a "conduit" that will be "destructive there", towards those seen as "with Paganism guiding" them.
12. "THE army lodged Not removed far away" from their enemies will use that close proximity to "violently sent forth" to the "North flows" of "destructively harmful darts".
13. These "cast" object will be like "vines" that are leashed to "rudely handled" beasts.
14. This "army lodged" will keep "concealed" these "biting" weapons through "vine leaf" camouflage netting, or naturally wild "grapevines", as well as use of "mountain curs", all of which will defend their "secret" lairs.
15. All of the anger that brings "THE army led" by "Him powerful" will be due to those "of Ethnic groups" not maintaining their connections to Christ.

Afterthoughts: This quatrain is one where it is important to see the religious thread underlying. The "virgin" can be seen as the Virgin Mary, but that figure from the New Testament did not arrive in coastal France, on a rudderless raft. The Saints Mary - Mary Magdalene, Mary Jacobe, and Mary Salome - should be seen as models of the "virgin" mother of Jesus. The trio are "vestal," as defined by the terms "chaste, clean, decent, immaculate, modest, pure, virgin, virginal." None of those terms are relative to the sexuality of the women, as they had all been reborn in the name of Jesus Christ, just as had been all the Apostles and followers of Jesus.

This realization makes the coastal area of southern France, at the mouth of the Petite Rhone be the point of focus in the main theme: Saints-Marys-of-the-Sea, in the Camargue. Still, those original figures began the true origin of Christianity in Europe, which would lead to that area being populated by people who were called "Cathars." The root word for that name is "New Latin, from Greek *katharsis*, from *kathairein* to cleanse, purge, from *katharos*."[11] The Cathar County is that area surrounding the Aude River.

---

11 Merriam-Webster.

This can then be seen in the secondary theme, where the influx of true Christians blended with the Gentiles of Gaul, living separately, but not far removed from one another. Much of the lore of the first saints (men and women on the raft) who settled there became sought by the indigenous people when troubling times brought them fear. By the time the twelfth century came, the Gentiles had become a mixture of forced Roman Catholics, Cathars, Jews, and Moors. The first Inquisition was a campaign by Rome, in league with the King of France, to annihilate the Cathars for refusing to convert; and, once that genocide was successful, the French Inquisition forced out the Jews and the Moors. Still, the place where the three pure women landed and the place called Cathar Country still in a "temple" where the people of that area have not forgotten.

When the terms of line four are then examined, *"getés fluves"* or "cast out rivers" can be seen as the floods that sent the Gentiles the Church of Rome did not want out of France. The symbolism of that is how the River Rhone sweeps soil out to sea, which gathers in the swampy land of the Camargue. Still, that is where the "vine" of true Christianity was planted and grew into a vineyard of faithful; all near to the Pyrenees Mountains.

The value of Osama bin Laden being allowed to stay in those mountains and plot the demise of the Christian West is he was totally committed to being an instrument that planned to begin a Holy War. His motivations are centered on the Moors being "cast out rivers" of people, but the whole theme of the story line of *The Prophecies* is the peoples around the world who have similar histories, also being cast out by those with bigger swords and a willingness to kill in the name of their gods. The Basque, the Catalans, the Muslims, the Eastern Europeans, and the Africans have all bent a knee to the European overlords historically. While the same feelings of oppression are felt around the globe, the Communist Russians and Chinese do not put up with it, like Western nations do. That makes allowing Osama bin Laden to find peace and quite in a perfect environment the greatest reason why someone should seriously investigate that region.

Chapter 14
Prosecution Exhibit J

For Death One Will Go To The Monts Pyrenees

The fourth of the five quatrains that state *"monts Pyrenees"* in the secondary theme line can be shown as stating (simply translated):

Par mort la France prendra voyage à faire,	By reason of dead there France will embrace journey in to act,
Classe par mer, marcher monts Pyrenées,	Fleet on sea, footing mountains Pyrenees,
Espaigne en trouble, marcher gent militaire:	Spain upon sedition, to march nation soldier-like:
Des plus grand Dames en France emmenées.	To them more great From-soul ones into France fetched unto ones.

This quatrain is primarily one taking the reader to another part of the puzzle, which borders on the aspect of Osama bin Laden going to the "Pyrenees Mountains" to hide in protective safety, planning a major offensive against the West. This quatrain is placing focus on what will take place before the eve of a surprise invasion upon Europe. Prior to that planned attack, Europe will begin to panic. The nations of Europe will realize a serious error has been made by having let down their guard. The secondary theme states that at the time of Europe taking action, it will be too little, too late. The stronghold in those "mountains Pyrenees" will have long been secured.

Due to the futuristic nature of the information this quatrain holds, most of the lines do not play a significant role as evidence that Osama bin Laden is in the "mountains" along the France-Spain border. The importance of this whole quatrain is that it acts as evidence of the motivation for that presence. It shows how Osama bin Laden did not choose the "Pyrenees Mountains" simply because it was a safe place to heal and tape audio and video threats. This quatrain shows Osama bin Laden is in those "mountains" to establish a strategic command center. Once his plan of action begins, he will be at the front to coordinate the moves.

I will do a full interpretation of this quatrain. It is important to see what will be happening before it becomes absolutely too late to prevent a coming war. There are other quatrains that develop the story line of fear waking up Western Europe, which has been referred to as "sleeping" (*"duero"* = "she sleeps"). By touching on the highlights of each line, I will assist one in seeing how the European guard will be let down. The lack of a sense of urgency to secure against a domestic threat will have aided bin Laden's presence among those "great ones."

Beginning the interpretation again with the secondary theme, one finds it stating, "Fleet – on – sea – , – to proceed – mountains – Pyrenees". As one can see from the presence of mid-line punctuation (a comma) this is a theme with two parts. This means the second part can be seen as subsequent in time to the first.

The important initial focus is placed upon the capitalized word *"Classe"*. In French, this word means "a rank, order, or distribution of people according to their several degrees; in schools (wherein this word is most used) a form, or lecture restrained unto a certain company of scholars, or auditors." This meaning makes it appear this secondary theme is beginning with an important "Classification", which would then be seen as relative to some information presented in the main theme. However, this is not the primary translation intended.

The word *"Classe"* is rooted in the Latin word *"Classis,"* which is the root for the French version, as it too means "a group as summoned, a division, class." The primary meaning comes from seeing the Latin word also bearing the meaning, "the armed forces, especially a fleet." This is where the secondary theme is found to be focused, as an important statement about a "Fleet", which makes the main theme take on greater meaning. The capitalization elevates this *"Classe"* to the level of being a recognized "Fleet" of warships, as would be assembled by a nation. The use of Latin is also a hint as to where the "Fleet" is going. The implication is to Italy, where Rome is the home center for Latin. The singular number makes this word indicate one important nation's "Fleet". That nation is identified in the main theme line as "*France*".

In reference to the translation as Latin-based, the translation of "*Classe*" as relative to "*Classis*" is like another word we have discussed. That word is "*copie*", which has been shown to be rooted in the Latin translation that mean, "supplies, provisions, troops, and/or forces". In both cases, the French version was not commonly associated to those military meanings. Because one has to go to Latin to find the best applicable use, which activates the surrounding words in a context of warfare, the system of Nostradamus leads one to look for a higher (religious) meaning as the purpose for those words being selected. This is because Latin is the language of the Church of Rome and in turn Christianity. Seeing this connection to Latin words of warfare becomes significant, especially when the theme of The Prophecies is an unholy Holy War (Armageddon).

This use of "*Classe*" means the initial action that will take place, in the secondary theme, is the "French navy" will travel "by sea" (from the following words, "*par mer*"), as the "Fleet" will be "on" a "sea". Certainly, the use of "*mer*" could make this half statement mean any "sea" in the world, even an ocean, as "at sea" generally means to "set sail on the water." However, as a secondary theme statement, relative to the main theme focus set on "France", one would have reason to see the "French Fleet on" a "sea" with which "France" shared a coastline. The choices, in that scenario, would be the North Sea, the Ligurian Sea, or the Mediterranean Sea. By seeing the use of Latin as giving an Italian bearing, the most likely "sea" is then one around Italy.

An inference of this nature has reason to be considered seriously. That reason is the quatrain that stated "by sea Tyrrhenian enclosed" in its main theme. The same words, "*par mer*" were stated in that quatrain. With the Tyrrhenian Sea being the body of water one would have to sail to reach Rome, one can make that leap in judgment by linking the two quatrains together. Without being a direct statement about Italy, this quatrain's use of "*Classe*" as "Fleet", from the language of Rome, leads one to get a feel for that destination. By seeing the link to a quatrain that makes a direct statement, "by sea Tyrrhenian", such an idea here is justified. Clues of this nature are how one is assisted to reach logical conclusions about the meaning in *The Prophecies*.

Confirmation of which "sea" the "Fleet" will sail is assisted by the next word in line two, which is *"marcher"*. This word *"marcher"*, according to the 1611 Old French-Old English dictionary, can bear the same meaning as the word *"marchiser"*. The word *"marchiser"* meant, "to border, to adjoin, or to lie so near each other that one touches another; to abut, and/or to bound one on another." While a comma does separate *"mer"* from *"marcher"*, one cannot help but realize the "Fleet on sea" is sailing a "sea adjoining France".

That acceptable meaning acts to confirm a "sea" relative to "France", but it primarily acts to show that a major "Fleet" has been prepared to set sail, loaded with foot soldiers, who are "to march" upon the ground of their destination. As such, the "Fleet" is "to proceed" to a point of military activity. The comma then introduces the subsequent phase of a "Fleet" being sent to "sea", which is "to go, walk, pace, step, tread, and/or to foot it." This strongly implies a foreign landing, in a land that is not "France". In that regard, one must see how "by sea and to march" (where the comma acts as a conjunction) can mean going to the same place by two modes of travel. Italy and Spain are the only two places the French would have reason to sail and march troops, both going to the same place separately.

When one remembers the two quatrains that stated, *"Par mer & terre"*, *"Par terre & mer"*, along with the one stating *"par mer Tyrrene close"*, one sees this is not the first reference to travelling "by sea". It brings focus to the main theme that stated, "Close by to them she sleeps [a reference to Spain] by sea Tyrrhenian enclosed [a reference to Italy]". It becomes clear now that travel to Spain is over "land", while travel to Italy is "by sea", through this quatrain's secondary theme's divided statement. Thus, the secondary theme is stating that *"France"* will first sail troops to Italy (referencing *"par mer Tyrrene close"*), in defense of Rome (the use of Latin). Then, following that *"voyage"* (pulled from the main theme), there will be land troop movements ("to march") toward the "mountains" of Spain, along and leading up to the border in the "Pyrenees Mountains".

Once one sees this meaning in the secondary theme, the third line clarifies that *"marcher monts Pyrenees"* is on the Spanish side of those "mountains". It does this by emphasizing "Spain" (from the capitalization of *"Espaigne"* as the first word). That then follows by saying "Spain" is "in trouble". This takes the focus of a "voyage" (from the main theme line) on the Mediterranean Sea and means "France" is not focused on its side of the "Pyrenees". It implies difficulties "marching" troops from "France" to "Spain", as line three can state how it would indeed be "troublesome to march military" personnel there (from line three stating, "*trouble, marcher gent militaire*"). However, line three, like line two, is separated in the middle by a comma, which makes the "trouble in Spain" be prior to the "march" of "people warlike" (alternate translation of "*gent militaire*").

The second half of the secondary theme thus becomes relative to the second half of the supporting details of line three. As such, "to march mountain ones Pyrenees" is precedent and relative to "adjoining people soldier-like" (alternate translation of "*marchiser*", present participle). In between those statements one sees that "Spain", importantly (capitalization) has fallen "upon sedition" (alternative translation of "*trouble*"). This acts to explain the kind of "trouble Spain is in".

This means that "Spain" has played an important role, as has another "great one" of Europe, "France". Unlike "France", "Spain" is unable "to march" because of "paramilitary" groups, or "citizens armed" (from "people" being "military like"). This means that the "mountains" targeted include the "Pyrenees Mountains", but not exclusively. Since most of the "Pyrenees" are on the Spanish side, "Spain" will be chosen "to march" to the "mountains" about the "Pyrenees", with its national troops. As that action is planned, "France" will send its "Fleet on sea" to another location where "mounts, hills, and mountains" are an important feature necessary "to step" upon.

All of this information then forces one to look at the main theme line, to see how all of this relates to that theme. The first line can be seen to read, "By reason of – death – there – France – to embrace – journey – with – to commit". In this way, one can see a progression of cause and effects that sets up the whole quatrain. It immediately shows the importance of "Reason" (from "*Par*" meaning "By reason of") that a "Fleet" and foot soldiers will need to respond militarily. It shows how two will be called upon to agree to act in unison (from the preposition "*à*" being read as "with"), via a commitment made to show strength "by land AND sea".

The motivation is shown to be due to a summit in "France" (from "*là France*" meaning "there France"), relative to some "death" (from "*mort*") that either took place "there" or more likely affected them by "death" elsewhere. This aspect can be seen as viable through the news of kidnapped French miners in Nigeria having had an affect "there" in "France". Thus, "Through" (alternate translation of "*Par*") some act that resulted in "death" or "dead" people from "France" (from "*la France*" also simply meaning "France"), a decision would be decided upon in "France", as to what actions "will be undertaken".

The secondary theme and third line each having two halves represents two separate directions of action, related to the main theme. Thus, two separate entities would be required "to commit" and "to act" militarily. A summit in "France" would indicate "France" to be one of the two; and, the naming of "Spain" in line three shows who the other committed party will be. These two will be sent on "journeys" to prevent, intercede, and/or encounter a danger that will have resulted in "dead" or a significant action "Of death" (alternate translation of "*Par mort*").

The fact that "Spain" will have "trouble", by attempting "to set foot on" (alternate translation of "*marcher*") the "mountains" leading to hostile areas of the "Pyrenees", is evidence that a preexisting force was there beforehand. Movements by the Spanish military, on their own soil, towards their own citizens, would then act to cause "sedition". The statement of "people joining near together" (from "*marcher*" sharing the meaning of "*marchiser*"), becomes relevant to the information in the last quatrain discussed.

There, one read about an "army lodged" (from the main theme) in the "Pyrenees" (in the secondary theme), which was kept "hidden" (from the third line). Here, the reader is shown the circumstances that existed prior to the Spanish government's troops going in to secure a situation they would not be prepared for. Therefore, "Spain" is "stopped" (from "*troublé,*" past participle of the verb "*troubler*") cold in its tracks.

This statement in line three confirms that the regions along the "*Pyrenees*" will have been building an "army" of "folks" ("*gent militaire*"), who are of "kindred" spirits (alternate translation of "*gent*"). Those "people" will be willing to go to war against the "great" (from "*grand*" in line four, as well in other quatrains). Likewise, those "people" will be willing to be killed, "For death" (from "*Par mort*") to come to those who lord over them.

The last line is one with a degree of difficulty to interpret, due to the use of the word "*Dames*". This word is clean French, as the plural number added to the word "*dame,*" meaning "lady, mistress, and/or dame". The capitalization gives the word a royal or aristocratic air, as a proper title. This, however, is misleading, and that is part of the reason why this quatrain has been kept safe from a correct interpretation for centuries.[1]

---

1   One could not prove Osama bin Laden hiding in the Pyrenees before he was

The answer to how to read *"Dames"* correctly is to insert an apostrophe, such that it becomes *"D'ames"*. This is like one having the ability to accent an unaccented letter, as the system that allows this is based on the presence of many words found in *The Prophecies* that are obviously contracted words but are simply missing the apostrophe. This slight adjustment makes an important (capitalization) contraction appear, of the preposition *"De"* added to the plural of the word *"ame"*. The word *"ame"* means, "the soul, or spirit; also, a spirit, or ghost; also, the mould that is within the bore of artillery when it is cast." Thus, this becomes readable as "Of souls", or when the *"s"* is seen as an indication of the "one of", it can be, "From ones of spirit". This allows one to see meaning from line four, when it states, "To them – more – great – Of spirit ones – into – France – led unto ones."

Line four begins with the capitalized plural form of the preposition *"De"*, where *"les"* is added to make it mean "To them, Of them, With them, and/or From them". The word also can be used simply as stating, "From". Remembering that a word needs to be represented with different uses when it reappears within one quatrain, seeing *"Dames"* as *"De+ames"* means the preposition *"De"* is such a duplicate. Line four now contains two capitalized uses of *"De"*, when *"Dames"* is altered. This means that if the line begins with "From them", then *"D'ames"* will not mean "From spirits". The combination acts to show a "To/From" scenario. Regardless of the directions seen, one must realize how the *"les"* part of *"Des"* is relative to "them", as "France", "Spain", and the "people military".

Seeing that makes line four begin by stating "With them (France and Spain) more great". This means the line is supporting the second half of the secondary theme, while being an example of the second half of line three. It supports the secondary theme by stating the importance of both "France" and "Spain" having mightier numbers of men (and weapons), as "great" nations. They are "more" compared "To ones of spirit", whom "they" ("France" and "Spain") have committed to fight. As a clarification of line three (colon use), it shows that "To them more", as an influx of "people military", through a call to arms, that would make them "more mighty" (alternate translation of *"plus grand"*). That helps explain why "Spain" would be a "great in trouble". The capitalization of *"D'ames"* shows this importance by beginning the next series of words in the line.

When one sees the importance (capitalization) "Of ones of spirit", this becomes born, or had lived a life that would place him there to fulfill a prophecy.

how a smaller foe can challenge a larger one. This capitalized word then becomes an important statement about those in the "mountains", especially in the "Pyrenees" (supporting the second half of the secondary theme). Add this factor to "*D'ames en France*", and it shows an important call out for help, "To (kindred) spirits" that are also "in France". Those "people military-like" will be "in" there awaiting a call to arms. Thus, these are "From souls" willing to join a "kindred military" cause (alternate translation of "*gent militaire*") that is well known, but very secret.

The focus of this quatrain remains on "France" and "Spain", but many other quatrains explain where the "Fleet on sea" is headed, and it is not "Spain" or the "Pyrenees". "Spain" being in "trouble" is just the beginning, as all Western European nations will also have problems to deal with, shortly after the activity of this quatrain plays out. The major piece of evidence as to why Osama bin Laden will be in the "Pyrenees" is he has a master plan for revenge. This quatrain gives hints to that plan being set in motion.

The first word of line one's main theme is "*Par*". That word can translate to state, "By reason of". As a capitalized word, it is making the importance of "Reason" be the first word read. One must be able to see "Reason" as being from one's ability to think; and, thus a motive for planned action. It says the "Cause" of this quatrain is that which led up to this piece of the puzzle. Being followed by the word "death" shows it is a plan to bring something to an end (symbolic meaning of "death"). The word "*mort*" also can be used to mean, "murder", which is a planned act of violence. Thus, the main theme is telling about a planned "Cause", with a planned response that does not upset that plan.

This plan then involved preparing an army "to march", who are hidden in the "mountains" around the "Pyrenees". After the response solicited by a planned "murder", a "Fleet" sets sail and the troops in the "Pyrenees" are mobilized, by plan. This, in turn, is why "Spain" finds itself "in" the midst of a very "unsettled" (alternative translation for "*trouble*") situation.

Finally, those "Of spirit in France" represent willing immigrants, legal or illegal, which will have flooded (from "inundation of kindred humans", used in the letter to Henry II) Europe's free Western nations, in particular "France". This is not happenstance or because of hard times in the Middle East. The rule of a dictator or a war with an invader in their homelands is not why devout Muslims would leave their homes and go to lands where freedom of religion is advertised as a

PROSECUTION EXHIBIT J

good thing. They have flooded Western lands to bring one religion to where it did not exist before. Muslims have been sent to Europe by a *"grand"* master plan.

This plan is confirmed by the last word in line four, which is *"emmenées"*. This word (in the singular past tense) means, "brought, led, and/or fetched unto." The plural makes the statement mean, "those led" to be "in France", and that constitutes a plan. The "Reason" they will have been "fetched ones" will be to bring about "death there" of "France", when the timing of the plan is right. One makes the call to arms; but those "With spirits" to fight are thinking "Of souls" owned by Allah, who has ultimately chosen the one making the plan and the call. That one is Osama bin Laden.

To summarize the elements of this quatrain, which supports the evidence previously given while giving a glimpse of what Osama bin Laden plans for those "great" of Europe, is as follows:

1. The initial focus is on the "Reason of" the events that will follow, showing it to be the result of planning.
2. The element of "death" becomes part of the plan that starts the following activities.
3. The plan includes the objective of "death" of *"la France"*.
4. The topic of some who are "dead" becomes important "there", in "France", possibly due to French citizens having been "killed" elsewhere.
5. This notion of elsewhere is because of the actions "France will take", which is a "voyage".
6. This calls for a plan of "travel" that involves a partner, as someone "with France" will also "embrace" a "journey" they have "to act" upon.
7. One of the parties ("France") will send its "Fleet" of warships "on sea", into the Mediterranean, Adriatic, and/or Aegean Seas.
8. The other party ("Spain") is "to march" troops into the "mountains" of northern "Spain", and into the "Pyrenees Mountains".
9. After the French "Fleet" is at "sea", activity will begin in the "mountains" around the "Pyrenees", "to bound one unto another", as a mobilization of an army waiting for "France" to "commit" to an "action" that will weaken its home defenses.
10. The troops of "Spain" will encounter "trouble".
11. The "action" of the "Spanish military" will have raised the

"people" to "sedition".
12. A "paramilitary" response to the "march" of "Spanish troops" will have the "Spanish stopped".
13. Despite the "Spanish" having "With them more" soldiers, as a "great" nation of Europe, there will go out a call "To souls in France", "there By reason of" responding to the threat of "death", to come to the aid of those in the "Pyrenees".
14. All of the "military-like people" in the "mountains" and "To those" representing "more" mingled with the "great" make a "mighty" number of willing soldiers, all "ones led" by one man.

Afterthoughts: If Osama bin Laden was truly killed on May Day 2011, then that still does not take away from the picture Nostradamus painted, some four hundred sixty-five years ago. The main theme statement in this quatrain placed immediate focus on "death" being the reason for France to set sail. Italy is another land inundated by immigrants, legal and illegal. France has experienced a lot of terrorist acts that have resulted in deaths. Now, the world is facing a pandemic that is currently rising in Europe, in particular Italy and France. This main theme statement says a significant level of death will be the motivation for France to send troops somewhere, if not to Italy.

The presence of so many potential "simple soldiers" in the midst of French, Italian and Spanish cities, looking like poor migrants looking for a helping hand (many from the war in Syria, as of late) makes it impossible to figure out who is coordinating all the terrorism. Simply by announcing Osama bin Laden as dead (and then throwing the body away so no one can verify it independently), the Western world became lost, as to where to get intelligence to fight terrorism.

It makes the nine years he was not killed seem like an intelligent thing to do, as then they would know to hunt where the head of the beast might be. When Saddam Hussein was killed, Iraq no longer was able to counter the power of Iran. When Libyan leader Muammar Gaddafi was killed, floods of illegal immigrants began flowing through Tripoli. Also, when Egyptian leader Hosni Mubarak was taken out, the land was terrorized by the Islamic Brotherhood, until the Egyptian military took control and stopped that. Killing Osama bin Laden would have the same effect, which makes one ask, "Why could Barack Hussein Obama do what George W. Bush or William J. Clinton could not do?"

Maybe they knew it was best to let the leader be the leader, to keep stability?

Chapter 15
Prosecution Exhibit K

Reasonably Beneath Them Mountains Pyrenees

The last of the five quatrains that present the words *"monts Pyrenees"* in the secondary theme can be seen to state (simply translated):

Deux grans freres seront chassés d'Espaigne,	Two great ones brothers will be ones chased from Spain,
L'aisné vaincu soubz les monts Pyrenees:	The eldest put down by reason under them mountains Pyrenees:
Rougir mer, rosne, sang lemam d'Alemaigne	To grow red sea, rose-born, kindred theme with Germany
Narbon, Blyterre, d'Agath. contaminees.	Narbonne, the males of Béziers, the people of Agde contaminated ones.

As a theme statement that places focus on the "Pyrenees" and relative to the presentations so far, of evidence for Osama bin Laden hiding inside the "mountains" there, here we find the word *"soubz"* connected. The word *"soubz"* does not necessarily have a plural ending, as it typically is found spelled with the *"z"* at the end. That spelling is in the 1611 dictionary which translates the word, while also referring the reader to the spelling, *"sous"*. Both spellings mean, "under, beneath, and/or at the bottom of". The spelling with a *"b"*, which has

175

since become unique to Old French, is connected to the Latin root word, "*sub.*" The Latin meaning expands to include, "close under, at the foot of; in the power of; under cover of; the underside of, and/or down under."

If the "*z*" is seen to be indicating the plural number, then the word can be highlighting the "ones under". In that case, line two is making a statement about the "ones under the mountains" or the "those beneath them". This acts as a continuation of the "hidden", in "Overt veins" themes seen previously, where the "mountains" have been "pierced", with one "descending" a "mountain". This is confirming the theory of an army being housed "under" ground, with preexisting caves and mines known to be in the "Pyrenees".

The important element that leads to "those under mountains" is the capitalized first word, which is a contracted article-noun. That word is "*L'aisné*", which is usually seen as singular in number, as "The eldest". Because the attached article is capitalized, it announces "THE", as a sign of important singularity. The noun "*aisné*" means, "eldest, and/or first born," but it also can be used in a context that allows it to announce the "most ancient, foremost, and/or first in date."

This can act to make the statement that "THE one first in time" to be "beneath" the "mountains". In that regard, the secondary theme acts to repeat the mythology that is behind the name "Pyrenees", as the burial site for the princess Pyrene. The plural indication can then act to show "those under her power", who populated "those mountains". Those have been identified in the letter to Henry II and the first quatrain presented in this summary of evidence referring to them as "*Pyrennees*" ("ones born of Pyrene"). This makes the singular masculine representation of "THE first in history" to populate the "Pyrenees" be the Basque people.

The people of Greek mythology, to whom Pyrene was related, need to be understood. Pyrene was a daughter of a King Bebryx, whom Hercules visited in his travels, in order to complete his tenth quest of "Twelve Labors." King Bebryx ruled over the Bebryces, a mythical tribe of ancient Mediterranean Gaul (known as *Gallia Narbonensis*, in Latin).

In history, the Romans encountered a preexisting culture of people in Iberia and Gaul who were identified as "*barscunes.*" Some believe that word translates to state, "the mountain people,"[1] which would be apt for peoples living around the "mountains". Tests of Basque genetics prove they are the oldest pre-

1 Wikipedia article on "Basque people".

Indoeuropean tribe, with some scholars believing they have existed in Europe for 30,000 years.² The fact that there are Neolithic cave paintings in Basque Country seems to confirm that dating.

Regardless of an argument over who may or may not be the one specific "eldest" in the "Pyrenees Mountains", as multiple tribes are known to have predated the Roman expansion into that area of the world, the general name, "Basque people," represents all of the tribes along both sides of the "Pyrenees". They, collectively, are "THE first born" of the "mountains Pyrenees". This means the contracted "*L*" can represent "*Les aisné*", becoming the plural statement of "Them eldest".

The verb of the secondary theme is "*vaincu*", which is the past participle of "*vaincre,*" and means "vanquished, overcome, subdued, foiled, overmastered, surmounted; and also, convinced by reason, and/or put down in reasoning." This word controls how the secondary theme is read. With the following word being "vanquished", the secondary theme shows "The eldest" as having been "overcome". The past tense gives the implication of one coming later in time, after "The first born". This fits the concept of the Roman and Carthaginian conquests of the Iberian Peninsula; and later still, the formations of France and Spain. In these scenarios, those indigenous tribes became "overmastered" by larger and stronger forces.

This translation of "*vaincu*" makes it easier to see "under, beneath, and/or at the bottom of" as being a condition of subservience and domination, due to having been "surmounted". This word, especially when the "*z*" of "*soubz*" is seen to turn the meaning into the "ones under", states the yoke of a greater power. It shows how the need for a separate identity has kept "The first born" from blending in with those who "vanquished" it (or them). By not adjusting to this situation, a classification has kept "The eldest ones beneath" the larger class; and thus, they are seen as the least valuable segment of a larger society.

This is the plight of the Basque People, who have long sought to have their own autonomy, as a self-governed nation. The Wikipedia article on the "Basque people" states, "a significant part of Basque society are still attempting higher degrees of self-empowerment (see Basque nationalism), sometimes by acts of violence."³ This is directly related to them being "under" those who have "subdued" them. It also brings in the other meaning of "*vaincu*", as the violence

---

2   Wikipedia article on "History of the Basque people".
3   Wikipedia article, "Basque people".

of Basque nationalism is a result of having been "put down in reasoning". Neither the French, nor the Spanish (primarily the Spanish), have been willing to listen to the "reasoning" of the Basque, to the point that extremists have resorted to violent measures to get one's attention to a matter that has become unreasonable.

This is the same situation for many "overmastered" peoples around the world. The Irish Republican Army (I.R.A.) is a result of the English refusing to listen to any reasonable argument that is designed to allow Northern Ireland to be one with Ireland, as it was before the English took that land by force. India long desired its independence from Great Britain, before it was reluctantly granted, at a time when the British had been weakened by a global war. The American Revolution was fought for such independence. Tibet has been a government in exile for sixty years, due to the Red Chinese forcing their will upon the Tibetan people. However, the most pertinent parallel example of "vanquished" people being the "ones under", which is relative to the story line of the "Pyrenees Mountains", is that of Palestine.

The nation that was Palestine existed, in some size or name, deep into antiquity, including when it was generally known as the "land of the Philistines." Egyptian records name the land between Egypt and Greece as "the land of the Philistines." The area of land along the Mediterranean Sea coast (in particular Gaza) was part of the land of Canaan. The Philistines often dominated the Canaanites, with this condition continuing well after God had led the children of Israel to Canaan, their "Promised Land." In addition, after the vast majority of Jews had been forced from the Middle East (beginning with the fall of Israel to the Assyrians), the land named Palestine arose as a vassal under the Ottoman Empire. This is the way it was when Nostradamus lived. Much later, the nation of Israel returned, which forced the Palestinians into lesser land, with second-class status. For this reason, Palestine is another example of "The eldest born vanquished ones under them".

The question as to who came first thus goes to the origin of Arabs and Jews. Since both are known to be children of Abraham, Ishmael was "The first born" to him. The birth of his second child, Isaac, came to Abraham's first wife, Sarah, through a miracle of God. Ishmael was born to Hagar, who had been given to Abraham by the pharaoh of Egypt. Ishmael was banished by Abraham, as he was "put down by reason", based on the actions of Ishmael towards Isaac. With Hagar and Ishmael about to go "under" in the dessert, an angel (*halak elohim* - messenger of god) saved them by the miraculous appearance of a well of water. The angel told Hagar, "Lift the boy up and take him by the hand, for I will make him into a great nation."

This story makes the Palestinian descendants of Ishmael "The eldest" who were "put down in reason" by Zionist Jews' cunning and bribing. Returning to the land their ancestors had lost long before, with no way to use force to take it back, could only be accomplished through "reasoning". Their opening came when the Ottoman Empire accepted defeat at the end of World War I. Before thirty years had passed, they were able to put Palestine "beneath" Jewish feet. Once in control of Palestinian land, nothing the Palestinians said would matter, as all arguments have routinely been "put down in reasoning".

When one sees how the secondary theme stands alone to project all of this history, it is possible to draw it into the theme of Osama bin Laden hiding in the "Pyrenees". The reader is able to see "The eldest" as both the Basque people and the supporters of Palestine. Both of these groups plot violent ways to respond to those who will not listen to "reason", and together they will have placed the "mountains under" their control. An army of troops will be protected "beneath" the surface of the "mountains" of the "Pyrenees".

When this secondary theme is digested in this manner, one can look at the main theme line with a fresh set of eyes. The line can be read as (simply translated), "Two – great ones – brothers – will be – chased ones – from Spain". The immediate tendency that the wording brings to mind is "Two brothers", who are in some way related "to Spain". When one is looking for "Two brothers", seeing "The eldest" makes this quatrain appear to be about "Two" important individuals. However, that misdirection keeps this quatrain from easily being solved.

As one can see, "Two brothers" can equate to Ishmael and Isaac; but to get that view, the word between "Two" and "brothers" has to be overlooked, or seen as a superlative adjective. That is never the case in *The Prophecies*. That middle word is "*grans*", which has been seen several times now. It means, "great ones", and, the word "great" is always associated with a nation of tremendous power, wealth, and influence over the world. This means the main theme is initially placing focus on an important "Two" (capitalization), with those "Both" (alternative translation of "*Deux*") being "great nations". As "great ones", they are "brothers".

At this point, one needs to be aware of the translation possibilities for the word "*freres*". In the singular number, "*frere*" means, "a brother; and also, a friar." When seen in this light, one is able to see a Christian connotation, where "brothers" means, "those of the same religion." All of Europe has a history of being Christian, such that all European nations are "brothers" by sharing the same God, the Father.

This then makes "Two" an important number, which was emphasized in the last quatrain discussed. There, France and Spain were "to commit" to take action, because some "death" would have previously occurred. In fact, it was discussed that "By reason of death there France will take voyage" and they would act "with Spain", as both were seen "to act". The main theme of this quatrain is thus making "France" and "Spain" those "Two great ones", who would be "brothers" in religious beliefs, as well as in their oaths of commitment.

This distinction of "brothers" is then seen "being" focused on "chased ones", with a goal "being" to have the "pursued ones" sent out "of Spain". With this matching the commitment made by "France" and "Spain", where troops were "to march" to the "mountains" of the "Pyrenees", such as they will have "chased ones" that have come "to Spain", the opposite is also true. In the last quatrain, where it stated, "Spain in trouble", this quatrain shows the "brothers being chased ones", in particular those "brothers of Spain". This main theme statement explains the third line of the last quatrain and then leads us to the secondary theme of this quatrain, which tells of a hidden danger in the "mountains".

The secondary theme of this quatrain ends with a colon, making line three become a clarification of "The eldest vanquished under them mountains Pyrenees". Line three also, as the place for finding supporting details to the main theme, explains the "brothers being chased ones of Spain". This clarification and explanation is shown to be in three stages, due to the placement of two mid-line commas, stating, "*Rougir mer,*" "*rosne,*" and "*sang leman d'Alemaigne*".

The first stage is set up by the capitalized infinitive verb, "*Rougir*", which means, "To blush, and/or To redden". One must be able to see the symbolic nature of blushing, based on the emotionally connected physical appearance of redness in a face. While embarrassment is one reason for one "To blush", another is anger. In this sense, one importantly (capitalization) is flushed with anger.

When the meaning is seen as "To redden", this is the act of making something take on the color of red, with red not being the natural state. As such, the spillage of blood becomes the addition of the color red on a uniform, which was not red before. In all, this symbolism can show the major "Embarrassment" felt by the "Spanish", as well as the emotional "Anger" of those in the "Pyrenees", causing them to respond with warfare.

One of the systems of Nostradamus must be explained at this point. It refers to the use of color in the verbiage of the quatrains and letters. Three basic colors are often repeated, which are "white", "black", and "red." Nostradamus also used the word "yellow", which fits the same model; but that word was used rarely. All of these colors are symbolic of a level of religious belief and this is how they must be read for stand-alone meaning to come forth. As such, "yellow" represents the polytheistic eastern religions, "white" represents Christianity, "black" represents Islam, and "red" represents atheism. The use of "red" to symbolize communism (as Red Chinese and Russian Reds) is matched in the use of *"rouge"*, throughout *The Prophecies*.

In this light, the capitalization of *"Rougir"* becomes an important statement of someone changing from one religious belief, "To no religion" believed. For those who may have been converted to Christianity, as would be the case for all classified as *"d'Ethne"* (as "to Gentiles" taught the Gospel); they would not be limited by a belief system that punishes those who break the Commandments, such as killing from "Anger" would do. Thus, this word of importance is clarifying those of the "Pyrenees" and supporting those "of Spain" doing the chasing.

The second word, of a two-word first stage, is then *"mer"*, which only means, "sea". This should bring back memories of the quatrains that had "sea" surrounding an ampersand, along with "land". The last quatrain's secondary theme began with the importance (capitalization) of a "Fleet on sea". This was seen as the French "Fleet", but this quatrain is giving information that comes after that sailing of their "Fleet", so that the French have reached their objective by the timing of this quatrain. Now, the clarification of "The elder" can be seen differently, where Osama bin Laden is "The eldest" who has come to "vanquish beneath them" those attacking the "mountain ones" in the "Pyrenees". "The elder", or "The Arabian king", or the "One against", or "One king", or "the conductor of the army" (all terms used in past quatrains) will make the call "To redden" the Mediterranean "sea".

Some have seen this as drawing so much blood in warfare that the "sea blushes red"; instead, it means a call upon the allies of the Muslims, who are communist

181

("reds") and have their own "Fleet" of ships which are committed to assist in the invasion of Western Europe. Therefore, "To redden sea" is supporting the theme "of Spain" being the "ones chased", not only by the "mountain ones" but also by "sea", through mobilized troops being carried on Eastern European ships. Further, the troops need not be seen as being non-Muslim (figuratively "Red"), as Morocco and Tunisia ("Two" North African "brothers") have flags that are predominately "red", in the literal sense.

The second part of line three is a one-word statement, *"rosne"*. We have seen this spelling before, as an Occitan-Provencal spelling for the Rhone River; and, I have pointed out how this could become *"n'Rose"*, as "Rose-born". This word acts the same here but without the importance that capitalization brings, being presented now in the lower-case. In this regard, a "rose" must be seen as most often "red". Without the religious symbolism (capitalization raising a word to a higher meaning), a "born rose" would be an opened flower. As a flower of many petals, a rosebud expands with maturity; this then symbolizes an out flowing of heartfelt emotion, of which "To redden" would be "To anger". In this scenario, roses also have stems with thorns and crowns made from those stems could be figuratively applied to the "great ones", causing them to panic and run. To "The elder", seeing the "sea Redden" would be a sight of beauty, as the bud of a plan would open and spread wide.

The third part of line three states, *"sang lemam d'Alemaigne"*. This can be read as, "kindred theme with Germany". The key to this reading is the word *"lemam"*. The earliest edition with this quatrain in print shows *"lema"*, with the *"a"* having a wavy bar above it, as a printer's indication of abbreviation, meaning an *"m"* or *"n"* should be added. Most people read this as *"leman"*, which is the original Latin name for Lake Geneva, as *"Lacus Lemanus"*, which the French continue as *Lac Léman*.

The problem with that translation is twofold. First, the word is not capitalized, as would be a proper name. In the lower case, the meaning for the name would be its meaning as *"leman"*, such that Lake Geneva itself would not be a necessary focal point. This meaning is uncertain; the French believe the root comes from the Celtic language.

The second problem arises when one sees the 1568 edition of *The Prophecies* (which I believe is the accurate copy from which to proceed), and finds the unabbreviated word is shown as *"lemam"*, not *"leman"*. The people "of Spain" do have a word *"lema"*, which is from the Latin word *"lemma"*. The Latin word *"lemma"* makes *"lemam"* a perfect simple anagram; and, simple anagrams are one of the systems of Nostradamus. The anagram is moving the last *"m"* in front of the next to last letter, *"a."* Thus, the Spanish word *"lema"*, and/or the Latin word *"lemma"*, can be expected to make sense of this third stage in line three.

Wiktionary lists the Spanish noun *"lema"* as meaning, "motto; subject; headword, term, title; and as the Latin *"lemma."* The Latin word *"lemma"* means, "theme, title; an epigram."[4] As such, the meaning becomes "theme"; and, following the word *"sang"* means, a "kindred theme". This is the theme discussed here, about the collecting of Islamic "blood" in Western Europe for the purpose ("theme") of spilling Western European "blood".

When the last word (a contracted preposition-proper noun), *"d'Alemaigne"* is read as "with Germany", or "to Germany", one sees how the call of arms, by "The elder" in the "Pyrenees" goes out to all of his "race" in Europe, as far away as "Germany". This is commonly known to be a problem (rising Muslim immigration) in all of Western Europe, with "Germany" included. Thus, the third stage is the mobilization of Islamic forces embedded throughout all of Western Europe, including all of the "Germanic" nations. This then indicates the "German" element in Switzerland (on a secondary level), by seeing *"lemam"* as *Leman*.

In this regard, line three does not end with any punctuation, such that this Islamic call to readiness is continued into line four. Line four is where the supporting details to the secondary theme are found. With the main theme focusing on "brothers" (a term relative to "blood", thus "kin"), who "will be following ones" (alternated translation of *"chasse"*, as the present participle) "of Spain", the supporting details of line three show this being expanded to North Africa, blossoming fully open, until all Islamic "lineage" as far as "Germany" have been reached. Thus, with the secondary theme being relative to "those under the mountains", line four is adding to that meaning, listing three places in the shadow of the *"Pyrenees"*.

Again, seeing how each line following the colon at the end of line two becomes either an example or a clarification of that theme, line four is not so much

---

4   The Free Dictionary by Farlex shows "epigram" as meaning, "A short, witty poem expressing a single thought or observation; A concise, clever, often paradoxical statement."

chronological stages, as it is a list of examples, each separated by a comma. All examples are capitalized to show the level of importance they represent, as a continuation of the "born rose" of emotion, from an "Anger risen", to a "race" focused on one "subject", as far away "from Spain" as those mingled among those of the "Germanic race".

Line four lists three southern France communes, as being "Narbonne, Béziers, and Agde". As evidence for Osama bin Laden being in hiding in the "*Pyrenees*", it is not necessary for me to delve deeply into how "*Blyterre, d'Agath.*" (with "*Agath.*" seen as abbreviated) becomes "the males of Béziers," and "to the people of Agde". The important aspect is the capitalized first word, "*Narbon*", which has been seen previously.

I discussed the secondary theme of a prior quatrain which stated (simple translation), "In War Narbonne not will make resistance". While there were several ways to read those words, as a whole it clearly states that the people of "Narbonne will be" put in a position of refusing to fight. I have also stated in the analysis of this quatrain that ancient Mediterranean Gaul was known, in Latin, as *Gallia Narbonensis*. This was because the Romans initially founded the *Colonia Narbo Martius*, which became the capital of the southern region of Gaul that took its name.

This Latin history acts to link "*Narbon*" (line four) to "*lemam*" (as "*lemma*"), the Latin word of line three. Thus, "*Narbon*" has the importance of being the capital (main "theme") of a wider region where Muslims will find refuge. From that understanding, one can see the significance of "Narbonne" being in the French department of Aude, while both "Béziers" and "Agde" are in the neighboring department of Hérault. This area is the old French region known as Languedoc, which is today called Languedoc-Roussillon. This distinction of "Narbonne" being "The eldest" shows how it is an important seat from which "The elder" in the "mountains" operates.

The key word of action in line four comes from the pluralized past participle "*contaminée-s*". The root verb, "*contaminer*", means, "to defile, to pollute, to contaminate; to stain, to disdain, to violate." Thus, the addition of an "*s*" makes this mean the "ones contaminated, defiled, polluted, stained, and/or violated". The word "pollute" means, "To make unfit for or harmful to living things; to make less suitable for an activity, especially by the introduction of unwanted factors;

and to render impure or morally harmful; corrupt."[5] As such, the last example of line four makes the statement that, "the people of Agde [will be] contaminated" by the incorporation of harmful unwanted factors, who "will make resistance not" to Muslims, but to French authorities. The call from "The eldest" will be heard by "those harmful factors" already in place in southern France.

When one sees line three beginning with the capitalized verb, "*Rougir*", meaning, "To redden", the action of "*contaminées*" is then seen as "stained red ones". When the use of color is implied in this meaning, one sees "the people of Agde" as being "contaminated" by a lack of religious beliefs. As such, the Greek etymological root for the commune's name, "*Agathe,*" means, "Good." Nostradamus, through his use of color, depicts "white" as representing Christianity, with that color symbolizing "purity and goodness." This acts to make the last statement imply "the people of Goodness [are] stained ones." They have been "born rose red", thus unlikely to "resist" in a war between Muslims (blacks) and Christians (whites).

This quatrain adds greater depth to the cause for Osama bin Laden being in the "Pyrenees Mountains". It calls him "The elder", and connects that title to a plan that will have the "Two great ones vanquished under them". The central location of those "mountains" will reach south to North Africa, northeast to central Europe, and within the shadow of the "*Pyrenees*" to the ancient region of *Gallia Narbonensis*, where French Christians will be "contaminated" by Muslims called to a Holy War.

In summary of the key elements of this quatrain, the bullet point breakdown is:

1. The main theme is about "Two great ones" of importance, with one named as "of Spain".
2. The use of "brothers" brings a religious meaning to the main theme, identifying the "Two great ones" as Christian nations.
3. Due to the state of "being" Christian, the "Two great ones will be hunted ones".
4. The activities of Christian nations, as "brothers being great ones", will have "driven away ones to Spain".
5. Those with the distinction of being "The first born" civilization "of

---

5   Fair Use – The word "pollute" is commonly defined as the above, which was stated by the Free Dictionary by Farlex, utilizing The American Heritage Dictionary of the English Language.

Spain" are the tribes who can be called Basque people.
6. The Basque people have been "vanquished" by the governments "of Spain", and "put down in reasoning" as to being granted independence.
7. The religious theme of "brothers", where "The oldest" was "driven away", places focus on Ishmael and Isaac, the sons of Abraham.
8. The people of Ishmael, as Palestinian Arabs, have been "vanquished" from Palestine, and the Zionists who influence the Christian West have "put down in reasoning" the Arab claim of their land being stolen.
9. One who is importantly seen as "The elder", who has been "overcome" in his place of operation, will be "under" the protection of "them" in the "mountains Pyrenees".
10. This one seen as "The first born" to right wrongs for Allah will be "under the mountains" in a system of caves.
11. Those who have been "driven away" will be called upon "To redden" the "sea".
12. The "sea" separates those "of Spain" from North Africa, where two nations of Muslims fly predominately "red" flags.
13. Those who are lacking religious beliefs will act to sell ships to Islamic nations, designed "To bloody" enemy ships at "sea".
14. The mature "born rose" spreads open wide, and symbolizes fullness of emotions.
15. A "theme" of "kinship" tells of "brothers" placed in Western Europe, "from Spain" in the south, "to Germany" in the north.
16. Those in southern France, under the shadow of the "Pyrenees Mountains" will have been mixed with politics "To redden" one's devotion to Christianity and with Muslim males who act to "pollute" the "Goodness" the French people once had.
17. The commune of "Narbonne" is a stronghold of supporters for "The elder", with other southern French communes making a network "under the mountains" of France, who plan to have France "vanquished".

Afterthoughts: Narbonne, Béziers, and Agde are all close to the Mediterranean coastline, with the later two northeast of Narbonne. Carcassonne is slightly northwest of Narbonne; and Carcassonne was in Cathar Country. This makes the "rose born theme" be the pure Christians that originated Christianity in France. The Cathar men were called "*bonhommes*," or "good men."

Chapter 16
Prosecution Exhibit L

To the Pyrenees Without His Luggage

Having presented all of the quatrains that state "*monts Pyrenees*" in the theme statement lines (verses one and two), there are three remaining that make that statement in the third line. Since line three is where the supporting details to the main theme are found and also where the secondary theme is furthered (by example, clarification, or as sequential related events) it becomes important to see how line three's statement of the "Pyrenees Mountains" supports those themes. While line four is not necessary to interpret, it may add relative material that helps understand the premise that Osama bin Laden is hiding in those "mountains".

These last three quatrains all use both key words consecutively and in the same order ("*monts*" followed by "*Pyrenees*"), but they have some special characteristics that set them apart. The differences are relative to capitalization and the spelling of "*Pyrenees*". In this regard, two of the three I am about to introduce have "*Monts*" and "*Pyrenees*" capitalized, with "*Monts*" being the first word of line three. This adds important focus to the word "*Monts*", unlike what has been seen presented thus far. The final difference is in the use of "*Pyrens*", rather than "*Pyrenees*". This is similar to the presentations of "*Pyren-nees*" (in the letter to Henry II) and "*Pyrennees*" in the first quatrain exhibited. This places important focus on the history (or lore) of those "mountains".

The last of these, where Nostradamus wrote, "*monts Pyrens*", will be the first of the line three exhibits presented here for interpretation. That quatrain can be found to read as follows (simple translation):

187

Dessoubz Jonchere du dangereux passage	Beneath Work made of rushes to the dangerous strait
Fera passer le posthume sa bande,	Will act to pass the last born his company of soldiers,
Les monts Pyrens passer hors son bagaige	The mountain ones buried under the Pyrenees to proceed without his baggage
De Parpignam courira duc à tende.	With "Perpignan" will make hostile incursions owl in encamped.

When one looks first at line three, the words "*Les monts Pyrens **passer** hors son bagaige*" include an infinitive verb that is repeated elsewhere in this quatrain. That word is "*passer*", and it has been seen before in the quatrains presented. We first saw it appear in the main theme statement that stated, "*L'Aemathion **passer** montz Pyrennees*". We then found it used in the secondary theme statement that read, "*Pour **passer** outre vers les monts Pyrénées*".

Now it appears in lines two ("*Fera **passer** le posthume sa bande,* ") and three. Three of the four uses found are in the line that also contains the words, "*monts Pyrenees*" (in some spelling). If these four lines were placed in order, as if to compose one new quatrain, it would state (simple translations):

> "The Arabian king **to hold on a course** mountain ones Pyrenees-born ones,
> Because **to depart from** pierced towards them mountains Pyrenees:
> Will act **to pass away** him after-buried one's company of soldiers,
> Them mountain ones ancient descendants of Pyrene **to proceed** without his luggage"

When the words of those lines are translated in this manner (completely within the scope of meaning those words bear), it presents a main theme of an "Arabian king" who will not change his path, through the utilization of "those of the Pyrenees". This main theme implies a change is necessary, but the overall goal will remain the same. The use of "*passer*" is "to hold on a course".

The secondary theme then picks up on that change, as it states that the cause "to depart" will make it necessary for an alteration to the "course". The use of "*outre*", which means, "pierced", makes this relate to the "travel itinerary" quatrain, which states an important "Thrust through Alania" will take place. This also matches the secondary theme in another quatrain, which used *"percer"* to state, "Will come to pierce them great ones mountains Pyrenees".

In the above secondary theme (the one created by placing four lines together), one is seen as having been "struck through", even "sickly", while also "opened towards them mountain ones Pyrenees". It is making the idea of Osama bin Laden having been killed in the attacks of Tora Bora have merit, as he very well could have received a serious wound. If that were the case, he would need to find a safe place to be tended to medically. Thus, he is transported through Russia to the "Pyrenees", having been forced "to depart from" (*"passer"*) where a search for him still goes on.

The second secondary theme acts as the third line, since the other secondary theme ended with a colon. As such, one secondary theme line then clarifies the other. That makes the secondary theme that tells of the faking of his death, as a clarification of the "pierced" state causing a need to "depart". This secondary theme (acting as line three) tells how an important action "Will make" or "Will act" to have it appear that "he to pass away". This uses *"passer"* as a word of life passing, through death. That use matches the reports that the C.I.A. dug up graves and cut of fingers to test for Osama bin Laden's fingerprints or DNA, to see if he had died and was "buried" (from *"posthume"* being from Latin, meaning "after burial") with "his band" of men who had died in the attacks.

That action has made it appear that Osama bin Laden is still in the "mountains" of Pakistan, while the next line states, "The mountain ones native to the Pyrenees [descendants of the mythical Pyrene]" was where he was "to go" (*"passer"*), leaving in a hurry, "without his luggage". The word *"bagaige"* can also actually mean "carriage [supply train] of an army"; and as such, be a reference to the "muleteers" or "mule drivers". Those are the teamsters who lead mules pulling wagons of supplies; and, that implies soldiers who keep supplies for the troops. This becomes relevant to the story that Osama bin Laden escaped on muleback.

In that escape into Pakistan, the story shows that he traveled "without" all of those who furnished him with "his military equipment", thus he escaped unarmed and "without supplies". Still, the same words show that he traveled "out of" (alternate translation of *"hors"*) where he was and that would then be with "his luggage". The symbolism of reading these words in this way means Osama bin Laden had a bag already packed for travel. That represents an escape plan readied, which included assistance from Russians and a willing group in the "Pyrenees" ready for his arrival.

This "three-dimensional" view comes from one aspect of the story of Osama bin Laden's escape from Afghanistan, which is possible by linking four lines with one key word (*"passer"*). That one verb is connected to *"monts Pyrenees"* three times, with this one quatrain having it connect to *"monts Pyrens"*. That relates the information in this quatrain's line three to the story of bin Laden's escape from Afghanistan. As the third line is providing supporting details to the main theme, this quatrain is entirely focused on the story of that escape. With that realized, one can look at the main theme statement verse in this light.

The main theme statement begins with the capitalized first word *"Dessoubz"*. This word includes a word recently seen in another quatrain, *"soubz"*, with both words bearing the same general meanings. The word *"dessoubs"* is listed in the 1611 Old French-English dictionary as meaning, "(substantively) the bottom, lowest, or most underneath part", and as an adverb, "under, beneath, and/or below." I have discussed this repeating theme as being relative to underground passages in the "Pyrenees Mountains", as well as the known fact that al-Qaeda used elaborate tunnels and caves in the "mountains" of Afghanistan. The same meaning needs to be seen as the initial focus of this quatrain, as the capitalization means an important group (from the "*z*" ending adding "ones of") that are "those Beneath".

The second word is also capitalized. It is the word *"Jonchere"*, which is rooted in the French word *"Joncher"* (Old French *"Ioncher"*). That word, *"Joncher,"* means, "to strew; to spread or cover, as with rushes; to work or make of rushes; also, a liar, cogger [a flatterer or deceiver], foister [a falsifier], deceiver; to gull; to cog or foist with; to lie unto, deceive, give gudgeons, bear in hand with untruths, and also, to dally, jest or toy with." The French word *"Jonchére"* is defined as, *"Lieu couvert de joncs,"*[1] which says, "Place covered with bulrushes." This word, by its own normal meaning being connected to the importance of the "Beneath ones", is making a statement about "those Beneath" being in a "Place hidden by bulrushes". This is a statement about the importance of being hidden.

When one understands that capitalization acts to elevate a word to a higher meaning than would normally be seen, the "Place covered with bulrushes" can

---

[1] From the French website Dicocitations, under a search for citations on the use of *"jonchére."*.

be seen as reminiscent of the story of Moses. In Genesis 2:3, of the King James Version, one reads, "And when she [Moses' Israelite birth mother] could not longer [than three months] hide him, she took for him an ark of bulrushes". In the New King James Version, the end of that verse states that Moses' mother "laid it [the ark of bulrushes] in the reeds by the river's bank." While the two Hebrew words that are translated as "bulrushes" and "reeds" are different, a reed and a bulrush are generally the same. Both are the same plant, only in different states.

The "bulrushes" that were used to make the ark for Moses were cut and dried "reeds." As such, the biblical "bulrush" (Hebrew – gimel/mem/aleph – pronounced "*go-me*") is commonly called "reed mace."[2] Reeds are living and bulrushes are dead, each used for multiple purposes (including basket weaving and making papyrus). Thus, the French used "*Joncher*" as a verb that states the act of spreading something about to dry in the sun, in a strewn manner. This same scattering of reeds becomes symbolic of a way to cover something up.

The elevated meaning of "*Jonchere*" is to parallel the Moses story. The importance becomes relevant to a "Place covered with bulrushes", such that "Beneath" God (or Allah) one makes him or herself a "Credit" (alternate translation of "*Lieu*") through service to God (or Allah). This is then stating the importance of God protecting those mortals who will serve a purpose for God. Just as the baby Moses was hidden in the "Place covered with reed mace", he would not have survived had he not been found. The "covering with bulrushes" simply allows one to be protected from the threat (from "dangerous", a following word in line one) that put him there in the first place. Osama bin Laden was "Hidden" from a "dangerous" situation, allowing for "passage" to a safe realm, just as was the baby Moses. The main theme is stating he had the protection of a higher source.

The stories told by captured al-Qaeda soldiers, that Osama bin Laden has demonstrated supernatural abilities in their presence, are worthy of mention. Reports have been made that say Osama bin Laden avoided harm in situations where mere mortals would surely have died, in particular when a mortar shell (Soviet) landed just feet from him. He was unscathed in that blast, while others were wounded and killed. The soldiers say that Allah blesses him. This is certainly putting him on an elevated level, one that can avoid bombardments and deadly wounds, through protection by a higher source. As such, the main theme

---

2   Definition for "bulrush", second "Life Sciences & Applied Applications / Plants" definition, from Collins Encyclopedia, presented on The Free Dictionary by Farlex.

is stating that he used some form of cover to escape, which was as natural as "bulrushes"; but the essence of importance is that his escape (and not dying from wounds, if wounded) was by the grace of God.

The remainder of line one states, "to them dangerous passage". The French word "*passage*" bears the same meaning in English. It has to be seen as both a noun and a verb, where the noun offers uses that show movement from one place to another. Still, in mountainous terrain a "passage" is a "pass". This has been discussed before, in the previous escape quatrain, where the verb "*passer*" shows that movement as "to pass". The element of the "passage" being "dangerous" shows both the difficulty of movement (as would be a mountain pass), and the difficulty of not being detected moving (causing one to go "Beneath" to a "Place covered with bulrushes"). Both of these scenarios fit the story of the Tora Bora escape of Osama bin Laden.

The secondary theme is a continuation of this escape, as noted by the lack of punctuation at the end of line one. Line two takes a different focus on the escape, by what other aids (other than "*Jonchere*") made the escape go undetected. In this line, as was discussed earlier, those left behind to fight the allied barrage (and die), "Will make" it seem Osama bin Laden ("*le*" as "him") was "to pass away" in that battle. His "posthumous" audio bites and video clips made it appear he resurrected "after death and burial". This is another element that brings on the idea of bin Laden having god-like powers.

Still, the reality is that many al-Qaeda soldiers died fighting, so bin Laden could escape. Included in this plan was the wherewithal to make quick burials of those who did die, to make it look like "his company of soldiers" was trying to hide evidence of "his" being dead. When the word "*posthume*" is seen to mean "born after his father's death" one sees how Osama bin Laden acts as the "father" to "his band" of followers. This means that regardless of how severely defeated al-Qaeda was at Tora Bora, and over the subsequent years, the real "company of soldiers" that will be "his" will be "born after Osama bin Laden's death" has been feigned. That "band of men" will be "Them mountain ones born of the Pyrenees Mountains".

The fourth line of this quatrain is not necessary to interpret fully as evidence that Osama bin Laden is hiding in the "Pyrenees". For that reason, not all of the words will be discussed here. However, one word will be presented as support for the translations previously submitted, of "conductor" and "king", as well as to "Goshawk" and "eagle".

That word is "*duc*", which has two meanings. The first, and most common, is as "duke". In the lower case, the meaning is not of a royally decreed "Duke," just as a lower-case "*roy*" is not a bloodline "King." The lower-case spelling calls for the 1611 dictionary explanation, which went along with the basic translation as, "A Duke."

That explanation mentioned the root word being Latin, as "*duces.*" That explanation stated: "When the French Kings had chased the Romans out of Gallia [they] found some of the provinces governed by certain martial commanders, termed duces". Italians used this term as a title for Benito Mussolini, who was called, "*Il Duce.*" The word means, "leader," such that Mussolini had to have a nickname like "*der Fürher,*" given to Adolph Hitler. Still, the word is rooted in the Latin word "*dux*", which means, "a guide, conductor; a leader, ruler, commander." Thus, line four is supporting the secondary theme's use of "*le*" and "*sa*" ("him" and "his") by making the title of "conductor" match "him". This is relevant to the first quatrain discussed, which mentioned "the conductor of the army".

The word "*duc*" is found used twenty-seven times in the quatrains.[3] This number of repeated uses makes it an important word to understand. It appears both in upper and lower-case spellings and indicates an important person of general rank, while also one of official title. The use in line four of this quatrain is not focusing primarily on the aspect of one person having an official title. Instead, it shows how one gains such a title through one's actions, to the point of a nickname being bestowed that conveys the meaning of title, through the symbolism of the name. This is where the second meaning for "*duc*" becomes important.

The word is shown in the 1611 French-English dictionary as "also" being known as a masculine noun referencing, "the great owl, termed a Horn-owl, or Horn-coot." It then states there are three categories of this "owl", with one being the, "*Grand duc,* which is the great Horn-coot." This is then described as being "bigger than a goose, and keeps always in forests and deserted places." This word gains greater meaning through realizing known "owls" of southern France, the type of bird an "owl" is, and the symbolism the word "owl" conveys.

The genus *Bubo* includes Old World Eagle-owls, of which the Eurasian Eagle-

---
3 Alphabetical Nostradamus Index.

owl (*Bubo bubo*) is one of the largest types of "owls" anywhere. An article on the Eurasian Eagle-owl (Wikipedia) states it "is found in mountains and forests with cliffs and rocky areas, usually nesting on cliff ledges."[4] Their known regions of habitation include Afghanistan, Pakistan, Iran, southern Russia, and the southern region of France (ancient Languedoc), the "Pyrenees Mountains", all of the Iberian Peninsula, and the North African coastal areas of Morocco and Algeria (Africa closest to Spain). The "owl" is certainly a bird of prey, just as is an "eagle" and a "Goshawk", but it is nocturnal, rather than diurnal.

This distinction of "*duc*" as an "eagle-owl" makes line four match the bird of prey uses in prior quatrains discussed here. It acts to show how Osama bin Laden can be "against the eagle" by being "opposite the eagle". The element of preferring night operations to those of the day shows this "opposite" aspect. As such, day and night become relative to Christianity and Islam, according to the systems of Nostradamus. Christianity is symbolized as being ruled by the sun (Jesus as the light), with Islam ruled by the moon (symbolism of the Crescent Moon). The nickname of "owl" shows the same strength as an "eagle", but it represents a power that obeys a different light.

The French name for the Eagle-owl (searchable in Wikipedia as "Horned owl") is "*Bubo*", which is the Latin classification name. However, the Catalan language name is "*Duc.*" This becomes important when one realizes the Catalan language is spoken primarily in Catalonia, which is the northeastern region of Spain, bordering France in the "Pyrenees".

In line four the (seeming to be) proper name "*Parpignam*" is found, which is certainly designed to represent the extreme southern French commune "Perpignan." This town is in the region now known as Languedoc-Roussillon, but the Catalonians view Roussillon as a part of France that should be joined with Catalonia. The French department *Pyrenées-Orientales* (Pyrenees Eastern) is also referred to as Northern Catalonia. The "Pyrenees Mountains" are so close to "Perpignan" (roughly 25 miles), an "owl" trained as a "messenger owl" could make the need for a cell phone and cell phone towers unnecessary. That would be a good way of being undetected by satellites spying, especially when one is making supply requests and commands for troop training.

For those who are avid Harry Potter readers, the symbolism of an "owl" as a messenger (Hedwig, a Snowy Owl) is nothing new. American Indians of the

---

[4] Wikipedia article, "*Eurasian Eagle-owl*".

northwest depicted "owls" in totems; and, they saw them symbolizing messengers, omens, prophecy, reincarnation, and wisdom.[5] The Ainu people of Japan see the eagle-owl as a messenger of the gods, or a divine ancestor.[6] Most adults recognize the symbolism of wisdom in "owls", through fables and nursery rhymes. Owls are associated with "elders," such that "The elder" would naturally be a "wise one." However, in Greek mythology the goddess Athena was often depicted holding an "owl" on her arm. The symbolism of Athena is wisdom, while she is also the "virgin" goddess of war, and in particular war strategy.[7]

All of this symbolism plays into the meaning of "*duc*" in line four, where the word becomes supportive of the "posthumous" recreation of "his company of soldiers". Osama bin Laden will have been able to be resurrected, after thought dead. It points to one male who will be like a "martial commander" in the province that includes "Them mountain ones born of the Pyrenees Mountains", like a "duke", or "*duce*". He will be the "conductor of the army" from the heights, acting like a great nocturnal bird of prey, the "*duc*" of Catalonia. He can communicate without the need for traceable devices. He will be wise as an "owl" in his planning the demise of the "eagle", as symbolized through the strategy wisdom provided by the goddess Athena.

This quatrain then progresses from an important escape from danger, to a level of safety, which comes from a holy wisdom. In Christian terms, one being "Beneath" the LORD means one has submitted oneself to being filled with the Holy Spirit; and thus, being capable of doing what normal people could never possibly do. Osama bin Laden's escape, via a "Place covered with bulrushes", and leaving "his band of men" to fake his demise, to keep his pursuers (another "company of soldiers") from finding him, is an act of divine providence.

It is like the movie plot from *Clash of the Titans* (1981), where Athena has Vulcan (a.k.a. Hephaestus) forge a mechanical "owl" that would make Perseus invisible, to assist in his quest to slay the Kraken. This film represents unfounded mythology, but the element of a mechanical "owl" was to replace the helmet of invisibility that was crafted by Hephaestus, which was used at various times by Hermes (the Messenger god), Athena (the goddess of war), and Perseus. The word "owl" then represents God's ability to hide a brave hero, through the aspect of God that is shone through the goddess Athena (who is synonymous with

---

5 Life Paths, Spirit of Owl.
6 World Owl Mythology – Japan .
7 Wikipedia article on "Athena".

"owl"). It shows that God will give such a hero all the tools he needs to escape and plan an act requested by God.

To summarize this quatrain in the bullet point format, this quatrain presents:
1. The quatrain begins with the capitalized word meaning "Beneath" and "Undermost part of", which emphasizes something "Below" the surface.
2. This initial importance is then enhanced by another capitalized word, one meaning, "Place covered with bulrushes", which is an important element of deception, relative to being "Beneath".
3. The word "*Jonchere*" introduces the element of the story of Moses, who escaped death by being hidden in an ark made of "bulrushes".
4. The escape is made due to "dangerous" circumstances, one of which includes "passage" that by itself is "dangerous".
5. The main theme is continued into the words creating a secondary theme, where "dangerous passage" is possible by what "Will cause" the escape "to hold on course".
6. This that "Will act" is relative to the appearance of one "to pass away", or "to decease".
7. The death is to one, who is identified as "him", and there will come those who "Will make" tests "posthumously" to confirm it is "him".
8. This individual is recognized as the "father" of "his company of soldiers", with a new "band of men" being "born after the [Lied unto] death of the father".
9. The one identified as "him" will be "born after death" as a form of resurrection, or rebirth.
10. The new "company of soldiers" that will be "born after the death of the father" will be "Them mountain ones born of the Pyrenees Mountains", as descendants of Pyrene.
11. To go to the "Pyrenees", he will be seen "to depart without his luggage", meaning a rushed departure.
12. To go to the "Pyrenees", representing travel that means, "to go out of his band" of influence, with "his luggage", shows a plan of escape.
13. This individual will be a "martial commander", as a "conductor" of "his company of soldiers".
14. This individual will be like a nocturnal bird of prey, in particular the Eagle-owl of the Catalonian "Pyrenees".
15. The symbolism of an "owl" represents one "Beneath" the protective umbrella of God, in a secure "Place covered with bulrushes", as having

the invisibility and strategic planning abilities of Athena the "owl".
16. The symbolism of the "*owl*" identifies "*him*" as a wise man, such as "*The elder*".

Afterthoughts: Holy Moses! From the clear 20/20 perspective of the year 2020, I wish I had edited my book nine years ago. The idea that Osama bin Laden's death was faked, so he was allowed to survive from a higher power, forget about giving God (YHWH) that nod, as President Barack Hussein Obama would fit that billing. Forget about Tora Bora. This quatrain explains the ruse that was a May Day 2011 public announcement.

The main theme statement begins with two capitalized word, saying "*Dessoubz Ionchere*," which is a most important "Cover-up." When I first saw my interpretation of "*Ionchere*" while editing nine years after having written this analysis, my mind immediately went to the Camargue, as that silty river basin area would be a natural area for reeds. The question, however, was how that could be justifying capitalization.

Then it struck me! Washington D. C. becomes a perfect metaphor for Bulrushes. Forget about that capital city not being built on swamp land (although it is called "the swamp"). It is a city **known** for the sleazy "Underneath" goings on and the scattering of "Bullshit" that hides the truth so well. With that realized, this quatrain takes the focus off Osama bin Laden and places it somewhere in the government of the United States of America. God knows, no one with a history in that place will ever come forward and freely admit having been a major "Liar" (one of the uses of "*Ionchere*") in the May Day "death" of Osama bin Laden.

Simply by seeing that written in to capitalized words at the beginning of the main theme statement, the word "*dangereux*" takes on a whole new light of meaning. The French words "*du dangereux passage*" are no longer painting a picture of heroic Osama bin Laden standing amid Navy SEAL stealth helicopters, night-vision goggles, assault weapons, and hard-ass military boots on the ground, as if that "dangerous" attack he somehow escaped "from." Instead, the same words now calmly say, "to the dangerous passage." Osama bin Laden now becomes the "dangerous" one, leading "dangerous ones" (if the "*x*" ending acts like a "*z*"), when he was never in Abbottabad, never in danger, like that which befell his body double and sacrificial family members and friends. "*Allau Akbar*," I imagine they said before being murdered (a meaning of "*mort*").

The main theme statement then paints a picture that agrees with the concept that Osama bin Laden escaped alive (maybe wounded) from Tora Bora, as these quatrains have proposed, and got well in the Pyrenees Mountains. There, he would be up on all the latest French news and be able to order some acts of terrorism, against the Great Satans of Europe. Rather than keep giving the intelligence agencies of the West tidbits of evidence that he was alive and well and still plotting Death to America (*et al*), all he had to do was put a tight lid on all his operations. The point would then be that he was in his strategic position (as the brains of a Trojan Horse), waiting for the perfect time to strike for the kill.

The lack of punctuation at the end of line one says the secondary theme is a continuation of that "non-escape," just as Bugs Bunny never came up behind Elmer Fudd, looking battered and bruised. The capitalization of "*Fera*" (the future tense of the verb "*faire*") says some major "Fabrication" will take place, which "Will counterfeit" or "Will imitate" (viable translations of "*faire*") "him posthumously" or pretend that "he [is] posthumous." The 1611 Old French to Old English translation of "*posthume*" as "born after a father's death" can relate to the fact that "bin Laden's adult son Khalid" was one of the others killed in the raid. (Wikipedia article "Killing of Osama bin Laden") A father's sacrificial lamb, so some believability so the "Lie Will work" (alternate translation os "*Fera*," combined with "*Ionchere* ").

This also allows "*posthume sa band*" be a statement of secondary theme merit that says, "posthumously his company of soldiers." One can only possess ("his") a "company of soldiers" (alternative meaning of "*bande*"), if one is still alive. Even if part of faking his death meant allowing others to assume the powers of command (and be the ones killed by C.I.A. drone strikes), so "his company of soldiers" followed his orders through others in command, it only says Osama bin Laden has played the role of playing possum perfectly

When line three is known to be supporting details for the main theme statement, the element of "*bagaige*" being read as "supplies for an army," this relates to those "*Dessoubz Ionchere*," or the powerful "Distraction Liars" in the swamp of D.C. Anyone remember Charlie Wilson? He was a swamp rat that provided Osama bin Laden all the surface-to-air missiles the Mujahideen could handle. This means someone, somehow, is loading up mule trains of weapons that are walked up the Pyrenees Mountains, to their nice, safe storage cave (a.k.a. armory).

This leads to a deeper investigation of the misspelling of Perpignan, as what is published is "*Parpignam*." The word "*Par*" can immediately be separated, leaving two words: "*Par pignam*." The word "*pignam*" can them become a simple anagram for "*m'pigna*." The 1611 dictionary, under "*pigne*," refers the researcher to look up "*peigne.*" This makes "*pigne*" become "*peigné,*" and acts as the past tense form of the infinitive "*peigner*". The "*a*" ending then converts the word into the future simple tense, so the word "*pigna*" (or "*peigna*") becomes "will comb." When added to the capitalized words "*De Par,*" with no punctuation ending line three, is what "supplies" come "To" "his company of soldiers." Those will arrive "By reason of" ("*Par*") "myself will comb" with that which "will pass very quickly" (all coming from "*De Par m'peigna courira*").

The figurative use of "comb" (from "*peigne*") says a symmetrically arranged order. When one is talking about tools of war, this very well could be a multiple rocket launcher. I just watched a video on YouTube of a TOS-1A Solntsepyok - 220mm MLRS Multiple Rocket Launcher, which was a 24-rocket launcher on top of a tank (I assume Russian-made). There have been nine years for the "Beneath Liars" in the political world to stockpile the caves in the Spanish Pyrenees with quite a few such "combs."

The $50-Million Reelection Gift • *Robert Tippett*

Chapter 17
Prosecution Exhibit M

Mountain Ones in the Pyrenees He Will Be Restoring

This quatrain is one of two that capitalizes the word "*Monts*", placing it as the first word in line three. This capitalization acts to heighten the meaning to a level of strength, much greater than simple "mountains" as the lower-case indicates. The proper name "*Pyrenees*" is still capitalized, which gives it the singular importance of identifying a specific mountain range, while also bringing in the mythology and history that surrounds that area of the world.

As the presentation of evidence comes in line three, it represents the supporting details for the main theme and the natural flow of information subsequent to the secondary theme. Still, it is best to look at the information coming in line three separately, before seeing how that information fits with the information in the other lines.

The whole quatrain can be translated as (simply translated):

Un regne grand demourra desolé,	One rule great will change from death abandoned of company,
Aupres del Hebro se feront assemblees:	Close to the Ebro oneself will be acting calling soldiers to report:
Monts Pyrenees le rendront consolé,	Mountain ones Pyrenees him will be restoring comforted,
Lors que dans May seront terres tremblees.	In that time then in May will be countries quaked ones.

When line three begins with "Mountains", it gains higher meaning by seeing the "s" ending as the addition of "ones" to the singular importance of "Mountain". Rather than the simplicity of "ones of the mountains", which could be generally any people who live in the "mountains", this is elevated to represent great numbers of people. Thus, the word "mountain" can be defined figuratively as "a huge quantity."[1] The capitalization acts to make this even greater in importance, as a "Mountain of people".

This immense number of people (not necessarily from mountainous terrain) will then become part of the "Pyrenees Mountains" community. In effect, the combination of the two capitalized words shows a massive influx of people to the "Pyrenees", which is in addition to the "mountain ones" native to the "Pyrenees". This relates to the evidence previously stated that shows an army of soldiers being raised along the border between France and Spain.

The next word is the 'article' "*le*", which is actually translated as the personal masculine pronoun, "him". This is a connection to one male related to this story focused on the "Pyrenees". It is "he" that is central as the attraction of "Mountains" of people going there. This word is then connected to next word, which is the third person plural, future tense of the verb "*render.*" As such, the actions of "him" will be affecting all of them "Mountains" of people, as well as those of the "Pyrenees". His affect "will be restoring" to them, as in taking them to a position of past glory. His affect will also be to instill a sense of "making restitution", for what has been lost since those original times. He will be gathering them for the purpose of "paying back" those who caused a need for "restoring". This becomes an implied sense of retribution, if not revenge.

From these emotions elicited, by "him" to "Mountains" of people in the "Pyrenees", all are then found to be "comforted". This nurturing aspect, where one provides "solace" to the others, shows that pain has been an affliction born by all, including "him". It makes it possible to see how Osama bin Laden could have been wounded during the attacks at Tora Bora, but found the "Pyrenees" a place where his wounds could heal. He would have then received help and assistance from the people who welcomed "him" there. Additionally, from the original meaning of the French word "*conforter*", it makes the statement that "strengthening" will take place. This would be relative to "him" physically, and

---

1   Fair Use - Many dictionary sources use the same definition for one common word of the English language.

to the "Mountains" of people in the "Pyrenees", as the numbers continue to grow larger.

With this view of the meaning that comes only in line three, that information needs to be connected to the main theme. Having seen "him" in the supporting details, we see the main theme begins with the capitalized word "One", which denotes a very important individual. We have discussed two other quatrains where the secondary theme statements also began with "*Un*", with those stating, "One king will be who will come to see France", and "One against the eagle great forces to direct". This "One" was also seen identified in another quatrain by "One" name, as "*L'Aemathion*". That individual was "An Arabian king" found in Greek mythology. Simply because of all of these quatrains are linked by the key terms, "*monts Pyrenees*", the "One" of this main theme can be expected to be about the "One" of all, who is Osama bin Laden.

The second word of the main theme is "*regne*", which is the masculine noun meaning "kingdom, realm; also sovereign rule; dominion, government; also the continuance of that government as a reign." As the past participle of the verb "*regner*", it means, "reigned, ruled, and/or governed." Thus, as a noun it becomes the "dominion" of the "One", which is detailed in line three as being the "Pyrenees Mountains". However, as the past tense verb it leads to seeing another "One" who has "governed" the "great" (the next word in the main theme line).

The "great" are the ones who own the past, which is the history leading to this quatrain. That history is relative to "One" rising to have "dominion" in the "Pyrenees". As such, the "great" will have "administered public policies and exercised sovereign authority, through controlling actions, and political maneuvers" (all paraphrased definitions of "govern"), within the "realm" of the "One". In reference to "The Arabian king", Saudi Arabia is a kingdom where the "great" nations, Great Britain and America, have "governed" in such a manner that Osama bin Laden (as well as many other Muslims) see the United States' government as the "great" Satan. After that steadfast translation as the noun meaning "the great" has been interpreted, another translation of "*grand*" can next be examined.

The French word "*grand*" can mean, "big, large; huge; mighty; substantial; and also high, lofty, and/or stately." When one knows the third line is focusing the supporting details to the main theme on "Mountains" of people, it becomes necessary to see "*grand*" as bearing these other meanings. The sense of "might" is important to realize when an army is being built, whereas safety in numbers is one thing, but "strengthening" (alternate meaning of *"consolé"*, found in line three) implies getting to the point of being "mighty". This meaning is the core reason for all who have become elevated to the level of "greatness", as it comes from "great" power, wealth, and influence over others.

The next word is archaic in its use, as modern French dictionaries will not display the word *"demourir."* This word is the rare Old French root verb that conjugates to the third person future tense version, *"demourra"*, which is found in the main theme line. The French website Wiktionnaire (Wiktionary in English) shows this to be rooted in the word *"mourir"*,[2] which means, "to die, to decease, to depart this life; to perish; and/or to decay". Because the word has the Latin prefix of *"de-"*, meaning, "taken from, changed from, following from, or after," it makes *"demourra"* state a condition where one is saved from dying. As such, Wiktionnaire says the word *"demourir"* is a "non standard [form of] *ressusciter*,"[3] meaning, "resurrection". This means *"demourra"* translates as, "will be taken from to die", thus implying one who will be returned to life.[4] This word brings a wealth of meaning to the main theme.

When the third line states *"consolé"*, meaning "comforted", and with "comforted" being defined as being helped physically in a time of fear, that use implies "help" recovering from a physical injury. The use of *"demourra"* is a statement that the "One" who will be "comforted" will first be "taken from death". That, minimally, confirms an injury to the point that "death" did occur and Osama bin Laden (the "One") was "taken from [that scene of] death", still alive. It also makes it possible to see how he very well could have been injured to the point of appearing "to die", only to be "taken from" the battle zone to a "Place covered with bulrushes" (from the last quatrain's main theme) where he was "resuscitated".

The element of "resurrection" acts to confirm the thoughts that the "One" is "Under" (the first word of the last quatrain's main theme) the protection of God (or Allah), where the "Place covered with bulrushes" was seen as synonymous with the story of Moses and protection from death coming from divine providence. The title of "owl" (from the last quatrain's fourth line) was seen as an association with the goddess Athena who symbolized wisdom and military strategy, with that nickname (*"duc"*) indicating one receiving assistance (definition of "comfort")

---

2   Wiktionary.org, French."*mourir*".
3   Ibid.
4   Wiktionary.org. French "*demourra*".

from a higher source. Thus, Greek mythological figures could occasionally sneak into Hades and return safely, as long as strategy made protections (like helmets making one invisible) available.

Middle Eastern mythology sees an "owl" as representative of "destruction, ruin, and death."[5] In Arabian lore, the "owl" is an omen of revenge, because the "spirit of a murdered man continues to wail and weep until his death is avenged."[6] As a sign of this spirit being reincarnated as a bird, an "owl" flies over the man's grave, continuing to hoot until the death has been vindicated. All of this symbolism is less representative of a Lazarus-style "resurrection" and more in line with a "restoring" to the way things were before an injustice had been committed. This is what line three's use of *"rendront"* ("will be paying back") indicates.

The final word in the main theme is *"desolé,"* which means, "desolate, deafly, desert; made solitary; abandoned of all comfort or company." This acts as a counterbalance to the use of *"consolé"* in line three. The main theme is thus focused on the loss of "comforting" surroundings, through acts that will leave "One", "after death", "abandoned of company". This matches the theme of Osama bin Laden escaping from Afghanistan, while leaving behind his place of residence for the previous twenty (or so) years. It also applies to his al-Qaeda soldiers who laid down their lives in battle for the "One" who "reigned" over them. They will be left "desolated".

The main theme then ends with a comma, making the secondary theme a separate focus on events that are subsequent to the "desolate" conditions from which Osama bin Laden escaped. The first word of the secondary theme line is the capitalized preposition that indicates the important direction that followed, "Next". The preposition *"Aupres"* is always followed by the preposition *"de"*, such that the two words mean, "Next to, Close to, Compared with, and or In the opinion of". This places it in a relationship with another, or in proximity to some place.

In this regard, Nostradamus utilized Spanish, as he did in the quatrain stating *"del duero"*, this time writing, *"del Hebro"*. The combined preposition-article *"del"* is Spanish, meaning, "to the, from the, of the, and/or with the". This use of Spanish makes the statement that "Next", after the "desolate" situation where "One" would be "taken from death", comes "One" "to them" of Spain. The inference of

---

5 World Owl Mythology.
6 Ibid.

Spanish is then confirmed in the next word, "*Hebro*", which is a place in Spain.

The proper noun, "*Hebro*" is seen as the "Ebro River", whose name is believed to be rooted in the Greek name "*Hèvros*". This makes it closer to the Latin spelling, such that "*Hiber*" (Latin) means a "Spaniard," or more precisely an "Iberian." Because the "*H*" is silent, the word becomes representative of the "Ebro", but the name is not Latin. The true Latin name for the "Ebro River" is "*Hiberus*."

The "Ebro", Spain's most voluminous river, runs parallel to the "*Pyrenees*" from the Cantabrian Mountains (just west of Basque Country) to the east through Catalonia, emptying into the Mediterranean Sea. The use matches the use found previously, of "*duero*". The Cantabrian region contains basins for both the "Ebro" and "Duero", with those rivers sourced in those "Mountains". The Cantabrian region sources a main river ("*Ebro*") and a major tributary to another main river ("*duero*").

This secondary theme's focus on Spain is then shown to be relative to "One", as the pronoun "*se*" is inserted. This pronoun means, "oneself, itself, himself, herself, and/or themselves". It relates with the personal pronoun, "him", found in line three. Thus, all three lines are making statements that focus on the activities of the "One".

The activity of the secondary theme is the third person plural, future tense of the verb "*faire*", that tells what "will be done". The efforts put forth "Close to the Ebro" will be those which "oneself" "will be making, working, forging, composing, effecting, causing, and/or forming". These actions will be found to be relative to "assemblies".

The word written, "*assemblées*", can be read as "assemblies, congregations, companies; meetings or drawings of people together, as at huntings; (hence) also huntings or troupes of hunters; also public proclamations or summons', or commands unto soldiers to meet, or make their rendezvous' at a certain place, and thence go into the field; and also the fight, coping, or encounter of two armies." Obviously, this word shows that "One will be effecting" many to respond to a call to arms, as has been seen relevant to other quatrains.

This secondary theme then ends with a colon, making "Mountains" act as the level of response to this call. The "assemblies" will be so large they will fill "Mountains" with soldiers readying for the call to action. That call will be made by "him", the "One" who "will be making restitution" to all who have suffered at the hand of the "great". From a position in the "Pyrenees Mountains", the people dedicated to supporting his cause will be "comforted" knowing Osama bin Laden is alive and well, having come back from near death.

Line four of this quatrain does nothing to add to the evidence of Osama bin Laden hiding in the "*Pyrenees*". It is an important line that links this quatrain to another series of quatrains that tell of severe earthquakes. Those earthquakes will change the face of the globe significantly. Thus, this quatrain is timed to be prior to those quakes. When those earthquakes occur (and they will be known to be the ones Nostradamus wrote of, because they will be larger than any known before), this call to arms, for soldiers to go to Spain for safe lodging and preparations, will be complete. The plan will be in effect and waiting for the word to "go."

This quatrain is another solid piece of evidence that a story is told by *The Prophecies*, and one of the stories that makes up that whole story is the one telling of someone very much like Osama bin Laden who will be hiding in the "Pyrenees Mountains". This quatrain connects to other quatrains, by the use of "One", and by the use of Spanish in the text. It directly states what has been seen implied before, which is the "gatherings of soldiers to prepare for battle". The purpose for all of this preparation is "to restore" the dignity of the small, who have been "left for dead" by the "governments" of those who call themselves "great".

A bullet point summary of this quatrain reads:

1. The initial focus is on an important individual, shown as "One".
2. The issue of "rule" is relative to this person being elevated to the position of "One", which is a position normally held by those "great".
3. The element of "death" is relative to the "One" and the "great", such that "One will be taken from death", or "resuscitated" back to life.
4. The "One" who "will be taken from death" will leave behind those who will have died, as he will be "abandoned of company".
5. Following this abandonment, the "Next" place arrived will be Spain, in the regions through which "the Ebro" River flows.
6. From Spain, the "One" "himself will be causing gatherings" of people, much like "calling soldiers to report for battle".
7. These "assemblies" will be "Mountainous" in volume, and they will go to the "Mountains" of Spain.

8. In the "Pyrenees Mountains" one will find "him", where he "will be bringing to pass" an army of men to "govern".
9. The "One" will be "comforted" in the "Pyrenees".
10. Those who will seek "him" to guide "them", who "will be making restitution" for past wrongs to "them", will be "comforted".

Afterthoughts: The main theme statement can be read as "One government great," where the importance of a capitalized "*Un*" can be like the saying, "We're number one!" Until the Russians and Chinese actually pass the United States of America, this quatrain can be seen as being relative to what is happening in the good ole US of A.

The last words of the first verse then lead one to see how that state of "greatness" has changed, with the "great" becoming no longer that, as there will come a significant "death" (from "*demourra*"). At the present time, the United States has some love of men in their seventies being elected presidents; so, it would not be a stretch of the imagination that one could die in office, causing "great will die" to make for a change of leadership that will completely leave the United States abandoned of allies, or it will abandon those it once had.

If that is the meaning of the main theme, then the important "Mountains" that begin the third line could not be people, as much as major problems set before America. This could then be based on "assemblies" of people protesting the changes, which keep America from helping its allies. One such ally would be Spain, which has come to its senses and realized all is not well in the Pyrenees. That then allows for "assemblies of soldiers" gathering in the Spanish side of those "Mountains.

Line four certainly implies an earthquake, from the words "*terres tremblees*," but a more realistic reading could be "lands shaken ones," where the loss of the "great One" as an ally has made Europe very nervous. That state of being would then be furthered along to the worse, should the United States of America suffer a catastrophic earthquake that would result in it being less likely to assist others.

Still, the use of "May" as an important month makes May Day 2011 need some closer inspection. The news of Osama bin Laden being dead made several "lands" in the Muslim world be "shaken." One would need to begin at the end and then work backwards, looking for known history to support what is written.

Chapter 18
Prosecution Exhibit N

Confused by Ambushes from the Mountains Pyrenees

This is the last of the three quatrains that contain some form of *"monts Pyrenees"* in line three. This is the second of two quatrains that capitalizes *"Monts"*, and does so because it begins that line. However, this *"Monts Pyrenees"* is a complete statement, by itself, because only those words appear before an ampersand divides line three in half.

The whole of this quatrain can be seen to state (simply translated):

L'ennemy docte, se tournera confus,	The enemy thoroughly instructed, itself will return disordered,
Grand camp malade, & defaict par embusches,	Great camp ill at ease, & broken by reason of ambushes,
Monts Pyrenees & Pœnus luy seront faict refus,	Mountain ones Pyrenees & Tunisian will be feat repulse,
Proche du fleuve descouvrant antiques oruches.	Adjoining with the river discovering ancient ones sedges.

Beginning the interpretation with line three, one has to see *"Monts"* as meaning more than "Mountains", just as we saw in the last quatrain when it began line three. Where the last use meant a large volume, it can mean the same here if the context of lines one and two calls for that meaning. As a stand-alone statement,

209

of importance, and along with "*Pyrenees*", those two words expand to a broader scope of meaning when "Mountain ones" is read from the plural ending. In that case, "Mountain ones Pyrenees" is making an important statement about a large volume of people in the "Pyrenees Mountains".

The definition of "mountain" also includes focus on the difficulty one can face when a problem seems insurmountable. This use shows how overcoming a figurative "mountain" represents a sizeable obstacle in one's path. When capitalized, the difficulty level rises significantly, especially when one is actually faced with the task of surmounting "Mountains", meaning more than one huge obstacle is before one. When one compounds this by seeing "Mountain ones" as a formidable group of people to overcome in the "Mountains", this adds to the difficulty one faces.

To understand how important "Mountains" are during a time of war, World War II offers some valuable historical perspective. That history mirrors how "Mountains" are an enormous obstacle to overcome, when the enemy holds the high ground. Going up a "Mountain" is hard enough, but when one finds "Mountain ones" preventing one from coming up the challenge is quite difficult.

During World War II, allied forces invaded Sicily in July (9-10) of 1943. Sicily is, basically, a mountaintop surrounded by water. The Germans held mountain positions, which caused the allies difficulties in their objective of taking that island. That island was secured rather quickly, however (on August 17, 1943), primarily because the Germans withdrew to the Italian peninsula, keeping their troops from being encircled. That withdrawal allowed the allies to take control the island. With Sicily secured, the invasion of the Italian mainland began on September 9, 1943; one month after Sicily was secured.

To make the necessary comparison, one must realize that the D-Day invasion at Normandy took place on June 6, 1944. Berlin fell and Germany surrendered on May 8, 1945, less than a year later. Part of the reason Germany fell so soon after France was invaded is because the path from Normandy to Berlin was through what is considered to be the "lowlands" of Europe. While forests and rivers created natural obstacles that were difficult to overcome and winter weather added to the difficulty of transporting armor, supplies, and troops, neither the Germans, nor the Allies had to train special "Mountain ones" to take and/or hold high ground. The high ground is a strategic advantage to have, when wars are fought over "Mountains".

Allied forces did not take the Italian peninsula until April 29, 1945, when a surrender agreement was reached. A complete surrender took effect on May 2, 1945, three days later. The surrender took place after German troops in the Alps of northern Italy realized it was futile to continue fighting. The end was inevitable because Berlin was under siege. The Italian Campaign lasted more than a year and a half because the Nazis made the Allies break through multiple defensive lines in the Apennines "Mountains". Those were very difficult "Mountains" to overcome.

Had Germany only needed to defend Italy, those Apennines "Mountains" would have taken much longer to overtake. This is known because the islands of the Pacific (more mountaintops surrounded by water) were expected to cost a million Allied lives, needing 100,000 troops to take each mountainous position held by 16,000 Japanese soldiers (estimated figures). It was also found that the Japanese "Mountain ones" had elaborate networks of tunnels in those "Mountains", particularly on Iwo Jima, Guam, Guadalcanal, and Okinawa. Because U.S. Marines had to take "Mountains" filled with "Mountain ones", terrible losses were incurred.

When this understanding is realized, one can see that the reason "Pyrenees Mountains" is stated in the plural is because there is a vast array of "Mountains" called the "Pyrenees." Every peak has its own name. Specific groupings include various ranges and chains, along the central line that makes up the border between France and Spain. All are part of the overall "Pyrenees" system, just as the Cantabrian "Mountains" (discussed in the last quatrain) are part of that system, but specifically separate. Each mountaintop in the "Pyrenees" is a potential "Mountain" of difficulty to overcome, especially in a time of war.

That stand-alone statement leads to the ampersand, which acts to signal the reader to expect an important aspect to come, in addition to the information offered by the first half. What follows the ampersand becomes its own stand-alone statement. The first word in this series is also capitalized, and is Latin. The use of Latin (a system of Nostradamus) is always an indication of higher meaning, based on the beliefs of the Roman Catholic Church.

The first word of the second half of line three is "*Pœnus*". This is the singular, masculine noun version of "*Pœni*," meaning, "Carthaginian". It also acts as an adjective, meaning, "Punic", which is descriptive of someone from Carthage.

Carthage was originally founded by Phoenician colonial seafarers. Today, that area is in ruins, on the outskirts of Tunis, Tunisia. The word "punic," due to it being associated with Roman history and their wars with the "Carthaginians" (three Punic Wars) also bears a meaning of "Treachery". This meaning is directly attributed to how the Romans characterized actions of "Betrayal" (synonym of "Treachery"), as being like those the North Africans repeatedly displayed. The "Carthaginians" deceived them to gain peace, while planning another war.

It is also worthy to note the history of those Punic Wars, as Rome's ultimate victory over Carthage gave Rome control of the "Carthaginian" empire. These holdings included the Mediterranean islands of Corsica, Sardinia, and Sicily, as well as much of Northwestern Africa, and Spain. The fact that the Moors were of Berber-Arab descent, which means they came from Africa, west of the Nile (i.e., not Egyptians), makes this statement be relative to the "Carthaginian" control of Spain. As such, that association connects well to the word preceding the ampersand, "Pyrenees", which is where the Moors had prevailed years ago, even into southern France. It also links this line and quatrain to the instructions in the letter to Henry II, which stated, "the ancient kingdom" would "not be removed from one place unto another". That "ancient monarchy" can be seen here as having "Carthaginian" roots.

The remainder of the second half of line three states, *"luy seront faict refus"* which says, "he, him, or it will be made refusal". The use of the objective case of the third person singular then identifies "Carthaginian" as the symbolic identity of an important one who "will be" from North Africa generally, and/or from Tunisia specifically. This person also "will be made, formed, framed, forged, fashioned, achieved, and/or accomplished" (some possibilities of the use of past participle *"faict"*), and led to "action", to do a "deed", to perform a "feat", and/or to put on a "performance" (some possibilities for the masculine noun *"faict"*). This person's ability to "act" is rooted in a "refusal" to be held back, as "he will be" expected to play a "part" (masculine. noun *"faict"*) in a "denial", as a "repulse" to the actions of others.

Seeing this half of line three roll out in this manner, it allows one to see how this North African "part" of "repulse" relates to the first one-third of the line three, in a previously interpreted quatrain, which stated, "To redden sea". The flag of Tunisia has an all "red" background, with a "red" crescent moon and star surrounded by a circle of white. The meaning that was discussed in the other quatrain was a call out by "The elder" in the "Pyrenees", to those far away to begin a naval invasion. This line in this quatrain makes it possible to see ships flying the Tunisian flag departing en masse. This also becomes reminiscent of the "ancient kingdom," where the Barbary pirates sailed the Mediterranean Sea as the Ottoman navy.

This second stand-alone half then connects to the first half as "Pyrenees AND North African". This links to the multiple quatrains that told of "By land AND sea". It makes the whole of this line three become a statement of "Mountains" of trouble being in the "Pyrenees Mountains", while additional (ampersand use) "Treachery" (variation of "Punic") will come from Tunisia, acting to "repulse" the people of France and Spain, sending them away from the "Pyrenees". It acts to confirm the concept of a naval invasion, with a land force previously established that surprises the forces of France, Spain, and Italy, preventing them from thwarting their enemies, by either "land" or "sea".

Certainly, to begin looking at line three and come to these conclusions, as to its stand-alone meanings, one needs to widen one's scope and see if those conclusions support the main theme. Then, see if it falls in line with the secondary theme. When one looks at the main terms that are present in those themes, it is easy to see the meanings of line three being as stated. The two themes are begun by stating the importance of "The enemy" (line one) and the "Great camp" (line two), which then spells out a "confused" condition (line one), relative to "ambushes" (line two).

The main theme makes a statement in two words (three counting the contracted article), where the presence of a comma makes those words stand as their own statement. Those words translate to say, "The enemy thoroughly instructed" (from "*L'ennemy docte*"), which can also be an indication of "An enemy skilled, learned, and/or cunning". An "enemy" is defined as being relative to a, "hostile power or force."[1] This is also a statement of a well-known "enemy", as "THE enemy", which is the importance (capitalized "*L*'") more than a small band of terrorists holed up somewhere.

In this regard, "The enemy" parallels the "Great camp" of line two, making it "The enemy" of the "Great". The main theme's partial statement, "The enemy skilled", is then supported by the first half of line three, such that "The enemy" is in "Mountainous" numbers, in the "Pyrenees Mountains". Additionally, it

---

1   Fair Use – Many dictionaries state the word "enemy" as being relative to this meaning.

is "cunning" as "thoroughly instructed Mountain ones" (based on meanings of "*docte*"). This then also acts to identify the "Great camp" as being Spain and/or France, who share a border at the "Pyrenees". The word "*camp*" can also denote a "field," in particular one where battle is being prepared by soldiers.

The second half of the main theme (following the separation of a comma) is then subsequent to the timing of "The enemy" having become "thoroughly instructed". The comma then acts to state that a period of time was required for "The enemy" to get into position first and then to be trained to the level of being "learned" as "An enemy". Having achieved this point of expertise, the second half states, "himself, oneself, itself, and/or themselves (from "*se*") will give in exchange or will return (from "*tournera*") confused (from "*confus*")". This acts to make two important statements, relative to the "him" in line three, and the "Great" of line two (in essence, "Them" to "The enemy").

When line three's objective pronoun "him" is supporting "himself" (from "*se*") in the main theme, it is identifying another "him", which is the one who "instructed The enemy". This links this main theme to the quatrain that told of the "conductor of the army", the "One king who will come to see France", and the "One against the eagle great troops to address". When "*se*" is read as "himself" it becomes a statement that the "learned enemy" will have been trained in tactics that "will return" a dividend, causing a "confused" state in one's opponent. This state of confusion makes that opponent weak and vulnerable. [This is the role Osama bin Laden played, as a leader of the Mujahideen in Afghanistan, against the Soviets.]

When the main theme's use of "*se*" is seen in the plural, as "themselves will turn confused," it is making a statement of cause and effect. With "The enemy thoroughly instructed", such abilities in battle will make those who they trained to fight against ("their "enemy") unable to fight. The training comes before the exercising of skills "learned". This is seen, when it next happens that the foe of "The enemy" trained to fight comes into a trap, set by their "cunning". That military group ("themselves"), once in the trap, becomes "disordered" (alternate translation of "*confus*") and "troubled" (alternate translation of "*confus*").

When a military unit is overwhelmed in battle, "they will turn" and run, "confused". This demonstrates how "themselves" will have been ill prepared for battle. This then becomes reminiscent of the quatrain that had its line three begin by stating, "Spain in trouble", which can be read as, "Spain – upon – turmoil". The word "turmoil" is an alternate translation of "*trouble*," means a state of "extreme confusion".

To confirm that those "confused" are not those identified as "The enemy", the comma at the end of the main theme separates it. The separation allows the secondary theme to be free to go in a completely different direction, as long as it is relevant to the main theme. The first word of that secondary theme is "Great", which is the word always used by Nostradamus to indicate nations with tremendous power, wealth, and influence over others. When that word is capitalized, it gains importance as those associated with the West, of which France and Spain are considered allies. The two words (the last one from line one, "confused", and first one from line two, "Great") act together to identify the reason why the "Great" were routed and "turned" away.

The reason is their "camp", which is where the "Great army lodged", was "*malade*", or "sick, diseased, crazy, out of temper, and/or ill at ease". The word bears the same meaning that "malady" has in English; it is an indication of being in poor condition. This can be an indication of a physical sickness, like the flu, which could be affecting an army's ability to maneuver and react in battle. However, it is more likely a word meant to convey an unwillingness to fight, which is a "malady" of today's "Great" militaries.

In view of how a military was run in the 16th century, versus how the United States military operates today, the differences are obvious. One could say that the modern "Great" armies have evolved to be the best ever; but such a statement could only truthfully be made if based on the level of technological advancements. Today there are airplanes of all kinds and weapons that are called "smart." When it comes down to the men that fill the tents in the "field" (alternative translation of "*camp*"), they may be "Great" computer experts, with "Great" rifles with night vision scopes and computer guidance technology, but they may not be all that they can be.

In this way, a modern military is "diseased", to the point that its "sickness" is an unwillingness to get dirty and bloody, winning in hand-to-hand combat, capable of cutting the throat of "an enemy". Modern armies are filled with career professionals, enjoying the benefits of military service, with families that stay in touch by e-mail and cell phones. It is not much different from a white collar, 9-5 job. That is because today's soldiers volunteer to serve, whereas the old armies constricted people, forcing them to be soldiers.

Another consideration along this line is the make-up of modern armies, primarily in the sense that women have taken up roles as soldiers. The recent issue of gays in the military, where homosexuals were previously allowed to serve only as long as they kept their sexual preference secret, is another sign of a modern army. Some European countries do not take their militaries as seriously as do other nations, perhaps because having a weak military keeps a nation from getting into a war it cannot win. These nations have slack standards to which their soldiers have to comply; and, those nations prefer to spend taxpayer funds on social programs, rather than maintaining huge defense budgets. All of these conditions that exist in our times can be seen as a "malady" to the "Great" nations.

Such examples of a "sick" army can be overcome through technology. For example, the U.S. military knows trying to take the Afghan mountains by sheer troop force would come with a casualty rate like those projected in the Pacific theater of World War II. The technology of smart bombs and drones that can be flown by a "pilot" 8,000 miles away, means the enemy can be tracked and attacked, without the enemy being able to kill any soldiers in return. These tactics make the point of this modern war game one of patience and endurance, where sudden attacks ordered by satellite surveillance can demoralize the enemy, and over time cause them to surrender.

This is a new kind of war. There are armies of human beings who are not emotionally charged about killing the enemy, nor are they worried about being killed. It is simply a profession to many. The ones pulling the triggers (or pushing the buttons) do not sense the kill, nor the danger of being killed. The United States went to war against Bosnia without setting a single soldier on enemy ground. They only did aerial attacks, in many sorties, destroying targets to the degree that those who were waging civil war called a truce and sued for peace. Those who see the actual carnage this type of warfare causes are the ones emotionally scarred for life. Seeing what war really means is how many wars come to an end. Wars end when one side has seen too much death to keep fighting. The will of the soldiers is broken at that point and the leaders know surrender is best.

When one sees this quatrain talking about a "troubled" army, filled with a "disease" that makes then "turn" and run, and when one sees how that fits "Spain in trouble", it makes it easier to see how Spain is not as modern as other European armies are. Due to the history that had Spain under a dictator for decades (General Francisco Franco), Spanish defense capabilities were left by the wayside. After thirty-five years (Franco died in 1975), Spain still has not caught up with modern warfare technology. While being one of the "Great" nations of European history, Spain has long been a poor country, with limitations placed on its ability to conduct modern military operations. Without the advantage of smart weapons in a terrain of "Mountains", the second half of the main theme points out such a limited circumstance. A "Great" nation's army "turns" from its mission, "confused", because its "field" capabilities are "sickly".

Line two's secondary theme is then separated from the remainder of the line by a comma. That makes the words that follow detail a subsequent element of the theme statement. The insertion of an ampersand, after the comma,[2] then acts to inform the reader that this subsequent element is important. However, the comma acts to disconnect the first half stand-alone statement from that of the second half, meaning the ampersand does not join the two as one statement, indicating similarities and/or differences surrounding a symbol for "AND".

The second half of the secondary theme states, "broken by ambushes". The verb, "*defaict*" has importance as if it were capitalized, due to the ampersand preceding it. The word "*defaict*" (which is a modern spelling used by Nostradamus, with the correct Old French spelling being "*desfaict*") means, "undone; broken; defeated, discomfited, overcome; ruined, destroyed, and/or overthrown." This, then, is an important statement that the "sick camp" will later reach a complete "undoing".

After having been "confused" by "The enemy" and forced to retreat without the ability to evacuate the territory of "The enemy", the "sickly" army is left at risk. To have no choice but to make "camp" while still in jeopardy will leave them "ill at ease". With their will to be "Great sick", they become easily "defeated by ambushes", which are "sudden surprises" (by definition).

The "sudden surprises" come from the call to "To redden (the) sea", such that an important "Carthaginian himself will be" coming to Spain, in an "act" that will "repulse" whatever military opposes his invading army. This attack will "deny" any of the Spaniards wearing military uniforms the luxury to quit playing soldier, if captured or surrendering. This means the second half of the secondary theme is mirrored in the second half of line three; between "The enemy thoroughly instructed" in the "Pyrenees", and the invaders called from Tunisia, everywhere the Spaniards "turn" they end up being "confused".

---

2   One will note that it is syntactically incorrect to place a comma and an ampersand back-to-back, as it becomes redundant, indicating, "and and."

Line four in this quatrain serves no purpose as evidence of Osama bin Laden hiding in the "Pyrenees Mountains". It makes a statement that is related to the invasion from Tunis, which begins a series of quatrains that tell of a war in Spain. This war will be plotted and planned by Osama bin Laden, but this quatrain introduces a "Carthaginian" who plays an important role as a general under the "One king", an "Arabian king", who will be the "conductor of the army". It shows that Osama bin Laden is connected to North African Arabs-Berbers-Moors. Many other generals are introduced in other stories of *The Prophecies*, with all showing the support behind him as being "Great".

To sum up the relative elements of this quatrain in bullet point fashion, one finds this quatrain stating:

1. The initial focus is on an important "enemy", which is "THE enemy" in opposition to the "Great" nations of the West.
2. An important state of readiness has been met, as "The enemy" has been "thoroughly instructed," to become "skilled" and "cunning".
3. This level of preparedness will lead to an encounter with troops who "will be turned back" in a "confused" and "disordered" state.
4. Those who will be "confused" are identified as being one of the "Great" nations of the West.
5. The "camp" of the "Great", which is both the physical troops in the "field" and the overall state of it military being able to keep a nation "Great", will be "diseased" and "sick".
6. This "ill at ease" state of the "Great camp" will lead to it being utterly "defeated".
7. The leader of "The enemy" is identified as the one who will have the "Great defeated", and "he" will accomplish this "by surprise attacks".
8. "The enemy" will be trained in the "Mountains", with "Mountains" of soldiers becoming "skilled Mountain ones".
9. The specific "Mountains" where "he" will train troops are identified as the "Pyrenees Mountains".
10. The soldiers in the "Pyrenees" will have their enemy "defeated by ambushes", while a "Carthaginian will be" called upon to "act" to "deny" the "Great" from getting well.

Afterthoughts: The words "*L'ennemy docte*" can mean they possess the same technological advantages of "smart weapons." These would have been purchased from those they will be used against. That becomes a "sickness" in the "Great."

Chapter 19
Prosecution Exhibit Q

There Moon in the Plain of Night Above the High Mountain

Originally, I informed the reader that the word "mountain" appeared in the quatrains (one quatrain has two uses) in some form fifty times. This was enhanced by the presence of the word "mountain" also appearing once in the letters of instruction written by Nostradamus. In those fifty-one examples, eleven of the quatrains, along with the one stated in the letter to Henry II, had the word "*Pyrenees*" (capitalized, in some variation of spelling) along with the word "*monts*" (or "*montz*"). All of the eleven quatrains had the two words together, in the same order, as "*monts Pyrenees*". The letter to Henry II showed "*mont Iouis*", later followed by "*Pyren-nees*". All are thus linked by these common elements.

This work, to this point, has been an analysis of one segment from the Henry letter (three strings of words, separated by punctuation marks), in regard to how it establishes an explanation for what can be found presented in the eleven quatrains stating "*monts Pyrenees*". In addition, two quatrains have been presented that match the criteria of an escape from the "mountains" (with Afghanistan relative to Tartary), making one important person link to both Asia and Europe. Everything presented has been evidence that Osama bin Laden is the focus of all of this that was written and published in 1555. This produces a prediction about where Osama bin Laden can be found; and, if proved, the words of Nostradamus will be realized to be truly prophetic.

This section is a continuation of evidence toward this end, by using three of the quatrains that state some form of the word "*mont*" in them. Without the specificity of the "Pyrenees Mountains" being present, the next three quatrains will expand on the themes developed previously. They will enhance the story of one man's presence in "mountains", his association with "mountain ones", and his awareness of the strategic advantage a "mountain" presents. All will point to the one person now known for "mountain" guerrilla warfare, which is Osama bin Laden. He is believed to have been hidden away in "mountains" for at least the last nine years; and, he developed his reputation over a twenty-year period prior to that, by fighting the Soviet occupation of Afghanistan and developing a group of jihadists in those same "mountains".

The period between the Soviet withdrawal from Afghanistan (February 15, 1989) and the attacks of September 11, 2001 (12 years, 7 months) gave Osama bin Laden plenty of time to plan for war with another "Great" opponent. Over that same period of time the Soviet Union broke apart, into Mother Russia and many freed poor nations. All those smaller countries were sent begging for capitalist dollars. The only thing of value they had to sell on the open market was Soviet-made weaponry.

After the first Gulf War (1991), it was announced that Iran had contracted with Russia to purchase ten Soviet Kilo class attack submarines (1992). The United States protested that sale and Russia agreed to delay delivery of the subs for ten years (until 2002). By 1995, Iran had received three of those vessels and intelligence cannot determine how many the Iranians now have on hand (2010). What has to be seen in the factual news releases is how they play into the stories written into *The Prophecies*, which show a long-range goal of arming Muslim nations for the purpose of a major war effort.

In that vein of thought, one must realize that Osama bin Laden is a wealthy Saudi (albeit one on the lam) and many oil-rich Arab nations have plenty of dollars to make it possible for a good, proven planner (like bin Laden) to have everything he needs to defeat the "Great" Satan. The story of "One" in the "Pyrenees" is certainly an individual "Great", with power through wealth and influence. He and his Islamic supporters have an agenda that will make the world realize the only true "Great" is their god (Allah); and, their plan is to prove that no nation or group of nations are unconquerable, when they have turned their backs on such a divine power.

These next three quatrains will add to the evidence already presented, such that key terms will be repeated or restated synonymously. Most of each of these quatrains will add pertinent information to the story line, relative to the themes already established. In all cases, the use of the word meaning "mountains" is not limited to the specific "mountains" named "Pyrenees". The accompanying theme statements and information presented in the supporting detail lines will show an association to the "mountains" of Afghanistan, more strongly than those "mountains" of Europe. They act to define the essence of a man like Osama bin Laden and tell why such a man would take to the "mountains".

All of these three quatrains have the word "mountain" ("*mont, montz,* or *monts*") in the main theme line. This shows an importance that flows to every subsequent line. Those lines that assist in the development of the theme of Osama bin Laden having reason to choose the Pyrenees Mountains as a base of operations will be interpreted fully. However, those that veer onto other themes will be left largely alone.

When an artist paints a picture, the first step is to set down broad strokes as background, upon which the details will be layered. So too is it true in writing. An introductory paragraph gives broad views of what will be detailed later. As such, in *The Prophecies* there are quatrains laid out in a way that makes them speak in poetic metaphor of what is to come. Still, the metaphoric words provide quite detailed information, when one sees the depth that metaphor allows.

There is an entire series of quatrains that lay out the whole story line of *The Prophecies* in broad strokes that confirm the general details of the letter to Henry II. These quatrains use the Sun, Moon, and other planets as symbolic characters. Many appear as beautifully written poetry, capturing a glimpse or essence that needs more details provided to be fully understood. These become crystal clear in hindsight, after one understands the systems and the terminology presented. The first presentation here now is an example of one of these.

The entire quatrain states (simply translated):

| *La Lune au plain de nuict sus le hault mont,* | There Moon from the plain with night above him high mountain, |

The $50-Million Reelection Gift • *Robert Tippett*

Le nouveau sophe d'un seul cerveau la veu:	A rare wisdom from one single brain the vow:
Par ses disciples estre immortel semond,	For his pupils to be everlasting summons,
Yeux au midy, en seins mains, corps au feu.	Eyes at the midday, upon hearts hands, body in the fire.

This almost dreamy poem is one that past interpreters of Nostradamus have written off as nothing more than an "occult" vision, with "occult" defined as "hidden from view." They see it as too generic to be anything related to a specific predictable event. When reading the lines as if they were run-on sentences, it just appears generally mystical, as if some guru were sitting on a mountaintop contemplating the "Moon", while experiencing warm fuzzy feelings. That could happen to many people, right?

This quatrain, when read according to the systems of Nostradamus, becomes quite clearly a statement about one man of such important following that an entire quatrain is dedicated to explaining him. That man is Osama bin Laden. The use of "mountain" in the main theme links "him" to that word. The key to being able to see that comes from seeing "*La*" and "*le*" as an adverb and pronoun (in that order), rather than a couple of meaningless "the" fillers (as the articles they seem to be at first glance).

The capitalized first word is "*La*". This can be seen as an important "THE"; but reading the word that way makes it incapable of having stand-alone meaning. As an important article, it only has meaning when connected to a following noun. However, it has individual meaning when read as "*Là*" (the systems of Nostradamus allow for accent marks being added, but not subtracted), which is the adverb meaning, "There, Here, and/or Then".

When the main theme statement is seen to begin with "There", it is immediately placing focus on a place. From Nostradamus' perspective in southern France (he wrote *The Prophecies* in Salon-de-Provence), "There" would be some place other than France, and "Here" would mean France. However, he followed the word "*Là*" with another capitalized word, "*Lune*", which means "Moon".

This means "THE Moon", represents a place "There", where the "Moon" is all-important. In all cases where the "Moon" is stated in *The Prophecies*, it is a reference to Islam. Thus, "There", where the "Muslim" people are native, is the initial focus of this quatrain. With the capitalization acting to elevate the implication to the most revered place "There" of the "Moon", one is led to find a place that represents their religious center. Such a place is Mecca; and, Mecca is in the country now called Saudi Arabia.

The following words, "*au plain de nuict*", can state "in the plain with night", but these translations have to be founded on the place of the "Moon" being Mecca. As such, the combination preposition-article, "*au*", makes a statement about how the "Moon" is revered "to them", to the point that a pilgrimage to Mecca is held yearly, called a Hajj. This ritual gathering is modeled after the path Abraham (Ibrahim) took, before he banished Hagar and Ishmael, leaving Hagar to look for water for her dying child. The timing of this yearly event is in the twelfth month of the Islamic calendar, which is "Lunar" based.[1]

Along the path that devout Muslims take in their pilgrimage two "plains" become important, one at Mount Arafat and the other at Mina. The one that stands out the most is Mount Arafat's "plain". The fourth stage takes them "to the plain" at the base of Mount Arafat, which is the one step that a Muslim must make in order to validate one's pilgrimage. This essential step becomes the most important place, as Muslims must remain "There" praying and reciting the Qur'an until after sunset.[2] During this time "at the plain", many Muslims contemplate how their future lives should be coursed.[3]

They stay the "night in the plain" with their religious tradition teaching that Muhammad delivered his "Farewell Sermon" from "above" where they pray, on the hill called Mount Arafat (only 70 meters of elevation).[4] This "*mont*" is "high" in the sense that it is revered because of Muhammad's presence there. To Muslims, "he" (Muhammad) is most "high" or "most glorious" (alternate translation for "*hault*").

It has been said that faith will move "mountains," and faith is the purpose for the Islamic Hajj. There is also the proverb that states, "If Muhammad cannot move the "mountain," the "mountain" will move to Muhammad." The meaning of that message is that if things do not change to be like one wants them to be, then one

---

1   Wikipedia article on "Hajj".
2   Wikipedia article on "Mount Arafat".
3   Wikipedia article on "Hajj".
4   Wikipedia article on "Mount Arafat".

must make the changes that one wants to come. This means the word "mountain" is relative to all obstacles that stand in the way of Islam ("Moon"). The way one gets "over" obstacles, as seen by Muslims, is by following the messages "he" (Muhammad) left behind, in the Qur'an.

When one sees the main theme being an important statement about Muslim devotion to their religion, one must realize that Osama bin Laden is a most religious Muslim. He is native to Saudi Arabia and known to have enjoyed camping with his father in the desert around Jeddah, which is on the coastal "plain" just west of Mecca (roughly 55-60 miles). He has gone from the "flat" surface of "smooth" sand (alternate translations of "plain"), that of the deserts of Saudi Arabia consist of, to rise "above" those who pilgrimage "There" as devoted Muslims. The faith of Osama bin Laden is seen as so "high" that "he" represents a new one who is "most glorious" to Islam. It is "he" who has come to climb "high", ready to go to the "mountain".

This main theme then leads to the secondary theme, following a comma. The comma acts to separate the main theme from the focus of the secondary theme, although it is relative to the theme of Islamic devotion. This is then focused on "Him" (capitalized "*Le*"), or "He", as a significant "One" (as "A" or "THE", seeing "*Le*" as a most important article) who is "rare, fresh, recent, new, and/or unheard of before" (alternate translations of "*nouveau*"). This makes the secondary theme begin its focus on a very important person, who is Muslim, and a phenomenon.

This person's phenomenal abilities come from a "new wisdom", where things "strange" and "uncouth" (alternate translations of "*nouveau*") are attempted, not based on standards of thought. This "wisdom" is called "out of the box thinking," such that this one is known for finding "new" solutions to old problems. This is then explained to be a special trait, as this "wisdom" is "of one". It shows how "He" possesses a unique grasp of "wisdom", one that exceeds a normal person's abilities to think and do typical problem solving. This ability relates the "One" of the secondary theme to the main theme of Islamic reverence to the "Moon".

Nostradamus was an astrologer; and thus, he understood the esoteric meanings associated with all the heavenly orbs. In the solar system there is only one light source, the Sun. Still, from a geocentric perspective, the visible equal in the sky (by apparent size) is the "Moon" and it is a source of reflected light. Thus, "in the plain of night", when the "Moon" is "above high", one can get a better sense of where to walk, unlike when it is pitch black out, due to no "Moon". The symbolism of this is reflected onto the "Moon", so that astrologers see it as the "ruler" of intuition and the unconscious mind.

Due to this meaning being applied to the "Moon", someone like Osama bin Laden can be seen as having "rare wisdom" through an ability to "feel" or "sense" what needs to be done, regardless of how much rational intelligence he also possesses. Nostradamus also had such insight, which he explained (in his letters of instruction, and some quatrains) were due to being able to hear the "good angels".

In other words, Nostradamus explained that he was filled with the Holy Spirit when he prophesied. That spirit guided him, without conscious thought, to pen the words he wrote. Although he was conscious of the words as he wrote them, and conscious of their meaning, he was writing from a higher "wisdom". The secondary theme is placing focus on an ability that can only be explained as being God sent.

The words that show this focus state "from one sole" source, as well as "to one alone" (variations with the translation of "*seul*"). When the capitalization of "*Le*" is then seen as "Him", it bears a higher meaning. As such, "Him" becomes representative of God. When the main theme is known to be directed towards Islam ("There Moon"), God is then called Allah. The capitalization of "Him" represents the one who sends insights, opportunities, and protection to Osama bin Laden. Because "He" (bin Laden) consciously knows Allah is the source of all his successes, Osama bin Laden is acting for "Him", and thus becomes "Him". Still, Osama bin Laden cannot claim that any power he possesses comes without that divine assistance.

The same can be said of Nostradamus, such that this quatrain acts as a metaphor for all prophets. Because it fits Osama bin Laden, in particular through the linking of "him the most glorious" with the word "mountain", and then connecting "mountain" to the capitalized "Him", we can see "He" is like Moses and Muhammad. Moses talked directly to God, in particular by going to the "mountain" named Sinai. Muhammad received the message that became the Qur'an from inside a cave on a "mountain". It says that Osama bin Laden is a "mountain" man (literally), a "high mountain" of reputation (metaphorically), and a prophet "high" on a "mountain" (figuratively).

When the word "*sophe*" (from Greek and Latin, "*sophia*") is seen as "wisdom", and that word known to be defined as "good judgment", one sees it is relative to knowledge. That is a function of the "brain". It states that the conscious power to discern insight requires turning ideas into plans of action, based on knowledge, experience, understanding, common sense, and insight.[5] This is the general description of "wisdom". It naturally comes with age in most human beings; but line two states this is about "wisdom to one single brain there".

The repeating of the word "*la*" (in lower-case, in line two) must be seen the same was as the first word of the quatrain was seen, where "*La*" was translated as "*Là*". When the choices as an adverb were "There, Here, and/or Then", one simply needs to not repeat the usage from line one. Since "There" makes the main theme have greater meaning, line two can be best read as stating, "wisdom to one single brain ... then ... vow".

This is making a statement that "He" who receives this "wisdom" knows its source as it fills "Him". After having been so filled, "then He" acts to thank the source. It says, "He then made a vow, He then made a solemn promise, He then prayed" (all alternate translations of "*veu*"). This is significant in the way it addresses who will be a prophet of God, because it says God chooses a "single brain" to access and "then" that "one alone" thanks God for the privilege. God controls who becomes filled with the Holy Spirit, not man.

The word "*veu*" is also the Old French spelling for the past participle of the verb "*voir*," which makes it mean, "viewed, seen, perceived, beheld, overlooked, surveyed; marked, heeded, observed, regarded; examined, searched into, and/or considered of." It even had adverbial application as, "considering, seeing, and/or in respect of." This makes the statement then focus on a vision "seen" that is quite important. It is the source of Osama bin Laden's plans to overthrow the West and convert it to Islam, through the instruments of war.

A colon follows the last word of the secondary theme, making line three become a statement that clarifies or provides examples of the "vow" made, as well as of that which has been "seen". The capitalized first word is then the preposition "*Par*", which means, "By, Through; Of, By reason of; For; and/or On." This shows an importance relative to how the "vow" will be honored, how the

---

5   Fair Use – From one definition of "wisdom" listed on the Free Dictionary by Farlex.

"solemn promise" will be upheld, how the "prayer" will be answered, and how the "vision" will materialize.

The remainder of line three states, "his disciples to be immortal summons". On a whole view, that makes a statement that the realization of the "*veu*" will be "Through disciples", or "By pupils", or "By reason of learned ones". All of that confirms the main theme focus on "The enemy thoroughly instructed, learned, skillful, and/or cunning" (in the last quatrain discussed). It also allows one more clarity to the secondary theme in another quatrain that stated, "One head man of a company [lower-case alternate for "*roy*"] will be who will come to see there Beaten-down-with-a-pole [alternate translation of "*Gaule*"]". The "vision" is of harsh justice, to shatter the clay pot (symbolic for infidels) with a rod of iron (symbolic for weapons of mass destruction), "Through" those who are still connected to Allah "By prayer", the "disciples" of Islam.

Line three's use of the verb "*estre*" (modern French "*être*") states the infinitive, making the point of what is "to be, to subsist; to stand, to remain, and/or to rest." This is then a statement about what was "seen to be", before it will have been. The word then also takes on its noun usage, as "a substance, a subsistence; an essence, a being; and/or a state" that was "seen" coming "Through disciples". This means it is a prophecy of what will come to pass, if allowed "to be", without divine intervention preventing that "vision" from happening. Thus, the use of "immortal" is reference to God, or Allah, as only the heavenly is "eternal, everlasting, ever-living, never-ending, and/or all-enduring."

The last word of line three has been translated here as the third person singular present version of "*semondre*", which means, "to bid, to invite; to summon, to warn, and/or to cite." As such, it reads as, "to be immortal summons", "subsistence eternal warns", and/or "state everlasting invites". This acts to clarify the "vow" as being a response to a divine request, such that God (or Allah) is asking one to make the future come "to be". However, the use as "warns" takes one to the edge of sensing the purpose of prophecy. It is a warning to avoid a future, rather than "to be" taken to the point that a "vision" becomes reality.

In this sense, one can look at the letters making up "*semond*", and "view" them as a simple anagram. This is allowable because by 1611 the word "*semondre*" was already being replaced by the spelling "*semoncer*." The simple anagram becomes the third person singular present version of the verb "*esmonder*", which means, "to cleanse, to purge, to clear, and/or to make clean." It is rooted in the

Latin word *"emundare"*, which adds the term "purify" to those French translation possibilities.

This translation acts to make the statement that God (or Allah) does not want a future of doom and gloom for humanity. As such, God (or Allah) wants a corrupt state "to be cleansed", rather than continue in that state. That purification can come from the world suddenly being able to share a "vision" from God "immortal", such that it voluntarily "frees (itself) of (the) dirt" the corruption has caused. Otherwise, without such a self-cleansing, "disciples" of God (or Allah) will carry out that future "seen".

When the anagram possibilities are drawn off the Latin spelling, one sees *"s'emond"* appear. In Old French, both *"esmonder"* and *"emonder"* meant the same thing, as the *"s"* was disappearing to be replaced by an accent mark. As such, the freed *"s"* can simply become detached from *"semond"*, becoming *"s'emond"*. The abbreviated *"s"* then acts as an attached *"se"* at the beginning, combining so the word then states, "oneself cleanses", "himself purifies", and/or "itself purges".

This last variation works in agreement with the *"ses"* at the beginning of line three, such that the plural number is continued with *"se emond"*. That is an indication of those needing to be "cleansed" doing the cleansing "themselves". This allows line three to state an invitation from God (or Allah) to clean one's own house, before it becomes "cited" as an offense before God (generally called an "abomination"), leaving the "vision" to play out as foreseen.

Line three then ends with a comma, making that supporting statement be separate from the following supporting statement of line four. Line four is then divided into three segments, due to the presence of two internal commas. In this case, the commas act to separate the segments into subsequent events.

The first of these segments begins with the capitalized first word *"Yeux"*. This word means, "Eyes", as it is the plural form of *"Oeil"*. The plural number shows more than one set of "Eyes" are involved, and acts to support the use of *"veu"*, in line two's secondary theme. It represents both the All-seeing "Eye" of God, along with the two "Eyes" of the one human being who had a divinely inspired "vision". This is then the insight of the "Moon in the plain of night" allowing one's "Eyes" to feel what is ahead, as well as see what is now.

The complete first segment then states, "Eyes at the midday", or "Eyes in the noon (time)". This is developing a contrast from the main theme, where the word "night" was used. When one sees "night" as the subconscious state, enlightened by the "Moon", then one sees the "midday" as the conscious state, enlightened by the Sun. Just as it was discussed that the "Moon" represents Islam, the Sun represents Christianity (Jesus is the Light). This means that the segment stating, "Eyes at the midday" is supporting the "vow" and the "vision" as targeting those led by Christianity.

This is in no way a value statement about Christ, as He is the true Light of God, sent to spread the Truth to all humanity. Those who have their "Eyes opened to the light of day", meaning a professed claim to be Christians, will have their "Eyes" blinded by staring "at the Sun", and not being in-tuned to their inner heart. The heart is where Christ truly "rests" and "summons" one to act right. It is therefore a statement about the "vision" being of those with "Eyes" that see, but cannot (or will not) see the evil of their ways.

The second segment of words states "upon inward minds public authority", "into depths of the heart hands", and/or "on gulfs of the sea the grapples of ships". This supports the "wisdom" of the secondary theme, where "inward minds" is relative to "brains" left "alone" in thought. It mirrors the intuition and emotional attachment of the "Moon" to one's "heart". It even shows the "vision" including the use of a navy to get "into" the "middle" of those places where the "midday" light warms them. It also states that Christians must place their souls "into" God's "hands", through "Eyes" opened to the atrocities of their "public authorities".

The final segment states, "*corps au feu*", which can translate to state, "body in the fire". This translation must be seen as the "body" of Christ, who opened the "Eyes" of the world to the one (and only) God. That "body" is more than a church; it is all who profess membership in the Church of Christ (not a denominational distinction). To see that "body in the fire" means Christians must get "fire in the bosom" about acting Christian. One must realize that "fire" is the gift of the gods to mankind, as "fire" provides man with light, warmth, and a way to an elevated stature on earth. The essence of "fire" is also transformative, such that matter is changed from a solid state into ashes that release gases and light. It symbolizes the death of the "body" for a higher realm.

In that sense, the Old French also used the word "*feu*" to mean, "dead, deceased, and/or departed". Modern French still shows this use as a reference to "late", which means someone who has passed away. As such, *"corps en feu"* can equally mean, "corpse upon dead". That is a statement about everything material remaining on the earthly plane. All that is released from the "body upon death" is the soul, with no one able to hold onto any possessions of this realm. Whatever comes "into (one's) lap (held tight by one's) hands" stays behind with the "corpse to the departed."

This quatrain is very profound in its meaning, and quite detailed in how it applies to the Christian world, its persecution of the Islamic world (in particular its disregard for the Arabs of Palestine), the lack of religion leading one's "heart", and the turning of one's back to God bringing about the end of the world. It makes it clear that the vehicle ("Him") who will use "disciples" to bring about this end is Osama bin Laden, the "mountain" Muslim imam. Still, it tells everyone that the "vision" need not come true, if one's "Eyes" are indeed "with the light", which comes from within the emotional self.

To summarize this quatrain into bullet points, it breaks down as such:

1. The initial focus of the main theme is "There", with that place being identified as relative to the "Moon".
2. The "Moon" is elevated in meaning to represent Islam, such that many Muslim nations fly flags that depict crescent moons.
3. The use of the word "plain" and "night" is relative to the Islamic Hajj (yearly pilgrimage to Mecca), where a devout Muslim must stay the "night" on the "plain" at Mount Arafat.
4. The use of *"le"* identifies one male Muslim as "him" who will be seen as "most glorious" in his worship to Allah "above"
5. The word "mountain" identifies "him" as a devout Muslim, who models Muhammad, through his use of "high mountains" to achieve greatness.
6. The secondary theme immediately identified "Him", which is relative to "him" in the main theme as earning a reputation as "high" as a "mountain".
7. The capitalization of "Him" elevates to mean God, who has assisted "him".
8. The focus goes to "He" with a "rare wisdom", which comes "from one" being in touch with God's voice.
9. The focus of the secondary theme is on one "alone" in touch with God, as a prophet and messenger of God.
10. The one of focus has a "brain" that allows "Him" to be conscious of his

subconscious thoughts.
11. The "brain" is able to discern a "vision" from God, as well as give "prayer" of thanks for having been chosen.
12. The "vision" will unfold through "disciples" dedicated in their religious spirit, "to be pupils" of the one led by the "everlasting" deity.
13. The "disciples" will be called to act by "summons", with the intent being to "cleanse" the world of the impure.
14. Christianity is seen as the target of this cleansing, because the "Eyes" of Christians being led "to the light" of the Sun.
15. The spirit of Christ lies "in hearts", such that those who put their lives in God's "hands" will be saved.
16. The church of Christ, his "body" must see the reward being on a transformative plane, symbolized by "fire".
17. The corruption of the world is because of the "public authorities" controlling the "bosoms" of Christian nations.
18. The "corpse" of Christianity will burn "in the fire" of retribution.

Afterthoughts: When one delves into the merits of religion, it is easy to get lost in one's personal idea about right and wrong, based on the teachings of one's sect or denomination of preference. The Muslims believe their way is the right way, as they kill in the name of Allah. The Jews believe their way is right, when they kill in the name of Yahweh. Christians believe their way is right, when they kill in the name of God, through Jesus Christ. When everyone thinks they are right, then everyone is wrong.

In the Old Testament are plenty of stories about God siding with His faithful and many people who challenged those faithful were destroyed. Americans decry the Old Testament as the root of all the world's problems today, trying to play gods by demanding guns be taken away from anyone who would own one. Besides that concept of man being part of the reason why an invasion of Europe will find mass destruction of weaponless French, Spanish, and Italians, tell me what type of gun Cain used to slay Abel. Mankind is a bunch of born killers and the only thing that keeps mankind from killing is religion, one that places God in the hearts of the faithful.

For this plan shown to Nostradamus by God's All-seeing Eye, no man is led by that God to be a killer of many, with persecution being the plan for the torturous deaths of millions more. The God of Jesus will not be empowering someone like Osama bin Laden to wage war successfully. His success will be due to

Christians (those calling themselves such) will have turned so far away from God that someone worshipping another god will have their way with them. That is the repeating story in the Old Testament, after Moses dropped the Israelites off at the Jordan River and said, "As long as God is your King, that land will be yours, regardless of who thinks different." From then until David, it was forty years of being faithful, followed by forty years of getting their ass kicked by people seeking revenge, because they turned away from God. God always came back to help when they regained their faith and repented.

Osama bin Laden is not supported by God. He is supported by wicked, evil men and women who want to see the West demeaned, as repercussion for being wealthy while there are poor, for thinking they are better human beings than people elsewhere in the world, and by all means for allowing Zionist Jews to steal Palestine (with military assistance from big powers). Osama bin Laden is more aided by karmic debt owed by the West, than a god that hides in caves, whispering to his prophet.

Again, after seeing how Nostradamus prophesied the faking of the death of a leader, who is now shown to be Muslim, with a devotion to his god that few Westerners can match, Osama bin Laden is aided by the gods running the government in the United States of America. In the nine years since he was announced dead, Muslims have infiltrated the government of the country they openly declare to be evil and in need of destruction, all the while they sit in a seat in Congress. This is a sign of the malady that faces the one said to be number One.

I repeat what I have said before. The enemy is within. If giving back Palestine to the Arabs and displacing the Jews one more time (a historical act of repeating itself), perhaps God will shine His light of protection over a country that one boasted "In God We Trust." Finding Osama bin Laden in the Pyrenees is not reason to begin a war the West is ill-prepared to wage. It would be, however, reason to say, "Time out!" and then realize how close to Satan we are, having turned a complete about face to God.

Chapter 20
Prosecution Exhibit P

There Great Troops Will Pass Them

Mountain Ones

This quatrain is the second that has the word "mountain" in the main theme line. It is not a quatrain that is about the "Pyrenees Mountains"; but, instead, it tells of the "mountains" that brought Osama bin Laden to his initial prominence. It is one that tells of the "mountain ones" of Afghanistan, who have a long history of defeating invading forces. That history of success is simply because it has been impossible for invaders to conquer those "mountains".

This quatrain is a very interesting one, in that it deals with the Soviet occupation of Afghanistan and the actions that happened which made them leave. This is where Osama bin Laden became a popular name on the American nightly news. He was a thin young Saudi fighting with a group called the Mujahideen, in a war against the Soviets. The verses holding the supporting details are where this quatrain offers insights about the collapse of the U.S.S.R., which tells a different story than that which is believed to be the case about that breakup. However, those details become peripheral to the focus on evidence of "mountains" being relative to Osama bin Laden; so, only the first two lines will be interpreted here.

The whole of this quatrain states (simply translated):

La grand copie que passera les montz,	There great troops that will surmount the mountain ones,

THE $50-MILLION REELECTION GIFT • *Robert Tippett*

Saturne en l'Arq tournant du poisson Mars:	Saturn upon the Archer returning to the sacrifice March:
Venins cachés sous testes de saulmons,	Poison ones kept secrets beneath self-willfulness ones from salmon ones:
Leur chief pendu a fil de polemars.	Their chief hanging with rank to war ones.

This quatrain begins with the capitalized article "*La*", just as the last quatrain was shown to do. Accordingly, this use also has to be read as the adverb "*Là*", so the word can stand alone and have meaning. In the last quatrain discussed a translation of "There" is the same read here. In the last quatrain "There Moon" represented all places where Islam reigns. The use of "plain" and "mountain" took the focus to Saudi Arabia, as to where "There" was. With the word "mountain" combined with "great troops" in this main theme, "There" is relative to all places the "great" nations have placed "troops" in mountainous foreign lands.

In the story line of *The Prophecies*, such a place suggests Afghanistan, but only in a secondary sense. Here one sees "There" is the place of "them mountain ones" (due to the presence of a "*z*" ending). This is identifying "There" as a place known for "mountains", where a "great" nation had to conquer "those of the mountains". In this work, only one other quatrain has "montz" spelled with a "*z*".[1] That quatrain interpreted had a main theme that stated "*L'Amethion passer montz Pyrenees*"; and, it was discussed as representing "mountain ones" left behind in "mountains", with new "mountain ones" moving to the "Pyrenees Mountains".

In both scenarios, the "mountain ones" were the soldiers under "The Arabian king", who is Osama bin Laden. That statement makes "mountain ones" be an identifying factor to that man. It is another way of stating the "disciples" he has surrounding him. Thus, the main theme of this quatrain can be expected to be about some "mountains" where Osama bin Laden has been known to operate and where the "great" have sent "troops". This makes Afghanistan the best fit as "There".

---

1   There are only three quatrains with the spelling "*montz*". The other quatrain does not add to the evidence of Osama bin Laden in the Pyrenees Mountains. However, it is relative to what happens after the war begins, as that other quatrain mentions "*assemblez*" is stated twice. Use of that word links it to the quatrain interpreted that had the secondary theme stating, "*Aupres del Hebro se feront assemblees*".

When this focus takes one to that portion of the Middle East most known for its "mountains", the qualifier that differentiates between Afghanistan and Pakistan comes from the words "great troops that will transport over". No "great" nation has invaded Pakistan in recent history. It is a historical record that Afghanistan has been invaded by the "great" of U.S.S.R. (1979 – 1989), and the U.S.A. (with allies, 2001 - present). Thus, the main theme is about one or both of those invasions (with one being the primary focus and the other secondary, if both).

Once again, one finds the future tense of *"passer"* (*"passera"*) used in connection with "mountains". That verb makes this statement show "troops" (from *"copie"*) moved by the "great", such as "that" (from *"que"*, referring to the use of "troops") will act "to go; to proceed, hold on course; to depart from; to surpass, overrun, surmount; to suffer, give way unto; to omit; to transport over; to strain through; to wither; and/or to vanish away". This movement of "troops" then refers to "them", which is a statement about the "great" and the "mountain ones".

The word *"passera"* (or the infinitive, *"passer"*) has been found in three of the quatrains mentioning *"monts Pyrenees"*. Each of those had an association with movements from Afghanistan to those other "mountains". In the case of Osama bin Laden moving from Afghanistan to the "Pyrenees Mountains", this is a secondary reference to the invasion of the "great" United States. Still, *"passer"* meant movement of "troops" at Tora Bora, prior to his escape.

The primary meaning of *"passera"* in this quatrain comes from realizing the history of the Soviet's war with the "mountain ones" of Afghanistan. It became a constant movement of "troops", because the Afghan soldiers were poorly armed for a long time. That is the primary function of guerrilla warfare, such that ambushes and surprise attacks require forces to be constantly on the move. The use of *"les"* as the plural pronoun "them" indicates the movement of the "mountain ones" and the opposing "troops". This is then indicating the eight-year problem the Soviets faced, from more than one person or group of guerrillas.

The main theme makes it clear that a "great" nation will be "There" with "troops", but the timing of this event needs to be narrowed down. One needs to be sure which "great" the main theme is focusing on. This comes from the separate focus (comma use at the end of line one) that is found in the secondary theme. Line two is free to focus on elements specific to the main theme of an invasion by a "great".

The secondary theme is one seen as an astrological-astronomical statement. This means the whole of the line has been read in one gulp, so that some think it says, "Saturn into the Archer (symbolic for the sign Sagittarius) turning to the fish (symbolic for the sign Pisces) Mars". There is something to this; the astronomical movements of planets shown in that series of words do act to time the events relative to an invasion; but one cannot grasp the full meaning of *The Prophecies* by grabbing handfuls of words and thinking that is the whole truth.

The full meaning of this line is developed on multiple levels of interpretation, by looking at the full meaning of each word written. When one does that, one sees depth coming from the symbolic associations connected to astrological analysis. By slowly reading the astrological elements, it becomes possible to see the Sun's movement being inferred by the sign changes. Each word acts as a progression of time, while also explaining what happened during that progression. Everything becomes precisely definitive of one historic period of time, which coincides with only one "great" invasion of "troops" into Afghanistan.

The first word of line two is "*Saturne*", which by being capitalized is seen as the planet of that proper name. The importance of capitalization is masked by the fact that "Saturn" is commonly capitalized. That name representing a planet is only one aspect of the word's meaning; and, capitalization always acts an elevation of meaning a word bears, which can only come from expanding beyond all limiting aspects a name of a person, place, or thing implies.

The 1611 Old French–Old English dictionary lists the names of each of the known planets (seven at that time). Those listings show them to all have an alchemical association to a particular metal. The listing for "*Saturne*" shows it to represent "lead". In the hindsight view of modern times, looking back on the times when people were seen as foolish for their beliefs, most people hold onto the notion that alchemists strove to turn "lead" into gold. As such, "lead" is a common metal, of little value; and, it was commonly used as an additive to paints, as well as to shape into bullets. In that sense, "Saturn" stands for "Lowliness", as alchemists saw "Lead" as the "Lowest metal".[2]

What are not easily determined by the typical person are the astrological associations tied to the planets. As the furthest known planet from the Sun (in the 16th century), "Saturn" moved the slowest through the signs of the zodiac,

2   Royal Society of Chemistry (RSC.org) article on "Lead".

and thus lingered the longest in each sign. It was related to the planet "Mars" as a "malefic" planet, meaning its placement often represented the hardships of life, making it appear to be the harbinger of bad "Times". The planet "Saturn" was called the "greater malefic" because its perceived damage lasted longer and did more harm. From this association, some astrological key terms for "Saturn" are, "Form, Discipline, Responsibility, Restrictions, Limitations, Sorrow, Delays, Patience, Timing, and/or Wisdom".[3]

From realizing this higher meaning of the name "Saturn", one can first look back at the beginning of the main theme line and associate "The great" as being mirrored in the planet "Saturn". From the meanings discussed, one can apply "Lowest" of "The great", the "Greater malefic" of "The great", and "The great" who acts to "Limit, Restrict, Delay" and bring "Sorrow" upon its own people, as well as those it invades. This meaning allows one to see the Soviet Union as the "Saturn" of "The great".

This then shows evil being spread onto "the mountain ones", because "Saturn" is the first word following the comma at the end of line one. While marking a separation, the two words become linked. It shows the importance of "Patience" and "Responsibility" being forced upon "them mountain ones", following the invasion of "great troops" into their land.

The proper name "Saturn" then reflects a completely separate focus, as the astronomical planet visible in the sky by the naked eye (when available for viewing at night time). It is not always in the same place, so the particular time that it goes "into" the sign represented by "the Archer" becomes an important timing factor. The planet "Saturn" takes roughly 28 years to make a complete trip around the Sun, meaning it spends around two and one-third years in each sign of the zodiac. This means that the time of "Saturn in Sagittarius" only occurs between three and four times per century. To put that into perspective, that celestial occurrence has only happened somewhere around 16 or 17 times since 1555, which is not very often.

When one realizes that the focus of the majority of the stories of *The Prophecies* are contemporary to the 20th and 21st centuries, there are only two relevant time periods to consider, based on when "Saturn" is, was, or will be "in the Archer". One still has not occurred, but it is relatively close to now. That time will be between late December 2014 and late December 2017, with a period in 2015

---

3   Universal Sky website page on "Saturn in Astrology".

spent back into Scorpio. The other happened between mid November 1985, and mid November 1988 (with a few months in 1988 spent back in Capricorn).[4] This last occurrence is the one most viable.

The time of "Saturn in Sagittarius" appears stated at the beginning of line two, following the main theme that tells of the "great troops that will transport over", into "There". This means that the period between 1985 and 1988 is representative of the separation (denoted by the comma at the end of the main theme line) from the initial invasion, which took place earlier in time. The Soviet invasion and occupation of Afghanistan began in 1979, and their "troops" aggressively carried out offensive campaigns in the "mountains" (including those of neighboring Pakistan), until early 1985. The period between 1985 and 1988 represented the "turning" point of that occupation.

A Wikipedia article on the "Soviet War in Afghanistan" states:

> "In May 1985, the seven principal rebel organizations formed the Seven Party Mujahideen Alliance to coordinate their military operations against the Soviet army. Late in 1985, the groups were active in and around Kabul, unleashing rocket attacks and conducting operations against the communist government."[5]

The article then goes on to state that the Soviets began withdrawing "troops" by the middle of 1987. This timing then acts to identify the secondary theme as a focus on "them mountain ones" having defeated the "great troops There". The main theme is then about the time that the Soviets kept "them mountain ones" always on the move, and defensive, simply trying to survive (leading up to the symbolism of "Saturn"). The secondary theme then states a following time, when "Patience" paid off, allowing the Mujahideen to go on the offensive, causing the tide of the war to turn.

From the article's snippet, which says the rebels began launching rocket attacks, this becomes representative of the capitalization of "*l'Arq*" (an abbreviation of "*Arquer*"). It shows a higher importance, as "the Bow" that shoots rocket arrows. This element must be seen as how the Mujahideen had a chance to defeat

---

4   Saturn was in Sagittarius between 1956-1959, and 1926-1929, while spending the first 10 months of 1900 there. Those times do nothing to bring meaning to this quatrain.
5   Wikipedia article on "Soviet war in Afghanistan".

the "mighty" (alternate translation of "*grand*") Soviets. The stealth of being "mountain ones" was impossible for the Soviets to defeat, but when technology was added to that hidden ability, the "great" knew it was time to pack it up and call it a day.

A report by the Congressional Research Service, entitled "Afghanistan: Post-Taliban Governance, Security, and U.S. Policy" states in its "Background" section:

> "The mujahedin weaponry included U.S.-supplied portable shoulder-fired anti-aircraft systems called "Stingers," which proved highly effective against Soviet aircraft. The United States decided in 1985 to provide these weapons to the mujahedin after substantial debate within the Reagan Administration and some in Congress over whether they could be used effectively and whether doing so would harm broader U.S.-Soviet relations. The mujahedin also hid and stored weaponry in a large network of natural and manmade tunnels and caves throughout Afghanistan."[6]

> "Partly because of the effectiveness of the Stinger in shooting down Soviet helicopters and fixed wing aircraft, the Soviet Union's losses mounted, turning Soviet domestic opinion against the war. In 1986, after the reformist Mikhail Gorbachev became leader ... (and) On April 14, 1988, Gorbachev agreed to a U.N.-brokered accord (the Geneva Accords) requiring it to withdraw. The withdrawal was completed by February 15, 1989, leaving in place the weak Najibullah government."[7]

This report, which acknowledges C.I.A. involvement with the organization of the rebels referred to as "mujahedin" (their spelling), shows how "There" in Afghanistan, when the Soviet "troops" invaded, the "great" United States had its own "troops" assisting the resistance. Until the time that "them mountain ones" could be adequately armed to fight a "mighty" foe, the C.I.A. was covertly training people like Osama bin Laden in the fine art of guerrilla warfare tactics: such as how to plant a roadside bomb. This involvement is what brought Osama bin Laden to prominence as a young member of the Afghan Arabs who went to

---

6   Congressional Research Service, RL30588, pdf.
7   Ibid.

Afghanistan to assist the resistance. All received training from C.I.A. operatives, whose enemy was their enemy. Thus, the secondary theme is showing the effect of a hidden (yet known) element of the "great", which acted to "Father" (the principle associated with "Saturn") "them mountain ones"; by showing "them" how to move "mountains" through terroristic acts and high-tech weapons.

The present participle verb *"tournant"* then shows the "turning" point of that occupation, but it hints at a much greater "changing, altering, and/or converting" that would take place. The Soviets would be found "returning" to their own land, but they would also be "returning" to the independent states and national names that existed prior to becoming a Union of Soviet Socialist states. The U.S.S.R. would crumble into Russia and the 14 smaller nations, all of which had been sovereign before 1922. The Soviet Union was "turning" into a milder, gentler superpower that wanted its people happy.

The secondary theme states "turning to the fish", such that the "fish" represents the astrological sign Pisces (symbol of two "fish" joined by a line). This segment of words then calls upon the esoteric meaning of Pisces, which suggests a "returning to the" characteristics of, "sacrificing, caring, empathy, selflessness, and/or understanding". There is a sense of "spirituality" also associated with the sign, such that the big bad wolf Soviet Union seemed to have seen the inner light of "intuitiveness'" and finally come to its senses. After a good defeat at the hands of shepherds in the Afghan "mountains", it was time for the Reds to "dissolve" (an alternate essence of Pisces).

During this time that the Soviet Union was "changing", Prime Minister Mikhail Gorbachev created the office of President of the Soviet Union. He assumed this position on "March" 15, 1990, (while the Sun was in the sign of Pisces) and he remained in that position until the Soviet Union ceased to exist on December 25, 1991. Soon after that initial step was taken, the planet "Mars" went into the sign of the "fish", and remained there between April and May 1990. This would satisfy the timing order stated in the secondary theme, meaning "Mars" went into Pisces and that ended the series of astrological events listed.

Still, the capitalization of the word *"Mars"* must always be seen as bearing the meaning of the Roman god of "War". This usage can turn the noun "fish" into the verb "fish", such that the "changing" is akin to putting new bait on a hook (a curved "Arrow"), in the game of "War". This is symbolic of a "turning" of the table, such that with the Soviets out of Afghanistan, only the C.I.A. was there

PROSECUTION EXHIBIT P

meddling.

The religious aspects relative to the sign Pisces is that "sacrifice" for a higher reward comes from being in touch with one's higher mind ("spirituality"). There was some appearance of the Russians making a "sacrifice" after they were left naked before the United Nations, without all their supporters (those formerly behind the Iron Curtain) urging them to veto anything the United States wanted to do. They "sacrificed" and let them all be free to call the Western nations for billions of U. S. dollars in aid. They even stepped back and bit the bullet in 1990-91, when the United States wanted to invade Kuwait and kick Saddam Hussein back to Iraq. They made this sacrifice when Saddam Hussein was a huge fan of the tactics of Josef Stalin and a former ally.[8]

Regardless of those facts, perhaps a better way to read the end of line two is as, "to the fish War". Seeing it that way makes a "fish War" become a "turning" away from being a "bear War." This states a reversal from focusing on "War" against atheist Communists on Afghan soil, to a "turning" against the Christian element on their soil, beginning a new "War". In case one has missed seeing those bumper stickers and auto emblems of the "ichthus fish", they are there because the "fish" is a very recognized symbol of Jesus and Christianity. To the Muslims fighting against the "great" in Afghanistan, victory getting the atheists off their land was a blessing from Allah, not from Stinger missiles nor from C.I.A. trainers. Allah had proved to them He can beat the "great ones", so why not go "fishing" for more?

The colon at the end of line two leads one to see the clarification of this use of "*Mars*" in line three. That line begins with the capitalization of the word "*Venins*", which means "Poisons, Venoms, and/or Poison ones". This word then leads to the word "*cachés*", which means "concealed ones, hidden ones, and/or kept secret ones". When the word "*Mars*" is used as a reference to "War", it becomes a link to important "Poisons" (capitalization) that are "kept secret". Such "Poisons" can be seen as weapons of mass destruction.

This clarification allows one to see a plan having been set into action, one that makes it possible to see how the Soviet withdrawal may have had ulterior purposes. In a "War" that caused the death of 13,400 Soviet soldiers,[9] due to

---

8   Frontline: The survival of Saddam – Secrets of His Life and Leadership.
9   From the Congressional Research Services report on Afghanistan, which cited Soviet statistics.

"secret Venoms" having been supplied by the "great" United States, that history demonstrates "secret deals" for "Weapons"[10] occurred. While this is shown to be associated with the subsequent "conversion" of the Soviets, line three's "secret Venoms" is clarifying a "fish War" and supporting a main theme about the Soviets dominating Afghanistan after invading it. It acts as "Weapons" of "War", or major importance (capitalization), being "hidden" for the purpose of surprising Christians.

Remember the reason the United States used to go into Iraq in 2002? It was to find "hidden Weapons of Mass Destruction". Reading this as a message in this quatrain helps explain why the southern Russians (in the "-stans") would assist the "passage" of Osama bin Laden to the "Pyrenees Mountains", as was seen in an earlier quatrain.

As stated previously, this quatrain is interesting and this "hidden" element assists one in seeing how the Muslim Iranians can deal so successfully with an atheist Russia, as far as arms deals over the past 20 years. Still, this direction veers away the purpose of showing evidence that Osama bin Laden is hiding in the "Pyrenees". For that reason, the remainder of this quatrain will not be interpreted. However, the two main themes, as well as the clarification to the secondary theme in line three, shows where Osama bin Laden "cut his teeth" as a military leader, proving his worth well enough to earn a devout following.

This quatrain indicates an important "turning" based on the "Punishment" (alternate meaning of "Saturn", as the "Disciplinarian") capability that comes from being "in" possession of "the Bow" that shoots "Venoms". This acts as explaining what is "beneath" the confidence Osama bin Laden shows in his continued messages to the world.

To summarize this partial quatrain by bullet points, it shows the following:

1. The initial focus of the main theme is on "There", which is a place of "mountains".
2. A "great" nation "will transport over troops" in the land of "mountains".
3. The "great will overrun them" who are described as "mountain ones".
4. The important ally of "them mountain ones" is found to be "Patience"

---

10   The alchemist view of the planet "Mars" had it representative of the metal "Iron". The word "*fer*", which means "iron", is symbolically used by Nostradamus to state "weapons".

and "Endurance" through "Hardship", as symbolized by the astrological associations with the planet "Saturn".

5. The planet "Saturn" identifies the "great troops" as those of "Lowest value", based on the alchemist association placed on that planet, which relates to the U.S.S.R.
6. The timing factor of "Saturn in Sagittarius" (symbolic meaning of "*l'Arquer*," in French) puts the secondary theme between November 1985 and November 1988.
7. The mujahideen of Afghanistan mounted their greatest damage against the Soviets between 1985 and 1987, due to anti-aircraft, surface-to-air missiles, making that be represented by "the Bow".
8. The U.S. authorized the C.I.A. to arm the mujahideen, making that become the "turning" point of the Soviet occupation of Afghanistan.
9. The Soviet Union also reached a "changing" after leaving Afghanistan, when it "dissolved".
10. The planet "Mars" went into the sign "of the fish" (Pisces) in April and May of 1990, after Mikhail Gorbachev became the first President of the Soviet Union, in "March" 1990.
11. The "turning of the Arrow" makes a "fish" hook, such that the possession of major "Weapons" allows "them mountain ones" to play the game of "War" from a position of strength.
12. The "fish" is a symbol of Jesus and Christianity.
13. A "fish War" would represent a "turning" from a "War" against Communists, and into a "War" against Christians.
14. "Weapons" of mass destruction, including those of "Poisonous" properties, have been "hidden" to avoid detection.

Afterthoughts: It is important for me to restate that astrology is a language that is similar to the writings in *The Prophecies*. The secondary theme statement in this quatrain is one of those that initially instilled a sense of urgency in my first nudges by God to "look here" and "look there." I found a timeline, based on what appeared to be astrological statements as found here; and that timeline went back to Oliver Cromwell, but really placed focus on the 20th and 21st centuries. I was sure the great war was going to begin around 2005 or 2006.

While I was (obviously) wrong, that had no impact on Nostradamus having been wrong, nor a true prophecy from the mind of Jesus Christ, sent by God to a prophet in His Son's name. My errors showed me that the whole of The Prophecies was in parts that needed to be put in the correct order. While my initial try at ordering failed, God was pleased with my first works. He was pleased with my faith and my enthusiasm based on faith.

In that regard, everything I wrote about the secondary theme is valid. Astrological language is expansive, to the point os being unlimited (to a degree) as to what more can be said. That more will also be valid. As I read verse two again, a fresh idea came to mind, which I feel is worthwhile to share now.

Saturn reflects the Father principle. Saturn is in many ways representative of the serious God the Father of the Old Testament. God sets expectations and then demands those be met. There is great reward when that happens, but great punishment when one fails. The punishment is always self-imposed, simply because one turned away from God by not meeting His expectations set. The reason is always, "Sin made me do it!"

In astrology there are two signs that reflect faith and religion and two signs that reflect true goals and true relationships. Those four signs are consecutive, stretching from Sagittarius to Pisces, with Capricorn and Aquarius in between. Sagittarius and Pisces are ruled by Jupiter, which can be seen (by Christians) like Jesus Christ. Jupiter rules the signs reflecting religion (Sagittarius) and faith (Pisces). Saturn rules the two in between: Capricorn and Aquarius. Saturn and Jupiter are two opposite principles, such that Jupiter is expansive and Saturn is restrictive.

With that basic setup, Saturn in the sign of Sagittarius is a bad placement. Strict religion is not good. Strict self-goals and strict associations with those who will help one reach expected goals is good. Likewise, loose goals and friends means goals can never be reached; and, strict demands on faith keeps one from hearing the voice of God within, because of the cleric hammering one's knuckles for not praying loud enough.

"Saturn in the Bow" (as a gulp of words reflecting one meaning) is a statement about the Taliban. Simply by seeing that as an important (capitalization) aspect of the secondary theme says, "Afghanistan." They grew in power after the Soviets were defeated, with many of them fighting with the Mujahideen. The Afghan Civil War becomes an element of "Mars" at the end of the verse. This means "turning to the fish" can be the Afghan government turning to the United States for help in fighting them, drawing America in further after the events of 9/11/2001.

Chapter 21
Prosecution Exhibit Q

French Mountains Will Come to Penetrate

This is the last of the quatrains I will present that have the word "*monts*" in the main theme line. This main theme is divided into two halves, as seen by the use of a mid-line comma. This usage is supportive evidence for the "Pyrenees", as it has verbiage that links to the quatrain that told of the itinerary from Afghanistan-Pakistan to France. In this sense, "*monts*" bears the meaning of "mountains" in both places, as well as the "mountain ones" who will be at both places.

The whole of this quatrain need not be interpreted as evidence that Osama bin Laden is hiding in the Pyrenees, but the themes of "piercing", "being under", and "secret" are found in the first three lines. Line four is important in supporting elements of the secondary theme, but it takes the focus away from the border between France and Spain. Therefore, the discussion will focus on relevant information in the first three lines and largely leave the deeper meaning that line four reveals alone.

The entire quatrain can be seen as stating (simply translated):

Gaulois par saults, monts viendra penetrer:	Of France through bounds, mountain ones will arrive to pierce:
Occupera le grand lieu de l'insubre:	Will usurp by force him place of to the home dweller:
Au plus profond son ost fera entrer,	With the more secret his army will cause to go in,

245

Gennes, Monech pousseront classe rubre.	Tortured ones, Monaco will be thrusting fleet red.

The first word is the capitalized "*Gaulois*", which means, "Of France, French, and/or Frenchman". As the name for specific peoples of a nation, the word is commonly spelled as a capitalized proper name. Still, the true meaning of the word is to state "Someone from Gaul", which is the region of Western Europe the Romans knew by that name.

The area that was "Gaul" was divided into territories, such as Belgica, Celtica, Gallia Cisalpina, Aquitania, and Narbonensis. Today, that territory covers Belgium, Luxembourg, Switzerland, France, and Northern Italy. On a higher level of meaning, "Someone" from all of these places puts an initial focus on being "Western European", even though "Someone of France" is heavily implied.

This use of "*Gaulois*" links this quatrain to the quatrain that stated "One king will be who will come to see there Gaul". In a sense, this is like the saying "When in Rome, do as the Romans do." When one is in "Gaul," one acts "*Gaulois*", without actually being "French" or even "Western European". Thus, when this word is followed by the words "*par saults*", it says that one is "of Gaul through leaps, jumps, skips, and/or bounds". This is making the first half of the main theme focus on the stages one will have gone "through" to get to Western Europe. This links to the itinerary quatrain, as the "jumps" were from "Tartary", to "Alania", to "Armenia" and then "Gaul".

The second half of the main theme, following the comma use, is indicating a subsequent event to the "leaps" that made one "of France". The first word of this second half is "mountains". As stated, this becomes an indication that the "bounds" one took went from "mountains" to "mountains". When the plural number acts to indicate those of a "mountain", one then sees that the "leaps" took someone from one set of "mountain ones" (al-Qaeda/Taliban) to another set (indigenous people of the Pyrenees, such as the Basque people).

The remainder of the main theme (second half) states, "will come to pierce into" ("*viendra penetrer*"). This is the repeated theme of "piercing", which has been seen stated by the capitalized word "*Transpercer*" ("To pierce through"), which was found in the itinerary quatrain. The secondary theme of another quatrain stated, "*Pour passer outré*" and this was also seen to translate (using the past participle spelling of "*oultré*") as "Because to pass pierced". Then there was another secondary theme that repeated "*Viendra percer les*", meaning "Will come to pierce them". Obviously, these links make this quatrain's use of "*monts*" and "*penetrer*" connect to the use of "monts Pyrenees" and acts of "piercing" in all of the other examples.

This whole main theme, where the two halves are seen in the broader view together, acts to make a statement to be "Of Western Europe" collectively. It went "through" a series of planned stages, where groups of non-Europeans will have made "leaps" from their homelands to the West. The cumulative effect will be "mountains" of immigrants flooding into "Gaul". This main theme matches the interpretation of the two quatrains where their third lines focused on "Mountains" in the "Pyrenees". It also matches the information in the letter to Henry II, which said "there third flood of kindred". The main theme is about a staged flooding of Western Europe, which "will come to penetrate" the lines of defenses that normally prevent invasions.

To confirm this train of thought, the comma at the end of line one leads to the capitalized first word of the secondary theme, "*Occupera*". This is making the important statement that following this "penetration", the major purpose will be to "Occupy; Busy, Trouble, Employ; Use, Posses, Enjoy; Win, Take, Usurp by force; and/or Seize on". All of these uses are put into effect over "leaps" of time, from the beginning of legal and illegal immigration. The people flooding Western Europe will become a major "Trouble" on western economies, as these people "Use" the benefits of the West to their advantage. However, the ultimate purpose will be found to be to "Usurp by force" Western Europe; and, that can only come through a major war offensive.

This makes the capitalized word "*Occupera*" have a higher meaning, but the ultimate height of meaning comes from seeing how this planned "Occupation" is an exact model of the Zionist movement into Palestine. That was a plan that was designed to infiltrate Palestine with Jews through legal immigration, and then through uncontrolled illegal migrations. This took place over decades of time (1900-1948), increasing greatly with the assistance of British and French mandates in the Middle East (1918-1946). The ultimate result was, as the Zionists had envisioned it, the "Usurping by force" of Palestine, to create the new Israel. That "Occupation" is the root of the "*Gaulois Occupera*" ("Will occupy people of Western Europe"). The higher meaning is how God allows for "turnabout (to be) fair play."

This major word ("*Occupera*") is then followed by the article "*le*", which once again must be seen as the personal pronoun, indicating "he, she, it, and/or him". As the non-gender use, "it" is pointing to that which "will be Occupied". As the masculine third person pronoun usage the word acts as "he" or "him", which relates to one masculine gender found in "Of France" (or "Frenchman"). That becomes "he" who reached that destination "through jumps" from "mountains" to "mountains" (i.e., Osama bin Laden). In either case, the objective is to "Usurp by force" the region that calls itself "great" and "mighty" (alternate translation of "*grand*", the next word in line two). The achievement of that goal will make "him" equally "great".

The secondary theme clearly indicates the "Occupation" is to be in a "great place" (from "*grand lieu*"), which Western Europe is, especially France. It also shows how "he" will be in a "high place" (alternate translation of "*grand*"), which is a good description of being in the "mountains". However, when the word "*lieu*" is seen to also mean, "seat, rank; calling, state; reckoning, and/or account", one can see how "he" will be the one to hold the "great" to a "reckoning" for their acts of aiding and abetting an "Occupation" of Palestine.

The final word of line two is somewhat of an enigma, in the sense that in the lower-case it is not a word. That word is "*insubre* and it is recognizable as the ancient people of the region known as Insubria, who were the Insubres. That region is in northern Italy. That acts as a secondary meaning, which relates to the information of line four. One is able to see "*insubre*" as one person from the region known as Insubria, because one sees the Italian city "Genoa" and the principality close to that, "Monaco", appear in the last line. However, the lower-case spelling indicates the true meaning goes to the root of the proper name, which would be descriptive of those ancient peoples.

The Insubres were Celtic "*Gaulois*", who were the first to invade northern Italy. They settled in the north-central region of the Italian mainland, in what is now Lombardy. The Insubres founded the city of Milan. The Celtic meaning of "*Insubres*" is "home dwellers",[1] which means they built their "dwelling place" (alternate translation of "*lieu*"). Thus, the secondary theme is putting focus on why "he Will occupy the great". As a parallel, that "great place of their dwelling" (to "Western Europeans") is as important to them as was the "home dwelling" of

---

[1] From Total War website, "The Celts" thread.

PROSECUTION EXHIBIT Q

the people who called Palestine "their dwelling place".

Line two then ends with a colon, making line three offer clarification on "the home dweller". This leads to the capitalized first word, "*Au*", which is a combined preposition-article ("*A+le(s)*") meaning, "To him, In the, With them, and/or At a" (in many combinations). In all possibilities of translation, a relationship is indicated between those who "dwell" in Western Europe and "him" who "Will occupy". As such, this relationship highlights how the "great place" that is made up of the nations of Western Europe includes those whose "place of dwelling" has been "Usurped by force" by the "great". This is the situation found in the Pyrenees Mountains and it is the situation found in modern Insubria. A movement for independence has been present in that region for centuries, albeit to a lesser degree than the efforts demonstrated by the Basque.

When the third line is seen as a separate entity, it begins by stating "With him more profound", where the word "*profond*" can also mean, "high, deep; of much capacity, of great receipt; secret; insatiable, and/or bottomless". This one word shows a relationship between "him" and those "*Gaulois* of the dwelling place", who "Will be occupied" by "the great". This relationship is "deep", allowing much "capacity" to keep "it" and "him secret", while being "penetrated deep" within the "mountains" they "Will occupy". This shows how Osama bin Laden can be "hidden" in the "Pyrenees Mountains".

The remainder of line three states "his army will act to enter". This is stating the singular masculine possessive circumstance, which links "he" to "his". The word "*ost*" means only "army", which is a direct link to the other quatrain that foretold of the "conductor of the army" ("*conducteur de l'armee*"). The use of "to enter" is supportive of the rhyming verb in the main theme, "*penetrer*", such that this "entry" will be to "pierce into Gaul" by "having access unto". This "access" will be prior to an invasion "entrance" (due to the order of words). The use of "to enter" then has military implications, because it "will be made" by a "profound army" (from "*profond ... ost*").

The elements of line four support the translation of "*l'insubre*" as Insubria, by focusing on two Ligurian coastal "dwelling places". Those two places were in ancient Ligum, controlled by the Ligurian people ("Monaco" was a colony of Liguria). Because Ligum is not the same as Insubria, one can begin to see that the word taken as meaning "Genoa" ("*Gennes*") can actually turn into a stand-alone statement, meaning "racked or tortured ones". This is because Old French shows the word "*genne*" as being the same as "*gehenne*", which bears that meaning of torture. Still, the implication holds a secondary meaning as two places that will become the focal points of a naval invasion, which is "to enter profound".

Seeing line four in this light brings one's attention back to the several quatrains that have been shown to prophesy major events "By land AND sea". It shows that "Of Gaul" includes France, Spain, and Northern Italy. The main focus of this quatrain takes shape by recognizing the stages that prepare for such a "deep penetration". It shows that a master plan is in effect and it requires a master planner.

The bullet point breakdown of the information of this quatrain is as follows:

1. The initial focus of the main theme is of "Someone of Gaul", which is collectively Western Europe, and individually France, Belgium, Luxembourg, Switzerland, and Northern Italy.
2. The main theme shows a passage "through jumps" to become one "Of Gaul
3. A focus of "mountains" states the "bounds" between "Gaul" and the "jumping" off point.
4. The main theme is telling of what "will come to penetrate Gaul" in stages, such that immigration becomes an important issue.
5. A major focus is placed on what "Will occupy the great", which parallels that which "the great Will usurp by force".
6. The issue of "Occupation" is relative "to the home dwelling" one is forced to share with another.
7. An important person is implied to have "penetrated" the "mountains of France", and this is supported by the statement that "he" is "With them" who "dwell" in a "place Occupied" by the "great", which seeks its own independence.
8. This important person has built "his army" in "secret", from "deep" within the "mountains" of "the great".
9. This "army" will assist "him" at the time that "he will cause" an invasion force "to enter" Western European countries.

Afterthoughts: Both the main theme and the secondary theme statements end in colons. This means the main theme of going to Gaul (France) for the purpose of penetrating it yields an example that is both the past (Palestine stolen) and the future (Western Europe stolen). Thus, "his army" is relative to Osama bin Laden.

Chapter 22
An Appeal in Defense
Against ~~Twenty-Five, Twenty-Seven~~ ... Fifty Million U. S. Dollars

Overall, 948 quatrains make up the ten *"Centuries"* of *The Prophecies*. From that whole, to this point I have presented parts or all of sixteen quatrains. That constitutes less than two percent of the total. I also presented one segment (three series of words) from the letter to Henry II, a document containing 4,500 words.[1] Those three series total 32 words or little more than seven-tenths of one percent (.007) of the total word count. That mirrors the minuscule percentage of the quatrains I have interpreted here. These figures show how the story that tells of Osama bin Laden being in the Pyrenees Mountains is just a small part of the whole story told by *The Prophecies*.

My one prediction has focused on where Osama bin Laden can be found. The evidence I have presented for that one prediction could be used in support of several related predictions. I estimate that roughly seven hundred prophecies are still fully waiting to happen. That figure is just under seventy-five percent. The sixteen quatrains I have presented have elements that have yet to happen, although the first parts are dependent on Osama bin Laden having already escaped to the Pyrenees Mountains. Those quatrains all link to other quatrains, which tell other related stories. This all goes to show that *The Prophecies* can produce a large number of predictions. It all depends on one's ability to read the instructions and then put the puzzles together correctly.

---

1   My document that has the French text of Nostradamus' letter to Henry II totals 4,500 words.

Each quatrain is a self-sufficient prophecy. Truth is contained in each one. By them connecting to one another, with all holding truth, a broader truth is found. The story that predicts where Osama bin Laden is hiding, as the evidence shows, is one series of true events that are linked into a long series of true events. Combined, the whole tells about the beginning of Osama bin Laden's rise, how Osama bin Laden gained a reputation that would build a following of devout Islamic soldiers, what he plans to do with those soldiers, and what will happen if nothing is done to stop him from unleashing his plan upon the world. Osama bin Laden is not the one creating this future, because the sum of the parts of the past is greater than the sum of the parts of Osama bin Laden. The past created Osama bin Laden and the past is creating the future.

Each new focus discovered is a consequence of something before. It then leads to something else happening, as a chain of events that are cause and effect; but this action is not linear, although it appears that way on a timeline. It is actually a back and forth movement, like a pendulum swinging. For every action there is an equal and opposite reaction. The result is like Newton's cradle, in which a ball is dropped against other stationary balls. This motion would go on for a long time if nothing is done to bring everything to a rest state.

Bringing everything to a rest state is the answer, especially when one is told that the future will be a direct result of the past. Nostradamus prophesied our future, from the rest state of his present. He was allowed to see what action would take place in his future (our past) and how it would continue to escalate the force of the pendulum, until everything would get so far out of hand that a rest state would come about through complete destruction.

Because prophecy is less believable these days and because people have failed to see Nostradamus as a true prophet of God, thus telling the truth when he named a book *The Prophecies*, his verses have been seen as "predictions." The problem we face now is that many people think that a prediction of future events must come to fruition to be believed. Anything short of perfection is just a lucky guess. Anything not coming true within one's impatient time expectations is then deemed completely false. That presumption is itself false, as stopping prophetic predictions from coming true is why God allows human beings to prophesy in the first place.

The quatrains are prophecies that are like dominoes, set up in rows so that when the first one falls over then all the rest will fall over. When an elaborate domino set-up has been "engineered" (as seen on TV) it takes a few minutes for the final dominoes to fall over. Life is on a slower pace than elaborate domino demonstrations. When the first domino falls in life, it may take years for it to make the second domino fall. Over time, all the dominoes will fall as planned, as long as they have been engineered correctly.

We are the engineers that set up the dominoes of life. God allows us to do that. When we set up a pretty domino arrangement, where only good things happen when everything falls down, God cheers us on; and, He might even blow in the places where one domino will lean a little off its angle, to help us out. However, humanity usually does a better job setting up bad dominoes that fall and hurt people. When that happens, God whispers in the ear of a prophet and tells that prophet to tell the people the dominoes are set up to do no good. In those cases, it is up to the domino engineers (us) to stop the dominoes from falling. If we do that, God will cheer us on; and, He might even help us hold a falling domino up.

We are now in the middle of a bad domino chain reaction, one than began way back around 1650, and slowly built up momentum over 350 years, but picked up the pace once 1900 came around. Now that the year 2000 has passed, the dominoes are falling much more quickly. We have engineered an elaborate array of dominoes, a single line of dominoes that split to about five circular lines back between 1948 and 1998. They are all about to come full circle. When that happens, then there will be points where many lines of dominoes converge. This means that the world cannot wait for a prediction about the end of the world to come true, in order to prove Nostradamus was a prophet of God. When the end of the world comes, what is the point of doing anything then?

The world has to see the dominoes lined up and remove those closest to the forward momentum, so that the most recent tipping point falls harmlessly to the ground, with the majority still left standing. To put that in clear terms, now is the time to do something to stop the forward momentum that is about to go out of control (in the near future), so the world can be saved. Proving that Osama bin Laden is hiding in the Pyrenees Mountains will do nothing to save the world. Osama bin Laden is not a domino. He is someone with his finger on the button of many dominoes, but anyone can replace his finger. The domino that needs to be stopped is that which makes Osama bin Laden do what he has done and what he promises to do. Believe me, Osama bin Laden is not a natural born killer that does what he does for cheap thrills, without any other reason. There is something bigger than Osama bin Laden behind Osama bin Laden.

The $50-Million Reelection Gift • *Robert Tippett*

At this point, one must realize that catching Osama bin Laden is not the point of this work. Proving he is in the Pyrenees Mountains will not be easy. If he were to walk out of some cave and turn himself in for the reward money today, putting him in a prison and then heaping all the evil deeds of the world upon his shoulders, like a scapegoat, will not save the world. The charges against him represent the pendulum swung by the actions inspired, led, or committed by Osama bin Laden. To cut off his head and then go kill everyone who might have known him, helped him, or plotted revenge with him, would be the pendulum swinging back once more (we actually have already done the killing of his friends part).

We have to realize that the actions caused by Osama bin Laden were reactions to actions taken by those who have made the pendulum swing before. That action was cheering the recreation of the State of Israel and then helping the Israelis win a dozen or so wars against Arabs. To catch Osama bin Laden would not remove the momentum that will make more dominoes fall, the most critical dominoes. The only way to stop the momentum is to stop, look, and listen. The answer is crying out to be heard, but everyone is so busy pushing the buttons that make the pendulum swing that no one can hear that cry.

The answer is not to have ~~$25-million~~ ~~$27-million~~ $50-million in reward money for turning in Osama bin Laden, dear or alive. That is blood money; and, it is paid in pieces of paper that have less and less value. All value that $50-million has is in this worldly dimension is an illusion, as no value will be carrying over into the heavenly dimension. The reward money represents the thirty pieces of silver Judas Iscariot took for turning in Jesus. As such, all rewards for giving information that leads to the apprehension or conviction of Osama bin Laden, a wanted criminal, is nothing more than a carrot on a string, leading the world to want that end. Osama bin Laden is not the end that justifies the means.

The answer is to have God save the world. This means the problem sensed by so many people, of the End Times being near (the History Channel can be referenced for the various genres of End Times sources) is because mankind has no inkling that God is the only way to save the world. An admission that the end is inevitable is an admission that humanity has collectively turned its back to God.

The leaders of the world have become like the Roman Empire overseers of Judah. The Sanhedrin assembly is like the United States government, which wants to try, convict, and execute Osama bin Laden. They want to kill him because he points at them and calls them out as being far from protectors of the holy temple. The Western world is like the Sadducees and Pharisees, who bend over backwards honoring the wealth, power, and position their knowledge of their religion allows them, while thanking God for not being like those who have nothing but misery. This is not a world of Christians seeking to find peace. It has become lynch mob mentality, with all kinds (Muslim, Christian, Atheist, Polytheistic, etc.) clamoring to let the criminal free and crucify the good. Everyone wants to see some human sacrificed to the gods, as a way of saving the world.

That was why Jesus sacrificed himself to the mob. He was God's sacrificial lamb that was presented to the world for inspection and found to be without blemish. He was sacrificed so that the world would know the way to God and never have the end approach. It only took 1,900 years for all hell to break loose. Now the insane ones have risen to take over the asylum. No matter how hard the weak pray for God to come save the day now, God is not going to remove the most critical dominoes that we have worked so hard setting up to fall. It is up to us (everyone in the whole world, together) to do that. The world has to show that we believe in God and are begging God to come save us. We have to act to stop the momentum, to steady the arm of the pendulum, and make peace rule over the land.

Evidence of God's intervention into human history is proven through realized prophecy. Thus, this work has presented its case in that regard. The prosecution rests, having given ample reason to believe that Osama bin Laden is hiding in the Pyrenees Mountains. He is there plotting the destruction that will lead to the complete collapse of a life-allowing planet. He plans retribution and persecution, on a level that plans to make those he captures face utter agony. He wants them to beg God to put them out of their misery.

All that is left now is to have a few believers convince the F.B.I. that they should look in the Pyrenees Mountains. By dragging the body of Osama bin Laden through the streets of New York City, the world will surely come to realize it was all possible by the word of God, nothing else. As that great day of celebration is taking place, some lucky winner will be at least $50-million richer. Go with throttle up Challenger and save the world by nabbing the most wanted international criminal. And, may God's love be with you.

Afterthoughts: From the 20/20 vision of hindsight, in the year 2020, we know the result of someone having been given a reward for the killing of a man and others in a compound in Abbottabad, Pakistan. Supposedly, the one who targeted that place was unknowingly doing so. There were reports of the fifty million reward having been paid, but then there are reports that nobody was given the reward money

On top of that failure to stand behind an offer for information that leads to the capture of a much wanted criminal, I imagine fewer will come forward in the future to help America weed out its enemies. There also was no corpse brought home and placed in a pine box, leaded up against the outer wall of the Pentagon, for all gawkers, onlookers, and people wanting their picture taken with a heinous criminal to help pay back the reward paid. They supposedly did that with the body of Jesse James, but then there came those reports that his death was another example of fakery, so the wanted could walk freely without worry.

The news of the Navy disposing of Osama bin Laden's body at sea, with some quickie DNA test having been done, is too much to swallow as truth. Even is test results were to come back within a few days (which was not the case), there would have been reasonable doubt as to whether or not the DNA was obtained properly and tested beyond any question. Even if it would have been absolutely confirmed that the corpse was that of Osama bin Laden, the dead deserve being released to their families for internment. To dump a body into the sea and say it was adhering to Islamic law sounds like America had all of a sudden turned into a Muslim nation.

As such, the defense would like to challenge this death as questionable, at best. It was no secret that Saddam Hussein employed body doubles for himself and his sons. The pictures I saw of the supposed corpse of Osama bin Laden did not look like him, as far as other pictures of him I had to compare those death pictures to. If it was Osama bin Laden, then he must have suffered some stroke or contracted sudden-onset yellow belly syndrome of chicken spine disorder, reduced to some lackey holed up in a Pakistani compound, within walking distance to the Pakistan military command center.

Finally, if God (the one Christians bow down before) had been on our side in this attack, there would be no questioning the identity and no stealth helicopter would have been crashed and left behind. It all smells to high heaven. The dominoes are still in their slow-motion fall.

Chapter 23
Defense Exhibit A

Whose Side Is God On?

To this point, some fainting goat Christians might have gone stiff over the comparison I have made, making Osama bin Laden out as a parallel to Jesus Christ. Let me assure everyone that Osama bin Laden is no Jesus Christ. He is quite the opposite, in many ways; but he is also similar.

Jesus had his devout followers, as does bin Laden. Jesus began a major movement; and, to some degree, so has bin Laden. Jesus was betrayed by one follower and killed; but despite the offers of reward, bin Laden is not in the custody of law enforcement officials. So far, there has been no Judas Iscariot stepping forward to turn him in, nor has Osama bin Laden offered himself up as a sacrificial lamb. Jesus led a faction of the tiny religion (comparatively) Judaism, while bin Laden leads a faction that amounts to roughly 24% of the world's population (1.7 billion [est.] Muslims, 7 billion [est.] total population). This all can be seen as similar aspects that result in major differences. If one had to sum up this comparison, Jesus is the Son of God (as the Messiah), while Osama bin Laden is the Antichrist. That name actually means, "Opposite Christ."

This is the important perspective offered by Nostradamus, one that needs to be considered before teams of prospective bounty hunters load up the pack mules and head to the Pyrenees Mountains. Evidence shows how Christians also have become opposites of Christ, by acting out lives that are far from being Christ-like. This is as anti-Christ as is Osama bin Laden being the Antichrist. In essence, Christians acting like antichrists means Christians have turned their backs to God, making the Antichrist possible. Therefore, we all need a prophetic lesson on how this opposite state was foretold by Nostradamus.

Nostradamus explained in his letter of preface that the events detailed in *The Prophecies* (the prophetic quatrains) would occur when the world had come to the point of being "diametrically opposite" to the way things were in 1555. This flip-flopping, or polar shift, was prophesied to be a change in the order of powerful influences over the masses.[1] He identified those three influences as "reigns, religions, and sects".

This meant the days when kings ruled nations, with the Roman Catholic Church acting as their equal (they influenced kings and had powerful armies too). Those two main powers then allowed power and influence to a thin (but ever growing) layer of non-royals/non-religious specialists. Those would have a level of influence over the people in common ways (architects, painters, astrologers, printers, military leaders, etc.). All had influence from being connected to God. The kings of "reigns" represented the royal bloodline. The leaders of the "religions" represented the royal body to lead. Those common people of talents (the "sects") represented the royal spirit. Collectively, they represented the rightful order of the Trinity.

That order changed when the common man began cutting the heads off kings, denying the Church influence over a government (separation of Church and State), and allowing those of common birth to land in the tops seats of power, over nations and empires. It was a time when Camelot lost its way. The Holy Grail (i.e., the Trinity) was missing and Arthur (Christ the King) was without Excalibur (the Church of Christ). The world began a slide towards apathy and depression, which allowed evil to overtake the kingdom.

The quatrains tell stories (just as they tell the story of where Osama bin Laden is in hiding), which detail the corruptions that would symbolize the last straw, when each of the three, "sects, church, and royalty", would turn their backs towards God. Those who have no significant connection to Christ, either by blood (royal bloodlines of Christ), by body (the apostles of Christ), or by spirit (those given talents by the Master), will ultimately cause the end of the world. We have been in those times for quite awhile now.

1   Nostradamus wrote in the Preface, "*pource que les regnes, sects & religions feront changes si opposites, voire au respect du present diametralement, que si je venois à resere ce qu'à l'advenir sera ceux regne, sect, religion*". This [quite oversimplified] says, "therefore that them reign ones, sect ones & religion ones will be making changes so opposite ones, to see in the respect of the present diametrically, that so I have come at to reveal this that in them to come will be those rule, sect, religion".

In the letter to Henry II, Nostradamus wrote a separate series of words that gives one an overall perspective of how the time of those dismal days will be recognized. Nostradamus wrote in his letter of explanation to Henry II,

> *"qui feront par leur ignorance seduitz par langues qui trencheront plus que nul glaive entre les mains de l'insensé le susdit regne de l'antechrist ne durera jusques au definement de ce nay pres de l'eage"*.

This states (most generally speaking),

> *"who – will be making – by reason of – their – ignorance – seduced ones – through – tongues – which – will be cutting – more – than – no – sword – between – them – power of authority – from – them incensed – him – aforementioned – reign – to – the antichrist – born – will endure – until – with them – wasting away – with – this – ship – close – of – the age"*.

It should be realized that this is one uninterrupted string of words appears between two punctuation marks. There are no marks interfering with the flow of meaning coming from each individual word written. The evidence presented so far in this work has repeatedly shown how important it is to read each word slowly, digesting each word's full scope of meaning. From looking at these words, as they have been translated, this string is stating a more detailed synopsis of what will happen when this "diametrically opposite" state is in place.

Rather than give a full analysis of all the meanings these word convey, due to each word's contextual translations creating an enormous matrix of possibilities allowed[2], it is best to see how the flow generally develops. This series of words begins at a comma, meaning it is a continuation of thought related to a prior string of words. In this regard, the flow that begins by stating, "who will be making their ignorance" is such that "who" (*"qui"*) becomes relative to that previous statement. The previous statement makes it very clear that "who" is the Church of Rome, shown there as, "Kings – temporary ones". That makes "who"

---

[2] In my yet unpublished book, *"The Systems of Nostradamus"*, I introduce how a matrix of translation possibilities can be produced for each quatrain. In another yet unpublished book, *"The Poetry of Nostradamus"*, I arrange all 948 quatrains, one per page, with each quatrain spread out as a matrix.

represent the line of popes. This flow is then stating a prophecy that the times of a "diametrically opposite" Church will be recognized when the popes will be more concerned about "their" position in the world, showing "ignorance" of their vows to Christ and God.

The next flow tells, "seduced ones through tongues which will be cutting more than no sword". This is explaining the seduction that popes will fall prey to, as far as worldly lusts, which in turn turned into seduction of those who looked to them as pious and connected to God. The use of "tongues" (from *"langues"*) is representative of the talk that will spread about those seductions, to the point that people will lose all confidence in the Church, "cutting it asunder". It also applies to the "talk" of the Church appearing as little more than being "seduced" by its archaic beliefs, which made the Church appear to be "ignorant" of science. These two corruptions have already occurred (1939 – present), with the Church having been cut to shreds, worse than any "sword" could do. Still, on a most literal and vulgar level, "seduced through tongues" is an appropriate summary of the scandals the Church has become mired in over the past thirty years, in reference to child molestation accusations.

Following that, the line continues to state, "between them powers of authority from them incensed". The word "incense" has been translated to appear close to the word spelled (*"insensé"*), as the meaning of both is similar. It means a state of extreme anger, rage, and fury. This is then a statement about the Church being overtaken by corrupt elements, who would share that position over all Roman Catholics (and the power, wealth, and influence held by the Vatican). This reached a peak in the late 1970s, causing those who cared for the Church, and who saw through the sham that was taking place, to be outraged.

When the string then states, "him aforementioned rule to the antichrist born will endure until in them wasting away with this ship of the age", this is talking about the subsequent time that will come, after the ruin of the Church. That time will be when one man will become elevated to the "power of authority" (from *"main"*), because of the "wasting away" (from *"definement"*)[3] of Christian values. The "ship" (from *"nai"*, with *"nay"* being an alternate spelling) is symbolically representative of the Holy Church, which is where the fishers of men's souls sail. With that influence for good corrupted, "the antichrist" will be "raised" to right

---

3   The 1611 Old French-English dictionary lists under the word *"definement"*, as being used in the sentence *"Le Definement du monde."* as translating to state, "The later end of the world." Thus, "wasting away" is relative to a "later end."

that "ship", in the ways told of in *The Revelation of John* (his *Apocalypse*). It will be righted by the release of the Four Horsemen. The one human being who now holds that "rule" is Osama bin Laden. Thus, he is the embodiment that is representative of all acting "diametrically" as an "antichrist".

It is important to understand the word "aforementioned" better (from "*susdit*"), which is a loose translation, although an accurate one. The word "*susdit*" was coined by combining "*sus*" (as a form of "*dessus*", meaning "above, over, upon, aloft, and/or on high") with "*dit*" ("*dict*" being preferred in Old French), which is the past participle of "*dire*", meaning, "said, spoken, delivered, uttered, expressed, shown, told, declared, signified, and/or reported unto." In other words, this word is saying, "as told before in prophecy", from "told on high". That word being found before the use of "the antichrist" is referencing *The First Letter of John*, (in particular 1st John, 2:18) which told of "the antichrist coming."[4]

In John's prophecy from his later years (*The Revelation*), he referred to the "beast," but not specifically to "the antichrist." Many believe the "beast" is a different way of stating "the antichrist," much like many see Paul's "man of sin" (2 Thessalonians 2:3) as meaning "the antichrist." These assumptions have led most to believe that John wrote the actual word "antichrist" in his prophecy. In fact, that word does not appear in his *Apocalypse* anywhere.

John wrote the word "antichrist" in four verses, with one also using the plural form of that word. He wrote,

> (1 John 2:18) "Little children, it is the last time: and as ye have heard that antichrist shall come, even now are there many antichrists; whereby we know that it is the last time." (KJV)

> (1 John 2:22) "Who is a liar but he that denieth that Jesus is the Christ? He is antichrist, that denieth the Father and the Son." (KJV)

> (1 John 4:3) "And every spirit that confesseth not that Jesus Christ is come in the flesh is not of God: and this is that spirit of antichrist, whereof ye have heard that it should come; and even

---

4   1st John 2:18 states fully, "Little children, it is the last time: and as ye have heard that antichrist shall come, even now are there many antichrists; whereby we know that it is the last time." (KJV)

now already is it in the world." (KJV)

(2 John 1:7) "For many deceivers are entered into the world, who confess not that Jesus Christ is come in the flesh. This is a deceiver and an antichrist." (KJV)

The words written by Nostradamus, "him aforementioned rule of the antichrist" should be seen as a reference to those statements by John in his letters. Those statements say that "the antichrist" is everyone who denies Jesus is the Messiah.[5] It was in the world then, meaning that the word depicts all who will be in power before the return of Christ, as long as they deny Jesus. All Muslims deny Jesus, as do most Jews; but many Christians do not hold up the truth of Jesus, as demonstrated through their actions. Thus, they are "liars denying the Father and the Son."[6] All are disconnected from God and Christ, so all will act against the nature of Jesus.

The French spelling, and thus the one written by Nostradamus, is "*antechrist*", rather than "antichrist". Although that is an acceptable French spelling that translates as "antichrist", it represents a combined-form Latin word, saying, "before Christ" (as "ante-Christ"). This means that "the rule of the antichrist" will come before the return of Christ. That makes a connection to "the antichrist" and the End Times.

Continuing the flow of words from Nostradamus' letter to Henry, one finds that "the antichrist" and his "rule will not last". This says that this "beast," or "man of sin," will perish before the prophesied return of Jesus. He will rule "before Christ" returns, up "until" the time he sees his war machine "waste away this" world that has turned its back on God. The "birth" of a sick world will let everyone know the return is "close", but "the age" of rebirth in Christ will not mesh with "the age born" that will have caused the "antichrist" to rise. This means Osama bin Laden is serving the purpose of cleansing the world before Christ will return.[7]

---

5 When a true Christian is defined as one "in the name of Jesus Christ," the meaning is one becomes the resurrection of Jesus, as the Christ reborn. All who deny that receipt of the Holy Spirit within one's own being (a marriage of soul to God, resulting in His Son reborn in the flesh) is therefore an "antichrist" by definition.
6 A "liar" is then one not becoming the Trinity in one's body (the merger of Father, Son, and Holy Spirit), while professing to be "Christ"ian.
7 The meaning of "Christian" is the return of Jesus Christ, which began with the twelve Apostles. The imagery of The Revelation, which is seen as the return of Christ, is more in line with the return of an Old Testament God, than the 'sweet Jesus' people

This means the world will be cleansed of evil by evil.[8]

When one sees this perspective of one specific "antichrist", it becomes a perfect fit for Osama bin Laden. However, when one understands this is more than Nostradamus making this claim, it is John, an acknowledged prophet of God, that then means taking down Osama bin Laden might not be possible through ordinary means. After all, John told of multiple "antichrists".

So, if Osama bin Laden is one, with him gone, it then stands to reason that another would take his place. If that happens, nothing is gained by catching Osama bin Laden. If God is allowing Osama bin Laden to remain free, where does that leave us?

Afterthoughts: Again from the 20/20 perspective of 2020, knowing what we lowly Americans are allowed to think we know, even if Osama bin Laden was killed on May 1 (technically 2), 2011, then nothing changed. In football, that mentality is "Next Man Up." Nothing changed because some other human being will always rise to take the position once held by Osama bin Laden. If he was not killed, only sent into hiding, where he can plot evil deeds against America without the danger of being hunted, someone else will still become his outward replacement and field general.

This is where the concept of "antichrist" has to be realized as not a human state of being. We hear the word "Christ" and immediately think of Jesus, the man-god. Likewise, people hear the word "antichrist" and think of historical figures, such as Napoleon, Hitler, and Osama bin Laden. In reality, the Christ is the spiritual state of God in a human form. Jesus the man was the Christ, but then all twelve who were filled with God's Holy Spirit on Pentecost Sunday were all duplications of the Christ in human form. This is how John's reference to "antichrists" is an equivalent duplication, only it is against those who are reborn as the Christ.

This means anyone in human form who bows down before Satan (or whatever name you apply to "the devil") is an "antichrist," which means each serves self, not God. For as much as Osama bin Laden was on the F.B.I.'s "Ten Most Wanted

---

like to see him as.

8   A God-like man of long white hair, riding a white horse, with a double-edge sword coming from his mouth, says "Christ" is God's presence within one's being, as Jesus was God incarnate (the Christ). Thus, John wrote a vision of God coming back 'all Old Testament style', where justice will be administered by a sword.

List" for almost a decade, judged as evil because he took credit for the events of September 11, 2001, he can easily be seen as an "antichrist," as a Muslim who vows "death to America!" Still, the one who gave the orders to have a compound raided and people murdered on foreign soil (in the name of justice) and had to have approved the dumping of a corpse into the sea, so nothing can ever be proved beyond question, is he not also qualifying as a self-worshipping human being?

When Jesus was quoted in the Gospels, he often began a statement with the words, "Truly I say." Jesus the man was speaking those words, but he was not the one authoring that which was the truth. Jesus spoke the truth of the Father, keeping his own opinions to himself, as those opinions were secondary to those of God's truth. The truth is always a signal for the Christ. Those who offer lies as truth must then be seen as "antichrist."

The spiritual essence of Osama bin Laden became greater when he was claimed to be dead, becoming spiritually elevated as a martyr. This means that the one who had him killed played a role in making some old man who appeared to be feeble-minded and too incompetent to lead a revolutionary army of jihadists be suddenly revitalized and eternally youthful. If Osama bin Laden was not that man who was murdered on May Day 2011, then he would be foolish to come out and declare, "That wasn't me!" Barack Hussein Obama immortalized Osama bin Laden, whether or not Osama bin Laden was indeed killed.

There is evidence that Barack Hussein Obama is an "antichrist," simply because of his recorded words and documented deeds, which belittled Christianity and empowered Muslim nations, while relaxing defenses against Communist powers. Still, Barack Hussein Obama is a politician, which is the epitome of selfishness; but he is like Osama bin Laden, in the sense that both men play important roles in ideologies that are much larger than themselves could ever be, as mortals.

The element of God speaking through Nostradamus, who was another in the line of Christs reborn into the world, to be Prophets, is not to motivate human beings to seek out individuals and murder them. It is important that each individual realize the call for each is to not be an "antichrist." To even begin to reach the state of being that spiritually is the rebirth of the Christ in one's being, one has to have faith in the message God sends through all His Prophets. Faith sees believability, without the need for proof. Belief that Osama bin Laden is dead, without proof other than hearsay, is not faith in God. It is faith in man; and, that is why Nostradamus was told to write *The Prophecies*.

Nostradamus wrote of the leaders of Christianity reaching a state of being "diametrically opposite." Nostradamus was one who was representative of a "sect," as a man of faith who helped others during the Black Plague times in France. He practiced astrology, but one should see that as a private study, not a business that he sold. God had Nostradamus give to the community of France and Europe prophecies that were based on his insight, which was spurred to reception through the art of astrology. Because God was behind that inspiration, the people were attracted and amazed, calling Nostradamus a "prophet." Because so-called Christians besmear the name of Nostradamus, along with atheists, calling him a liar and a charlatan, the mirror of time reflects how those people today are looking at the past and seeing themselves as prophesied. They cry out insults just as the demon spirit cried out to Jesus, "What business do we have with each other, Son of God? Have You come here to torment us before the time?" (Matthew 8:29, NASB)

The Church of Rome murdered the last pope who was sent by God to restore it (Pope John Paul I).[9] The Roman Catholic Church has sealed itself as forever being "diametrically opposite" from its original purpose, thus fulfilling the prophecy of Malachy, whose line of popes ended with the Antipope Ratzinger (a.k.a. Benedict XVI, another co-conspirator that murdered John Paul I). The co-pope situation with the Socialist from South America, calling himself Francis, is nothing more than a Church being led by a corpse, with no life of God in it anymore.

The likes of Osama bin Laden, and all who decry America as the Great Satan, when the United States took great pride in being the land of Christianity, as the self-professed savior of the world, is nothing more than the truth being seen by the acts of America. It is just like the Church of Rome. It says it is holy, but its actions are evil. The world sees the actions as speaking louder than the lies. The West is therefore also "diametrically opposite" the way it professes to be. Osama bin Laden is given power, simply because he speaks the truth about how corrupt the world calling itself "Christian" has become.

The people believed Nostradamus was a prophet, but there are few Saints walking the face of the earth now, who can present the Word of God to the people, as

---

9   Pope John Paul I actually became the first pope to designate, purposefully, the number "First" to his choice of following in the names of the Apostles John and Paul. That should be seen as a prophecy of his own death coming, as his murderers would be aided by Pope John Paul II (a co-conspirator).

a messenger prophet. Because there are so few saints, the denominations of Christianity are led by hired hands that preach a "political party line," not the truth of Scripture. The people are then not being led to become saints. It is impossible for the blind to teach the blind how to see. Thus, the world is filled with the "sects" of science, philosophy, and art, none of which are influenced by the whispers of God's "good angels." Astrology is seen as trash, by those who calculate through algorithms the probabilities of the future. As of today, when the fear mongers are proclaiming COVID19 as reason not to go to church, which includes the bishops of denominations instructing their hired hands to deny their congregations sacraments of any kind, the gods worshipped are the media, politics, and those who are sellers of toilet paper, face masks, and hand sanitizer.

The "sects" have also become "diametrically opposite" the way they were in the 16th century. The result is a complete lack of faith, the likes of which were depicted in the Old Testament, when God sent prophet after prophet to tell Israel and Judah, "You're going the wrong way!" The people then were to busy enjoying their ancient equivalent to handheld smart phones to listen and say, "You mean, if I don't start doing what God told Moses I should do, then some foreign lands will come and destroy my nation and take me prisoner, bring great woe upon my being?"

Even while the news does take the time to report another natural disaster, another event of terrorism, and another foreign threat to freedom being exercised in dark, godless countries, nobody is willing to be the one who does anything against that direction to ruin. Osama bin Laden is thought to be dead, which takes him out of the present consciousness, so his image cannot be a reflection of owe's own state as the Antichrist, bring about the End Times. No one takes the end seriously.

Finding Osama bin Laden still alive in the Pyrenees Mountains is the least of our worries now. America has become so "diametrically opposite" that it now has a majority of antichrists running it. If they were to pull Osama bin Laden out of a cave and announce to the world, "We have caught the Antichrist," America would say, "Praise be to Satan! Long live the Antichrist!" Then they would make him the President of the World and bow down before his will.

The message of Nostradamus, as a true Prophet of God, speaking as Jesus Christ through divine insight says,"You need to see the evil in yourselves, if you ever expect to stop people from Osama bin Laden pulling out the double-edged sword." The last place people look to find evil is within.

Chapter 24
Defense Exhibit B

No Napoleon Here

Nostradamus wrote of Osama bin Laden indirectly, as a "mountain" one; but he repeatedly wrote of that individual because he is the one who represents "the antichrist". In the sense that John defined "the antichrist" as being one who denies Christ, Osama bin Laden, being a Muslim, qualifies for that position. Thus, Islam, in general, can be seen as "an antichrist", as can any non-Christian religion (monotheistic or polytheistic) and those who profess no religious beliefs of any kind. In that regard, there are many in opposition to Christ, but only one who received such detailed focus by Nostradamus, as the one plotting evil in the Pyrenees Mountains.

Much has been written about Nostradamus naming three antichrists. These people say Napoleon is the first antichrist, Hitler the second antichrist, and there have been a plethora of guesses about who number three will turn out to be. That line of thought is wrong, simply because there is method to Nostradamus' use of numbers (the systems again), which has been missed. To see Nostradamus tell of more than one antichrist, he would have to hyphenate each one, as "first-antichrist, second-antichrist, and third-antichrist", which he did not do. He did write "*second antechrist*" (in another place in the letter to Henry II) and "The antichrist three" ("*L'antechrist trois*", found in a quatrain), but each separate word must be taken as a stand-alone statement. Every reference shows "antichrist" separately, meaning there is only one, but numbers are associated with that one.[1]

In those attempts to make a false preconception of three "antichrists" appear

---

1   In Old French, the word "*second*" (as a masculine noun) meant "A second, or assistant in a single combat."

267

true, three evil villains of history have to be found. Napoleon is evil to the English, Austrians and Russians, so making the words of a quatrain fit him acts as evidence that supports the claims of English interpreters. It is doubtful that the French people see Napoleon as an "antichrist" and Nostradamus was French (pre-Napoleonic). Certainly, Napoleon has some parallel characteristics to Osama bin Laden, but because Napoleon came earlier in time, it is hard to erase that earlier notion and apply it to one more suited for the story line of *The Prophecies*.

One quatrain that has been erroneously applied to Napoleon is actually a perfect fit for Osama bin Laden. That quatrain is fully shown as (simply translated):

De soldat simple parviendra en empire,	From soldier simple will come forward in the world in empire,
De robe courte parviendra à la longue	To robe brief will thrive to there out-stretched
Vaillant aux armes en eglise ou plus pyre,	Valiant with the weapons upon church where more bad,
Vexer les prestres comme l'eau fait lesponge.	To vex them priests like the water done the sponge.

The quatrain states its main theme to be, "*De soldat simple parviendra en empire*", or basically: "From soldier simple will achieve upon empire". Those who believe this quatrain is placing focus on Napoleon see that primarily because Napoleon did indeed lead France to the level of empire (which it had been before). Still, they justify that connection by seeing the words "simple soldier" (a syntactical reversal of words through translation) as describing a member of the military, beginning at a low rank. That barely fits the fact that Napoleon rose from a Lieutenant in an artillery regiment in the army of Louis XVI, to become the Emperor of France. By the time he joined the Jacobin faction (another word for "*sect*") and their revolutionary army, he was given the rank of Lieutenant Colonel, in command of a volunteer battalion.[2] Obviously, that rank means "simple soldier" to those who see Napoleon in this quatrain's main theme.

The French word "*simple*" can translate to mean (among several other things) "unskillful". The full scope of meaning is, "simple; single, pure, mere, unmixed, uncompounded, of one sort, of itself; also plain, round, blunt, sincere, unfeigned;

---

2   From the Wikipedia article, "Napoleon I".

harmless, innocent, without guard; shallow, unskillful, ignorant, foolish; rude, homely, mean, and/or base." As one can see, "unskillful" is a good choice, when considering the context of the military. In this sense, all formal members of the military are more than "simple", once they have been trained to the point of being recognized as a "soldier". This means Napoleon was not a "simple soldier", as he was schooled at a military academy, to be a commissioned "soldier" of rank.[3] Osama bin Laden, before he went to fight the Soviets in Afghanistan, came from a history that was "pure" or "uncompounded" by military training. He was a "simple soldier". His "empire" has yet to manifest, meaning this quatrain is another prediction of prophecy, which one can expect to happen in the future.

The secondary theme of this quatrain states, "*De robe courte parviendra à la longue*", which translates to say, "From robe short will achieve to there extended". These words have been syntactically transformed to say, "From a short robe will grow into a long one". That change of robes (from short to long) has been interpreted as fitting the image of Napoleon transforming from the "short" tails of a military uniform, to the "long robe" of an emperor crowning himself. This is an example of how words can be made to fit a preconceived notion. However, as far as attire goes, Osama bin Laden, the son of a Saudi businessman, would better fit the everyday translation of "coming forward in the world" (from "*parvenir*"), after exchanging his business suit (his "compendious", or "succinct" [from an archaic meaning "girded"] meaning of "*courte*", and "*robbe*" as "coat, or garment") for an imam's ankle-length "robe".

The word translated as "robe" is actually a modern spelling. Old French spelled the word meaning, "robe," (English) with an extra "*b,*" as "*robbe*". This could be due to the fact that the Old French verb "*rober*" would be written in the past tense as "*robé*". That verb meant, "to rob" and is the etymological root to the English word "robe". However, when no accent mark is present, one is allowed to be added (only when already present is it not to be amended), meaning the secondary theme can then be read as, "To – robbed – low – will come unto – in – there – wearisome". In that case, there is no "robe" anywhere to be found.

From seeing "extended" as akin to that stated in the letter to Henry II, as "the antichrist born will endure until with them wasting away", it becomes easy to see the use of "wearisome" as matching that foreseen state of "wasting away". Line two can then be found saying the one who will find an "*empire*" (from the main theme) will go "To" those who have been "robbed" (Afghanistan, Muslims,

3   From the Wikipedia article, "Napoleon I". .

Palestine). He will arrive as a "low", "soldier simple", leaving his immense wealth behind. With the capitalized preposition representing both "To" there, and "From" there, one can see how he "will come unto" an "empire", one that was not his, but someone else's (i.e., Soviet Union, Great Britain, France, Spain, the USA). Once "in there", he will make life "wearisome" for those. With all of that meaning seen beforehand, it is then possible to jump to the conclusion that he will steal that "empire" as his own. Once that happens, payback will be hell.

One must then see that the main theme statement and the secondary theme statement repeat the word *"parviendra"*. This is the future tense spelling of the word *"parvenir"*, which can translate as, "will achieve, will attain, will arrive, will come unto, will thrive, will come up, and/or will come forward in the world." If "will achieve" is used in line one, then one of the other possibilities needs to be used in line two. All translations are viable, as long as the same translation is not repeated. When the secondary theme is focused on how one "will achieve To (an) empire robbed" (a stolen empire), then the use of *"parviendra"* (in the secondary theme) might best predict the future by saying, "will thrive in there long". The English word "thrive" is rooted in the Old Norse word that meant, "to seize". This matches the use of *"robé"* as "robbed".

The remainder of this quatrain has a slant towards the "simple soldier's" use of "arms upon a congregation of Christians" ("church" as the general body of people, rather than one building). These "weapons" are then described as "more worse", which is describing how an "empire" will be stolen. It will be through the use of "weapons" of mass destruction. It then goes on to talk about significant (capitalization) acts "To afflict them priests", which is another term specific to Christianity, although pagans also have "priests".

The last words, "like the water made the sponge", is then a reference to the Roman "simple soldier" who held "a sponge" soaked in bitter wine-vinegar-water to Jesus' lips, as he was dying. Jesus was thirsting as he was dying, but he refused to accept the bitter wine of his persecutors. This is a prophecy of "long" times of persecution that will come, after a "soldier simple will attain an empire". The question is then upon those Christians being persecuted in this future, as to whether or not they will drink from that "sponge".

The point of understanding this quatrain is that it identifies the antichrist through the details of the third and fourth lines, which supports an empire that is against Christianity. The objective of Osama bin Laden is the conversion of Christians to Islam, through willing subjection or through painful persecution. Those unwilling to convert will be punished severely, with no remorse. The objective of the antichrist of *The Prophecies* clearly becomes the antithesis of the Christ spirit.

Afterthoughts: The perfect 20/20 hindsight, from the perspective of 2020, is to see the greater value of this quatrain's main theme statement, found in the first line of this poem. While Osama bin Laden can be seen as someone with no military experience, thus a "simple soldier," that statement becomes the model from which all al-Qaeda is formed.

When Osama bin Laden led the Mujahideen in Afghanistan, against the Soviet Union, it was all about taking goat herders and teaching them how to ambush tanks and military helicopters. A "simple soldier" was trained by America's Central Intelligence Agency to realize all a goat herder needed to be effective was smart weapons. Since 1980, weapons have become much smarter.

After the destruction of Iraq and Saddam Hussein, "simple soldiers" began streaming in Europe as refugees. After the report that Osama bin Laden had been killed, the Syrian Civil War led to a reported 100,000 refugees crossing into the European Union in July 2015.[4] After the Libyan Civil War (2011), which was after Osama bin Laden was announced killed, the removal of Muammar Gaddafi led to an even greater number of African illegal immigrants to flood into Western Europe, with most departing from Libya. Wikipedia reports "estimates that around 4.6 million African migrants live in Europe" with another "7 and 8 million illegal migrants from Africa live in the EU."[5] All of those flooding into Europe are potentially "simple soldiers" waiting for someone to give them the tools of war.

The secondary themes in this quatrain need to be seen as related to the Vatican, where the pope rules over another "empire" that has dwindled to nothing of importance. In 2013, after Osama bin Laden was reported to have been killed, Pope Francis - a South American Socialist - was made the ruler of a religious institution that represents many Christians. During his reign, when Europe has been flooded with potential "simple soldiers," he has preached receipt of non-Christians into Europe and all Christian nations of wealth, with open arms.

---

4   Wikipedia article "Refugees of the Syrian Civil War".
5   Wikipedia article "African immigration to Europe".

The overall message of Nostradamus, as easily found in the quatrains of *The Prophecies*, is one that is a strategic equivalent of the Trojan Horse, where ruin is less about a direct assault, and more about stealth. This is a mirror image of the stealth that took place in the attacks upon the Pentagon and the World Trade Towers, with those modeled after bombings around the world, all of which have fallen under the general heading of "terrorism." George W. Bush declared a "war on terrorism," which is akin to fighting a ghost. A ghost is the epitome of a "simple soldier," but a ghost is again the element of spirituality.

The spirituality of all which claims to be Christian is as flawed as its leaders. The "simple soldiers" that wear robes and promote opening the doors and letting the enemy walk among us are "antichrists." The ghosts of terrorism America is fighting now, more than ever before the reported death of Osama bin Laden, are those that look like their are friends, when they are really foes. Once we begin to question each other, the enemy has won, without firing a shot.

Still, because this quatrain points to a "robe," which is the attire worn by a pope of the Roman Catholic Church (an empire), and that theme fits the supporting details given, of "church" and "priests," the word "short" ("*courte*") can be the time Pope John Paul I served the Catholic people. His murder, cover-up, and replacement the surprise election of a Polish cardinal (when Poland was a Communist puppet nation of the U.S.S.R, forbidding religion), who had a history of assisting the Nazi occupation of Poland, as a youth that did work at a concentration camp, becomes a reflection of the evil "weapons" (from "*armes*") Pope John Paul I "Valiantly" attempted to stop. The joke by Vatican insiders was calling Pope John Paul I "the Peter Sellers pope," because they saw him as a bumbling idiot, incapable of filling those papal "robes." However, he was placed in power by God; so, his murder will be expected to come through God's grace.

Osama bin Laden will be the "simple soldier" who "will come upon an empire" through his conquest of Rome and the Vatican, with whatever pope left standing will be the one placed on the cross of persecution and forced to sip the gall soaked into a sponge. Again, pay back is hell.

Chapter 25
Defense Exhibit C

The Empire of the Antichrist will Commence

The story line of *The Prophecies* can be seen as parallel to that of *The Revelation of John*. Because the Antichrist is associated with the fears of Armageddon, the person who will act as this figure is an important person to identify. John was not allowed to write in terms that were as clear as what Nostradamus wrote. John used heavy metaphor to convey the horrors to come. Nostradamus was given more freedom in this regard, as it is clear now that he wrote about what is recent history. That makes identifying the antichrist possible to determine. That character can be identified in multiple quatrains of *The Prophecies*.[1] The history of the man known as Osama bin Laden matches the verbiage of *The Prophecies*, which leads me to conclude that he is the antichrist.

To this point, I have already presented one uninterrupted string of words that contained the word "antichrist". It came from Nostradamus' letter of explanation addressed to King Henry II. In all, Nostradamus wrote the word "*antechrist*" (both in lower case and capitalized) five times in that letter, in three different segments. While I culled one series of words that uses that identifying noun, the series of words that leads up to that string, and those which extend beyond, give a deeper picture of what can be expected to be found relative to the person acting as the "Antichrist".

When all three segments containing the five references are placed together, they tell one continuous story. The story introduces "the Antichrist" as an entity rising to his appointed time on earth and then alludes to events that lead up to his story.

[1] I have attributed twenty-five, not counting the "Pyrenees Mountains" quatrains presented in this work.

Those events are parts of other stories and are not completely told in the story of "the Antichrist". This story begins with a capitalized first letter in the first word, which is a signal that a new story has begun. One finds that many capitalized first words in the letter to Henry are "And, But, Because, After, and Then", because they link to something before. This story begins with the word "Then".

I will present the French text for these segments first. I will then present the basic translations, with some notes included. I also will spread those translations out in the segments they appear (between marks of punctuation), so each series of words acts as its own line, similar to those of the quatrains. This helps one see the text of the letter in a similar style. I will also add hyphens between each translated word, to force the reader to slow down and notice which words have multiple meanings in translation.

At the end of each of the three segments, I will give an interpretation. This interpretation will touch on the high points stated in these words, not deeply explaining every nuance. It will be good practice for the reader to read along slowly and let images form in one's mind as each word is read. The reader may pick up on valuable points that will not be covered in the interpretation.

Segment One (French)

> "*Puis le grand empyre de l'Antechrist commencera dans la Atila & Zerses descendre en nombre grand & innumerable, tellement que la venue du saint Esprit procedant du 48. degrez fera transmigration, deschassant à l'abomination de l'Antechrist, faisant guerre contre le royal qui sera le grand vicaire de Jesus Christ, & contre son eglise, & son regne per tempus,*"

Segment One (English, segmented)

> "Then – him – mighty [from "*grand*", "great"] – empire – of – the Antichrist – will commence – within – there – Attila [symbolic of Attila the Hun, and the region of Eastern Europe]
>
> & [importance] Xerxes [symbolic of an Iranian Emperor] – to lay down – in – number – substantial
>
> & [importance] innumerable,

so much – that – there – coming – to him – holy – Spirit – proceeding – to the – 48th – degree ones [the 48th degree of north latitude runs through northern Europe: France, Germany, Austria, Slovakia, Hungary, Ukraine, Romania, and Russia – as well as Asia, and North America. Paris, France has the coordinates of 48°. 52'.] - will make – transmigration [the act of passing from one country to another],

driving out of – with – the horrible thing – from – the Antichrist,

making – warfare – against – him – royal – who – will be – he – great – incumbent to do service unto the Lord ["vicar," from "*vicaire*"] – to – Jesus – Christ,

& [importance] against – his – church ["*eglise*" is not capitalized, making it symbolic of a body of Christians, as well as a lowered state – corruption – of Church],

& [importance] one's – government – for – the time [from "*per tempus*", which is Latin, conveying a Christian meaning, relative to the End Times],"

This segment begins with a capitalized first word "*Puis*", meaning "Then". A new piece of the puzzle is being explained, as "Then" implies other elements have previously been set before. It also introduces one to a new time, or phase in the overall story of *The Prophecies*. This next phase is prophesying the coming of the "empire of the Antichrist".

It is important to see that the first series of words leads to the capitalized name "*Atila*", which is the French spelling for Attila the Hun. That name represents the Hunnic Empire that warred against the Roman Empire. The homeland of the Huns was that territory north of the Danube River, in current Romania. The empire under Attila covered the Germanic regions east of the Rhine River (Germany, Austria, Hungary, and the Czech Republic, Romania), including the Slavic regions of Eastern Europe (Slovakia, Poland, Latvia, Belarus, Ukraine, and Moldova) and southern Russia. The Alans ("*Alain*"), the people of the Caucasus Mountains isthmus, represented the eastern reaches of this empire. Thus, the first series of words is telling of an "empire commencing" with Eastern European allies.

This leads to an ampersand, followed by the name "Xerxes" (written as "*Zerses*"), making an important reference that matches the ancient ruler "*Atila*". This is another name of a famous emperor from history. Xerxes I was the head of the Achamenid Empire of Persia, and is best known for defeating the Greeks. He accomplished that feat by utilizing soldiers from the many lands under Persian domination. Those allies included Egyptians, Assyrians, Babylonians, Indians, Phoenicians and Jews.[2] The symbolism here is that "Xerxes" represents modern Iran, inferring that Iran will be another ally to the "empire of the Antichrist". It also shows a model of recruiting soldiers from around the world, or from the vast sphere of Islamic influence.

By stating two vast areas of land that will support this person identified as "the Antichrist", Nostradamus is indirectly stating that "the Antichrist" will be neither pagan (a European) nor Persian (an Iranian). The nations that fell under the control of those two emperors will all come to support the cause of "the Antichrist". Many quatrains link to tell of this recruitment program.

This then tells one "the Antichrist" comes from some other place. All "empires" have a home base, such that Attila's base was in what is now Romania and Xerxes' base was in what is now Iran. Nostradamus names those two emperors as if they would be wing commanders of "the Antichrist", who has a different base. This then helps to identify Osama bin Laden as that leader. He is a Saudi Arab. His Islamic beliefs link him to Iran, but the mainly Sunni Arabs of Saudi Arabia are quite different from the Shiite Muslims of Iran. In addition, Iranians are quick to point out they are Persian, if mistakenly called Arab.

The ultimate meaning of an Arabian base is it represents an empire with a religious core (Mecca). It uses the power of Allah to link Muslims who hate Christians, with Eastern Europeans (atheist Communists) who hate Western Europeans (Christian Capitalists). It is all those who are "against Christ" that are then under the one "Anti-Christ."

The next word of importance (ampersand prior) is "innumerable". This is not simply a total of Iranians that will fall behind "the Antichrist", but a countless number of soldiers from all places. It means there will be no official count of how many soldiers are enlisted into the army he commands. Since there is no official army, the supporters are incapable of being counted. Still, the numbers

[2] From Wikipedia article, "Xerxes I of Persia".

of supporters is so vast that it is a figure impossible to guess.

This means that all news reports of al-Qaeda being too fragmented and disarrayed to be a significant threat (other than an occasional bomb attack here and there) are missing the point of how huge the support for Osama bin Laden is. He has allies throughout Europe, the Middle East, and Africa. He has allies that are Muslim, and non-Muslim. His messages come from this position of "innumerable" strength, such that he is quite sure his words are promises, rather than idle threats.

The next series of words tells why so many will come to him, in support of his cause. It tells how he is seen as "holy", such that he fills others with a higher "Spirit". They want to fight for a higher good, more than just hyped up with rah-rah enthusiasm. This is the "Spirit" of kindred blood, where religion has not been lost. The combination of words that say "holy Spirit" (from "*sainct Esprit*") is then a statement about what Christianity is supposed to have been, modeled after Jesus. This state that should be is reflected in the words of Jesus, when he said "the Holy Spirit, whom the Father will send in my name, will teach you all things and remind you of everything that I have told you." (John 14:26, New American Standard Version) To have "the Antichrist" be the one so filled and also be the one filling others with "Spirit" is a sign of the fall of Christianity.

Another element that shows the fall of Christianity comes when those filled with the "Spirit" are found "proceeding to" where "those of the 48th degree" are located. This must be seen as a sweep to the north, by those who will be "there coming" from a more southern latitude. The latitude of Tehran is 35°40', Baghdad is 33° 21', Cairo is 30° 03', and Damascus is 33° 30' (all north latitude). The "48th degree" (written as "*48. degrez*") of latitude runs through northern Europe, with several major cities within one degree of that latitude: Paris (48° 52'), Munich (48° 08'), Vienna (48° 13'), and Budapest (47° 30'). This latitude also goes through Canada, Mongolia, Kazakhstan, as well as Ukraine and southern Russia; but the only "48th degree ones" (with "ones" being cities) of merit are in Western-Central Europe. This number is then prophesying how far north the "empire of the Antichrist" will reach; and, it is a fact that Muslims and Eastern Europeans have been filling Western European countries, en mass, since the early 1990s.

The next series of words repeats the capitalized reference to "the Antichrist", but makes the statement, "driving out of with the horrible thing" that has been placed "with, of, and/or to" (use of the preposition "*de*") "the Antichrist". This, in turn, becomes "the horrible thing from the Antichrist" (alternate use of "*de*"). The word that means, "the horrible thing" needs to be fully understood.

The combined article-noun word written is "*l'abomination*". The word "abomination" is shown in the 1611 Old French-English dictionary as translating to, "an abomination, a detestation, a horrible or execrable thing." An English dictionary defines "abomination" as, "hate coupled with disgust."[3] Some synonyms for "abomination" are evil, crime, horror, plague, and curse. I have chosen to use the translation as "the horrible thing" because the word "horrible" implies "horror," and a "state of dread."

That "thing" which fits all of the above descriptive terms is a nuclear weapon. It can also be a biological weapon or a chemical weapon. In short, "the horrible thing" is a weapon of mass destruction. All are "horrible" if ever used, because their past uses have created "horror" and the world "dreads" the time when they will be used again. In the quatrains, Nostradamus often refers to the use of one of these "abominations" as a "monster".[4] This term implies "something with a strange and frightening appearance," as well as "one who inspires horror and disgust."

This series of words is making it clear that these will come "from the Antichrist". Once one realizes Osama bin Laden is that entity, one can then see how he not only has "innumerable" people ready and willing to go to war for him, he has the weapons that will make their goal easier to achieve. The link to Eastern European mercenaries ("Attila") becomes the source for some of these weapons, and the oil money from Iran ("Xerxes") buys the rest from Russia.

The next series of words confirms "a horrible thing" is a weapon, because it says, "making warfare against". This is "against him royal who will be the great vicar to Jesus Christ". This is a statement that Europe considers itself Christian and is thus led by the pope of Rome. As "warfare against" Christianity, "the Antichrist" is identified as being "anti-Christian". This also identifies the "warfare" as a Holy War, making the name Armageddon be associated, as the "warfare" of the End Times.

---

3   Fair Use – Many dictionaries use the same common descriptive words to define the same root word.
4   Nostradamus wrote the word "*monstre*" eleven times, once each in eleven quatrains.

The use of the word "great" is shown associated with "he" (personal pronoun use for "*le*"), which becomes the one who has power, wealth, and influence throughout the Western countries. As the leader of the largest church in the Christian world, the pope is representative of "the great" (use of "*le*" as article). Because no popes have used their greatness to promote Palestine being returned to the Arabs because that land was stolen from them, "he" is not acting "great". Because the "vicar" is the caretaker "to" the words of "Jesus", "great" powers are granted to "him" who becomes the "incumbent to do service unto the Lord". When the Lord becomes someone other than "Jesus" (money, possession, fame, power, and other tricks of Satan), then "warfare against him" who has been elevated to "royal" status "will be" so "he" ("the Antichrist") takes the place of "greatness". Through war, the corrupted papal seat will be burned clean.

It is also a fact that throughout the centuries the popes of Rome have sanctioned "making warfare against" the ones who lived in the land surrounding Jerusalem (the Crusades). In addition to "him" (those popes), the "royal" leaders of Europe (the Kings) have assisted in this "warfare against" Muslims. This union between the two "royal" groups (kings and church) has been one that has proven to be a quest to see "who will be the great Curate" of Jerusalem and the surrounding regions, due to their belief in "Jesus". They believe Jesus is the Jewish "Messiah" (Hebrew "*Mashiach*," meaning "the anointed," in Greek "*Christos*"), but they prefer the Greek title, "Christ", as it takes the Jews out of the mix too. Because of this history begun by a pope, the European mind has not, will not, and does not see the Holy Land as Arab, in any sense. This has allowed them to support Israel's right to exist, adamantly, "against" holy law that says "Thou shalt not steal."

The next line emphasizes more that is relative to this papal "warfare against" Islam, showing more reason why someone like Osama bin Laden will rise and be "the Antichrist", simply to say "Enough is enough." That reason is to be "against his church". Following the words "Jesus Christ" ("*Iesus Christ*"), which ended its series, is a comma that separates "Christ" from the next. That is then followed by an ampersand (", &"), which is a combination symbol the announces an important element follows, one that goes along with the "vicar to Jesus Christ". This makes the possessive pronoun ("*son*") become relative to the pope, meaning the pope is "against his church", that of Jesus Christ.

When the word "church" appears in the lower-case, it takes on the general root meaning for what constitutes the Roman Catholic Church. This means that the "church" is the body of people who are specifically Catholic and generally Christian. It prophesies that the pope is corrupt; but this announcement can specifically indicate the one "incumbent to do service unto the Lord" at the time of "the Antichrist".

I will not go into all of the elements that lead one to realize the current pope, the one prior to him (especially), and all of the popes going back to the corruption Pope Pius XII allowed (particularly in 1939); but collectively they have brought about a rapidly degrading Church. Many Catholics left because they turned "against his church", seeing the Church no longer as the Church of Jesus Christ, instead becoming the pope's "church". The scandals have piled up over the years that have occurred during this decline. Still, one has to see how "the Antichrist" becomes a tool of God, as one allowed to strike down a "church" that has become a promoter of evil, more than good. We are in those last years of "his church" and the Roman Catholic Church has deemed the prophecy that listed all popes, up until the last pope, as divinely inspired.[5] According to that divine prophecy, we are near the end of the papal line.

The next series begins after another comma-ampersand combination, adding one should take note of "one's government" (from "*son regne*"), where the ampersand makes this statement about "one's rule" be important. As the last important series was about the pope, this is another important statement about the "pope's reign". This is then confirmed by the last two words being written in Latin, the language of the Vatican.

Those words, "*per tempus*", literally translate to state, "throughout, in the course of, during, through, along, over" (from "*per*") and "a division, section, space, period, moment, time" (from "*tempus*"). As such, the Latin elevates the meaning "for time" to a level that makes "time" relative to Biblical prophecy. This becomes relevant to the "end times," which are unknown as to when they will occur. Jesus said, "It is not for you to know the times." (Acts 1:7, New International Version).

One must be prepared for his or her personal "end time", "*in the course of*" one's "*time*" on earth. Thus, the Latin is saying the pope who will be "vicar" "during" the "time" up to the End Times will be ruling corruptly, as though he would last "throughout time". This is a statement of unpreparedness, minimally. It moreover shows a pope who does not believe that Judgment Day will come to all

---

5   The prophecy of Saint Malachy named all of the popes from his visit to Rome (1139), until the last pope. We are at the next to the last pope now (2011).

humans, himself included, when individual life comes to an end.

The last series of words in this first segment is then also preceded by an ampersand, making the following words important. Again, the words of this series are in Latin, making them elevated as words of repeated prophecy. Those words say, "*in occasione temporis*", which translates to state, "towards – opportunity – at the right time". This is referencing the "end times", as the statement says the march is "towards" that end; and, time will be afforded the "opportunity" to reach that threshold. The end will be based on an "opportunity at the right time". This is where Osama bin Laden being in the Pyrenees Mountains plays a significant role. He will have been there for a considerable length of "time", training troops, and organizing those soldiers based in Europe living there as immigrants. He will have them prepared to be ready for his call to arms, "at the right time".

With this segment completed and before going into interpreting the next segment, let me make the reader aware that the last two series of words, both used Latin, referred to "time". The next segment begins with a short series of words that also includes the French word "*temps*", which means "time". The last segment ended at the top of page 10 of the letter to Henry II, as it appeared in the 1568 Lyon edition (page 138 of the .pdf copy of that document). The next segment begins at the bottom of page 18, in that same edition (page 146 in the .pdf source document). About 1,750 words separate these two segments.[6]

Because both segments include the use of "antichrist", they are connected pieces of this puzzle. The pieces are divided by method, based on punctuation present in the text. It is not coincidence that one segment ends with "time" and the next begins with the same word. This is evidence of how the systems allow one to cut this letter apart and then put back together in the correct order.

Segment Two (French)

> "*& dans iceluy temps & en icelles contrees la puissiance infernalle mettra à l'encontre de l'eglise de Jesus Christ la puissance des adversaires de sa loy, qui sera le second antechrist, lequel persecutera icelle eglise & son vray vicaire par moyen de la puissance des Roys temporelz, qui seront par leur ignorance seduitz par langues qui trencheront plus que nul glaive entre les mains de l'insense le susdit regne de l'antechrist ne durera que jusques au definement de ce nay pres de l'eage*"

[6] The Word Count of my copy of the French text shows 1,757 words.

Segment Two (English, segmented)

& [importance] "within – he – time

& [importance] upon – the same man – countries – there – army – infernal – will set – in – the shock of enemies – to – the church – of – Jesus – Christ – there – mighty – from them – adversaries – from – their – law,

which – will be – him – assistant in combat [as the "second" in a duel] – antichrist,

which – will persecute – the same man – church

& [importance] its – true – vicar – by reason of – moderator – of – there – power – to them – Popes ["*Roys*" capitalized means "Kings" or "Popes"] – temporal ones [means those limited in the time they rule, due to being mortal],

who – will be – through – their – ignorance – seduced ones – by – tongues – which – will be hacking asunder – more – than – no – sword - between – them – powers of authority – of – the extremely angered – him – aforementioned – reign – with – the antichrist – born – will endure – that – until – at them – wasting away – to – this – ship – from – the age"

This segment includes (as its last series of words) the previously interpreted mention of "the antichrist", which was explained in the last chapter. It was explained as a presence being brought on due to the corruption of the papacy. When one reads this entire segment (slowly, of course), one gets a better feel for how Islam has developed a hatred of Christians over "time". Thus, the first series of words in this segment states, importantly (ampersand use) "within times" (from "*dans ... temps*") of "he", which states: the "times" of Christianity ("he" is Jesus); the end "times" (when "he" will return); and, the "times" of retribution (where "he" comes with "fire in his eyes and a double-edged sword coming from his mouth"). In this way, "he" is both Jesus and "the Antichrist".

When the word "*dans*" is seen to imply the similar word "*dedans,*" which adds the meaning, "inwardly," one can begin to see this word stand-alone as an intuition, emotional feeling, or inner uneasiness. This becomes a sixth sense that all will not be right in the world, when "he" has entered his "time". The word translated as "he" is "*iceluy*", which also is translatable as "the same man". In modern French, this word is seen as "*celui-ci,*" which is the masculine form of "this one" or "that one."

This is a word that then points back to a connected segment, in order to understand who "the same man" is. In the first segment we ended with the statements "against his church," "his reign during a condition of things bad", and "in at the right time". All three statements were important (preceded by ampersands); and, all three are referring to "the Antichrist". Thus, the second segment is beginning with a "theme" statement that this segment is about "that one," "the same man".

The image of *The Revelation of John*, which comes from chapter 1, goes like this:

> "(13) and among the lampstands was someone "like a son of man," dressed in a robe reaching down to his feet and with a golden sash around his chest. (14) His head and hair were white like wool, as white as snow, and his eyes were like blazing fire. (15) His feet were like bronze glowing in a furnace, and his voice was like the sound of rushing waters. (16) In his right hand he held seven stars, and out of his mouth came a sharp double-edged sword. His face was like the sun shining in all its brilliance."[7]

In verse 13, where the quotation marks are setting the text apart from another biblical quote (see Daniel 7:13), where the Greek text is found stating "*homoios huios anthrópos*" (in Greek, "ὅμοιος υἱός ἄνθρωπος").[8] If one reads this prophecy of John as one reads the prophecy of Nostradamus, those three words, which have been translated syntactically to state, "like a son of man," one finds they actually say "like – a son – a man".

In the Book of John, translators show "Son of man" written eleven times.[9] In actuality, the Greek states, "*huios ho anthrópos,*" in ten of those verses and simply "*huios anthrópos*" in the eleventh. The placement of "*ho*" (in Greek,

---

7   New International Version
8   Biblios Greek Text Analysis, "Revelations 1:13".
9   The Book of John shows "*huios ho anthrópos*" the following verses: 1:51, 3:13, 3:14, 6:27, 6:53, 6:62, 8:28, 9:35, 12:23, 12:34, and 13:31.

"τοῦ") allows for a translation (literally) that states, "a son of a man." The Greek letter upsilon is not found in the upper-case form, meaning "Son" is best shown as "son." In the ten verses where "son of man" is found in the Book of John, he was recalling how Jesus prophesied the coming of God, such that He (God) would be descending (and ascending) upon the "son of man." The capitalization in translation is then added to identify this as a name for Jesus.

In the first verse quoted from *The Revelation* (verse 1:13) there is no presence of a Greek word indicating "of." This makes the text stating "*huios anthrópos*" match the use found in the one verse from the Book of John that had the same lack of "*ho,*" or "τοῦ."

That one verse is found in chapter five, verse 27, which is commonly read as,

> "And he has given him authority to judge because he is the Son of Man." (New International Version)

The literal translation of this verse, per Strong's Greek, says, "and – authority – he gave – him – judgment – to execute – that – son – man – come." This is not referring to Jesus as "the son of man" in the way the other verses make that identification. By saying "God gave Jesus authority to judge", Jesus is understood as "him," but the one who is "to execute that judgment" is identified differently, which is "like" Jesus. The executioner will be a male "of the Father" (a divinely led "son"), but he will be simply a "man" that will "come." That "man" is then described further (as having "white as snow hair," "fiery eyes," "bronze feet," etc.) in *The Revelation* as that "man" of "judgment." That description also seems "like" Jesus, but it is not Jesus.

The difference can be seen because this will not be "the Son of man" foreseen in *The Revelation*. The above description is not of Jesus Christ, but of an angry God, which has given his power for "judgment" to a different "son." In that regard, the word "*homoios*" means "like, resembling, and/or the same as." This means that who John saw in his vision was not Jesus, but "resembling" him. In the symbolic sense that this snow-white haired man will bring justice to a corrupt world, it conveys a meaning that one will have the "wisdom" of God as his protection (remember the "owl"?). The inference to Jesus comes from "*huios anthrópos*" appearing to be "resembling" "*huios ho anthrópos,*" which it does; but it is not "the same man".

This means one will be able to identify when we have entered a "time", or come "within" the end "times", when "he" will rise. The first series of words in this second segment uses the French word "*iceluy*" (meaning "he"), with the second series then found repeating this word in the feminine gender, stating "*icelles*". This means the same thing, only it is plural in number and connected to a feminine noun. Both forms can also translate to state "the same man" or "the same person". This is a reference back to the first segment, which began by identifying "him" as "the Antichrist". It is "within the same man's time". As such, when that "time" is "upon" the world, "the same man" will rule over "countries", not those where "he" will be from, but those "there", where judgment will be made.

This person will have raised an "army" from hell, as one will find an "infernal" fire from nuclear weapons that "will set in" upon those "countries". That will be "the shock of enemies" never expected; and, it will come "to" those who make up "the church of Jesus Christ" or the "body" of all who claim to believe in "Jesus Christ" (i.e., Christians). When "the Antichrist" is "then mighty" (from "*là grand*" as "then great"), "he" will have taken power "from them" who are his "adversaries". At this point, when "the Antichrist" will be in full control, he will persecute Christians, just as they have done "to" others, by forcing the will of "their law" upon the world. This means "the Antichrist" will use a farce called "law" to punish Christians, just as the farce of "law" allowed the theft of Palestine to stand.

The next series of words states "second antichrist"; and, this small part of the letter to Henry is where those who specialize in wrongly promoting Nostradamus on television say they have reason to state that Nostradamus saw three antichrists. This is where it must be recognized that the first segment used a capitalized "Antichrist", but this segment shows a lower-case version. The "antichrist" is thus not the Biblical version, as is "the Antichrist".

The lower-case version represents those who will carry out the commands of "the Antichrist", such that their actions will be an extension of those desired by "that one man" (alternate translation of "*iceluy*"). This means there will be many underlings that will execute his judgment, being "those same men" (alternate translation of "*icelles*") who helped raise "the Antichrist" to power. This is how the word "*second*" takes on the meaning "assistant in combat", becoming the identification of a "second", as in a duel. It also is indicative of a "double", where many "will be him", by the decree and authorization of "the Antichrist". However, they will be "second antichrist", not first.

The next series shows how those representatives of "the Antichrist" will be the ones who actually "will persecute". The persecution will be towards conversion, from Christianity (the "church") to Islam. The model of this, "which will persecute" as an "assistant antichrist", is found in the history of the Islamic Revolution in Iran, after the return of the Ayatollah Khomeini. He was able to sit in a tent and decree one head after another be lopped off, all while his hands stayed clasped in a position of prayer. This history will mirror how "the Antichrist" will also be free of the blood of persecution, although he will be on the front lines of the war he initiates, as an "assistant in combat antichrist".

This is then followed by an ampersand that shows the important "true" reason many will assist in the persecution. In this series, the word "*vicaire*" is used, having it be a repeated word that was presented in the first segment. Following the previous series of words, which ended with "church", it is making a statement about where the "true power" of a "vicar" (or one who is "incumbent to do service unto the Lord") comes from. It comes "by the reason" of the "medium of them" who allow one to be seen as more religious than all the rest. This series shows how the "persecution" will specifically target the "Pope" in office at the time of this Holy War; but it also shows how "the Antichrist" will be given "power by them", as himself then "King", "for" the purpose of "moderating" (variation of "*moyen*") the "power of them Popes", making them "temporary ones".

The use of "temporal" means several things. It acts to show the "limits of time" that will be placed on more than one "Pope" (due to the plural number). It shows that the persecuted "Pope" will be shown to be, or forced to become "worldly ones," lusting for material things. It further allows one to see the mortality of any human rising to "power", as we are all here on a "temporary" basis. Finally, it shows how the persecuted "Popes" (one at a time) will not be elected based on their dedication to the Church, but instead will come from a "secular" base. This persecution acts to mirror the state that the papacy had fallen into, causing it be condemned to become a caricature of its "temporal sins".

In regard to the "Pope" of this end "time", Nostradamus wrote quatrains that tell stories of several. In particular will be the one who will be the reigning pope (the current pope), at the onset of this coming Holy War. He will die attempting to escape, at which time another (an associate to the pope) will be announced as pope by his captors. He will represent the last pope. He will be persecuted by being forced to commit acts that publicly ridicule the Roman Catholic Church and all who call themselves Christian. When that pope finally refuses to do as commanded, he will be executed. Then, a completely false pope will follow him, who will have absolutely no qualification for leading anything. Many quatrains detail this persecution of the Roman Catholic Church, through the false pope. These popes will all assist in persecuting those who still believe in a man as god (like a Roman emperor), rather than acting as the "true vicar" who is the "medium to the power" that comes from a heavenly source.

The end of the second segment is the series of words presented in the last chapter. It refers to the past corruptions of the Church, now allowing one to see how the past will continue to be reflected into the future. The Church that has been seen as "hacked asunder" by its failure to tend it flock's needs, while allowing its own leaders to be "seduced" by corrupt "tongues", will be further degraded. Its popes will be physically "cut into pieces" and they will not find God coming to their rescue, as "no Excalibur" (variation on "*glaive*") will be "between their hands". The kingdom will be forever lost, as the "wasting away ship" will have ended "an age" when people could trust in religion.

Before interpreting this next segment, it is important to know that there are 530 words between the last word of segment two, and the first word of segment three.[10] The last word of segment two appears on page 19 of the letter to Henry II, as it appears in the 1568 Lyon edition (page 147 of the .pdf reproduction). The first word of segment three then appears on page 21 of that document (page 149 of the .pdf copy). This again shows that the letter is scrambled and must be placed together properly.

These three segments are presented in the order that they appear in the letter to Henry. In this order, they read logically and correctly. The first segment containing the word "Antichrist" begins with a capitalized first word, and the linking next series' reference the previous segments, beginning with punctuation that indicates a need to link to something else. This next segment ends with a comma. That indicates there is more information that is relevant to this overall chain, beyond these three segments. Only a segment ending with a period mark will make this story line complete.

---

10   Word count function used on my French version of the Letter to Henry II.

Segment Three (French)

"tournera estre Sancta Sanctorum, destruicte par paganismes & le vieux, & nouveau testament seront dechassez, bruslez en apres l'antecrist sera le prince infernal, encores par la derniere foy trembleront tous les Royaumes de Chrestienté"

Segment Three (English, segmented)

& [importance] "will turn – to be

[switch from French to Latin] Consecrated – One who enacts [from Latin idiom, "*Sancta Sanctorum*", means, "Enactor of Sanctity", and is thus a title for one holding Christian powers, like a pope],

subverted [or "utterly destroyed, absolutely ruined, and/or completely overthrown"] – for – paganism

& [importance] him – ancient

& [importance] new – testament – will be – expelled ones,

& [importance] [as "*bruslé-s*"] burnt ones [or discredited ones] – in – after – the antichrist – will be – prince – infernal,

again – for – final – faiths – will be trembling – all – them – Kingdoms – to – there – Christendom [or "Christianity"],

This third segment is fairly easy to follow, if one has followed the story line to this point. It is referring to the false pope, which importantly (ampersand use) "will turn" the Church of Rome to the state of being "absolutely ruined" (from the third series of words). It will have revolved back to its true roots, which were the "paganism" beliefs of a polytheistic people making up the Roman Empire. There then appears to be an important statement about "the old & new testament" (when read syntactically, as a continuous run-on of words), but this is actually stating something quite different. The first series ("*le vieux*") is stating, separately, the importance (ampersand use) of "him ancient", who is Satan, the Destroyer. The church will have turned to worshiping Satan in a "new will" (as a document "will") that will be read after a death.

Those who believe in the "new testament" (Christians) "will be those expelled" from living in the Europe they knew and loved. Many quatrains develop this theme of expulsion, as well as the debauchery that the "new covenant" between man and the devil will bring about. Those who will be in the Church, still believing in Jesus Christ, also "will be expelled". The rumor of scandal that circulates about the Church now will be nothing then, as this "new" church will be openly corrupt.

The next word, following the ampersand (thus announcing importance), tells of "burnt ones". This has to be seen as the pagan ritual God said would no longer be required, which is that of "burnt" offerings. The important factor, following "expelled ones" (or "chased away ones"), means this "new" practice will include human sacrifice.

The continuation of this series then again shows the lower-case version of "antichrist", making the statement read: "in after the antichrist will make them prince infernal". This is a statement of souls being sold to Satan. It also is a prophecy of what will come when the days of happy debauchery come to an end and those times without worry of a Day of Redemption will not last.

The places of the world outside of Europe will mount a fierce offensive to rid the world of Muslims and those whom they have allowed into power. These will come "into" power, "after" the model of the "assistant antichrist", such that they "will be forced" to defend against a "prince" who will make "them burn" in hell. The use of "prince" becomes a double-edged identification of the "prince" of darkness, versus a true "prince" of royal blood rising to defend against evil. Finally, the use of "infernal" can be seen as more deployments of nuclear weapons, in a "slash and burn" style of retreat. This becomes reminiscent of the way Hannibal salted the soil of Italy when he could no longer enjoy its fruits.

The use of "final" in the last series of words (from "*derniere*"), along with "faith" (from "*foy*"), is a statement about the end of religion, of any kind. It says that all of the "*Kingdoms of Christianity will be trembling*". This is a condition of fear (a sign of lost "*faith*" in God), where individual Christians "*will be trembling*". It will be the state of the world when survivors are found, just as were the prisoners found in Nazi concentration camps, "trembling" from a complete lack of care. The news will make all "tremble". However, it will also prophesy a condition of earth shocks, as "Kingdoms will be trembling" physically, all over the globe. It is prophesying cataclysmic changes in the world.

The message of all of this that has been shown as the linking pieces of one puzzle explaining another puzzle, which is the purpose of the letter to Henry II, is that it confirms Osama bin Laden as "the Antichrist". It says what will happen if "the Antichrist" follows an unrestricted path to an end that has been foreseen happening. The question now becomes, "Will that end be averted by the capture, trial, and conviction of Osama bin Laden, after he has been found hiding in the Pyrenees Mountains?"

Afterthoughts: This is powerful information. I highly recommend the reader go over it again (and again).

Chapter 26
Defense Exhibit D

The Antichrist

Three Quite Quickly Ones Annihilated

In a word search of all the quatrains, two come up with the word "*antechrist*" in them. One has it stated in the main theme line, with the other in the supporting line to the main theme (line three). Both quatrains will be interpreted in regard to their identifying Osama bin Laden as being that person. One will garner more attention than the other, based on the amount of evidence each holds. What is imperative to understand about these interpretations is both quatrains deal with the time that is beyond the point of no return. For that reason, nothing presented should seem as a prediction to prove Nostradamus as a prophet. That would serve no purpose.

Some may think that with the lengthy detail that was discussed from the letter to Henry, where "the Antichrist" was presented as a main character, many more than two quatrains would be thought to be found with "antichrist" as part of the text. It could seem that many quatrains would be needed to confirm all of that information, particularly since the verses add a greater level of detail than the general overview found in the letter. In regard to that presumption, one has to realize two things.

First, the evidence of Osama bin Laden hiding in the Pyrenees Mountains was compiled from many quatrains, but none of them identified him by name. The words of the quatrains detail the known history that surrounds the rise to power of Osama bin Laden, his being attacked in Afghanistan and his inability to be found. In those many quatrains presented as evidence, an important person was repeatedly identified, but called several names.

We saw how a capitalized "One" indicated an important person, particularly "One against the eagle" and "One king ... who will see France". We saw someone was named "The Emathion", symbolizing an Arabian king of myth. We saw someone identified as the "conductor of the army", one called "The eldest" and another an "owl". The point that is gained from that multiplicity is there are more than one title given to Osama bin Laden, meaning there is more than one way to identify "the Antichrist" than by that one name. Therefore, with two quatrains stating that specific word we all recognize ("antichrist"), many more could also name the same person another way.

Second, the story told by Jesus, recounted by John, was of a time when "a son a man" was coming. In the prophecy of John (*The Revelation*), as discussed, this "a son a man" was described as coming with hair of white wool, feet of brass, fire in his eyes and a double-edged sword coming from his mouth. The appearance of "the Antichrist", in the text of *The Revelation*, came only after Jesus (the Lamb) told John to write letters to be sent to the seven churches. Those letters were warnings that they had veered off the path of righteousness, having gone the wrong way; they all (maybe not one so much) needed to get right with God.

That warning by Christ came before the coming of him "like" Jesus. The detailing of that "a son a man" was a vision (dream) of what would come, should the seven churches fail to listen to the warning Christ told John to write. The *Book of the Revelation* is the letter sent to the seven churches; and likewise, the *Book of the Prophecies* is from the same source, telling the same story, as told by another prophet. The letter to Henry II and the two quatrains naming "the Antichrist" are also telling us that the dream does not need to come true.

That means Osama bin Laden is not "the Antichrist" until that day he actually pulls the trigger and knocks over that critical domino, which is going to knock over all the rest. It is more important to see him as the "One Arabian king" and the "conductor of the army", because he has already gained those titles. It now is the responsibility of the seven churches, which represent all branches of Christianity, to keep the dream from materializing.

The whole reason for *The Prophecies* is to tell a story that leads to understanding the warning that says: "We are going the wrong way!" God inspired Nostradamus to put His words in a letter, so it can be sent to the seven churches, just as John was instructed. The seven churches represent bodies of believers in Christ. The message of Nostradamus must be realized BEFORE the white wool-haired guy comes down with the Four Horsemen. Everything that has not happened yet is fiction, if we believe and act from faith in the warning as being truth from God, in order to keep "the Antichrist" from making that appearance. To do that, we have to have a clue about what has gone wrong, so those wrongs can be fixed. That is the ultimate purpose of this work of mine (not to win anyone reward money).

With this understood, the defense in this mock trial is against going out to catch Osama bin Laden (if he could be caught). The defense is instead designed to make everyone aware that he is the last person that the world needs to focus on fixing first. The clock is ticking and nine years have already gone without him having been caught. Osama bin Laden is actually telling us he would prefer not being given the title of "the Antichrist". Islam prophesies one too, named Masih ad-Dajjal, which literally means, "The Deceiving Messiah". He is making an effort to tell Christians what they need to do, so he will not have to go to that point of no return. We need to listen to that and work on solving the problem that has become a problem much larger than Osama bin Laden.

God is the source of *The Prophecies*, discerned through the Holy Spirit sent by Jesus Christ, which fell upon Nostradamus (as him being a saint). This next quatrain should then be seen as a warning and not as a promise. It tells of a time beyond the point of no return. Visualize Osama bin Laden and all that has been read as evidence related to him up to this point, as I explain the words of this prophecy.

The whole quatrain reads (simply translated):

L'antechrist trois bien tost annichilez,	Him-before-Christ three quite quickly brought to nothing ones,
Vingt & sept ans sang durera sa guerre,	Twenty & seven years kindred will sustain his war,
Les heretiques mortz, captif, exilez,	Them heretics killed ones, captive, exiled ones,
Sang corps humain eau rogie gresler terre.	Blood corpse human water funeral pyres to hail earth.

The first capitalized word is the combination article-noun, "*L'antechrist*", which says, "The antichrist", but can equally be defined as "Him-before-Christ" (from the Latin roots). As stated before, when the first word of a line is a capitalized article that is connected to a noun the article becomes emphasized, as "THE". This means "THE antichrist" has to be seen as "THE" one and only "antichrist". This is best shown as "the Antichrist", but because it is the first word of a line, the article has to be capitalized. Still, the meaning is "The Antichrist", the one named in the first segment of the letter to Henry II.

As one of only two quatrains that have the word "*antechrist*" (French spelling) in them, and as the only verse that has it in the main theme line, the appearance as the first word plays a significant role. By stating the importance (capitalization) of being given the title "The Antichrist", the order this quatrain falls into, in the overall story line of *The Prophecies*, represents the time when "a son a man" has been elevated to become "the Antichrist". All of the quatrains that told of terrorism and wars against terrorists and a terrorist leader escaping and going into hiding, et al, is prior to the time when "the Antichrist" prophesied by John will descend upon the world. Those types of acts of violence were occurring when John was alive, leading him to call them the lower-case "antichrists."

The first word of this quatrain signifies a change of title. For example, the quatrain discussed that had the main theme stating, "The Emathion to hold on a course mountain ones Pyrenees," that also states a title in the first word (with a combined article). Before that prophecy came into being a real part of the story line, Osama bin Laden was simply a "conductor of the army" in Afghanistan, a "soldier simple". He later became the embodiment of "THE Arabian king" of myth. His "army" had gone beyond "mountain ones" in Afghanistan, to having devoted followers around the world. More than local rebels in Afghanistan assisted in his escape to the far away "Pyrenees Mountains".

That figurative title will hold into the future, until "the empire of the Antichrist will commence". That quatrain, beginning with a title from mythology, parallels the one that prophesied: "One king will be who will come to see there Gaul". The title of "king" was repeated. Both of those quatrains link to this quatrain, where a title from *The Holy Bible* acts as another progression, potentially in the life of one individual.

The word that follows in line one, "three", is one of those numbers that has fooled many into thinking Nostradamus predicted "three antichrists." John made that statement, as he said there were already false antichrists in his times ("even now many antichrists have come" – 1 John 2:18). In that sense, people like Napoleon and Hitler can seem like models for "the Antichrist", such that they become "Antichrist one," Antichrist two," with "Antichrist three" being next in line. However, that is a syntactical error playing tricks on one's brain, causing one to miss the true point of the word "three" in this quatrain.

If one has followed the story line of Osama bin Laden being in the Pyrenees Mountains, he is there training a land-based army that will assist at the time of a sea-based assault on the parts of Europe that have shorelines on the Mediterranean Sea. Nostradamus has inferred "three" nations that are "great" (directly referencing two) which will be the focus of that naval invasion. Those "three" are Spain, Italy, and France. This means that at the time Osama bin Laden is elevated to become "The Antichrist" then "three" nations will "quite quickly" become "annihilated ones". The point of no return gets passed and all dominoes are set to fall.

The third word of this main theme statement is "*bien*", which we have seen before as the capitalized first word of a main theme, in the quatrain that began, "*Bien contigue des grans monts Pyrenees*" ("Possessions near adjoining to the great ones mountain ones Pyrenees Mountains"). In the discussion of that quatrain, it was determined that "*Bien*" meant "Possessions" (as a noun), which linked that quatrain to the letter to Henry II, where he wrote "*mont Jouis*", which translated as "mountain Possessed-ones". Seeing this word now in the lower case can alter the focus of this main theme to state: "three" defined by "wealth"; or, "three" supposedly for "good". This becomes the essence of why those "three" will have been considered "great ones", because (as Christian nations) God blessed them. However, this main theme shows no reference to "three great", because those "three" are nothing close to that descriptive term.

The next word, "*tost*", says that "quickly, presently-suddenly, and/or swiftly" the "riches, possessions, wealth, substance, goods; benefit, and/or favor" (some of the noun uses of "*bien*") of "three" will be "annihilated, annulled, and/or brought unto nothing" (as translations of the next word, "*annichilé-z*"). Those "three" will "presently-suddenly" find their connection to "good office" (as rewarded luxury by God, as Christians) "brought to nothing" as they will be "annihilated ones".

This is a very powerful main theme statement that goes along with everyone's perception of the swooping down of a "Mean Christ," as he unleashes the Four Horsemen in the breaking of seals. It is a "sudden" happening, meaning it is a complete surprise that will bring about "annihilation." The word "annihilation" means, "completely being destroyed, reduced to nonexistence, defeated decisively, and/or vanquished."[1] The unleashing of "the horrible thing" that is only used when "making war" brings on this "sudden" state of nothingness (from the letter of Henry II, related to the actions of "the Antichrist"). As discussed, that "abomination" is weapons of mass destruction, here found used in preemptive strikes upon "three", "suddenly and quickly" becoming world history-changing events.

The main theme ends with the plural past participle word, "*annichilez*", "ones [three] facing utter destruction," with that followed by a comma. That punctuation separates the main theme from the secondary theme, allowing the secondary theme to be a different focus on that "annihilation," as subsequent events. It still relates "those completely destroyed" to the first word of the secondary theme, which is the capitalized (showing importance) of another number, "Twenty".

People who have translated Nostradamus in the past, without an awareness of the purpose of his punctuation (which includes ampersand usage), see his surrounding an ampersand with numbers as a way of stating a higher number. For instance, in the secondary theme here, the line begins with, "*Vingt & sept*". This translates to state, "Twenty AND seven" (in one simple possibility), but many simply use this as a way of stating, "Twenty-seven." This is not the case.

In fact, the use of the word "and" between two numbers is an indication of a decimal point being represented. Reading the words "twenty and seven" would mean, "twenty point seven", or (numerically) 20.7. The systems of Nostradamus make this reading possible only as a distant secondary meaning. The primary purpose is to make "Twenty" stand alone; and, then emphasize "seven" as important [introduction by ampersand], in its own stand-alone series of words. Thus, "Twenty" is an important stand-alone number to understand, first and foremost.

---

1   Fair Use, paraphrased from the definition of "annihilate" presented by the Free Dictionary by Farlex. Their definition comes from the American Heritage Dictionary of the English Language, but other dictionaries they list have similar words defining the same word.

DEFENSE EXHIBIT D

Following "three ... annihilated ones", the importance of "Twenty" is the subsequent number of "abominations". This very well could mean "Twenty" more weapons of mass destruction have been deployed. It is known from the main theme that those "presently-suddenly" found targets will be in "three" nations. However, the elevated meaning of "Twenty" (from capitalization) can increase the number of actual "abominations" deployed; meaning "Twenty" nations also will be "annihilated ones".

If this later possibility is the case, any number of those weapons could be used. There are quatrains that indicate more than "three" countries affected by such "monsters" appearing. One quatrain in particular states in the third and fourth lines (simply translated):

| *Qu'il mettra foudres, combein en tel arroy* | That he will thrust into thunderbolts, how many upon such array, |
| *Peu & loing puis profond es Hesperiques.* | Short & far off moreover deep into the Western ones. |

The use of a capitalized "That", beginning line three, is related to the last words of the secondary theme, which are, "them Celtic ones" (*"les Celtiques"*). One then must be aware that the Romans knew most of northern France, most of Switzerland, all of Luxembourg and Liechtenstein, and parts of southern Germany and western Austria as *Gallia Celtica*. This is then followed by the future tense word *"mettra"*, which means, "will put, set, lay; place, pitch, plant, situate, ground; thrust into; also will bring, reduce, and/or send".

Because the following word is *"foudres"*, meaning "thunderbolts" (from the Old French spelling, *"fouldre"*), these are as "sudden" as "lightening", matching the use of *"tost"* in the "Antichrist" quatrain. That connection makes the translation of *"mettra"* most justified as "will thrust into". This act of "thrusting" then links to all of the quatrains telling of a plan "to pierce".

The "thrusting" of "thunderbolts into the ones of Celtica" means four nations of Western Europe are most likely prophesied as being attacked by missiles in the future (France, Switzerland, Austria, and Germany). That is more than "three". When line four of the "thunderbolt" quatrain says, "far off moreover deep into the Western ones", this is stating still more than four "Short" distant countries. The "Western ones" were the Spanish, during Roman Empire days; but the word takes on a much further meaning, given the times of these attacks. Minimally, this would include the United State (then the New World), with Great Britain inferred. Several quatrains tell of both nations being attacked by "fire in the sky".

The point is that "Twenty" could represent the number of countries who will be "annihilated ones", along with the "three" of the main theme, who will "quickly" be hit, simply from being closer to a launch point ("*Peu*", in the "thunderbolt" quatrain). Those "three" will also be the place where soldiers on the ground will be acting, such that the surrender of those "three" could cause "Twenty" nations to also surrender, as if a hostage situation existed. Those "Twenty" nations affected probably would not want to return fire, if that return fire could mean killing their allies. This means a plan of attack will have been designed to cause such "sudden annihilation" that a major assault on "three" will lead to "Twenty" defeated.

As a secondary meaning, the use of "Twenty" can act as a timing factor. Just as was seen before, when the capitalized number "Seven" began a line (verse three), a number can be seen as important as the year of a millennium. In that quatrain, it was shown how "Seven" could mean the year 2007. In such a scenario, the number "Twenty" could mean the year 2020. This, again, would have to be considered a secondary meaning, only determined after the fact. If it should turn out to be a timing factor, it will have prevented nothing because Jesus said, "It is not for you to know the times or dates the Father has set by his own authority." (Acts 1:7, New International Version)

The second half of the secondary theme, following the ampersand, states, "seven years will endure his warfare". The use of "*sept ans*" repeats a previous quatrain, where the capitalized number "*Sept*" was also followed by the word "*ans*". As discussed prior, the use of the French word "*sept*" includes the month of "September". Due to that possibility, "*Sept ans*" was explained as capable of representing "September year ones", which identified those who committed the acts on September 11, 2001, as well as the group known as Black *September*. The same meaning can apply in this quatrain, but without the importance of acting as that specific group.

In the lower-case, it implies the same people, as they "will endure" (from "*durera*") until this time of future "warfare"; but the primary meaning is "seven years" of time will follow the surrender of "Twenty". During that time, the people who cheered the attacks of September 11, 2001 "will continue, persist, sustain his war" (from "*durera*"), the war of "the Antichrist", Osama bin Laden. It also states that for "seven years" the "three" and the "Twenty" "will suffer" at the hand of "his" (from "*sa*"), in a continued state of "strife, contention, discord, and/or debate" (alternate translations of "*guerre*", typically meaning "*warfare*").

This becomes a statement that the reign of "the Antichrist" will last (another translation of "*durera*") for "seven years". This makes this statement relate to the "forty-two months" stated by John, in chapter 13, verse 5, of *The Revelation*. He wrote, "There was given to him a mouth speaking arrogant words and blasphemies, and authority to act for forty-two months was given to him." (New American Standard Bible) The time covered by forty-two months is three and a half years, but people who have studied biblical prophecy see the *Book of Daniel* and his reference to the "seventieth week" as reference meaning "seven years".

The remainder of this quatrain tells of the horrors that will be committed against those termed "heretics". There will be a series of persecutions against Christians, where "deaths" and "captivities" will lead to "exiles". Many quatrains detail these horrors. They link to this quatrain, showing how this quatrain acts as an anchor for a series of stories that will tell of the effects "the Antichrist" will cause. It is not important to get into those details in this quatrain, as it is enough to show the broad scope that acts to reflect the plans devised by Osama bin Laden, while inside "mountains".

Afterthoughts: From the crystal clear perspective of hindsight in the year 2020 it screamed out to me as I read what I wrote in 2011, "TWENTY!!!" A stand alone, capitalized word saying "Twenty" could very well be relative to the numbering of a year. Since it is already deep into that year, it is not denoting when THE Antichrist will begin firing nuclear weapons into the West. However, it certainly make that year be important in some regard to that scenario.

This then makes "seven years" make the period of time between 2020 and

2027 a secondary theme of importance, relative to that main theme statement. This year might mark the line of no return.

Seeing how I did mention the possibility of the year 2020, with in now realized not to be a marker year for a great Holy War, it makes me readdress the meaning of the main theme. Again, everything I wrote in 2011 holds merit, as it is an interpretation of words that have defined parameters of meaning. Within those parameters are a prophecy of The Antichrist as Osama bin Laden planning a most devastating war of revenge. Still, the parameters allow for expansion, based on the hindsight of nine more years of history to consider.

Certainly, the year 2020 stands out as a year unlike any known in my lifetime. It has been declared a year of fear, where a pandemic has spread around the globe. While it seems to mostly kill old people, it seems old people are the only ones maintaining some semblance of religiosity in the world. The more old people die, then the less religion there is that keeps the End Times from coming closer. As such, the capitalized first word "*L'antichrist*" can be seen less as a projection upon Osama bin Laden and more as a projection on those who supposedly put their faith in the God of Jesus Christ (i.e.: Christians).

This retains the lower-case spelling of "*antechrist*", making it one of the many John pointed out. The capitalization is then the abbreviated "*L*" that requires important translation focus. This takes one to the translation offered: "Him before christ," which places focus on the pope. That makes the main theme be relative to a series of popes, numbering "three." With the secondary them stating the importance of "Twenty," the "three" popes that will rapidly bring about the insignificance of the papacy become (counting backwards): Pope Francis; Pope Benedict XVI; and, Pope John Paul II. The numbering of three can then make "L" be an abbreviation of "*Les*," the plural form, stating that each of "Them" was individually "The antichrist," who collectively would bring about the end of the Church of Rome as anything connected to God. "They" are all "against Christ."

Simply from seeing this new possibility does nothing to diminish the threat Osama bin Laden represents to the Western world, in particular the three nations of Europe mentioned: France, Italy and Spain. It says those popes helped give rise to "the Antichrist," by having murdered a man sent by God to navigate a sinking ship to safe harbor and then covering it up with actions completely against the intent and purpose of the Church of Christ.

When I first began writing this book (2010) and when I first published it (2011), there was no inkling of a Pope Francis. He was not sworn in a pope until March 13, 2013, or two years after I first published this book. As early as 2002 I was seeing the quatrains tell of the murder of Pope John Paul I (1979), which then led to true antichrist being made pope. He even had the audacity to take the name of the one who he helped murder, if only by keeping their secret hidden. Pope John Paul II. Pope Rat, "second antichrist", was elected on February 28, 2005; and he was more closely connected to the murder, if not the one who slipped the poison onto Pope John Paul I's nighttime snack. In 2010-11, I was not focused on this quatrain naming the Anti-pope, even though I thought that when he was elected. Therefore, "three" was still too early to realize.

The third verse, which was not discussed here, due to it being after the beginning of a great Holy War, needs to now be addressed as the supporting details to this new view of the main theme statement. This verse begins by importantly stating *"Les heretiques,"* where the capitalized first word is *"Les."* This supports the abbreviation of *"L'antechrist"* as being *"Les antechrist,"* where *"Les"* was a number designation as "three." All "three" were individually an "antichrist" (of the lesser variety).

That capitalized importance as "Them" can only reflect back on the number "three," who then became "the ones brought to nothing." What "They" "brought to nothing" was the Roman Catholic Church as an institution of religion. "They" "annulled" any agreement with God, in the same way Israel and Judah "brought to nothing" their Covenant that acted as a deed to the land that would become Palestine.

This means the word *"heretiques"* needs to be more closely examined. "They" are identified as "heretics," which is a word (in the singular number) that means "a person believing in or practicing religious heresy." By definition alone, "religious" points an important finger to "Them," who numbered "three" and were "anti-christ." When the word "heresy" is seen defined as meaning "belief or opinion contrary to orthodox religious (especially Christian) doctrine,"[2] this further points to "three" who were "contrary Christians" or "anti-Christ ones."

The next word in line three, "*mortz*," makes more of a statement about the "deaths" of "three antichrists," even though Popes Rat and Fran are not far from a free trip to eternal damnation. The word "*mortz*" must be seen as the "ones of death", which reflects back in support to "the one who brought to nothing" or "the one annihilating" the Roman Catholic Church. The comma following "*mortz*," is then a marker of separation that says those "murderers" (where "*mort-z*" can be a statement of "murder-ones") made Roman Catholics "captive" (from "*captif*") to their polluted religious decrees and (another comma placed) made them welcome "*exilez*" into their midst.

The use of "*exile-z*" is a clear statement of the immigration that has flooded Western Europe, especially after the Syrian War displaced so many refugees. The Wikipedia article entitled "Refugees of the Syrian Civil War" states, "In August 2012, the first Syrian refugees migrated by sea to the European Union," adding "Large numbers of refugees cross into the EU and by mid-2015 there are 313,000 asylum applications across Europe." This flood has been so great that many European countries refused to allow more and incorporated steps to reduce this number of "exiled ones" among them.

To listen to Pope Fran speak, the Socialist from Argentina, he wants the Western nations (those professing to be Christian) to open its arms and allow the whole, wide impoverished world to come take everything they worked a lifetime (through government finagling) getting for themselves. Such giveaways being endorsed by a pope will be the "deaths" of Europeans, leading to many being "captives" of invading soldiers and "exiles" sent to the islands of the Mediterranean (millions), where they will be starved to death. In one place Nostradamus wrote they would be striping the bark from the trees to survive.

The popes will be dead by then. That makes verse three speak of bin Laden.

2   Google search definition, of "heretic" and "heresy," with results listed as "Oxford Languages."

Chapter 27
Defense Exhibit E

The Subsequent False Antichrist

The second of the two quatrains that states the word "*antechrist*" shows it at the end of line three. It does not have an article attached to it, so it stands alone as simply "antichrist". Because the name is not capitalized and does not have an indication of specificity (as "the antichrist"), this presentation matches the lower case versions shown in the letter to Henry II. In that case, this second quatrain is not about "the Antichrist", but instead is about those who will model their actions after that lead figure. It is about the "assistant antichrist" or "second antichrist".

The quatrain that this appearance of "antichrist" is in offers no evidence of Osama bin Laden. It infers a time after "the Antichrist" has descended upon the world and denotes that the events related to the information stated in this quatrain is "before-Christ". Nostradamus wrote about the return of Christ in *The Prophecies*, which will occur after the carnage of "the Antichrist" has ended (the end of the world, as we know it). However, this quatrain is not focused on the actions directly related to those initiated by Osama bin Laden's command. This quatrain tells of a response to those actions, when the pendulum will swing back in the opposite direction, with a vengeance.

The whole of the quatrain can be presented as:

Le chef de Londres par regne l'americh	The head man of London by reason of government the soul-rich
L'isle d'Escosse temptera par gellee,	The isle from Scotland will test through frozen wide,

Roy Reb. auront un si faulx antechrist,	King Rebel will be containing one in sort also antichrist,
Que les mettra trestous dans la meslee.	Who them will thrust into everyone within there combat.

Because the word "antichrist" is found in line three, it can be expected to be a detail in support of the main theme. Due to the main theme having the capitalized name "London" (from *"Londres"*), along with the capitalized pronoun "Him" (from *"Le"*), the main theme is focused on England. With "Scotland" (from *"d'Escosse"*) found importantly stated in the secondary theme, it becomes obvious this quatrain is not about an Islamic occupation of Europe. Instead, it is focused on what will happen in Great Britain, as a result of that occupation.

This quatrain also contains the combined word *"l'americh"* in the main theme line, which is not a clean word in French, Latin, or English. In addition, there is a capitalized abbreviation,*"Reb."*, which is the second word of line three. Both words could mean many possible things. This means much debate as to the clear intent of these words would make a written interpretation lengthy. The point of presenting this quatrain is not to enter that rabbit hole. Therefore, I will only address the meaning of "antichrist" in the broadest sense of interpretation.

Line three begins with the capitalized word *"Roy"*, which means it is identifying a true "King". This is not a pope, because the main theme is identifying England. England is the last nation with a true royal family, even though it has been corrupted and made little more than tabloid-gossip significant. Still, the presentation of "King" in line three balances the quatrain's beginning with "Him head man (of a political party) to London". This is descriptive of who rules England, which is someone not a "King". This "chief" (alternate translation of *"chef"*) will have come "by" (from *"par"*) the "rule" of England, as the leader of its "government" (from *"regne"*). This is a form of "rule" that was unknown to Nostradamus.

England currently has a queen, Queen Elizabeth II. In April 2011, she will turn 85 years of age. He son, Prince Charles, is the first in line to become the next royal head of Great Britain, as a would-be "King". Charles has a brother (Prince Andrew) and two sons (the princes William and Harry), which means the next royal head of England will be a "King". Line three is prophesying a time when the rule over England will have passed to "an Eldest" male heir (the previous half quatrain [the half not shown] began with the first word "*L'aisne*", and ended with "son of the King"); and with the current queen's age, and knowing the information of this quatrain takes place after the beginning of "the rule of the Antichrist", one of the before mentioned people is most likely the "King" of line three.

The word "antichrist" is related to this male who will be "King". Disregarding the presence of "*Reb.*", the remainder of line three states "will be having, holding, occupying, using, possessing, enjoying, containing, and/or to be (all from the meaning of the root verb, "*avoir*") one in sort false, lying, untrue, treacherous, and or deceiving (all from the meaning of "*faulx*")". This then connects to the word "antichrist", which causes the mind to want to see the primary intent being on a "false antichrist".

That meaning can certainly be read into this supporting detail line, but that is only on a secondary level. The primary meaning is show a future "King" of England, who will be discovered to be "one even as (alternate translation of "*si*") treacherous" as "the Antichrist", being an "assistant antichrist" (from the letter to Henry II, which stated, "second antechrist", as a lower-case "antichrist"). This line acts as an explanation for why "the Antichrist" would come into being in the first place.

As I have stated before, Nostradamus stated in his letter of Preface that the grand scope of why the end of the world would come was because a "diametrically opposite" state would take over. This was concerning "reigns, religions, and sects". The "King" of England falls under the heading of "reigns", and that word is listed in the main theme ("*regne*"). One has to understand that the state that existed during the times of Nostradamus (regardless of how much corruption our hindsight sees from the perspective of the present) was when "reigns, religions, and sects" all faced God and Christ, and recognized that as the true source of their power, wealth, and influence.

This means those people who ruled the world were "pro-Christ." When those guardians of the masses would turn their backs to God and Christ, they "would be having one" quite opposite in their hearts. They would be corrupted by "one so false", "one" who is called Satan. After being corrupted, they would become "antichrists", as John said were already present in the world in his days. However, when those of the blood of Christ ("reigns"), the body of Christ ("religions"), and the Holy Spirit of Christ ("sects") would become "anti-Christ", then the world's masses would have no leaders directing them to God or Christ any longer. This state is what will be calling upon "the Antichrist" to end it.

From that perspective, one can see line three telling of the corruptive state of the British royal line. Due to that lack of being connected to God and Christ, as an "antichrist", the evil of "the Antichrist" (Osama bin Laden's beginning of retribution and persecution) will have fallen upon England and Scotland. As such, line four is saying (simply translated), "That (the state of an "antichrist King") – them (the people of Great Britain) – will thrust into – everyone (the whole world included) – in - there – mingled (standard translation of "*meslée*").

Remembering the use of "*mettra*" in the "thunderbolt" quatrain, the same future tense verb is used in line four. Line four then begins by stating (importantly), "That" (a reference back to line three, and the "antichrist", will have "them" (the English) "thrust into". This is a statement about an attack by the "abominations", or weapons of mass destruction. This detail of line four is then supporting the secondary theme of "Scotland", while also maintaining a focus of the main theme, and "London".

This is saying that "everyone in" (from "*trestout dans*") all of Britain (minimally), are feeling the effects of a resulting state of war: nuclear rain, the collapse of its economy and local governments, etc. Many dominoes will have fallen over once the point of no return has been reached. In turn, "all" will be "put among" one another (alternate translation of "*meslée*") as equals, with "all mixed" up due to being turned away from God and Christ. It means "everyone" will become an "antichrist". The collapse of man's law depends on each individual's inner moral law for civility to rule; but in a "melee" (derived from the French "*meslee*", and meaning, "a violent free-for-all") there will only be "everyone" for himself or herself.

The main prophecy of this quatrain is more in line with the end of the tale of Arthur. After the kingdom has been almost completely overcome by the forces of evil, the Holy Grail having been found awakens Arthur (who symbolizes Christ). Upon that renewal of spirit, good returns to challenge evil in one last "battle" (alternate translation of "*meslée*"). This is found in the translation of "*lamerich*" (in line one) as "*l'ame – riche*", meaning "the spirit-rich". By having realized a corrupt "King" and having acted to recognize him as "treacherous" (alternate translation of "*faulx*"), "The head of London" will lead "by government" that recognizes "the soul riches" are more valuable than earthly possessions.

This quatrain is relative to the passages from *The Revelation* and *Daniel*, which tell of the period of time "the Antichrist" will rule, during a "false" peace. After either three and a half years or seven years, Osama bin Laden's "empire of the Antichrist" will begin to crumble. The one who will "head" this final "battle" will be from England. However, the true power of this quatrain comes from knowing the meaning of a lower-case "antichrist".

We are "all, everyone" an "antichrist" if we allow Osama bin Laden to elevate (or descend) to the title of "the Antichrist". The fact that we have been warned of a time when our leaders will be turned away from God and Christ, we are the ones responsible for saving the world. We have to stand up for what is right, just as Galahad did, and be knighted by Christ, with the power of the Holy Spirit upon us. We can find the grail. We are now living in the critical times when we must turn away from our corrupted leaders and face God. We must stop pretending to be Christians and act to find the answer to the sorry condition our Camelot has fallen into.

The Holy Grail is not a material carrot on a string, or an illusion of fame and happiness that will come following our leaders' promises of wealth, power, and influence. Our leaders are no longer connected to God. Because of this prophesied "diametrically opposite" condition, it is the Holy Spirit that alludes us. The Holy Grail is ours for the asking, if we make the true efforts of Sir Galahad. It will mean suffering; but with God's help, we can achieve our goal. As "antichrists", we are not seeking the power of God to lead us to bring about a solution that is otherwise impossible.

Afterthoughts: From going over what I wrote in 2010-11, it becomes valuable to add from the clarity of hindsight, nine years removed, so the 20/20 vision of 2020 can be seen. The mayor of London, beginning on May 9, 2016, became Sadiq Khan, the first ethnic-minority mayor in the history of that city. He was born in England, the son of Pakistani parents and Indian grandparents, who raised him as a Sunni Muslim. He has been a strong advocate for the consolidation of British Muslims, as a voting bloc, and he is deemed a Social Democrat. Without a doubt, he fits the naming by Nostradamus as *"Le chef de Londres."*

When one sees how a major male (*"Le"*) leader (*"chef"*) has taken control "of London," this element as a main theme statement is directly related to the secondary theme (due to a lack of ending punctuation) that speaks of "The island of

Scotland." In 2014, the Scottish voted not to become independent from Great Britain, by a 55-45 margin. While that took place prior to Sadiq Khan becoming the mayor of London, his predecessor (Boris Johnson) had announced he would leave that office, leading to Khan attempting to become a government minister through organizing the Labour Party in 2014. This linking of the two as one, with two foci, makes 2014 a time when Scotland was "frozen" in its relationship with Great Britain.

Because the Queen of England is still alive and in power (now 94 years of age), her son Charles (age 72 presently), is not yet the king. As the third line being supporting details to the main theme, relative to the secondary theme, it may or may not have anything to do with a Muslim mayor of London and the Scottish voting for independence. Those are change in history since I first published this book. However, this history can be seen as how the "antichrist" will relate to London, Scotland and a new King of England, on the throne of Great Britain.

Relative to the possibility that Charles might not last long as king (hints to that end are in the quatrains), the former prince Harry has departed England for Hollywood (de-titled). Further, Charles' brother, Prince Andrew, has been removed from his position in line to the throne, due to his history with pedophiles having recently surfaced. All of this goes to further the notion that the royal family has become corrupted by "false" blood, which makes anybody who might ascend to the throne of England be a "King" that is not truly royal.

The only reason for royalty is bloodline. There is quatrain evidence that implies Charles never consummated his marriage to Diana Spencer, meaning both of the children she bore be bastards, perhaps not even partially of royal (mixed) blood. In the 1611 Old French dictionary, the word *"Rebours"* is followed by "'A reb. (Adverb.)," which appears to be a statement that this word is "abbreviated reb." If that indeed is the case, then the capitalization of *"Reb."* importantly says the "King" will be "Arsward, backward, preposterously, oblikely [obliquely], awry, overthwartly, quite contrary, full against the course, wool or hair inside out upside down, clean ham [leg]." In other words, the next King of England will be Charles, who has a closet full of secrets that his momma knows all about; so, she is not planning of dying and leaving England in the hands of one who is already known to be "lying, untrue, treacherous, and deceiving," most certainly "against Christ," therefore not what kings are made from.

Chapter 28
Closing Arguments

From the segments of the letter to Henry II it becomes clear "the Antichrist" will rain terror upon the Roman Catholic Church and all the domains through which Christianity has been spread. The person named Osama bin Laden has called the West "The Great Satan." He does so because it acts contrary to the religion in which it purports to believe. In that regard, he is pointing out how a Church born from apostles, made divine by the Holy Spirit through their devout faith in God, has long since lost that connection.

In one quatrain Nostradamus tells us a "King" of England will be named an "antichrist", because he "will be containing one so false". That comparison to Satan is, in effect, a statement that we have become "the Antichrist". With the collapse of the Roman church, with popes no longer representative of the saints of Jesus Christ (the royals no longer his blood), we have no one but ourselves to follow spiritually. It means we have reached the point of being "diametrically opposite" to the way things used to be; and, that is an "abomination" in the eyes of God that will be punished.

The two quatrains that directly state the word "antichrist" give specific details about what will be the result of Christians having lost faith. Nations will be "annihilated" by weapons of war that will unleash horrors upon the world. Attacks will come "suddenly", without warning, and everyone will be put into a state of panic. England and Scotland, as well as "deep into the Western nations", the lands will be struck by "lightening". This will lead to "seven years" of Christian persecution, because Christians will have forsaken their God and His Son.

What Nostradamus wrote is warning everyone that when "the Antichrist" comes he will be armed and accompanied by allies, for the purpose of persecuting that which has become itself "the Antichrist". The persecution will be designed to turn pagan worshippers into Allah worshippers, so the world will no longer be dominated by the powers of Satan. Those are represented by the weapons the West holds as its true sign of greatness, being nuclear weapons – the "infernal powers". The irony is that the enemy of Christ (the antichrists) also will be filled with the powers of Satan and thus just as wrong as Christians have been.

When these explanations are connected to a plan to occupy the Pyrenees Mountains, for the purpose of mounting a war against Western Europe and their allies, one sees the details that add to the generality of "the Antichrist" found in the letter to Henry. Osama bin Laden plots a surprise attack, by land and sea, utilizing very powerful allies and weaponry. It all links to his presence being required in the Pyrenees Mountains, where the quatrains show a command center will be established by one most powerful individual.

The stories that unfold from "One who will be king" make significant connections to the explanation of an "empire of the Antichrist". Empires are the result of one very charismatic leader (Napoleon, Xerxes, Attila, etc.), who has countless soldiers willing to make their leader's dreams become reality. Osama bin Laden has this charisma. The stories are all linked together (letter, quatrains, current history), such that each acts individually, but also as a whole. The greater picture is that America's Most Wanted fugitive has been identified by prophecy to be "the Antichrist".

Part of the awe and admiration that Muslims have for bin Laden, especially as told by those who have fought alongside him in Afghanistan, is that they see how clearly Allah protects him. Members of al-Qaeda have said they personally witnessed a bomb land and blast only feet from where bin Laden stood, only to have him walk away without a scratch. One could call that luck and logically explain how the trajectory of bomb shrapnel can entirely miss one person, while killing twenty others. However, in a story of prophecy, such events take on a much greater relevancy.

Separate from knowing anything of what stories *The Prophecies* tell, human beings on the planet are talking real stories of a man who is attempting to do the impossible. They believe Osama bin Laden will succeed in making that mountain move, through the help of Allah. That is one story found in *The Prophecies*, which tells of an unnamed man who will "achieve his empire", beginning as a "soldier pure". This is comparable to the letter to Henry stating, "will commence the empire of the Antichrist". The two are the same, at least until someone proves otherwise.

This is why the *"antechrist"* (in lower case) is non-specific. It is a general statement about a condition that will encompass the world of the future. That future has become our present. Nostradamus was shown this future and instructed by divine insight to write about what is to come. He could only do so by being filled with the Spirit of Jesus Christ. It is a warning that tells what will bring about the end of humanity; but the warning comes from God's love, for the purpose of us recognizing the "antichrist" within us, so we can turn back to Him.

In the letter to Henry II, when Nostradamus wrote *"qui sera le second antechrist"*, he was telling about this "assistant in combat" who will be "against Christ" ("anti-Christ). The same words tell what state will come into the world "before Christ" ("ante-Christ"), by saying it is everyone "who will be him", as a "double". A true Christian has accepted the Holy Spirit and been married to God, so one's soul is reborn as His Son; but to receive that Spirit, one must sacrifice self-ego and become a devoted servant to God (as was Jesus). "Before" that conversion takes place, all play the role of "antichrist," being against that transformation. This makes everyone fearing the future, our future, play a role as this "second antichrist".

This is not simply a numerical association to "the Antichrist", but all who have acted to support corruption in the world. All those in favor say, "Aye." All those opposed say, "No!" If only it was so simple to voice a collective opinion, but it is not. We vote to accept corruption through apathy and fear of standing up for what is right. We turn our backs to God and Christ when we do not face up to wrongs done, especially our own. We second the motion of evil in the world.

That failure to act as Christ would have us act as what has brought about the one person who has been prophesied to come to destroy the world ("the Antichrist, the son a man, the son of sin, the beast"). This then confirms the truth in how Muslims see America and the West as the Great Satan. They are warning us that they are willing to "assist in combat" to defeat the sinners, the so-called Christians, who have demonstrated a willingness to "assist in combat" their leaders, who use anti-Christian methods against Muslims. The separation of Church and State makes our government a "second antichrist", as it places government "against Christ". That government has often stomped around the world, taking whatever it (government officials) deemed appropriate, from whomever, all in the name of the Lord. The Crusades have never stopped; and thus, the pendulum keeps on swinging to and fro.

That makes Osama bin Laden nothing more than a derivative of the conditions set forth before him. If not him, then someone else like him would have popped up to challenge those conditions. Capture or kill Osama bin Laden and someone else will rise to take his place. The world has made Osama bin Laden what he is; and, Osama bin Laden has said that it does not matter who, or how many of his brothers will be felled in their Holy War. The movement has begun and it cannot be stopped by an "anti-Christ-like" response to him, personally. He is confirming that the time has come to end the way the world has become.

This is Osama bin Laden – a Muslim – a non-Christian, but a believer in the prophet Mohammed and thus prophecy – who is confirming his times are the times prophesied long ago. His view is based on the requirement of prophecy happening as prophesied. He is preparing the destruction and persecution of a world that has become too evil to continue in that godless state. However, the views of a true Christian must realize true prophecy comes from God's love for His creations, not hatred.

A true Christian will see opportunity coming from belief in prophecy, thus willingly be motivated to change, away from where prophecy says the danger awaits. Certainly, the world must change now, as the times of evil have taken the world to the precipice, with no time left to debate casually why nothing should be done. Christians can have a positive impact on the outcome, even if much hurt is still the result. Keeping nuclear weapons from being used means showing a serious attitude about peace, through admission of guilt and a sincere display of penitence before God.

Osama bin Laden once promised the Muslim world would cease its war of Jihad against the West (in particular that directed towards America) and call everything even, if America would see the error of its ways. One step in this direction must be to cease its blind defense of the State of Israel. The Arab view has always been that the Jews stole Palestine (something David Ben-Gurion admitted).[1]

1   From the Wikipedia article on "David Ben-Gurion" – quoted from Nahum Goldmann, 'The Jewish Paradox', translated by Steve Cox, 1978, ISBN 0-448-15166-9, p. 98, p. 100, p. 99 – Ben-Gurion said, "If I was an Arab leader I would never make terms with Israel. That is natural: we have taken their country ... There has been anti-Semitism, the Nazis, Hitler, Auschwitz, but was that their fault? They only see one thing: we have come here and stolen their country. Why should they accept that? They

Therefore, nothing short of the return of that stolen property (ALL of it) will have them cease their attempts to regain what was stolen.

The Islamic view is the same, as they support the Palestinian cause. They know first hand how covert American-British activities have been designed to weaken or eliminate the theocratic forms of government Middle Eastern nations hold dear. The union of Church and State in all Muslim nations (and one must realize Israel also has a theocratic form of government) has been threatened by the rouse of "democracy" being a better way of government. Democracy is the will of the majority ruling and true democracy can lead to a Theocracy, but only if the majority of the people want their religion to be one with their government.

When one understands how the end of the world will come to destroy our wonderful lives, one's eyes slowly begin to open and realize (from the cartoon strip *Pogo*), "We have met the enemy and he is us." As long as the enemy is allowed, unchecked, to be the enemy of the world, the world will come to an end by a separate but equal enemy. Osama bin Laden simply reflects that, as "The enemy" of "The enemy". If he is caught, that will not eliminate the enemy that caused Osama bin Laden. Until we realize Osama bin Laden is nothing more than a man holding up a mirror, reflecting our own image back to us, we will never act to cease the insanity that is about to destroy the world and all who live within it. Osama bin Laden represents "wake-up time." If we wake up, everything in the future becomes just a bad dream.

Nostradamus is a prophet who laments in the verbiage of the quatrains, just as did most Biblical prophets. Too often, the prophets are not recognized as true agents of the Lord until well after their words have come true. This dawning comes after much grieving and pain from suffering. We can look back at the Bible prophets and see how foolish it was not to listen. We have to learn from those visions of past biblical prophecy. Those futures that came to pass will mirror our future that will come to pass, if we repeat a past failure and ignore a divine warning. What was true then will always be true. Truth is a constant; and, as the axiom says, "Those who do not learn from history are doomed to repeat it."

From Sunday to Sunday, I sit in a pew at a church and hear the words of the Bible read aloud. Each week I lament the pains of the past stories, as they tell of the pains that are to come again, in our future. The pains came then, and the pains

---

may perhaps forget in one or two generations' time, but for the moment there is no chance. So it is simple: we have to stay strong and maintain a powerful army."

will come again, because few are willing to listen to the stories of prophecy until it is too late.

The prophetic story told by Nostradamus is not sanctioned by holy men who determine what is to be believed and what is to be shunned. Nostradamus has been portrayed as something he was not; thus we are told he cannot be seen as a prophet of God. We have no belief that makes us willing to act to save ourselves from suffering, much less act to help the pain of others. I have lost track of how man Sundays I have heard the warnings posed by Nostradamus be echoed from the warnings of past prophets and saints; but each time I hear the words of those sanctioned as holy, I know in my heart that Nostradamus was touched by the divine.

In this exposé that offers the reader the chance to get a big cash reward from the F.B.I., I have quoted *The Prophecies* rather extensively. While much more could be said from what is written, I have at least offered a reasoned approach to where that hiding place is. I have also offered evidence that Osama bin Laden is not a person that can be defeated by evil means. He is a character written into eschatological prophecy. Therefore, in closing this work, I would like to quote from a prophet that also fits that genre, whose words are said to have been written in the seventh century before Christ.

The prophet is Habakkuk, who wrote before the Babylonians overtook Jerusalem. His words were read aloud in church, soon after I began to write this work. As I heard them read, the words resonated inside me. I felt his pains as my pains, coming from my efforts to get someone, anyone, to listen to what I have to say; only to have my words go unheeded. I want to repeat those words for you to ponder.

Habakkuk laments to God,

> "Why do you show me iniquity, and look at perversity? For destruction and violence are before me. There is strife, and contention rises up. Therefore the law is paralyzed, and justice never goes forth; for the wicked surround the righteous; therefore justice goes forth perverted." (Habakkuk 1:3-4, World English Bible)

This is a parallel to our times; and it is a mirror image to the stories told in *The*

Prophecies. It is telling of times when the right way had become "diametrically opposite."

Then, God replied to Habakkuk, saying,

> "Write the vision; make it plain on tablets, so that a runner may read it. For there is still a vision for the appointed time; it speaks of the end, and it does not lie. If it seems to tarry, wait for it; it will surely come, it will not delay. Look at the proud! Their spirit is not right in them, but the righteous live by their faith." (Habakkuk 2:2-4)

That is excellent guidance, both then and now. However, the prophecy continues, although this was not read in church:

> "Indeed, wine betrays him; he is arrogant and never at rest. Because he is as greedy as the grave and like death is never satisfied, he gathers to himself all the nations and takes captive all the peoples." (Habakkuk 2:5)

This is a prophecy about those who deem themselves as "great". It is the story told in the quatrains that tell of "mountain ones" who never felt a part of the nations that lorded over them. The story of Osama bin Laden is as a hero to these "captive people."

Still, Habakkuk goes on:

> "Will not all of them taunt him with ridicule and scorn, saying, Woe to him who piles up stolen goods and makes himself wealthy by extortion! How long must this go on? Will not your creditors suddenly arise? Will they not wake up and make you tremble? Then you will become their prey." (Habakkuk 2:6-7)

This is the same warning given to John, as the bad things done by the seven churches, which Christ was not accepting. It tells of the Western intrigue in the Middle East, which includes sanctioning the theft of Palestine for Zionist Jews. The question is from God, "Do you think I will allow that to go unpunished?" That question is echoed by Osama bin Laden.

Then, Habakkuk wrote:

> "Because you have plundered many nations, the peoples who are left will plunder you. For you have shed human blood; you have destroyed lands and cities and everyone in them. Woe to him who builds his house by unjust gain, setting his nest on high to escape the clutches of ruin! You have plotted the ruin of many peoples, shaming your own house and forfeiting your life. The stones of the wall will cry out, and the beams of the woodwork will echo it. Woe to him who builds a city with bloodshed and establishes a town by injustice." (Habakkuk 2:8-12)

This is the essence of "turn about being fair play." It stated the evils of Judah, which were against God, rather than against those of Babylon, who had taken their kingdom away leaving Jerusalem to lament. Still, it perfectly mirrors the trail of blood the United States has left since the end of World War II, especially since dropping two "abominations" on the Japanese. It echoes the axiom, "He who lives by the sword will die by the sword." That is why the image seen by John, "like a son a man," had a double-edged sword coming from his mouth.

This image of an angry Christ is Osama bin Laden, "the Antichrist". There is a vision of where Osama bin Laden is in hiding, written in *The Prophecies*. I have written it here, so that vision comes into focus. I make it clear so all who run to the F.B.I. can be able to know how to make it become their own vision. He is hiding in the Pyrenees Mountains because he has a vision of a time when an invasion of Europe will occur. That vision is the beginning of the End Times. It will truly come if all bury their heads in the sand and do nothing to stop it now.

The End Times have long been "tarrying", to the point that it seems to be a trick; but some do wait for it to come. Some actually relish that end coming so they can see the wicked punished, while themselves are happily raptured up to Heaven. But alas, their end will come too, along with all who do not act from their hearts.

True faith means works from faith. True Christians know God can work miracles through those who believe and act. Some people are too proud to admit they have played a role in this coming destruction, falsely thinking they have long been fast-tracking to Heaven. They want the wicked punished. That spirit is not right. That is the spirit of Osama bin Laden, who plans his version of how the wicked should be punished. The righteous live their faith through acts of faith, without grumbling about how little that leaves them to hold over others. After all, the reward is not in land investments, oil sales, paper money, or gold bullion. The reward is on the other side; and ~~$25-million~~ ~~$27-million~~ $50-million will not pay for that transition.

Afterthoughts: In the nineteen years that I have been led by God to slowly understand more and more about the man who was Michel de Nostredame (a.k.a. Nostradamus) and what the meaning was to what he wrote, relative to *Les Propheties*, I have encountered vile responses by many who professed to be Christians. People in churches that I was a member of would shun me and talk behind my back about how foolish I was. Often, I heard someone say, "I have the Bible. I believe that. I do not believe Nostradamus." Unfortunately, this is a trial and the evidence presented must be weighed and a verdict determined.

I have come to realize that is Jesus Christ was to fly down from the skies, riding a white horse that landed in the parking lot of an Episcopalian church, with him dismounting so he could go inside and stand on the altar, dressed in a blood-stained white robe, with his double-edge sword in hand so he could talk, if Jesus Christ were to say, "Change your ways now or roast in hell for eternity!" The priest would call the police and everyone of the attendees (saying it is not a Cornoavirus fear day, set aside only for a social media live streaming service) would stand up and take phone pictures of "some crazy guy stormed into the church today," to send to their Facebook friends.

The truth of Christianity is that every saint, since Peter stood with the other eleven on the first Christian Pentecost Sunday sermon, has been Jesus Christ reborn. Nostradamus was a saint who was reborn in the name of Jesus Christ. Every true Prophet of God (YHWH) has been the "Son of man," as the Son of God, Jesus Christ before Jesus was born, after he died and resurrected, and forevermore. It is the duty of a saint to speak the truth, just as Jesus did, as Jesus Christ reborn, being Jesus without looking like his pictures in the coloring books of Christianity.

Christians today make the terrible mistake of thinking God stopped sending prophets and saints into the world, when somebody in Vatican City said, "No more! The book is full!" Even the last prophet of the New Testament (John, imprisoned on the island of Patmos) is shunned, because, "His words scare me!"

Few priests dare preach a sermon about the End Times, as they leave all that stuff up to the Baptists and Pentecostals. That means the flocks are shepherded by hired hands (or worse). The blind are leading the blind to a huge hole in the ground, a hole that leads to hell on earth.

Jesus told the Sadducees (who were not believers of an afterlife), "He is not the God of the dead, but of the living, for to him all are alive." (Luke 20:38, NIV) That goes over everyone's head, because the red herring was the Sadducees asking who would be the husband of a widow who married seven men, never having any sons. People think Jesus said, "God is not concerned about those who died and went to heaven; he is only concerned with those still living on earth." That is a belief heading towards that big hole in the ground.

Souls are given to bags of dirt, called human flesh. Human flesh is death waiting to happen, as it happens eventually to all mortals. That means a soul in a body that has not been filled with God's Holy Spirit and a walking, talking Jesus Christ reborn is a walking dead bag of dirt. God is not the God of walking dead bags of dirt, because God is only the God of those who can truthfully claim to be His Son, in the name of Jesus Christ ... reborn into one's soul. That presence is what gives the truth of life, meaning God is the God of those who are His Son reborn.

John was one of the living when he wrote *The Apocalypse*. Daniel was one of the living when his story was written into the book bearing his name, which was before Jesus was born into the world. Nostradamus was one of the living when God told him to write *Les Propheties*. Over and over again the dead go to buildings and listen to dead men and women recite passages of truth from those who were living. The purpose is for someone to actually hear, believe, and become reborn as Jesus Christ.

Christianity, overall, to the greatest degree now is dead. God is not the God of the dead. It is time to wake up and let every individual take upon himself or herself the role of seeking God personally, praying for divine guidance. One must repent everything one has ever done first. Then one has to realize ego is no longer allowed. Ego leads one to sin. When Jesus said you cannot serve two masters, God is one that will not allow you to think you are His equal. You can worship you all you want; but if you do, know you are a god of the dead, not of the living.

Chapter 29
Conclusion

In this work, I have referenced 20 quatrains. In none of those references did I make a connection to a *Centurie* or number by which the reader can look up those quatrains and check my representations as being accurate. I have not included that numbers because those numbers have nothing to do with the correct order of the stories.

Imagine you are in the car parts profession and you have to store car parts to sell. Before you actually get any inventory to sell, you have to build some shelves, on which you will store the parts. This storage area is pre-numbered, such that each box on the shelf has a number, whether there is a part in it or not. After the parts come in, they are placed in a slot and the number of that box is entered into the inventory, matching a storeroom number with a part. When a customer comes in and asks for a specific part the storage number has nothing to do with the part. A customer will ask for a part by name, not your storage number. Additionally, storage rooms are not set up to look like an automobile, such that the order of the parts is the same as one would find parts on a car. The windshields are on a row where the slots are big enough for fenders and axles. The various nuts and bolts, radio knobs and antennas are mixed in various slots, next to boxes filled with headrests, sun visors and air filters.

The analogy is the same as to how *The Prophecies* is presented. Ten "shelves" have been constructed and each of those ten is divided into 100 slots, or pigeonholes. The quatrains have been divided into 948 individual pieces, scattered into no particular order, and then placed into the slots in an unorganized manner. Aisle seven (a.k.a. *Centurie Seventh*) has over 50 empty compartments. Therefore, the number a quatrain was assigned when it was stored (in publication) has nothing to do with how the quatrain fits into the making of a completed puzzle.

That is why it as unimportant to explain as I interpreted each quatrain in this work, "You will find part number (fill in the blank) valuable." It has no bearing on the meaning, but can add to confusion. *The Prophecies* are already confusing enough. However, I will now address the part numbers specifically in a chart to follow.

In this chart, one should note how quatrains have been sorted into every *Centurie* (from Latin, meaning a division of one hundred), with the exceptions being *Centuries* one and seven. The numbers range from 1 to 99. Every group of ten is represented, with the exception being the twenties. The year each quatrain I interpreted was first published does not follow a chronological order. This shows a random presentation, although I welcome any statisticians to do a test of these numbers, to confirm this conclusion within a degree of reliability.

The Quatrains Presented

#	Serial Number	Key terms	Year 1st Published
The Escape series			
1	X-04	"*conductor of the army*"	1566
2	V-54	From "*Tartary*" to "*Gaul*"	1557
The "*monts Pyrenees*" series			
3	IX-64	"*The Arabian king*"	1566
4	VI-01	"*Eagle ... great ugly growth*"	1557
5	IV-70	"*Possessions joined*"	1557
6	II-74	"*From Judgment ... to the Rose-born*"	1555
7	III-62	"*Near to them she sleeps*"	1555
8	II-17	"*An army lodged ... to the pure virgin*"	1555
9	IV-02	"*By reason of death there France ... voyage*"	1555
10	IV-94	"*Two great ones brothers*"	1557
11	X-11	"*Beneath Place strewn with bulrushes*"	1566
12	VI-88	"*One reign great ... desolated*"	1557
13	VI-99	"*The enemy thoroughly instructed*"	1557
The "*monts*" series			
14	IV-31	"*There Moon in the plain of night*"	1557
15	II-48	"*There great army will pass them mountain ones*"	1555
16	IV-37	"*Of France through leaps*"	1555
Not Napoleon, but Osama bin Laden			
17	VIII-57	"*To soldier simple will achieve into empire*	1566

The Antichrist
18	VIII-77	*"The antichrist three quite soon annihilated ones"*	1566
19	IV-99	[Line three] *"he will put thunderbolts ... in such array"*	1557
20	X-66	[Line three] *"will be having one in sort false antichrist"*	1566

With this information known, let me reiterate how little I knew in 2002, when I offered my services to the F.B.I. I had seen the meaning shining through from some of these quatrains, but I am sure I would not have been able to compile a work of this magnitude as proof. I could tell the F.B.I. to go seek Osama bin Laden in the Pyrenees Mountains; but I probably would have made a fool of myself then, trying to explain how I saw that answer.

Since those days, the Internet has made so many tools available that have made it easier for me to expound on what I only had in my head then. For instance, I would have had to go through the one book I had on Nostradamus and write down which quatrains mentioned the Pyrenees. Now, I have my own database to search for that word. In 2002, I barely knew about the letters Nostradamus wrote, much less how to make sense of what they said.

I had only begun to formulate ideas about the systems of Nostradamus, although I knew some basic syntax. I had yet to do my own translations in 2002. I was going by the translations of one I expected to be an expert in French, which I was not and still am not. Even from that novice perspective, I could tell some words did not seem to fit; and, I could see how the few words I looked up made what I found more revealing to the meaning. What was obvious to me in the syntactical translations, from realizing the quatrains were pieces that told a story when placed in an order of understanding, was I could see that Nostradamus predicted Osama bin Laden would be in the Pyrenees Mountains.

In 2002, I had been an unchurched Christian for most of my adult life. While I knew Bible stories, I knew very little about biblical prophecy, other than what I had seen on television. Since I began to have more and more dawn upon me, about how to understand the words of Nostradamus, I have been led to read the Bible and understand it in ways that most other people cannot. All of this comes from realizing systems are built into prophecy. What a biblical prophet wrote has the same style as does what was written by Nostradamus. The systems are simple, once one realizes what they are; but they are complex when one's mind wants to read prophecy as one reads a typical novel. It was not from a preconceived notion that I thought it would be a good idea to dedicate my life to telling people I solved Nostradamus. It was not from some extreme position of eschatological belief that I tried to make *The Prophecies* fit my needs.

This work has used a logical approach. I have attempted to keep my emotions in check, so as not to slant my view on the words in a judgmental fashion. In the words of an old television show (Dragnet), "Just the facts." In that regard, I have relied heavily on what is a documented translation possibility, from the closest possible source to the 16th century. From those possibilities, it is dependent on a published definition for each word, including all forms of use. The systems are based on logical applications of language, only in a different way. A comma is defined by the rules of language, and, a comma works the same way, only as a direction marker, not part of a sentence. What leads me to see what I see as coming from the words is documented history that exactly matches the words; in the order the words are presented. That history being connected to words telling of what still has not happened makes the leap to prognostication a logical assumption, based on the past and past models.

I have been attempting to make it known that Nostradamus has a warning we need to be aware of, since October 2001. I have been trying to make it known that Nostradamus was a prophet of God, who encountered the spirit of Jesus Christ, since 2004. I have been trying to make it known that there is hope to avert this end, if faith is returned and we act upon that faith, since 2005. In all my efforts, I have lost money, friends, possessions, and had countless people tell me to do something else. I am not doing this for the money. I realized when the F.B.I. told me they did not pay consultants that my reward would come on a higher plane. I do this because I cannot stop; and, I will not stop, because I have been called by God to scream as loud and for as long as I can, "You are going the wrong way!"

I can feel the frustration of Jeremiah and Habakkuk every day. I only wish the world would not be so hard of hearing. Maybe the lure of $25-million (or $27-million, or $50-million) will get someone's attention.

It seems to have reach the president of the United States of America, somehow, some way. Unfortunately, rather than look in the Pyrenees, he killed a body double in Pakistan. So, the quest goes on.

Still, President Obama did a service to treasure hunters of the world. He kept them from reading this book and making the huge mistake of trying to find a nest of terrorists in the kind of terrain they excel in. So, one man was sacrificed, so many could live on. Sound like a familiar story?

The $50-Million Reelection Gift • *Robert Tippett*